At the Heart of the St

Anthropology, Culture and Society

Series Editors:
Professor Vered Amit, Concordia University
and
Professor Christina Garsten, Stockholm University

Recent titles:

Becoming Arab in London:
Performativity and the Undoing
of Identity
RAMY M.K. ALY

Community, Cosmopolitanism
and the Problem of Human
Commonality
VERED AMIT AND NIGEL RAPPORT

Home Spaces, Street Styles:
Contesting Power and Identity in
a South African City
LESLIE J. BANK

In Foreign Fields:
The Politics and Experiences of
Transnational Sport Migration
THOMAS F. CARTER

Dream Zones:
Anticipating Capitalism and
Development in India
JAMIE CROSS

A World of Insecurity:
Anthropological Perspectives on
Human Security
EDITED BY THOMAS ERIKSEN,
ELLEN BAL AND OSCAR SALEMINK

A History of Anthropology
Second Edition
THOMAS HYLLAND ERIKSEN AND
FINN SIVERT NIELSEN

Ethnicity and Nationalism:
Anthropological Perspectives
Third Edition
THOMAS HYLLAND ERIKSEN

Fredrik Barth:
An Intellectual Biography
THOMAS HYLLAND ERIKSEN

Small Places, Large Issues:
An Introduction to Social and
Cultural Anthropology
Third Edition
THOMAS HYLLAND ERIKSEN

Discordant Development:
Global Capitalism and the
Struggle for Connection in
Bangladesh
KATY GARDNER

Anthropology and Development:
Challenges for the Twenty-first
Century
KATY GARDNER AND DAVID
LEWIS

Organisational Anthropology:
Doing Ethnography In and
Among Complex Organisations
EDITED BY CHRISTINA GARSTEN
AND ANETTE NYQVIST

Border Watch:
Cultures of Immigration,
Detention and Control
ALEXANDRA HALL

Anthropology's World:
Life in a Twenty-First Century
Discipline
ULF HANNERZ

Humans and Other Animals:
Cross-cultural Perspectives on
Human–Animal Interactions
SAMANTHA HURN

Flip-Flop:
A Journey Through
Globalisation's Backroads
CAROLINE KNOWLES

The Anthropology of Security:
Perspectives from the Frontline of
Policing, Counter-Terrorism and
Border Control
EDITED BY MARK MAGUIRE,
CATARINA FROIS AND NILS
ZURAWSKI

The Gloss of Harmony:
The Politics of Policy Making in
Multilateral Organisations
EDITED BY BIRGIT MÜLLER

Contesting Publics
Feminism, Activism,
Ethnography
LYNNE PHILLIPS AND SALLY COLE

Food For Change
The Politics and Values of Social
Movements
JEFF PRATT AND PETER
LUETCHFORD

Checkpoint, Temple, Church and
Mosque:
A Collaborative Ethnography of
War and Peace
JONATHAN SPENCER, JONATHAN
GOODHAND, SHAHUL
HASBULLAH, BART KLEM,
BENEDIKT KORF AND KALINGA
TUDOR SILVA

Race and Ethnicity in Latin
America
Second Edition
PETER WADE

Race and Sex in Latin America
PETER WADE

The Capability of Places:
Methods for Modelling
Community Response to
Intrusion and Change
SANDRA WALLMAN

The Making of an African
Working Class:
Politics, Law and Cultural Protest
in the Manual Workers' Union of
Botswana
PNINA WERBNER

At the Heart of the State

The Moral World of Institutions

Didier Fassin

with
Yasmine Bouagga
Isabelle Coutant
Jean-Sébastien Eideliman
Fabrice Fernandez
Nicolas Fischer
Carolina Kobelinsky
Chowra Makaremi
Sarah Mazouz
Sébastien Roux

Translated by
Patrick Brown and Didier Fassin

PlutoPress
www.plutobooks.com

First published in French 2013 by Seuil
First English language edition published 2015 by Pluto Press
345 Archway Road, London N6 5AA

www.plutobooks.com

British Library Cataloguing in Publication Data
A catalogue record for this book is available from the British Library

ISBN978 0 7453 3560 5 Hardback
ISBN978 0 7453 3559 9 Paperback
ISBN978 1 7837 1311 0 PDF eBook
ISBN978 1 7837 1313 4 Kindle eBook
ISBN978 1 7837 1312 7 EPUB eBook

10 9 8 7 6 5 4 3 2 1

Typeset by Swales & Willis
Text design by Melanie Patrick
Simultaneously printed by CPI Antony Rowe, Chippenham, UK
and Edwards Bros in the United States of America

Contents

Part 3 Supporting

Series Preface

Anthropology is a discipline based upon in-depth ethnographic works that deal with wider theoretical issues in the context of particular, local conditions—to paraphrase an important volume from the series: *large issues* explored in *small places*. This series has a particular mission: to publish work that moves away from an old-style descriptive ethnography that is strongly area-studies oriented, and to offer genuine theoretical arguments that are of interest to a much wider readership, but which are nevertheless located and grounded in solid ethnographic research. If anthropology is to argue itself a place in the contemporary intellectual world, then it must surely be through such research.

We start from the question: "What can this ethnographic material tell us about the bigger theoretical issues that concern the social sciences?" rather than "What can these theoretical ideas tell us about the ethnographic context?" Put this way round, such work becomes *about* large issues, *set in* a (relatively) small place, rather than detailed description of a small place for its own sake. As Clifford Geertz once said, "Anthropologists don't study villages; they study *in* villages."

By place, we mean not only geographical locale, but also other types of "place"— within political, economic, religious, or other social systems. We therefore publish work based on ethnography within political and religious movements, occupational or class groups, among youth, development agencies, and nationalist movements; but also work that is more thematically based—on kinship, landscape, the state, violence, corruption, the self. The series publishes four kinds of volume: ethnographic monographs, comparative texts, edited collections, and shorter, polemical essays.

We publish work from all traditions of anthropology, and all parts of the world, which combines theoretical debate with empirical evidence to demonstrate anthropology's unique position in contemporary scholarship and the contemporary world.

Professor Vered Amit
Professor Christina Garsten

Acknowledgments

This research is the fruit of a five-year scientific program funded by an Advanced Grant from the European Council for Research awarded to Didier Fassin (for an overview of the program and a complete list of the publications and events which resulted from it, see http://morals.ias.edu/). Both the French version and its English translation have been the product of the close collaboration of the ten contributors in the theoretical conception, the empirical approach and ultimately the writing of the research. We therefore consider that this book has a genuine collective authorship. We are grateful for the comments we received from colleagues and friends when presenting our initial findings, particularly during the conference "Au Coeur de l'État. Comment les Institutions Traitent leur Public," which was held at the École des Hautes Études en Sciences Sociales in Paris, as well as during seminars and discussions at the Institute for Advanced Study in Princeton. We wish to thank in particular João Biehl, Fabienne Brion, Manuela Ivone Cunha, Vincent Dubois, Benoit Dupont, Anthony Good, Carol Greenhouse, Bernard Harcourt, Fabien Jobard, Bruno Karsenti, Danièle Lochak, Steven Lukes, Gérard Mauger, José-Luis Moreno, Adriana Petryna, Richard Rechtman, and Marc-Henri Soulet. We also wish to thank Estelle Girard, Émilie Jacquemot, and Monique Da Silva in Paris and Donne Petito and Linda Garat in Princeton for their assistance in the various stages of this project. We express our gratitude to David Castle for his warm support of the project at Pluto Press and to Patrick Brown for his patient and careful translation realized in collaboration with Didier Fassin. Finally, we wish to recognize all those whose willing participation and generous availability have made this work possible—the police officers and commissioners, magistrates and lawyers, prison guards, counselors and directors, social workers and special educators, psychologists and psychiatrists as well as the publics of the institutions that we have studied.

Can States Be Moral?
Preface to the English Edition

What is a state? Answers to this question vary, depending on whether they are provided by a political philosopher, a political scientist, a legal scholar, or a historian. In the present book, we propose our own response as sociologists and anthropologists. But rather than in its disciplinary configuration, the specificity of our approach resides in its method: ethnography. A political organization governing a given territory and its population, the state is generally studied in terms of its formation, structure, functions, laws, and relations with other similar entities. Such an approach presupposes not only a macropolitical perspective, which tends to produce a relatively abstract representation from above, but also an a priori definition, which delimits the scope of the study.

Our method adopts a symmetrical view. It is inductive, micropolitical, and from below. It is based on the participant observation of various institutions through the routine work of their agents and the everyday interactions with their publics. We do not determine in advance what the police, the justice system, the prison apparatus, the welfare services, and the mental health facilities are, but we examine the situations and problems which the people who belong to these institutions are confronted with, and analyze how they manage them: our theory of the state is therefore constructed empirically. We do not presume that it is a unified entity, but explore the diversity of its rationalities: we analyze, for instance, the tensions and contradictions existing between the logics of security and rights, the principles of coercion and responsibility. The state, we believe, is what its agents do under the multiple influences of the policies they implement, the habits they develop, the initiatives they take, and the responses they get from their publics. By inverting traditional perspectives, whether they be normative or deductive, ethnography thus offers a unique way of approaching the state.

But the question "what is a state?" only makes sense within a given national context at a particular historical moment. The word "state" does not mean or evoke the same thing in France, where our study was conducted as it does in the United States, where it may be discussed. In the French context, there is a certain self-evidence of the state, built over a thousand years. It benefits from an enduring legitimacy and raises high expectations. Strong and centralized, it defines most norms and policies. In contrast, in the United States, the word can suggest either the federal state or one of the fifty entities which comprise it. In the first case, it is an institution with limited prerogatives and declining legitimacy in most domains, except those of national security and foreign affairs. In the second one, it is only a component of a larger political set but has a substantial autonomy as far as executive, legislative and judicial powers are concerned. Consequently, to mention the state when referring to the justice or prison system implies the government of the whole country in France and of only one of its fifty parts in the United States. The same expression thus corresponds to entirely distinct realities not only in terms of denotation (what it means) but also of connotation (what it evokes). The reader should keep this dual difference—of meaning and evocation—in mind when going through the various chapters.

But even within a national context, both denotation and connotation evolve over time. Thus, in the case of France, what the state is and what it does as well as what image is associated with it has changed over the last half-century in France, transforming from an authoritarian Gaullist regime at the start of the Fifth Republic with its planned economy and nationalized companies to the Conservative and Socialist governments of today which are equally beholden to neoliberal ideology and anti-Keynesian policies: not only has the role of the state changed, summed up by the famously disheartening phrase of a prime minister "the state cannot do everything," but so too has its legitimacy, which today is increasingly challenged. In other words, the state is always situated both geographically and historically.

Classical theories of the state, from Bodin and Hobbes to Marx and Weber, tend to represent it as a distant entity and even as a sort of "cold monster." Seen through an ethnographic lens, however, it becomes a distinct reality. The proximity with the agents reveals the warmer side of the state, so to speak. It is more than a bureaucracy with rules and procedures. Officers, magistrates, guards, social workers, mental health specialists also act on the basis of values and affects. Justice and fairness, concern or indifference, empathy or indignation, admiration or distrust are part of their experience in their relations, not only with their public but also with their colleagues, their superiors, and their institution. They inform their daily decisions and actions but are also informed by the ethos of their profession and the ethical climate of the public sphere. Professional principles of rigor, respect, accountability—or the lack thereof—and public debates stigmatizing certain behaviors, blaming certain populations, insinuating suspicion toward certain groups—or adopting the symmetrical perspectives—influence what the agents think and do.

At the macrosocial level, moral economies correspond to how values and affects are produced, circulate, and are appropriated around a given situation that society construes as a problem: immigration, asylum, crime, punishment, etc. At the microsocial level, moral subjectivities reveal the values and affects involved in the ethical issues and dilemmas faced by the agents with respect to these problems: freeing an undocumented foreigner or keeping him in detention, granting a claimant refugee status or rejecting his request, arresting a suspect for a minor offense or letting him go, applying mandatory prison sentences or choosing individualized punishment, etc. Moral subjectivities are influenced by moral economies, which in turn reinforce, contest, or displace. The way immigration, asylum, crime, and punishment are publicly debated weighs on the decisions of the agents, whose actions confirm, challenge, or inflect the terms of the debate. Thus, values and affects insinuate themselves everywhere in the government of populations: it is this moral life of the state that we are interested in.

Because these populations are socially, economically and often legally precarious, their government involves three rationalities: the welfare state, which protects the subjects from the hazards of life; the penal state, which decides which crime to punish and how, and the liberal state, which mobilizes simultaneously individual rights and individual obligations. In the past decades, the decline of the welfare state has been paralleled by the expansion of the penal state, while the liberal state has appeared as a way to legitimize the former evolution by invoking the responsibility of the subject and to mitigate the latter trend by introducing minimal legal guarantees. This ambiguous moral configuration is a unique feature of the contemporary state.

Didier Fassin
January 2015

Introduction

Governing Precarity

Didier Fassin

Three police officers from an anti-crime squad are cruising the streets of a downtown area in an unmarked car when they come across a van with two non-European-looking men inside; they decide to turn around, stop the vehicle, check the identities of the driver and his passenger, both Kurds, discover that the latter does not have a residence permit, and arrest him despite the pleas of the former, bluntly informing him that they are only doing their job. When they arrive back at the police station with the arrestee, their colleagues begin to crack jokes about their tendency to achieve their quotas by arresting undocumented immigrants rather than real criminals, like they are supposed to. The squad leader replies that he at least is defending his country against illegal immigration.

A young man of African descent listens to the charges of theft brought against him at an immediate appearance trial. Stopped and frisked in the lobby of his apartment building as he was returning home, law enforcement agents found in his possession several lunch vouchers in someone else's name. The man is further accused of insulting the police officers and resisting arrest. Although the prosecutor requests a one-year prison sentence and the lawyer for the officer demands punitive damages, the magistrates decide not to hand down the minimum sentence prescribed in cases of recidivism but instead determine on the basis of the social worker's report that the youth's family context and employment situation allow for a three-month suspended sentence. This will permit the judge overseeing the execution of the man's sentence to assign an alternative punishment rather than incarceration.

A disciplinary board comprised of a prison administrator and two guards judges an inmate accused of possessing of a cellular phone at a correctional facility. The man, an immigrant who had entered the country illegally, admits to the facts of the case, while his court-appointed lawyer attempts to offer an excuse, explaining that, isolated and marginalized, he just wanted to communicate with his family. While in deliberation, the three officials agree to consider that the man, a victim of the local prison gang, confessed in order to protect himself from reprisal. Hesitating over a sentence which would also take into account his vulnerability, but also confronted with a lack of space in the less restrictive seclusion cells, they end up placing him in solitary confinement, albeit for a shorter time than is called for according to disciplinary guidelines.

A counselor at a Youth Employment Center feels hindered in her job by the racial and religious discrimination that her clients must endure. Left with no other option but to explain to young Muslims that they must shave their beards or remove their veils if they are to stand a chance of being hired, she often faces resistance on their part for having to deny who they are in order to adapt to the expectations of their potential employers. Aware that her insistent suggestions only perpetuate illegal hiring practices by evaluating individuals based on their appearance rather than their abilities, she finds the situation all the more difficult because she too is sensitive to the unequal treatment of minorities on account of her own family background and university studies.

A team of psychiatrists and psychologists treats troubled teenagers at a so-called Home for Adolescents located in a public hospital. Although they understand that the behavioral issues which triggered their referral stem more from the situation of their families, which are almost always of immigrant origin, from the socioeconomic constraints weighing on their parents, and from the exclusionary practices of the school system, the mental health specialists gradually limit their intervention to relational aspects which they feel authorized to treat at the risk of validating the same injustices which beset these adolescents. In doing so, they nevertheless offer them a means to avoid alternative measures, notably legal ones, which would penalize them even more.

* * *

Though the scenes described above may differ in their institutional settings, they offer insight into the "heart" of the state. The police, the courts, the prisons, social services, and mental health units all represent the dual dimension of order and benevolence, of coercion and integration, or, better yet, illustrate the multiple aspects of a notion as central as it is ambiguous in contemporary societies: security, a term which signifies the protection of persons against criminal and delinquent activities when classified as "public," or alternatively against the hardships and vicissitudes of life when qualified as "social." This tension between the penal state and the welfare state is never as strong as when the population the state is dealing with is characterized by its precarity, be it economic or legal. Indeed, the line between dangerous categories and categories in danger, between those destined for repression and those who inspire compassion is thin and permeable. The same holds true for the populations that the institutions in these examples must handle: immigrants and minorities, recalcitrant inmates and troubled adolescents, undocumented foreigners and young people from the projects. Depending on their interlocutors at the time—police officers or magistrates, prison guards or special educators—they easily slip from one side of this moral line to the other, from the role of suspect to the status of victim and vice versa. Exploring the heart of the state therefore means, literally, to penetrate the ordinary functioning of public institutions, but also, metaphorically, to examine the values and affects underlying policies and practices.

The populations concerned, sometimes deemed illegitimate and worthy of contempt, sometimes vulnerable and in need of assistance, and sometimes both, call the state's very *raison d'être* into question. If, as Weber affirms, the state holds the "monopoly of legitimate use of violence," signifying that the latter is not its sole means of acting, but that it is "its specific means," by contrast, for Durkheim, it is also the "organ of social justice" through which "is organized the moral life of the country."[1] The public of the institutions considered in this present book fear the state as well as implore it, dread its punishment as well as demand its assistance. Moreover, if one considers their trajectories over time, many individuals essentially bounce from one service to the other. Certain adolescents follow an almost straight path from police station to court to prison that is in large part determined by their racial and social origins. Likewise, certain immigrants unwillingly follow almost parallel itineraries, with distinct stops depending on whether they are undocumented or seeking asylum, only to end up in the same detention centers as they await deportation. But all—whether teenagers or immigrants—frequently interact also with special educators from youth protective units or social workers from welfare services, counselors from employment centers or probation officers from correctional facilities, and sometimes mental health specialists. What ties together these institutions through which we attempt to grasp how the state functions is therefore empirical: they constitute the government of the precarious.

Attempting to comprehend the heart of the state while studying marginalized populations that occupy marginal territories of the urban geography and benefit from policies mustering only marginal resources might seem like a contradiction. Yet what we are defending is precisely the opposite, namely that it is in its margins, comprised at once in terms of populations, territories, and policies, that the contemporary state can best be captured—in the way that it deals with its poor and its delinquents, its immigrants and its detainees, in the manner that it administers sensitive urban neighborhoods and waiting zones at the border, correctional facilities and detention centers, in its use of practices at once opaque and spectacular, deviant, or illegal. Like Veena Das and Deborah Poole, we too are forced "to distance ourselves from the entrenched image of the state as a rationalized administrative form of political organization that becomes weakened or less fully articulated along its territorial or social margins."[2] Indeed, a number of the state's exclusive functions, notably police and justice, find their most complete realization in the administration of these marginal populations and spaces, whereas, even at the center of the state apparatus, institutions can contravene the laws that the state enacts and the norms that it promotes.

Thus, the state is not just a "political association" which rests on a "relation of men dominating men" as Weber maintains or a "sovereign force" which prevents other social forces from "being subordinated to individual interests" as Durkheim proposes—the former interpreting the state through a logic of power and the latter through an imperative for the public good. Beyond the idea of abstraction and neutrality which tends to be associated with it, the state is a concrete and situated reality. In other words, it is simultaneously embodied in the individuals and inscribed in a temporality. These two elements are essential to the ethnography of the state we propose. Rather than focus on the dematerialized "body politic" and the impartial "administration" described in dictionaries, we turn our attention to the physical persons who constitute the state and to the historical reasons which account for its development. No analysis of the state can ignore power relations, ideological evolutions, electoral outcomes, or the singularity of each national context. Far from being a readily essentialized entity that exists in a sort of permanence, the state is at any given moment a product of its time.

To study the state—in this case, the French one—within a specific historical period is therefore to present what the agents do when working for it and to consider the policies which it implements. It is the police who perform the identity checks in order to achieve the deportation goals set by the government under its immigration policy. It is the magistrates who at immediate appearance trials arbitrate between mandatory sentencing and the individualization of sentences under pressure from an executive denouncing their supposed leniency. It is the correctional officers who on a daily basis face the tensions between repressive policies leading to a constant increase in the number of incarcerations and new regulations meant to better respect the rights of inmates. It is the employment counselors who attempt to assist young adults by ensuring that their physical appearance is in line with the expectations of employers at the risk of reinforcing discriminatory rationales. It is the psychologists and psychiatrists who are increasingly expected to compensate for the failures of the education system and provide answers based on listening and mediation. The state reveals itself through these professionals as they simultaneously implement and produce public action.

A common representation of the state—particularly in France, given the role that it has historically played and the centralism which characterizes its structure—is that public policies derive from decisions made by the government and laws passed by legislators while civil servants simply implement them. This top-down reading does not allow for a complete understanding of the functioning of the state. But the bottom-up interpretation is no less reductive. It considers that grass-roots organizations or service deliverers are the real producers of policies—the former through their mobilization, the latter through their discretion. The approach that we develop could instead be regarded as a dialectical one, which is all the more justified considering that the state governs precarious populations. Indeed, its agents are confronted with explicit and implicit expectations formulated in discourses, laws and rules while keeping sizeable space to maneuver in the concrete management of situations and individuals. So it is in the actions of the agents within public institutions that the politics of the state can be grasped. In the scenes we previously mentioned, the police officers could decide whether or not to arrest the undocumented immigrant; the magistrates had the choice whether or not to apply minimum sentencing guidelines for a repeat offender by taking into account the social worker's report; the disciplinary board at the prison was in a position to consider or to ignore the context in determining the punishment for the offense committed by the inmate; the job counselors at the youth center allowed themselves to determine whether or not to send their clients to employers whom they knew to be habitual discriminators in an effort to anticipate their frustrations; and the psychologists and psychiatrists were able to acknowledge or to overlook the social etiology of the difficulties faced by the adolescents they treated—needless to say, they did not extricate themselves entirely from the symbolic and practical authority emanating from the state's directives and legislation.

One could go even further. It is not just a question of maintaining that the agents have room to interpret and freedom to act with respect to the injunctions of ministerial and parliamentary texts defining the modalities of their intervention. To do so would be to limit the focus to "tactics" which, according to Michel de Certeau, imply that the agents, without mastering the rules of the game, can only subvert them, whereas "strategies" suppose a certain autonomy to define these rules.[3] In reality, whether through over-zealousness or conviction, the agents often extend the realm of policies well beyond what is requested. In a sense, they are not content simply with implementing the policy of the state—they make it. They are the state. When a liberty and detention judge inquires into an undocumented person's past or present situation as the basis to request for their release, she exceeds the strict delimitation of her role and resists the repression of immigrants. When magistrates in charge of determining the merits of claims made by asylum seekers adopt a stance that is systematically suspicious of the applicants, their negative decisions contribute to the production of government statistics and public discourse on so-called "fake" refugees. When a probation officer evaluates the effectiveness of reintegration projects for inmates applying for parole with a certain leniency, she actively participates in the alternative sentencing policies and prevention of recidivism programs developed by her service. When social workers involved in youth protection adopt a long-term approach to their educational interventions rather than conform to the authorities' expectations of immediate and quantifiable results, they redefine the terms of adolescent supervision and delinquency prevention.[4] And in each of these institutions, it is of course also possible to observe attitudes symmetrical to those described which produce opposing policies: ones that are less concerned with the violation of the rights of immigrants, more liberal in the evaluation of requests for asylum, more apprehensive about the risks of recidivism, less reluctant to follow official technocratic injunctions.

In other words, it is not just the state which dictates a policy to its agents, it is also the agents themselves who make the policy of the state, by feeling more or less constrained by the scope of their job and resources, by taking more or less initiative with respect to the regulations imposed on them, and ultimately by politicizing in the fullest sense of the term their actions, that is, by giving them political significance. As a result, the state is no more an ethereal place where one works impartially for the common good as supposed in the classical tradition than it is a coercive apparatus merely serving the dominant as maintained by Marxist theorists. Ideas—notably that of the common good—and interests—especially those of the dominant—are of course defended in the state, but the state is neither idealist nor interested in a monolithic way. Following Pierre Bourdieu, one can analyze it as a "field," that is, a "space structured according to oppositions" which "correspond to the division of its organizational functions."[5] Various institutions defend differing ideas and interests. Their agents therefore do not represent the common good in the same manner: even if both value the protection of society against crime, the police and the magistrates do not achieve that goal by relying on the same values because order and justice are often in conflict with each other. But these institutions are themselves also divided by tensions and disagreements which are a partial reflection of their contrasting relationships maintained with the dominant classes: one need only look at the strained relations with police unions or the suspicions surrounding the nomination of certain prosecutors. Therefore, to speak of the politicization of the state does not entail the supposition of one agent's exclusive dominance, even in a politically polarized context, as was the case when we undertook our research between 2007 and 2012. Instead, it means privileging debates and conflicts over the abstract integrity which some claim to embody despite evidence to the contrary and whose demise others deplore while overlooking divisions and resistances.

* * *

The institutions—be they the police, the justice system, the correctional facilities, the social services, or the mental health units—are thus the site where the state is produced. This production does not occur in a vacuum: it operates in an ideological environment and under regulatory constraints. Nor does it exist in abstraction: it proceeds from the individual and collective actions of the agents. The institution precisely interests us insofar as it is at the intersection of policies and practices, at the interface between what occurs in the public sphere and what reflects the professional habitus. In the cases we studied, the police officer, the juvenile judge, the prison guard, the special educator, the social worker, and the mental health specialist are all agents of the state working in public institutions within a legal frame and with specific objectives. It would be beneficial to clarify this dual dimension.

On the one hand, institutions have their actions framed by legislation, by the allocation of resources, and by the organization of the means which determine at least in part their modalities: the rationales defined in the organic law governing public finance, the statistical tools for evaluating performance, the evolution of personnel assignments, the transformation of structures operate like constraints which circumscribe the possible but also foster innovation. On the other hand, the agents of these institutions also work in reference to a certain professional ethos, to the training they have received, to an idea they have of their actions, and to a routine they develop: the principles of justice or of order, the values of the common good and public service, the attention to social or psychological realities, or the ignorance of one or the other, all products of their professional habitus, influence the manner in which they will respond to state injunctions and behave towards their publics. Indeed, both institutions and agents are permeable and susceptible to the discourses about the populations they deal with and to the debates provoked by the implementation of their own mission: the stigmatization of undocumented immigrants, the distrust of asylum seekers, the indictment of judges accused of leniency, the incentive to promote a sense of responsibility, or the recognition of the banality of discrimination—in the cases provided here—are all likewise elements which pervade daily practices, provoking adherence, adaptation, or resistance.

Because they occupy this specific space where action is produced at the intersection of the national and the local, institutions allow for the theoretically delicate and methodologically uncertain operation of interconnecting the macro-sociological and micro-sociological levels, a problem long faced by the social sciences. As Aaron Cicourel writes, "Neither micro- nor macro-structures are self-contained levels of analysis, they interact with each other at all times despite the convenience and sometimes the dubious luxury of only examining one or the other level of analysis."[6] Most often, sociologists have examined either social structures or social interactions, thereby situating themselves either at a certain distance or inversely in close proximity. Institutions, because they function both at the macrosocial level of public policy and at the microsocial level of individual practices, represent an appropriate position and an apposite scale from which to observe these two levels. Thus, the study of law enforcement agencies makes it possible to grasp at once the security rationale of the government as well as the work of a police officer, the former defining the latter, but the latter giving content to the former. The same could be said for the justice and prison systems or for the socio-educational and medico-psychological services.

For several decades, the study of institutions has benefited from a significant renewal of interest in the social sciences, political theory, and economic history. While the individualist approaches which have long dominated these disciplines stress the choices made by supposedly rational actors and describe the aggregation of behaviors necessarily predisposed to a certain volatility, institutionalist approaches privilege the comprehension of what it is that makes "institutions endure," as Elisabeth Clemens and James Cook write.[7] Indeed, what is striking is the stability of institutions over long periods of time, be it justice or police, asylum or prison. And it is possible to take this even further: what is remarkable is not only that these institutions last, but that society is produced and reproduced through them. Agents do not behave like free electrons, but find themselves trapped within networks of meaning and action that are inscribed within the institutions. In that regard, institutions have a dual dimension with contradictory effects: their constraints impose limits on the liberty of the agents, whereas their frame enables them to live together. In the words of Judith Butler, we are both subjected and subjectivized by the institutions, notably by the most visible of them: the state.[8] Power in general and that which is inscribed within these institutions in particular produce subjects (in the fullest sense of the term) who obey rules and norms all the while being constituted by them.

At the same time, this stability of institutions is put to the twin test of variation and change. Firstly, institutions differ according to national, if not local context: the common law of English-speaking countries built upon the accumulation of jurisprudence and the civil law of the Roman tradition based on the passage of legislation produce remarkably distinct justice systems from the point of view of the role of magistrates; police forces which must account to local officials and therefore to the public for their actions in the United States and the national police principally answering to its hierarchic authority within the state apparatus in France employ specific modes of regulation. Secondly, institutions evolve over time under the influence of multiple factors: some are internal and related to conflicts of rationales, as is the case for the appeals system for asylum seekers which has been reformed to reinforce the independence of the court toward the administration and the fairness of the rulings with regard to existing discrepancies; others are external and fall under the transformation of political orientations, as has been seen with prison probation officers, who shift from social assistance to sentence enforcement. Thus, admittedly, institutions endure, but they also vary according to national traditions and change depending on historical circumstances.

Works that focus on the permanence of institutions as well as the variations within them and changes over time generally highlight on the one hand the rules and procedures and on the other hand the interests and competitions. Yet the question remains: how can one understand the ways in which the rules and procedures come to be imposed and the interests and competitions defined as such? To answer this question, sociologists and above all anthropologists have sought to study the culture in which institutions are inscribed and consequently the norms on which they are founded and the rationales from which they are derived. Thus Mary Douglas wonders "how institutions think": not that she would attribute a sort of magic virtue to them by implying that they are endowed with an autonomous reflexive capacity; instead, she simply maintains that they are more than the sum of the individual decisions of the agents who compose them.[9] By showing how they operate through analogy and classification, how they make life or death decisions, she essentially concentrates on their cognitive dimension. However, institutions do more than just think, they also implement values and affects, judgments and sentiments. It is this moral dimension, rarely discussed, that we explore in our inquiry: how institutions assess and feel, so to speak.

In this regard, Durkheimian and Weberian analyses generally lead to a vision of the state as an impartial and dispassionate institution. This cold rationality is personified in bureaucracy. In his study of the western administrative apparatus based on the case of contemporary Greece, Michael Herzfeld observes this paradox: societies that have the most ancient and most generous traditions of hospitality can also be those whose bureaucracies prove in practice to be the most indifferent toward the populations that they are supposed to serve, if not the most aggressive toward those categories whose exclusion they succeed in legitimizing.[10] To mention indifference or aggressiveness is to underline the affective side of bureaucratic work, including when empathy is suspended or even reversed—a tendency clearly associated with an evaluative component through which agents judge their public. Indeed, moral questions always associate the rational with the emotional and the judgments with the sentiments. As rigorous as they try to be, magistrates not only apply the law at a trial, they assess the sincerity or the duplicity of the arraigned, they feel sympathy or antipathy toward the accused. As professional as they consider themselves to be, employment counselors do not only adhere to managerial rationales, they gauge the young applicant, they feel angered by the discriminatory practices of an employer. To grasp this moral dimension of the institution, we turn to two concepts: moral economy and moral subjectivity.

Moral economies represent the production, circulation, and appropriation of values and affects regarding a given social issue.[11] Consequently, they characterize for a particular historical moment and a specific social world the manner in which this issue is constituted through judgments and sentiments that gradually come to define a sort of common sense and collective understanding of the problem. Thus, one can speak of the moral economy of asylum to characterize the transformations of values and affects around the question of refugees: positively valued and emotionally charged in the 1970s and 1980s, when persecutions by Latin American and Southeast Asian dictatorships turned them respectively into heroes or victims, the figure of the asylum seeker was gradually modified to make way in the 1990s for the image of the "fake refugee," stirring mistrust whether he or she came from the Democratic Republic of Congo or Chechnya, Bangladesh or Haiti. Obviously, it is less the objective reality of the persecutions that has evolved than the subjective approach that one has of it. In the same way, the moral economy of punishment involves the appropriateness and fairness of the sentence, which change over time: the rehabilitative paradigm of the sanction, which was dominant until the 1970s, has been replaced by a retributive one, but this punitive turn has disproportionately affected disadvantaged minorities by focusing repression on certain types of offenses, such as drug use, while overlooking others, such as financial crime. As can be seen, moral economies do not characterize a specific group or activity—we do not speak of the moral economies of judges or of justice—but of a social fact—here, asylum or punishment.

Moral subjectivities refer to the processes by which individuals develop ethical practices in their relationships with themselves or others.[12] They attest to the autonomy and freedom of agents, notably within contexts in which opposing values can come into conflict, contradictory sentiments can create tensions, or political injunctions can run counter to professional ethos. They may be conscious exercises stemming from reflections on a dilemma or they may be ordinary gestures stemming from a sense of care. Thus, the members of a prison disciplinary board can decide not to apply sentencing guidelines to an inmate who is found in possession of a telephone or who angrily replied to a guard by taking into account both the necessity to recall the authority of the rules and the singularity of the individual situation; likewise, the police can lend a sympathetic ear to the plight of an undocumented immigrant whom they have arrested or psychiatrists can express their concern with regard to an African father destabilized by his son's delinquent behavior. In discussing subjectivities, we do not seek to encroach upon the field of psychology, which is not ours, but to signify the sociological production of subjects both as subjection and subjectivation.

Relating these two concepts, as we propose to do here, allows us to combine the two major approaches to moral questions in the social sciences inspired by Kant and Aristotle, namely the ethic of duty and the ethic of virtue, respectively.[13] According to the first paradigm, any society is characterized at a given moment by a set of norms and values which defines a moral code to which individuals must submit themselves either out of an obligation to accomplish their duty or out of a desire to do good. According to the second paradigm, any individual can develop virtuous practices with respect to him or herself and with respect to others independently of the rules that are collectively imposed. The first approach underscores constraint, the second freedom. But moral economies and moral subjectivities offer insights into the moral world of institutions that differ in some way from these philosophical legacies. Unlike codes, which are fixed and stable, moral economies permit us to grasp the changes in time and the appropriations by agents: norms and values are not simply imposed upon them, and furthermore they are associated with emotions and sentiments. Unlike virtues, which ultimately refer to practices focused on seeking to do good, moral subjectivities integrate all forms of practices having moral content whatever their valence and thus include resentment or indignation as well as compassion or admiration.

Moral economies and moral subjectivities are connected in the daily activities of institutions through the values and affects which crystallize around social issues and the responses that are given in concrete situations: for the law enforcement agent, the immigration judge, the probation officer, and the job counselor, they are respectively the insecurity embodied in the adolescent from the projects, the suspicion in the asylum seeker, the dangerousness in the inmate considered for parole, the unemployment in the discriminated young adult. These professionals face each of these cases through evaluations and emotions, judgments on what is a true refugee or a good prisoner and indignation over a lack of respect or a need for justice. To describe the moral work of institutions is therefore to account for both the tensions within the public sphere surrounding these problems (moral economies) and the actions in the professional world charged with resolving them (moral subjectivities). This moral work is therefore inseparable from the political stakes which underlie both of them—at the heart of the state.

Notes

1 See Max Weber (1994 [1919]: 310–11) and Émile Durkheim (1986 [1900]: 48).
2 See Veena Das and Deborah Poole (2004: 3).
3 "A tactic insinuates itself into the other's place, fragmentarily, without taking it over in its entirety, without being able to keep it at a distance" writes Michel de Certeau in *The Practice of Everyday Life* (2011 [1980]: xix).

4 In this respect, our conception of the role of agents in the implementation of actions by the state coincides with the sociological approaches developed regarding what Michael Lipsky coined as "street-level bureaucracy," implying that "the actions of most public service workers actually constitute the services 'delivered' by the government" and that "when taken together the individual decisions of these workers become, or add up to, agency policy" (2010: 3). For a recent overview of the literature on these approaches, refer to the case studies directed by Evelyn Brodkin (2011). Within the French context, this literature has contributed even more so than in the American academic environment to a renewed interest in analyses of the state, notably in the works of Vincent Dubois (2012 [1999]), and Alexis Spire (2008) on the relationships at welfare centers and immigration services respectively.

5 In Pierre Bourdieu's lectures at the Collège de France from 1989 to 1992 published under the title *Sur l'État* (2012: 40).

6 The difficulty lies in the fact that the macro-sociological approach seems too far removed from real practices, while the micro-sociological approach appears to ignore structural rationales (Cicourel 1981).

7 The interest in institutions (Clemens and Cook 1999) developed through different trends in history, sociology, economics, and political science as "new institutionalisms" (Hall and Taylor 1996), focusing on the role of norms, procedures, and systems; however, these approaches did not entirely supplant the "old institutionalism" (Stinchcombe 1997), more attentive to the role of actors in the production of institutions.

8 Developing Michel Foucault's analysis, Judith Butler writes: "This 'subjection' or *assujettissement* is not only a subordination but a securing and maintaining, a putting into place of a subject, a subjectivation" (1997: 90).

9 In fact, Mary Douglas even believes that "the individual tends to leave the important decisions to his institutions while busying himself with tactics and details" (1986: 111).

10 As Michael Herzfeld writes: "How and why can political entities that celebrate the rights of individuals and small groups so often seem cruelly selective in applying those rights?" (1992:1).

11 A thorough analysis of this concept is presented elsewhere (Fassin 2012a). I will not redevelop it here, but simply recall that moral economies had first been described by the historian of the working class E.P. Thompson (1971) to account for the systems of norms and obligations which govern traditional economies and whose rupture is liable to bring about protests and revolts, and that they were subsequently reformulated by the historian of science Lorraine Daston (1995) to discuss networks of values and affects which feed the work of agents of a given social world. Although these two versions might seem incompatible, my own definition partially draws on both, retaining the critical edge of the former and the affective dimension of the latter.

12 The understanding of morality in terms of subjectivation corresponds to the "ethical turn" in Michel Foucault's work, especially in *The Use of Pleasure* (1985 [1984]). Alongside conforming moral codes and individual behaviors, the author of the *History of Sexuality* identifies ethical conduct in reference to the actions of work on oneself through which the subject transforms his or her relationship with him or herself and with others. This approach has led to important developments in the anthropology of ethics (Faubion 2011).

13 For a presentation of these two paradigms of morality in the social sciences, notably within the domain of anthropology, see the seminal article by James Laidlaw (2002) as well as my recent synthesis (Fassin 2010).

Part I
Judging

CHAPTER ONE

The Right to Punish

Assessing Sentences in Immediate Appearance Trials

Chowra Makaremi

So how many hours of sleep did you get last night since you had to be in court? Want to know if you'll see your kids tonight? That all depends on how many cases you have … That's what we talk about with colleagues. You have such a huge caseload that you almost become a robot. You make decisions when you're only half-informed about the cases. Numbers are what's most important: you make choices, you take risks for yourself and others. You take a look at the file and think, "So-and-so is clearly guilty," except that anyone who has more time to read the file sees that it is much more complicated than that. But you don't have time to read the case closely and can miss things … It's really frustrating.

This was how one deputy prosecutor working in a large court district in the banlieues of Paris where we conducted our research[1] described his job. His words illustrate the extent to which the rise in the number of immediate appearance trials has increased the pressures placed not only on the day-to-day activities of his job, but also on the very meaning of what he does and what is at stake. As a result of several newly enacted laws and changes to penal policy guidelines, the number of immediate appearance trials rose by 43 percent between the years 2002 and 2006. This new form of judicial procedure has three major characteristics: it is a way of prosecuting minor offenses quickly, is aimed at offenders with prior convictions, and usually leads to a prison sentence (in 2010, 45 percent of all prison sentences handed down stemmed from immediate appearance trials).[2]

Immediate appearance trials are held in cases where the individual is accused of having committed an offense punishable by a prison sentence of six months to ten years. The trial occurs within 48 hours of the defendant's arrest, while he or she still remains in police custody. It is a so-called assembly-line type of legal procedure used today in nearly a third of all court hearings.[3] This "prosecution in real time," as it is termed, is based on a penal system that operates under constant pressure, involving actors and institutions from various fields: the police officers who arrest the defendant, the prosecutors who decide whether or not to refer the case to trial, the psychologists and social workers who conduct social reports, the criminal court judges who preside over the trial itself, and finally the sentencing judges who are responsible for adjusting the sentence either immediately after it is handed down, or while the convicted offender is serving it out. The social and political implications of this penal system have been consistently highlighted by sociological studies on the topic for several decades:[4] it is a harsh and swift form of justice characterized by particularly high rates of conviction following a trial that rarely lasts more than twenty to forty minutes.

Immediate appearance trials exemplify the political uses of the penal system as a key tool in the fight against crime. Two processes are at play here: first, the judiciary is reorganized to ensure the swift prosecution of offenses; second, penal policies are devised to target recidivism. Since the 2000s, the latter process has given rise to new tools in the systematization of convictions, such as the application of mandatory minimum sentences. These two stances are not unique to immediate appearance trials: prosecution in real time prompts a wide range of penal responses, and the prevention of recidivism is a fundamental consideration in the judgment of both felonies and misdemeanors since mandatory minimum sentences are applicable in other judicial procedures as well. Yet immediate appearance trials are "seen as quintessential to swift prosecution,"[5] and it is during these trials that most mandatory minimum sentences are required and applied. Thus, they offer a privileged vantage point from which to observe the logics at play in the handling of offenses. By examining the judiciary in light of this legal procedure, we will show how the penal response has become a way of governing social problems and how it has evolved since the 1980s within the context of security policies.

The above-described logics portray a judgment molded by constraints. How do these constraints shape the sentence which is at odds with other principles of justice such as the right to a defense, the individualization of the sentence, and the prohibition of administrative detention? And with regard to the actors and their daily practices, how do such constraints frame the judgment and determine, if not override, it, and how do judges reclaim their function within this system?

First, I will analyze the history and functioning of immediate appearance trials in order to understand how the handling of petty crime is conceived of as a social and moral project specific to the state's governing of populations that are characterized by their precarity. In this context, the actual exercise of justice is organized around a question that is at once moral, legal, and political: that of automatic versus individualized penalties. I will subsequently explore this tension through a qualitative examination of criminal hearings. A courtroom ethnography shows how the work of the actors negotiates between two opposing tendencies: on the one hand, the systematic nature of the sentence, be it an effect of the organization of the large-scale penal machine or a technical tool for repressive public policies, and, on the other hand, the necessity for the individualization of sentences, which is enshrined as a fundamental principle of criminal law. When, why, and how do magistrates decide to rely on the tools of individualization to soften the determinative effects of mandatory sentencing? What room for discretion does the interplay between systematization and personalization offer the actors of the justice system? Lastly, what is the conception of the offenders underlying this judgment, and which subjects of penal action do these mechanisms produce?

The Penal Handling of Offenses: Between Social Control and Moral Regulation

The quick and widespread judicial procedure known as immediate appearance trial took shape through the sedimentation of two rationales which still lie at the heart of this system today. On the one hand, the penal apparatus is reorganized around the concept of recidivism, and on the other hand, it is oriented towards the management of influxes. A look at the genesis of the French penal system shows how these two notions—recidivism and prosecution in real time—are historically rooted in the social and political will to regulate "floating populations" in the nineteenth century. This targeting of populations identified by their urban and social marginality helps us to understand why and how immediate appearance trials were reformed, expanded, and presented as a political response to the question of "insecurity" associated with youths from immigrant backgrounds beginning in the early 1980s.

The Repeat Offender: A Subject of Judicial Intervention

In light of contemporary laws promoting the repression of recidivism, this "creative obsession"[6] of the nineteenth century has been the subject of increased attention in recent years. Studies devoted to the concept of recidivism indicate that it is a relatively recent one, emerging at the end of the eighteenth century only to be imposed on judicial practice over the course of the next century.[7] According to Mario Sbriccoli, the reflection on the causes of "criminality" is driven by the first crime statistics and their dissemination, albeit in embryonic form, through the nascent press in the second half of the eighteenth century. His analysis is thus inscribed in the perspective proposed by Michel Foucault, who showed how statistical tools helped to construct the population as an object of government.[8]

Studies on the notion of recidivism highlight its absence in penal systems prior to the Revolution. The category is only imposed over the course of an important evolution in the social organization that underlies the forms of control: the transition from mutual acquaintanceship to anonymity and the increase in geographic mobility through the urbanization and industrialization of the country. Thus, according to Frédéric Chauvaud, the interest of criminal lawyers in recidivism only took off in the early nineteenth century, when France experienced an initial period of industrialization.[9] While local societies lost their power to manage conflicts and maintain order, the "national state" found itself "first in line to ensure the safety of people and their property," contends Philippe Robert.[10]

The importance of recidivism and the figure of the recidivist are thus the result of transformations in modes of legal, political, and social regulation. They echo an evolution not only in the exercise of justice, but also in the philosophy of punishment. They point to a shift in the conception of the offender, the dangers he presents to society, and the ways in which he can be reformed.[11] From these discussions emerges the fundamental principle of individualized sentencing.

The Paradoxes of Sentence Individualization

In his work on the birth of the prison, Michel Foucault traces the genealogy of an early nineteenth-century reform movement that developed a new approach to sentencing, marking a break with the idea of punishment.[12] The sentence was aimed at the rehabilitation of the offender from a humanistic and utilitarian perspective. In this view, the social reintegration of the deviant individual was both a more effective form of protecting society, and a practice of coercive power mindful of the value and dignity of the subject on whom it is exercised. This movement was embodied by the French Penitentiary School, or the Prison Society, founded after the restoration of the monarchy at a time when philanthropic enterprises were taking off.[13] The thought of individualizing punishment was gradually integrated into the philosophy of criminal law beginning in the nineteenth century, eventually becoming a fundamental principle thereof.[14] The principle of an individualized sentence, built around the offender as a person, around his individual responsibility, and around his potential for moral reform was introduced into the French legal tradition through a seminal text published by the criminal lawyer Raymond Saleilles in 1898. The text enshrined in the law a reversal in the definition of the "right to punish," which took place over the course of the century: the sentence was not only the retribution of one wrong for another, as established by Christian tradition, but also a right that remedied a wrong. The idea of individualized sentences was imposed as the practical application of this shift. It concerned as much the goals of reform and socialization attributed to the sentence—at once useful to society and desirable for the individual convicted— as it did the perception of the offender on which this enterprise was based: a responsible person who will be the subject of a moral transformation prompted by the evaluation process entailed by individualization. This, argues Saleilles, was in fact motivated by

> the now indispensable need to take into account the individual himself and therefore the necessity to proportion the sentence less according to the act he has committed or the external wrong that he has produced, than on a wrong which is inside of him, on a kind of latent and potential criminality which makes him a danger to others, on his degree of morality or, if it can be said, of normalcy, and on the chances of rehabilitation he can offer.[15]

In practice, the principle of individualization increased the amount of discretion in sentencing, offering judges more autonomy in the choice of sentence and in the elements that could be considered during adjudication. The last point has two consequences: first, individual responsibility is assessed by taking into account the intention; second, the personality of the individual (his moral sense, manners, and character) becomes part of the judgment beyond the act committed. As Saleilles points out, "Individualization and specialization of the sentence would have to take into account the whole individual, not the fragment revealed by the crime."[16] So individualized judgments echo the paradox that lies at the heart of Foucault's genealogical work on the prison: while the conditions of punishment may have been softened, the humanist and utilitarian approach is also more intrusive in so far as the sentence focuses on the offender as a moral subject.

But the attention paid to recidivism reveals another paradox: the principle of sentence individualization is concomitant with the Law of May 27, 1885 on the banishment of recidivists, which establishes "perpetual internment" in penal colonies for delinquents and criminals who exceed a certain threshold of violations. The promotion of convicts' capacity for moral reform goes hand-in-hand with the assumption that a fraction of them remain forever incorrigible. Seen as a critical threat to social order, the notion of recidivism born out of this new penal policy thus suggests a perception of both crime and the criminal rooted in the hesitation between two conflicting imperatives: the integration (or objective reentry) of the offender into the social body and the exclusion (or definitive distancing) of individuals deemed incapable of amending their ways.[17] Examining the convict profiles found within "reports of recidivism" kept by the archives of the Paris courts, it becomes apparent that between the restoration of French monarchy in the 1830s and the start of the Third Republic in the 1870s, an itinerant "population" of recidivists came into being, living in poverty on the margins of society, pushed beyond the walls of Haussmann's Paris.[18] It is precisely with regard to the management of this population living in urban marginality and wage instability that the police and the judiciary develop in the intervening period a method of handling the constant flow of offenses, a method later legalized as "*in flagrante delicto.*"

The Origins of Real-time Prosecution

In flagrante delicto judgments were introduced by a series of penal reforms in the second half of the nineteenth century. René Lévy shows how the Law of 1863 instituting this procedure formalizes and legalizes judicial and police practices gradually introduced during the Second Empire.[19] This procedure appears as a functional necessity, allowing for a response to key transformations in the courts, namely the importance and autonomy acquired by prosecutors as well as in the police, particularly through changes in law enforcement methods, the redeployment of police officers and gendarmes, and the creation of police files. The handling of offenses in real time via a simplified investigation conducted by the police thus appears as a tool to "adapt to the productivity of the judiciary to that of the police."[20]

Analysis of the legislative debates accompanying the institution of in flagrante delicto highlights a fundamental issue: is it possible to reconcile freedom and security? This question will color subsequent developments in the law even until today. First conceived as a solution to the problem of preventive detention for those who posed a flight risk, in flagrante delicto restricted the controversial use of pre-trial detention for "itinerants," which had become an increasingly widespread practice during the nineteenth century. However, far from correcting the social arbitrariness of imprisonment before trial, the law validated its use because the detention was justified by the risk that the accused would abscond and not by the gravity of the act. The deprivation of liberty was thus made necessary by the social precarity of the individual being judged, even if this deprivation proved groundless after the judgment. As the parliamentary debates on the adoption of the law in 1864 show, the in flagrante delicto trial was presented as a concrete system that would reconcile two conflicting concerns: on the one hand, the risk of undermining the respect for the freedom of "honorable citizens" potentially exposed to "persecutory acts," and on the other, the need to secure urban centers plagued by crime. The cause of this latter concern was attributed to a "floating population"—"people without hearth or home, without livelihoods, at odds with society, recidivists"[21]—which was made the target of criminal proceedings in real time. "Honorable citizens" versus "people without hearth or home": from its inception, the in flagrante delicto trial appears as a tool for the differential penal management of the population.

The Defendants: Young Men Often from Migrant Families

Handling crime in real time through the use of immediate criminal hearings is therefore part of the same structural evolution in the methods of social regulation that placed the notion of recidivism at the center of penal thought in the nineteenth century. Beginning in 1864, the procedure acquired a stable form, which lasted for more than a century until the reforms of the 1980s. In addition to this procedural stability, there also exists a consistency in the social uses of this prosecutorial form, as shown by the homogeneity of the population it affects. When immediate appearance trials were first instituted in the early 1980s, René Lévy observed that the penal clientele affected by this procedure was becoming increasingly younger and beginning to include more and more immigrants. Statistical studies conducted at the time explained that the over-representation of defendants with foreign backgrounds could be attributed to the choices of penalization determined by the police and prosecutors: "Even when they are French nationals, the probability [that these defendants] will be tried for in flagrante delicto is double that of French persons of metropolitan origin and 50% higher than French persons from overseas territories."[22] Relying on statistical data collected in the field, we can say that this trend has increased significantly, with an even younger public and even more people of foreign origin affected today.[23]

The population targeted by this criminal procedure is distinguished not only by social, racial, age, and gender characteristics that remain constant over time, but also by a degree of homogeneity in their backgrounds. In France, nearly four out of five defendants have a low level of education and a criminal record, which, as several studies have already established, is indicative of the formation of a judicial and police "clientele."[24] While the consistency in the profiles of those tried in immediate appearance trials comes as little surprise, the offenses in question have in fact evolved since the 1980s. The share of traffic offenses, charges of insulting a police officer or resisting arrest, and immigration violations has increased sharply. These evolutions are due to changes in legislation and public policies which promote the criminalization of certain offenses such as driving without a license or the lack of a residence permit. Yet they also stem from a managerial interest in resolving observed offenses immediately, in order to satisfy numerical objectives demanded by new methods of evaluating police activity. As for the nature of the sentences, half of them translate into hard jail time. And one cannot help but notice their severity, which has been highlighted by the quantitative analyses produced on the subject since the Second Empire.

In sum, the historical approach highlights two dimensions. First, the judgment procedure, which is both swift and severe, targets a homogeneous population that is socially excluded and portrayed as a threat. Second, it is closely linked to the constraints imposed on police activity. The function of social control assigned to this form of prosecution explains why it was used in the last decades and privileged over any other type of public action in the service of the fight against crime as it became a major political issue. With *in flagrante delicto*, the state management of social problems related to the modern condition (mobility, insecurity, urban marginality) acquired a penal dimension. This trend continues under the form of immediate appearance trials, even though the realities to which the social exclusion refers have since changed. The precarious margins of the nineteenth-century working class have been replaced by disadvantaged youth of immigrant origin: the racial question has been superimposed on the social question.[25]

The Penal Instrument of Security Policies

Public representations and actual categorizations at play in immediate appearance trials, as well as the function of social control assigned to them, inscribe this penal treatment within a broader project of "moral regulation."[26] Within this project, social relations are renegotiated over the course of major evolutions, like those experienced in France with post-colonial immigration and the settlement of migrant populations through multiple processes of exclusion.[27] Practices of moral regulation do not mask other forms of political and social control, but coexist alongside them, says Allan Hunt. They refer, according to the definition given by Philip Corrigan and Derek Sayer, to a "project of normalizing, rendering neutral, taken for granted, in a word 'obvious,' what are in fact ontological and epistemological premises of a particular and historical form of social order."[28]

In recent times, two moments have come to illustrate the reconfiguration of the moral issues underlying the political uses of the justice system: on the one hand, the expansion and increasing usage of immediate appearance trials beginning in the early 1980s, and on the other hand, the repressive evolution of the legislative and judicial system since the 2000s.

Unreformed for over a century, *in flagrante delicto* judgments were significantly reworked by the Law of February 2, 1981, only to be subsequently revisited by the Law of June 10, 1983 which established "immediate appearance trials." These penal reforms came at a time when the fight against crime had become a major priority in public debates and policies, while the issue of insecurity established itself as a social problem and a matter of "common sense" spanning the left–right divide.[29] This was accompanied by the emergence of institutional and media discourses surrounding the question of "urban violence." According to Laurent Bonelli, the report presented by Minister of Justice Alain Peyrefitte in 1977 was a milestone in the gray literature produced on this subject. It marked the beginning of a global approach toward the "new general feeling of insecurity," which would prevail in the ensuing decades. The ministerial report's initial assessment was that "violence has taken hold in the heart of the city," especially "ordinary violence, as if life itself had become violent." Based on various institutional statistics and opinion polls, this approach was based on the assumption that affects and collective emotions were in a state of crisis or, as the report termed it, a "feeling of insecurity" that could be defined through four assertions: "The risk of being a victim breeds fear. The spectacle of violence provokes emotion. The tensions of collective life cause exasperation. Anxiety stems from the feeling that the situation is difficult to define."[30]

This line of reasoning was adopted by Alain Peyrefitte in order to justify his Liberty and Security Act of 1981, which reformed the *in flagrante delicto* trial (giving the procedure its present form), while at the same time amended the Penal Code to include repressive measures like increased penalties for repeat offenders, constraints on suspended sentences, and limits placed on parole. Partial revisions to this law would be made by the new Socialist government when it later passed the Law of June 10, 1983, but the procedure of "direct referral to the criminal court" was nevertheless retained. The minister of justice justified the procedure's retention, arguing that it made "justice swifter." But the very name of the law and the introductory speech before the National Assembly presented these penal reforms as a response to the perception of political and social issues expressed as a "feeling of insecurity," the recurring theme of which had grown increasingly evident in the public and media debate.[31]

This discourse on insecurity reverberated throughout various public forums: expert reports, law commissions, the judiciary, the media.[32] The conversations that took place would determine the values and reference points from which security concerns would unfold in the ensuing decades. Following the legislative push of 1981, further adjustments were made to penal policies, including the Internal Security Act of 1994, which toughened penalties for certain traffic and immigration offenses (among others) by reclassifying them as misdemeanors. Between these two dates, securitarian common sense was compounded by a resurgence of xenophobic discourse in the public sphere directed against undocumented immigrants and French youth of immigrant origin living in low-income neighborhoods.[33]

The handling of crime has undergone several significant reforms since the establishment of immediate appearance trials, especially in the last decade: more than fifty criminal laws have been enacted between 2000 and 2012. These laws follow a general trend marked by two characteristics: on the one hand, the expansion of police powers over deferment to the courts, and on the other, the diversification and strengthening of legal tools for the punishment of recidivism. The latter responds to a desire to enhance the deterrence effect of the sentence by relying on theories of crime and society like the "broken windows" theory. Imported from the United States, this theory views disorder—be it qualified legally or not, as in the case of "antisocial behavior"—as an invitation for crime. As a result, acts presenting a potential for social disorder, beyond the threat that each of them poses individually, collectively become the object of public action for the prevention of crime. This prevention is in turn based on an exponential increase in the cost of the offense for the offender, who is perceived as a rational actor.[34] The Law of December 12, 2005 on "the prosecution of repeat criminal offenses" increased the prison time as well as the probation time when the offender was in a state of legal recidivism. The Law of August 10, 2007 "strengthening the fight against recidivism in adults and minors" introduced a major reform in the French legal system by including mandatory minimum sentences for repeat offenders. One effect of this reform was the systematization of convictions, as sentences were to be determined from then on by a minimum based on the existence of prior convictions. While mandatory minimum sentencing was applicable in other penal procedures, its impact on the immediate appearance trial was particularly important, since the latter targets a population of young offenders who have already been in trouble with the law. According to the quantitative data collected in the field, 65 percent of people judged in immediate appearance trials were in a state of legal recidivism (meaning the second act was of the same legal category as the previous one), while 85 percent of them had prior convictions (meaning the second act was not specific).

An initial assessment of the application of the 2007 Act underscores its impact on the increase in the country's prison population: the number of people in custody in France grew from 63,000 in 2006 to 68,000 in late 2007, and the average overall length of prison sentences went from 7 to 16 months over the same period.[35] However, magistrates can waive minimum sentences if they provide a justified decision. Judges do use this practice, which allows them to preserve the French ethic of "individualized sentences" within a new rationale of automaticity. There is indeed a tension between the principle of individualization enshrined in French penal law and the introduction of mandatory minimum sentences as part of a technical arsenal standardizing penal responses in cases of recidivism. This tension produced much controversy and resistance. First proposed in 2005 by the Conservative Party which was in power at the time (at the initiative of Minister of the Interior Sarkozy to the dismay of Minister of Justice Perben), the draft law on minimum mandatory sentences was initially rejected on the grounds that it opposed the French tradition of sentence individualization.

Personalizing the Investigation

The principle of individualization was first imposed through the discretion granted to judges in assessing a sentence depending on the character and previous history of the defendant. Since its inception in the late nineteenth century, this principle has been subjected to different changes. The most notable ones were inspired by the post-World War II criminal lawyer Marc Ancel, who would have considerable influence on Minister of Justice Robert Badinter, and the reforms of criminal procedure in the 1980s and 1990s. Championing a rehabilitative and humanist approach to criminology or, as he called it, the "new social defense (*défence sociale nouvelle*)," Ancel revisited individualization, favoring instead the concept of the "personalization" of the sentence, which was introduced under his influence in the new Penal Code of 1994:

> Within the limits set by law, the court hands down sentences and determines how they will be carried out according to the circumstances of the offense and the character of its author ... The nature, length, and way in which the sentence is carried out are determined so as to reconcile the effective protection of society, the punishment of the convicted, and the interests of the victim with the need to promote the integration or reintegration of the convicted and prevent the commission of further offenses.[36]

Reference to the "person" rather than the "individual" is indicative of a moral approach to the reform of offenders,[37] explicitly demanded by Christian concepts of "charity" and "redemption" introduced in the philosophy of sentencing. The emphasis on "moral rehabilitation"[38] turns the sentence into a process by which the accused is held "accountable for his actions" by the judicial institution. In practice, the evaluation of the person responsible for the criminal act requires systematic assessment methods that go beyond the subjective interpretation developed by the judges during trials. To do this, psychological and sociological thought was introduced into the judicial analysis, making room for social backgrounds and formations of character. Introduced in France in the early 1980s, the "brief social report" provided this method and became the specific tool in the implementation of sentence personalization in adjudication.

Brief social reports were established as part of an initiative of the Ministry of Justice with the aim of testing in France a method that had been previously experimented with in the United States.[39] In 1960, the Vera Institute of Justice, a private entity located in New York City, established a survey method for assessing the social integration of defendants who did not have sufficient assets to post bail pending their trials and were therefore remanded into custody, even if the severity of the offense of which they were accused did not justify such a deprivation of liberty. The United States has no legal equivalent to immediate appearance trials, which were of course conceived as a response to the issue of provisional detention. The studies conducted by the Vera Institute presented information on the financial situation, living arrangements, career paths, and family situations of the accused, which allowed judges to assess whether those who were too poor to afford bail were nonetheless integrated into a social network and would therefore be likely to appear in court.[40] The experiment was exported to France in 1980 by a team of investigators trained by the New York experts to assist judges in their decision whether or not to grant bail to persons held in custody. This method was quickly extended to *in flagrante delicto* trials, proving useful to the magistrates, while its application to provisional detention was abandoned.[41] Since then, the brief social report form has become a full-fledged tool for judging in real time. And while the apparatus has not been incorporated into service of the state as originally planned, the association created to consider the arrangements and adaptation of this practice to a French context still continues its activities with several courts in the Paris region. Elsewhere, reports are delegated by each court to socio-legal non-governmental organizations grouped together at the national level by the federation "Citizens and Justice."

The way in which each organization in charge of these reports operates depends on local habitats and the size of the jurisdiction. In the court I observed, the brief social report was based on a fifty-minute meeting that took place between the investigator, usually a psychologist by training, and the accused, when the latter had been transferred from the police station to detention facilities pending trial. The interview consisted of questions about the professional, legal, and family situation of the accused. The investigator then contacted employers or family members to verify this information, which he or she would summarize in a two-page memo sent to the prosecution and placed in the case file submitted to the judges. As will later be seen, this information was read and sometimes discussed at trial.

Initially conceived for trials of young adults (18–21 years) by the Act of July 6, 1989, which amended the Code of Criminal Procedure, the brief social report was made a requirement for all defendants under the Law of March 9, 2004. The repressive trend of which the latter is part is thus accompanied by a systematization of the instruments for the individualization of sentences. Within the context of a penal policy focused on recidivism, the systematic use of brief social reports has paradoxically perpetuated and strengthened the development of a personal and rehabilitative vision of sentencing.

This movement illustrates the tensions between swift prosecution, mandatory sentencing, and individualization at the heart of adjudication. What tangible system emerges from these different rules and practices underpinned by conflicting visions? How is this double imperative experienced by magistrates in their day-to-day work and what professional ethics are negotiated? I will now address these questions.

The Right Sentence

As stated in the assessment made by the government in June 2010, criminal court judges waived minimum sentences in half of the cases where they were applicable. Nevertheless, the study does show that this tendency declined from one year to the next as the new practice became normalized in the courts. Despite widespread opposition from various magistrate unions, this standardization made notable inroads in terms of legal precedents, since prosecutors were instructed by the Ministry of Justice to appeal decisions where the minimum sentence was not applied. In the court where I conducted my study, the prosecution made substantial efforts to normalize automatic sentencing, appealing decisions in which the law was disregarded 22 percent of the time, i.e., two-and-a-half times more often than the national average.[42] While mandatory sentencing is still being debated by judges, it has become a full-fledged tool in the day-to-day work of prosecutors, who are considered by the judicial hierarchy as the guarantors of its enforcement. To see how mandatory sentencing is actually applied or circumvented, let us take a look at a routine hearing in an immediate appearance court.

Mandatory Sentences and Their Circumvention

The defendant was a young, 22-year-old black man of French nationality, Elijah Traoré. The courtroom was half filled with the relatives of the 14 individuals on trial that day in a court session that would start at 1:30 p.m. and last until 9:00 p.m. The defendants were brought in groups of three or four from holding cells in the basement of the courthouse into a Plexiglas dock. Their cases were heard one after another, then the tribunal composed of three judges recessed to deliberate, after which it announced the verdicts in quick succession. Elijah was accused of having received stolen goods, "in the form of buying a packet of stolen lunch vouchers," and of insulting a police officer and resisting arrest. The trial began by returning to the circumstances of his arrest. The police had been on patrol in front of a building entrance when they saw Elijah Traoré enter. They recognized the youth as having been at the police station previously. They found his behavior suspicious since he had "put his hood up" and had looked around before entering the building.[43] The police decided to check his identity. The young man "removed his hood and got annoyed," after which the police decided to search him. This was when they found a packet of lunch vouchers not in the name of the accused. They arrested the man and took him to the police station.

We should now briefly reconstruct what came next. The suspect was placed in custody, that is to say, held in a police cell where his statement was taken by a judicial police officer. The latter then passed along his report to the jurisdiction's prosecutor. The case of Mr. Traoré (the charges against him, his statements, his behavior, his criminal record) and the cases of all those held in custody that night were outlined over the phone to the deputy prosecutor who determined the nature of the offenses and what legal action to take each time: release with a summons to appear before a criminal court or a plea bargaining commission (the defendant then agrees to "plead guilty" in the context of a simplified procedure without an adversarial trial); remand to custody and the ordering of an investigation; immediate appearance trial within 48 hours after arrest, etc. The suspect was subjected to this last procedure: he was charged with possession of stolen goods as well as for "insulting a police officer and resisting arrest" while in custody. The day after his arrest, he was transferred in the morning to the holding cells located in the basement of the courthouse. He met a deputy prosecutor for a face-to-face interview in the holding cell. Generally, the prosecutors read for the defendants the charges against them and ask them a few questions to complete the police records and prepare the indictment. Then, for nearly an hour in his cell, Mr. Traoré met with a psychologist responsible for drafting his brief social report.

In the early afternoon, Mr. Traoré was brought handcuffed into the courtroom, where his case was heard after several others. First, the judge looked at the two alleged offenses: buying stolen lunch vouchers, which the defendant admitted to, and assaulting a police officer while in custody, which he denied:

> I was the one hit. The police officer I had the altercation with left to execute a search warrant. I had to wait for him to return to confront him, and since I wanted to get out of there as quickly as I could, I confessed to the alleged assault. It's been three years since I've last been arrested and it was very hard for me to find myself back there. I'm trying to do the right thing, I've been trying for the past three years. I'm sorry, I'm ready to apologize to set everything straight.

The judge replied: "You are no longer in middle school." "I know," said Mr. Traoré, "but apologizing is something. Ever since my incarceration, I've only wanted to do the right thing and not end up in one of those cages again."

The brief social report, read aloud, specified that Mr. Traoré "was jailed in 2007 for 'gang assault.'" It went on to indicate that "Mr. Traoré lives with his mother, the family gets along, but he was traumatized by the death of his father. He is monitored by a social worker. He has tried to reintegrate into society since his release from prison and is currently training to become a wood turner." The floor was given to the counsel for the plaintiff, that is to say, the police officer who had brought suit and was demanding 900 euros in damages for pain and suffering. The prosecutor then gave his closing argument:

> No one forced the defendant to receive stolen goods, and no one forced him to threaten the officer. He has a selfish and self-centered outlook on life: he does what he pleases and the world must adapt. [Turning to the defendant] We respect others, especially a police officer, who does honorable work and deserves more respect than anyone else. The defendant has already been convicted twice. He was incarcerated and he says that he took court-ordered civic responsibility classes. How can we be sure that he has learned what it is

to be a good citizen? He faces a minimum prison sentence of one year without possibility of parole and cannot receive a suspended sentence with probation. The defendant loses his temper when he is in jail and should therefore keep a low profile. He is to take court-ordered civic responsibility classes to understand that our society requires that he learn certain values. It is not easy but that is how it is.

The prosecutor requested a twelve-month prison sentence, eight months of which were to be suspended, accompanied by eighteen months of probation with mandatory therapy sessions to manage his violent behavior and help fulfill the requirement that he find a job.

Mr. Traoré's court-appointed lawyer in turn made her case. In response to the prosecutor's arguments, she asserted: "It is not a lack of societal values, but a certain jadedness. This jadedness is understandable given the [social context]." She then mentioned the classes the defendant had started taking before concluding: "This is someone who surrounds himself with the right people. Are we going to ruin his efforts?"

The trial lasted a little less than forty minutes. The judges recessed to deliberate on the series of cases, which Mr. Traoré's had just ended. Half-an-hour later, the four verdicts were announced in the order in which each case had been heard. A 21-year-old adult of Algerian origin, convicted of stealing a handbag and who also had prior convictions, was sentenced to two years' imprisonment, eighteen months of which were to be suspended with probation with the requirement that he be treated for alcoholism and compensate the victim. A 30-year-old Congolese man convicted of driving while intoxicated was given a two-month sentence and a 500-euro fine. A 25-year-old man of Algerian origin convicted of credit card theft was sentenced to five months in prison plus seven months of a previous suspended sentence, accompanied by a fifteen-month suspended sentence with probation with the requirement that he be treated for alcoholism. Mr. Traoré was likewise found guilty of the charges brought against him and sentenced to three months of prison but was released pending execution of the sentence (that is to say, the defendant is not directly escorted by police from the courtroom to the jail). The judge stated that the minimum sentence would not be applied "on the grounds that the defendant shows promise of reintegration." It was, however, legally impossible to circumvent the prison sentence. Nevertheless, the magistrate handed down a sentence without immediate imprisonment, offering the possibility that the sentence would be adapted by the judge—another legacy of the individualized approach.[44]

The details of this trial illustrate three issues surrounding sentencing. First, the remit of the case as determined by the prosecution creates a situation wherein the defendant is held in custody for the mere purchase of stolen lunch vouchers. Then, following an altercation with a police officer while in custody, he is judged in an immediate appearance trial: a trial in which he systematically risks a prison sentence. This mechanism of prosecution is found in other situations like the theft of a cell phone, the breaking of a car window, the theft of two euros by a homeless man, or the use of a laser pen on a highway sign, all of which led to a public trial after custody. Almost every time judges were faced with sentencing guidelines they could not disregard, even when they gave a reason for their refusal to apply the minimum sentence in their decisions. In cases like these, which form the bulk of the court's docket, the gap between the act committed and the coercive form of judgment, as well as the extreme severity of the sentence incurred, raises a question: is it really the offense that is being judged (the theft of a few euros, the possession of stolen lunch vouchers)? The disproportion between the act and its prosecution raises yet another question: if it is not (only) the act that is being judged, who or what is being punished then? And what does the sentence mean?

Second, what is debated in the courtroom is not so much the defendant's guilt (the defendant is considered guilty *a priori*, unless proven otherwise as interviews with judges make explicit), as it is the assessment of a just sentence. This assessment is made within the many technical constraints, which leads to the severity of the penal response to recidivism—mandatory minimums are only one factor in the matter.

Third, the paradox is that sentencing has been legally redefined since the 2000s in a move towards ever more repressive response, while simultaneously, sometimes in sections of the same statute, the commutation of sentences is encouraged and facilitated. In other words, mandatory sentencing laws have increased the number of sentences handed down as well as their duration, whereas new measures have helped to reduce or commute the actual incarceration. This paradox creates contradictory demands that frame the work of the magistrates on political, ethical, and practical levels.

Evaluating the Offender's Criminal Record

The trial described above reveals the importance of the proceeding's time frame and the form of prosecution decided. The form of prosecution, the qualification of the crime, and the requisitions made by the prosecutor have three characteristics. First, the management of cases in real time systematizes the passage from police procedures to judicial procedures. The path of Mr. Traoré from his identity check to his conviction in criminal court suggests one thing: the delinquency that is being prosecuted seems to be constructed by the very system put in place to manage it. In a justice that is overburdened and perpetually lacking in resources, this issue is especially crucial. Second, in this swift prosecution, a moral discourse is realized through the hearing. What occurs in the courtroom is a small part of the entire process. The values on behalf of which the system works are publicly asserted: the importance of employment, the possibility of integration, and civic responsibility— and, more generally, an application *in situ* of individual responsibility. Within this framework, the adjudication is organized around the notion of recidivism: in a legal and technical way on the one hand, and in the assessment of the individual's background in addition to the acts committed on the other.

There are no specific categories of offenses that are judged at immediate appearance trials, but ones that are remitted to this form of trial by the prosecutor. The elements taken into account in deciding the form of prosecution are threefold. The first is the evidence established by the police report. The second is the legality of the police custody procedure; due process rules must be met or the counsel for the defense can appeal on the grounds of improper procedure, overturning the conviction and thus wasting the court's time and money: the prosecutor quickly anticipates this possibility and ensures that the charges "stick." The third is the length of the sentence faced by the accused, which must exceed two years in prison or six months in prison for *in flagrante delicto* offenses. However, the sentence incurred is itself determined by the state of recidivism, since the existence of a criminal record not only incurs a minimum sentence, but also doubles the length for the offense committed. The rules and practices of prosecution thus produce a judgment process, which prosecutes not so much the offenses as it does the offenders.

However, the problem of recidivism, around which prosecution is organized, exceeds the legal concept in the strict sense (having already been convicted of "similar" acts) to attach itself to a broader assessment of the criminal records of the offenders. One prosecutor stated:

> When a decision about the type of trial is made, prior convictions are one of the first things taken into account. "Recidivism" is a technical term: the person has been convicted of similar offenses. While this is certainly taken into account, what is more generally considered is the notion of repetition, even though the person is not a recidivist because he or she has not been tried yet. On the phone [during the conversation with the judicial police officer who gives the arrest report], it is one of the first things I consider. That's why I have the police records and the files that show the current cases.

However, in the reconstruction of an offender's background, the seriousness of each offense is blurred by a chain of relationships between the noted offense and the previous ones. As the same prosecutor points out:

> With prior convictions, it is the nature of the offense that is important. Say that someone has committed ten robberies and that for the first time, he or she is pulled over for drunk driving: I think that is much less serious than someone arrested two or three times for driving under the influence. Because it means that here is someone who is already used to this kind of dangerous and reprehensible conduct and is therefore liable to do it again. Whereas someone who has committed a lot of completely different offenses and who is caught drunk-driving for the first time is probably safer on the road than the one who has been convicted twice before for the same thing. I look at the nature of the offense first: was the same offense committed? When were they committed? Because someone who commits theft in 2000 and then again in 2010 is, for me, less worrying than someone who commits theft in 2009 and

then again 2010. And then there is the importance of the previous sentence. Someone who has received a warning and breaks the law again, that is not the same thing as someone who has been sentenced to prison for three years and breaks the law again because he has received a more serious warning: the severity of the first punishment is something I have to take into account when thinking of how I will respond.

From the different criteria for evaluation that make up the offender's criminal record—the repetition of the same offenses, the time between the offenses, and the nature of previous punishments—the figure of the repeat offender is constructed. This assessment of the accused's past not only takes into account the criminal record and other police files available to the prosecutor, but also the information available through the brief social report. As one vice president of a criminal court emphasizes: "In the two years between his first conviction and his second offense, what has the person done? If he looked for and found a job, if he has built a family, these are factors that lead us to disregard minimum sentencing requirements."

As we have seen, the prosecutor's job of determining the type of procedure is essentially tantamount to a "pre-judgment" carried out by a single agent from his office. The trial which follows this determination is itself divided into two parts: the examination of culpability according to the "judicial truth," which stems from the written record and questioning at the hearing, and the assessment of an appropriate punishment. Judges and prosecutors are in unanimous agreement that doubt is the cardinal virtue of their offices. Nonetheless, they take for granted that only cases in which the facts are fairly well established and the rules followed tend to be presented in immediate appearance trials:

> When there is doubt, it works the other way: we doubt [the accused's] guilt, not his innocence. The premise is that the prosecutor has information that gives him and the judge reason to believe that the accused has committed the offenses he is charged with; then, we check to see if we are convinced that the defendant committed those offenses.

This initial screening explains why the trial itself mainly focuses not on whether the defendant is guilty of the offense (in 2008, only 4.4 percent of defendants in trial were acquitted[45]), but on the assessment of the penalty incurred.

As explained earlier, the idea of a mandatory minimum sentence is not a break with, but the systematization of, a logic of punishment that existed prior to the law through other technical and legal tools. The novelty comes from the obligation it imposes on judges, where autonomy once prevailed.

However, the actual exercise of judgment once again reverses the pattern desired by the law. The trial undertakes an evaluation of the criminal record and the character of the defendant. This evaluation allows for decisions to be made prior to the application of the mandatory sentence or to its circumvention through the different legal tools available to judges. As one criminal court judge confirmed:

When deliberating, we start by asking: what does it deserve? Then, afterwards, we consider: does it incur the minimum sentence? If so, then we have to disregard it: how do we do that? (We have legal tools for this. If these tools are taken away from us, then we can't do it anymore.) Sometimes it is really difficult, but we prefer to think like that. Normally, this is not how we should think. We should be saying: he incurs the minimum sentence, does he meet the criteria for disregarding it?

As shown, the legal tools available to judges are, on the one hand, the personal circumstances of the accused, which provide a reason to disregard the application of a minimum sentence, and on the other hand, the adjustment of the sentence through the use of suspended sentences in conjunction with probation, but also through direct referral to the sentencing judge before the execution of the sentence.

The Rationalization of Moral Sentiments

Personalizing a sentence thus operates on several levels. With regard to the offense, the determination of responsibility is based on the intention behind the act and the circumstances. With regard to the sentence, the probation and the obligations that accompany the suspended sentence define the accused as the subject of a penal decision. Thus, the judges punish an offense, by handing down a sentence which takes into account the particular situation of the offender. Moreover, their decision aims as much to punish misbehavior as it does to normalize it. The convicted individual does not leave the judicial system with just the judgment of the criminal act, which caused him or her to enter it in the first place. He is also subjected to longer-term pigeonholing of his social life through the material, psychological, and emotional standards defined by the "obligations" that condition the adjustment of the sentence.

"Is it our job to judge social problems? A person who is totally unintegrated?" asked a former prosecutor who had become vice president of the criminal court, before continuing:

> Today, we must justify everything we do. Those who are not integrated because they do not have enough family support, for them, probation is the solution, like the follow-up measures stipulated by the sentencing judge. A long probation means that we are concerned and are trying to prevent a repeat. In that case, we will clearly specify the requirements, including treatment requirements if there is a psychiatric problem or an issue with alcohol: we specify it in such a way that we give instructions to the sentencing judge.

However, in reality, the judicial handling proves irregular, uncertain, and often without real implementation due to the lack of human and material resources, which results in an increasingly longer processing time.

But the personalization of the judgment also operates on another level, transversal to the two previously mentioned: that of moral sentiments like compassion, empathy, or indignation. Magistrates, however, tend to deny this, rationalizing their affective reactions through legal reasoning. As one former family court and current criminal court judge explained: "Not giving the person a harsh sentence because the person has a job is not a response to a sense of humanity, it is a question of prosecution: it is a way to avoid desocialization which is the quickest way to provoke a repeat offense."

An examining magistrate who was once a criminal court judge also touched on this distinction, which he situated between "humanity" and "compassion":

> Humanity is not compassion: compassion is taking out your handkerchief while listening to the criminal record of the person in front of you. Humanity is something else, and it is more difficult: it is the ability to hand down a penal response, which, taking into account all the elements, seems more appropriate. Humanity is not necessarily compassion but the taking into account of the difficulties of the person without showing any sign of weakness in the response that is handed down.

The presiding judge at the trial described above also noted the distinction between the values associated with good judgment and the affective dimension, which is excluded in sentencing:

> We do not become attached to the defendants because there are no affects, but we become attached insofar as they manage to turn away from crime. Their behavior does not enter into the decision because there is nothing personal and because we do not know each other.

The prospect of personalized sentencing thus offers a discursive and analytical framework that allows magistrates to dismiss or neutralize the emotional dimension of adjudication, so that it does not appear as such. One reason why this handling of affects through social and legal discourse seems necessary is that it frames and preserves the work of deliberation. Indeed, the decision of the judges assumes a margin of inner or subjective or, to put it more bluntly, arbitrary assessment. The erasing of the affective dimension maintains the conditions of possibility of this personal judgment by removing the specter of subjectivity, which, if made bare, might compromise the legitimacy of the sentencing and on a broader level the functioning of the public trials.

Adjusting and Transforming Sentences

After the verdict, the adjustment and monitoring of the sentence transform its nature. They replace the practice of harsh justice, in which the sentence is enforced at the end of the trial, with a much longer, more spread out, more dynamic temporality of modulating the punishment.[46] Criminal court judges who solemnly hand down their sentence at a trial are unaware of what will become of their decision and how it will be implemented; they sometimes have a rather vague idea of how the next phase works. The application of sentences thus benefits from a paradoxical status. It is considered by some magistrates as an act of "stewardship" of justice: an office activity that takes place in courts overloaded with pending cases, far from the decorum and symbols associated with the act of judging. Yet the application of sentences has an essential function in the criminal justice system as it determines what will actually become of the decision and the fate of the convicted offender. How do these practical developments in the enforcement of the sentence take into account the moral implications of the act of judging and how do they modify it?

Throughout the course of the interviews, several magistrates raised the dilemma of their "responsibility for people's freedom," as one of them termed it. This responsibility lies at the heart of the ethical issues raised by the act of judging in an immediate appearance trial marked by a sense of urgency, a lack of time, and lack of human and material resources—all factors leading to stereotypical judgments. As one examining magistrate, who was once a criminal court judge, pointed out, the work of preparing the verdict "still remains mysterious because there is the question of power behind it, a decision about someone's freedom: ultimately prison is still at stake. The law is technical, but you are still dealing with human beings." This responsibility implies a significant emotional burden, according to a magistrate who worked as a prosecutor and then as a criminal court judge:

> It means something, when you judge. It is serious, it is burdensome, it weighs on our shoulders. We know all the time that we are doing something serious: like a doctor who knows that what he or she is doing is serious, or like a diamond cutter who might miscut a diamond and slice it in two: what he is doing is serious.

In this context, the procedure known as "723-15," which systematically includes the sentencing judge in the course of the immediate appearance trial, and the transformation of the sentence into a flexible punishment with multiple possibilities in turn modifies the responsibility of the magistrates in the criminal courts. Their sentence becomes an element in a complex and time-intensive system whose outcomes they remain unaware of. During one hearing, for instance, judges were required by the law to hand down a prison sentence without suspension for the use of a laser pen by a driver, who for fun pointed it at highway signs. The offense was minor, but the offender had been previously sentenced to prison multiple times (once for several years for armed robbery). In these circumstances, the judges imposed a sentence of six months' imprisonment, but without immediate execution, which in practice referred the convicted individual to the sentencing judge with the expectation that the sentence would be adjusted before implementation. Splitting the penal activity between the official public trial and the application of the sentence held privately in the judge's chambers thus reevaluates and transforms the concept of "responsibility for people's freedom" involved in adjudication. It seems in fact that it allows for a compromise between this ethical responsibility and the repressive legal constraints.

Ultimately, the intersection between these adjustment practices and the systematic sentences is not necessarily graspable for either the observers or the actors of the justice system themselves. While, on the one hand, a rise in repressive laws since the 2000s increases the number of offenses which can be tried in immediate appearance courts and raises the punishments incurred, on the other hand the adjustment of sentences is extended to prison sentences of less than one year with the Act of November 25, 2009, and the completion date of sentences has been systematically altered since the Law of March 9, 2004. For some magistrates, this contradictory evolution boils down to "increasing the prison population, as a result of the law, and systematically adjusting the sentences, as a result of the law," while neither the prison system nor the application of sentences is provided with sufficient resources to manage both influxes.

One prosecutor did, however, propose an integrated reading of these different rationales. According to him, reintegration, so dear to the tradition of individualization, is reinterpreted through a logic of costs and benefits inherited from new theories of crime, including the "broken window" theory. From this perspective, the subject of penal action that aims to reintegrate is now a moral being who is governed and whose behavior is predicted through an economy of risks and interests. As the magistrate summed it up:

> What interests me is not sending people to the slammer for as long as possible; it's that they stay on track because it's in their interest and in the interest of the 64 million people around them to have someone who is not dangerous. There always has to be some punishment to serve as something of a deterrent for the person and for those who might be tempted to do the same. But the main goal is that the person doesn't do it again and to that end, we will look for punishments like suspended sentences with probation, the 723-15. Prevention of recidivism is achieved through the adjustment and individualization of the sentence. Minimum sentencing requirements go against the logic of adjusting the sentence, that's for sure ... A minimum sentence should be given to a person because you think the situation demands it: you play with the effects of deterrence that the sentence has. You're not going to do it again because you know that you're risking a lot. But after that, nothing stops you from: "We give you harsher sentences, but we can also adjust them more, so the stakes are more important for you to shape up after your conviction, because you know that you risk even more and what's more, you know that your sentence can be adjusted if you do shape up." It is a logic that is not necessarily contradictory. I know that I am in the minority with this view: many believe that applying minimum sentences on the one hand and expanding the adjustment of sentences on the other is contradictory.

The function of immediate appearance trials can thus only be understood in relation to their pre-trial stage—that is to say, police arrests and emergency prosecution—and their post-trial stage—the possibilities of monitoring and adjustment after sentencing. These different practices revolve around rationales that in the end point to the following question: how to control the habits, behaviors, and deviant actions of individuals belonging to a relegated population and governable according to the application of rational choice?

Conclusion

The swift and severe prosecution of offenses, such as is practiced in immediate appearance trials, has become a political response to security issues, as illustrated by the orders which the Ministry of the Interior gave during the riots of autumn 2005 to have all the individuals who had been arrested systematically tried in immediate appearance trials. This judicial handling of crime is based on an older justice "in real time" focused on the prevention of recidivism as a method for the social control of marginal and precarious populations. But the practice of *in flagrante delicto* underwent a major reorganization beginning in the 1980s. First, the number of cases handled that way significantly rose and continued to increase until the mid-2000s. Second, numerous legislative measures technically compelled a harsher response in penal decisions with regard to cases involving recidivism.

These developments pose a major problem for the magistrates involved in prosecution and sentencing: that of a judgment made in a situation of constraint, under the pressure of an accelerated time frame, and with limited means, a consequence of the increased number of immediate appearance trials and mandatory sentencing rules. The new norms were resisted by the judiciary as a whole when they were first enacted and have been denounced regularly since then as "contrary to the French tradition of the individualization of sentences," as judges I met in the field pointed out. Yet despite this opposition, the application of sentences with a mandatory minimum and which cannot be adjusted has been gradually normalized under pressure from the prosecution as was requested by the Ministry of Justice.

Yet this picture becomes more complex if one takes into account the fact that changes in judicial practice over the same period have incorporated elements of sentence individualization. These elements take the form, on the one hand, of brief social reports that allow for the systematic consideration, during the trial, of the character and social integration of the accused: their family background, their employment history, their relationships with their families and friends. On the other hand, they take the form of more systematic and more wide-ranging recourse to sentence adjustment. How can the use of these tools inherited from the tradition of individualization be understood within the context of the repressive penal and security policies of the last twenty years?

My research suggests that the systematized consideration of individual situations and, on a larger scale, the adjustment of sentences in practice provide the conditions under which judges can redefine their work within situations of constraint. Indeed, the information from the brief social report is enlisted in support of the refusal to apply minimum sentencing requirements. The individualization tool is not contradictory to mandatory sentencing; it is used to develop a differential management of its application. Similarly, the extension of sentence adjustment creates a form and temporality of judgment, which modifies the concept of "responsibility" weighing on the shoulders of the criminal court judge: the judges perceive the sentence as a multi-stage decision that can be immediately or subsequently adjusted. Such a process modifies, divides up, and projects into a new temporality the responsibility for the decision.

Notes

1 The empirical data stem from fieldwork conducted between May 2010 and May 2011 in a criminal court in the Paris banlieues, through ethnographic observation of the immediate appearance trials and a systematic collection of data from 230 trials; through an ethnographic observation and study of 80 criminal records at the Sentence Execution Services; and though interviews with 17 professionals in the criminal justice system: social workers, criminal court judges, sentencing judges, and prosecutors.

2 It is in this sense that we speak of a "penal clientele," an expression used by Fabien Jobard and Sophie Névanen (2007) to explain the considerable over-representation of ethnic minorities among those judged.

3 The statistics provided in the previous paragraph come from the *Annuaires statistiques de la justice* [*Annual Statistical Report of the Ministry of Justice*], 2006 and 2010, and from a report on immediate appearance trials by the information committee of the Senate's commission on laws (Zocchetto 2005).

4 See, in particular, the studies led by Philippe Robert and Pierre Lascoumes (1974), Denis Salas (2007), Camille Viennot (2012), or Angèle Christin (2008).

5 This is what resulted from a study devoted to prosecution in real time by Benoît Bastard, Christian Mouhanna, and Werner Ackermann (2007).

6 This phrase, often adopted by others, was what legal historian Bernard Schnapper (1983) used to designate the essential role that the concept of recidivism played in the formation of penal philosophy and the penal system such as we know them today.

7 See, for example, the collective works from the conferences "Récidive et récidivistes: de la Renaissance au XXe siècle" ["Recidivism and Recidivists: From the Renaissance to the Twentieth Century"], University of Geneva, June 6–8, 2002; "La récidive: représentations et traitement, XIXe–XXIe siècle" ["Recidivism: Representations and Prosecution from the Nineteenth to the Twenty-first Centuries"], University of Pau, December 9–10, 2009.

8 Sbriccoli (2006). The question of the formation of statistics as a government tool in relation to the emergence of the administrative and political concept of "population" is explained in Michel Foucault's lectures on "Territory, Security, Population" (2003).

9 Chauvaud (2006).

10 Robert (2009: 11).

11 See the reference works by Beccaria (1979 [1764]) and Mouton (1887).

12 Foucault (1979 [1975]).

13 This history is retraced in Schnapper (1983).

14 Though individualization might be qualified as a "fundamental principle" of penal law in judicial doctrine, it is not included in the "Fundamental Principles Recognized by

the Laws of the Republic" by the Constitutional Council, which has argued that it is a "constitutional principle" stemming from Article 8 of the Declaration of the Rights of Man and of the Citizen on the necessity of punishments (Decision DC No 2005-520 on July 22, 2005). It is interesting to point out that this inscription of the principle of individualization in the legal bedrock does not date back to the period immediately following World War II—the moment when the "fundamental principles" were drafted and the humanist values of criminal justice affirmed. Instead, it occurs thanks to a legal battle waged in 2004 against the procedure of plea bargaining as a tool in the systematization of punishments ("pleading guilty" is an import from North American judicial systems, which proposes a sentence negotiated with the prosecutor on the condition that the defendant waive the right to a defense).

15 Saleilles (1898: 16, 243). This text was republished in a critical edition accompanied by a series of studies on the contemporary uses of the concept of individualization by Ottenhof (2001).

16 Saleilles (1898: 243).

17 This point is developed in greater detail by Schnapper (1991).

18 This is the conclusion of the statistical study carried out by Jean-Claude Farcy on *in flagrante delicto* trials from the archives of the Paris courts during the Second Empire (Farcy 2006).

19 René Lévy studied the birth and evolution of this penal procedure in detail in the dissertation devoted to the topic.

20 Lévy (1985: 58).

21 Expressions used by the parliamentary rapporteur during the law's adoption, cited in Lévy (1985: 43).

22 Lévy (1985: 481).

23 The judicial "clientele" at the court where I carried out my study counted 57 percent who were less than 25 years old (34 percent in René Lévy's study) and 80 percent of defendants with either foreign last names or foreign citizenship (60 percent for Lévy).

24 These analyses were carried out by Bruno Aubusson de Cavarlay (1985) and Fabien Jobard and Sophie Névanen (2007).

25 The relationships between social exclusion and ethnic minorities and the way in which this articulation plays out in judicial treatment have been noted by numerous sociological works among which can be cited those of Jean-Claude Chamboredon (1971), Pierre-Victor Tournier and Philippe Robert (1991), Fabien Jobard and Sophie Névanen (2007), Didier Fassin and Éric Fassin (2006).

26 The concept of moral regulation, presented by Philip Corrigan and Derek Sayer (1985) is adopted and developed in numerous legal sociological studies among which, the works of Allan Hunt (2003).

27 These themes have notably been discussed by Gérard Noiriel (2007), Didier Fassin and Éric Fassin (2006).

28 Corrigan and Sayer (1985: 194).

29 See the analyses of Laurent Bonelli (2008) on this subject.

30 See the report presented by Alain Peyrefitte et al. (1977: 18–19, 37).

31 Philippe Robert and Marie-Lys Pottier have notably analyzed the emergence of new forms of security preoccupations beginning in the 1990s (Robert and Pottier 1997, 2004).

32 This movement has been analyzed by Laurent Mucchielli (2002).

33 This contemporary resurgence of xenophobic discourse has been analyzed for example in the works of Pascal Delwit, Jean-Michel De Waele, and André Rea (1998) and Gérard Noiriel (2007).

34 This theory, forged by the practitioners and experts of urban security in the United States is based on the idea that to deal with urban crime it is necessary to reduce and

control unruly behavior (e.g. "insecurities" in public policies terminology), the cause of social disorder. This "zero tolerance" towards antisocial behavior (Kelling and Coles 1998) imposes a conception of delinquency disconnected from its legal definition (the commission of an "offense" subject to punishment): the subject of repression and control are no longer acts, but more broadly behaviors and cultures referring to specific social affiliations. For a critical discussion of this theory and its spread, see Bernard Harcourt (2001) and Loïc Wacquant (2004).

35 Information report submitted by the National Assembly's commission on laws in December 2008: http://www.assemblee-nationale.fr/13/rap-info/i310.asp.

36 Penal Code, article 132-24.

37 "The new social defense doctrine is intended to take moral values into greater account since one of the essential goals that it attributes to the sentence is to make the individual aware of his human duties towards the collective," explains Marc Ancel (1954: 73).

38 Ancel (1954: 132).

39 As the genesis of the Association for Applied Criminal Policy and Social Reintegration, the first group in charge of this experiment in Paris, shows (Bonneau 2007).

40 The proven use of social reports is confirmed in a now-famous report by the Vera Institute of Justice (1972).

41 Interviews with the group's director, January 23, 2011.

42 These figures are those given by the Ministry of Justice. "Assemblée nationale, Peine plancher: statistiques. Réponse écrite de la garde des sceaux à une question de M. Éric Raoult (UMP)" ["National Assembly, Minimum Sentencing Requirements: Statistics. Written Response from the Attorney General to a Question from Mr. Éric Raoult (UMP)"], *Journal officiel* [*Official Journal*], Wednesday, June 29, 2010, 7352.

43 Unjustified identity checks are considered illegal.

44 Article 723-15 of the Code of Criminal Procedure introduced in March 2004 provides that when a person is sentenced to up to one year of jail time without immediate imprisonment, which was the case here, the case is systematically submitted to the sentencing judge by the prosecutor. The guilty party, after meeting with an officer of the Prison and Probation Service, is summoned by the sentencing judge. The purpose of this meeting, which takes place in the judge's chamber, is to determine the conditions of the sentence's execution. This may entail redefining the nature thereof and imposing alternatives to imprisonment, as Mr. Traoré's judges suggested.

45 Ministry of Justice, *Annuaires statistiques de la Justice, 2008* [*Annual Statistical Report, 2008*]. It may seem a little inconsistent to refer to different annual statistical reports (2008, 2009, 2010) throughout this chapter: the reason for doing so is that the different annual statistical reports are based on different data-gathering methods that change each year.

46 Mireille Delmas-Marty (1986) analyzed the new judicial temporality introduced by the adjustment of sentences.

CHAPTER TWO

Justice for Immigrants
The Work of Magistrates in Deportation Proceedings

Nicolas Fischer

It was almost six in the evening. A young man from Angola sat in a hot, cramped hearing room, waiting to appear before an immigration judge after having been detained in a waiting zone at the French border. He had been heading to Lisbon, for which he had a valid visa, but he lacked a hotel reservation, which is required to enter European territory under the Schengen Agreement. He had therefore been arrested while attempting to catch a connecting flight at Charles de Gaulle Airport. Also sitting in the room was a couple in their fifties. They were his aunt and uncle, the young man's lawyer explained when his case was finally called. Residents of Lisbon, they had traveled to France in order to attend their nephew's hearing. The lawyer submitted to the magistrate a reservation for a hotel in Lisbon, which had apparently been made a while ago but had only recently been confirmed. The judge was surprised: "If he has family there, why would he stay in a hotel? Can't they put him up?" In response to the question, the alleged relatives stated that their home was too small for them to be able to host him. The magistrate then asked them to verify their identities. They handed her two passports, both with the same last name, but not that of the young man. The lawyer insisted, however, that they were indeed the young man's aunt and uncle. After pausing for a moment to consider the case, the judge announced that she would allow the young detainee to leave the waiting zone. The lawyer defending the interests of the state waved his hands in protest. The judge turned to him and said, "Look, he's got a visa and everything else seems to be in order. Besides, I don't think these people would have come all the way here if they weren't related to him. I think that's enough to justify his release, don't you?"

On the face of it, this episode is an example of how an immigration court ordinarily operates. The judge uses the professional skills she has acquired through training and experience to determine the facts surrounding the situation of the young man who appears before her. Yet at the same time her judgment is also a collective endeavor. Throughout the hearing, her ruling is framed and guided by the arguments and justifications produced by the lawyers as well as by the relatives of the defendant, and relies on the affidavits and other supporting documents which they submit. So while the interaction at first seems to be restricted to the ordinary application of legal procedure, it is in fact much more than just a simple judicial process. Rather, it reveals how the various actors in the hearing come to reach a tacit agreement on what for them is a shared common sense: the fact that, for example, a traveler is supposed to stay with relatives who live in the country he is visiting rather than in a hotel, or that the long journey of two older individuals to help a young man is proof of the affective ties that they have with him.

But it is equally apparent how much these assessments are rooted in moral conceptions that operate on several levels. Certain assumptions like the correct attitude that relatives responsible for a young traveler should normally adopt, or the respect for legal obligations and formalities that can be expected of an honest migrant when he or she enters the territory of a foreign state make reference to a system of generally shared values. These values also incorporate a more immediately political dimension: for the state, it is the suspicion that the young man's entry could be fraudulent and an attempt to mask the desire to immigrate to France illegally; for the young man's lawyer, it is instead the concern for defending the rights of an honest individual who was unjustly arrested after getting off the plane; and for the judge, it is the desire to balance these two perspectives while at the same time respecting the values of her profession, which make her the guardian of both the law and civil rights.

It is the moral grounds of these immigration rulings that we will discuss in this chapter, and to that end, we will consider two types of judgment. First, I will examine the role of "liberty and detention judges," whose activities have already been outlined in the episode above. These judicial magistrates intervene in deportation proceedings that are completely administrative in nature, cases in which foreigners are detained either in waiting zones or in detention centers prior to their deportation. In these situations, it is in fact incumbent upon the judges, who are constitutionally defined as the guardians of individual liberties, to rule merely on the legality of the detention and either to extend it or to release the individual without assessing his or her administrative status. Second, I will consider the administrative judges who review the legality of the deportation measures adopted by the prefectures as they would adjudicate any dispute between an individual and a government agency, provided that the immigrant concerned files an appeal with one of these courts in due form.

Although these two types of magistrates differ significantly in the rules according to which they operate, we will see that they as well as the other actors involved in the trial are constantly faced with moral issues that are similar to, although often more dramatic than, those we have just presented. These dilemmas reflect a more general tension between two contradictory moral imperatives which the actors involved must arbitrate. On the one hand, for the agents of the state—the police in particular, but also the courts and social services—the restrictions placed on immigration since the late 1970s have generated an ever more insistent imperative to repress undocumented immigration. For the actors of the judicial world, this is viewed as an implicit demand that they be suspicious of any foreigner entering France or traveling through France en route to another destination who presents an irregularity and that, in cases where there is doubt, they ultimately be more stringent. In conjunction with this political imperative comes the moral disqualification of undocumented immigrants, whom the most repressive political discourses readily present as "cheats" seeking to circumvent the regulations in order to gain undue access to the national labor market or to take advantage of government benefits. But on the other hand, this suspicion is counterbalanced by a central principle of justice that has only recently been extended to foreigners: the respect for the rule of law and individual rights. This obligation is more strongly felt in the deportation proceedings handled by the two types of judges studied in this chapter. Long objects of mere administrative control, immigrants have only belatedly seen their subjective rights recognized by the state. These rights are all the more essential in these proceedings, since the individuals concerned risk being forcibly expelled to their country of origin, are sometimes deprived of their freedom, and may also find themselves in difficult personal situations—for example, being sick or having a family—for which there exist formally protected rights.

The magistrates as well as the lawyers are responsible for dispensing justice on behalf of a state which seeks both to return immigrants who enter its territory illegally and to protect those among them who are victims of a morally intolerable situation. How does this tension between repression and compassion translate into the day-to-day routine of these judicial agents? In what ways do they experience the moral conflicts they are confronted with, and how do they resolve them? What part does the law, but also their professional ethics or political ideas, ultimately play in the decisions they make? Such questions will be answered through a field study which combines interviews with judicial and administrative judges and ethnographic observations of the trial proceedings or their preparation.

To study these two types of magistrates implies not only describing what meaning the actors involved attach to the legal norms which simultaneously constrain and authorize their arguments and decisions, but also analyzing the tensions between the twin requirements of retribution and protection. Moreover, it means retracing the moral evaluations that these agents produce in order to issue a decision on each of the cases they are required to judge. And on a more general level, it means restoring the exchange and redistribution of the moral classifications and judgments concerning immigrants in the course of these same debates. In other words, it is to explore the underlying moral economy of the proceedings regarding the politics of deportation.

To explain this moral economy, I will consider the tension between the repression and protection of immigrants in order to envisage how it translates into dictates imposed on the professional ethos as well as on individual moral principles. There will be two steps to my approach. First, a socio-historical analysis will allow us to trace the tension between the repression and protection of migrants, in particular through the history of judicial oversight of deportation measures. Viewed as morally suspect for the whole of the twentieth century, immigrants were subject to the supervision of the police, whose power was limited only by the intervention of the courts beginning in the second half of the 1970s—which explains why the prerogatives of the courts have not ceased to be criticized, reformed, and restricted since then. Second, our examination of the marginalized position of the courts in what is essentially a police system of deportation will facilitate the analysis of how the tension between repression and protection operates on a local level for the judges involved in immigration trials.[1] These magistrates attribute different meanings to the professional role and ethos prescribed to them by the judicial institution in accordance with their own personal backgrounds, thereby creating individual value systems.[2] The moral dimension of the institution is, however, also evident in the practical categories and codified procedures as well as the social configurations or structures into which they are translated on a local level. The moral economy of immigration judgment is thus embodied in the hearings and debates of each court, as well as in the negotiated orders and professional interactions which make up those courts. That is what the fieldwork I conducted in a district court and an administrative court will show.[3]

Between Police Surveillance and the Defense of Human Rights

To analyze the position of judicial and administrative courts in the deportation system requires a brief review of the longer history of immigration control in France. We will begin by considering the origins of how immigrants came to be made objects of specific administrative control and then examine the resultant moral stigma experienced by this previously unnoticed segment of the population. Appearing in the late nineteenth century, this system of policing placed immigrants under the sole control of the police, gendarmes, and prefectural officers whom the state granted tools ranging from personal data files to detention or internment "camps" specifically meant to monitor them. Criminal and administrative courts would later intervene in this burdensome configuration—albeit in the second half of the 1970s—in order to define as well as to defend the "rights" of immigrants. While this relatively recent intervention does shed light on the tension between repression and protection, it also shows the isolation of the courts within the system of immigration control: in the eyes of the other actors involved, the judges import a heterogeneous legal rationality into a police logic of regulating populations that was developed and established over a century ago.

From Vagrants to Immigrants: The Invention of the Foreigner
as an Object of Policing

Appearing in France in the 1880s and 1890s, the control of foreign immigration is itself part of an older institutional and moral legacy which sought to control vagrants and other internal migrants whom eighteenth-century jurists filed under the rather generic category of "floating populations." As in other European states, the construction of the modern French state was accompanied by a desire to regulate population movements from region to region. To that end, special surveillance of so-called "tramps" and "unvouched-for persons" was first established under the Ancien Régime. It was from that point on that itinerancy as a lifestyle came to be seen as deviant and was imbued with the negative moral connotations evident in the two previous expressions. The instability of these floating populations was not merely geographical; it was also equated with the absence of stable employment and a steady income, as well as to a moral wavering which frequently led to the assimilation of migrants with highwaymen.[4] Beyond their differences, these populations shared at that time

> a number of common features that made it a privileged clientele of the police. Beyond their economic insecurity, they all occupied the streets and other public spaces. These undesirable populations were mostly in good standing with respect to the law. The specificity of the police mandate against them was therefore not related to their offenses. It was linked to the fact that these individuals were necessarily subjected to even stricter police vigilance because they committed no offense, that is to say, when law enforcement agents were not legally in a position to put an end to the social and moral disorder they created.[5]

Police control of these populations was therefore enforced within a system that lay at the margins of criminal law and judicial power. Individuals were policed not as a result of an offense, but due to the fact that their continued presence and free movement in the public space were considered moral dangers a priori. In fact, this "moral" policing of movements did not focus solely on vagabonds, but also on prostitutes and later, homosexuals and colonial subjects present in metropolitan France. Legal tools and resources were designed specifically to regulate them. This objective was central primarily in the birth of the police institution itself, which was built just as much around monitoring such deviant populations as it was around the repression of actual criminal behavior.[6] Moreover, there existed a series of practical techniques that were gradually implemented in order for the state to be able to exclude these stigmatized populations. Most notable among them was administrative internment which allowed for itinerant individuals to be arrested and imprisoned more or less indefinitely outside of the criminal justice system. This option was in fact commonly used by the police to arrest prostitutes, vagrants, or colonial subjects in metropolitan France.

The policing of foreigners when first instituted in the late nineteenth century can be seen as part of this general logic of controlling socially and morally stigmatized populations.[7] Initially, the need for the republican state to protect French citizens politically and economically led to the presence of foreigners being construed as a public problem. Addressing this "problem" meant implementing immigration policies, but it also required the establishment of an administrative police to identify foreigners and deny them access to social benefits, the labor market, and ultimately the territory itself. The introduction of passports, visas, and residence permits therefore marked the creation of the very first immigration controls and allowed for foreigners to be branded as ideal "police targets": rarely guilty of a criminal offense, their presence alone was considered problematic since they lacked the necessary permits to live and work in France. Deportation, the oldest repressive measure, was at this time complemented by administrative internment which allowed for the arrest of either isolated individuals or groups of individuals, thereby signaling the shift to a national logic of regrouping populations.[8]

Foreigners were therefore included in classic police systems of managing "floating" populations, but they were also targeted by the same set of moral stigmas, whether it be by evoking their burden on the economy and the welfare system from which they were seen as illegitimately benefiting, or by criticizing in possibly racialized terms their tendency for "nomadism" and their propensity to subsist on criminal activities.[9]

This management of foreigners through repressive policing and moral stigmatization is, however, the only form of control still to survive. As society's views on crime evolved, controls aimed at prostitutes or vagrants gradually faded away. Today, there exist only two forms of extra-penal imprisonment condoned by the republican state: the involuntary institutionalization of the mentally ill in psychiatric hospitals and the administrative detention of migrants. Use of this measure would continue to grow in the 1980s and 1990s as "irregular" foreigners became more stigmatized than ever before. But much like the institutionalization of the mentally ill, the detention of foreigners has also been criticized for its arbitrariness. Beginning in the 1970s, a series of legal fixes were implemented to prevent against abuse and to maintain the rule of law. It was within this context that the courts first intervened in the policing of foreigners.

The Addition of Judicial Review

When immigration controls were revived after France officially suspended labor immigration in 1974, the policing of foreigners remained largely an administrative task essentially enforced by police officers and local officials who enjoyed broad discretion and few legal limitations. It was under these legal circumstances that the issue of undocumented immigration was first raised in the late 1970s. This political discourse was accompanied by a series of moral evaluations that stigmatized undocumented immigration as both illegal and dangerous, drawing a continuum between illegal immigration and crime, if not, later, terrorism.[10]

However, this legacy of the first half of the century was quick to run up against an unprecedented move to *defend* the rights of immigrants, that can mainly be attributed to two important developments. First, a restrictive legal framework was created for policing immigrants, replacing the vague and poorly understood norms of previous decades. Law enforcement agencies thus lost some of their autonomy and at the same time also had to deal with actors who had traditionally been absent or barely visible in the management of immigration. Among these newcomers were judges and legal practitioners: the establishment of genuine "immigration laws" was essentially the result of a series of court decisions—from the lower courts all the way up to the Council of State (*Conseil d'État*) and the Court of Cassation (*Cour de Cassation*)—which in turn facilitated further legal challenges. Also new to the scene were activists: the move to defend immigrant rights was largely due to an increasingly denser patchwork of organizations seeking to change public opinion on the matter. Furthermore, the courts played an important role in the work of these activist groups: while concerned activists certainly used classic methods to promote their cause—from demonstrations to petitions—they also directly contributed the creation of immigration laws by turning to the courts to seek injunctions against certain practices.

Therein lies the tension described in the introduction to this chapter: on the one hand, undocumented immigrants have once again become ideal "police targets" due to the growing moral disqualification that they have experienced since the 1970s; on the other hand, they are simultaneously seen as possessing inalienable rights. These two perspectives have in turn had an effect on the institution's response to the issue, with the tension between protection and repression of foreigners echoed in the actual enforcement of immigration controls.

Administrative detention is perhaps the best example of this internal discord. Originally, arresting foreigners prior to their deportation was an informal police practice that went largely unnoticed by the general public. The police would routinely imprison immigrants at various sites for the time it took to prepare for their eventual deportation. This was done outside of any legal framework. The practice was made known in 1975 and soon thereafter contested in court. Cases traveled all the way to the Council of State and the Court of Cassation, both of which recognized the legality of the procedure, but also imposed a series of judicial safeguards. The detention of an immigrant was to be overseen by a judge—the future liberty and detention judge—whose responsibility it was to determine the legality of the imprisonment and to decide whether or not to extend it. When waiting zones for foreigners arrested upon entering the country were first set up in 1992, this same procedure was put in place. And even though arrests of undocumented immigrants continued to increase—the number of immigration detention centers went from 13 in 1988 to 25 in 2009, and the length of detention rose from 6 days in 1981 to 45 days in 2011—each individual case was subject to judicial review.

But the newly established judicial review process was also combined with increasingly repressive legislation that allowed for undocumented immigrants to be forcibly returned to their country of origin. A series of legal provisions did, however, define the categories of foreigners whose situation protected them against such deportation, namely the spouse of a French national or the parent of a French child. Interestingly, these developments gave foreigners being deported the possibility of filing an appeal with the courts—in this case, the administrative courts since they alone have jurisdiction to hear cases between an individual and a state administration—to have their legal protection recognized.

The institutional system of deportation had by the early 1990s fully integrated the tension between the protection and the repression of undocumented immigrants: the repression of immigration could not happen without judicial review under the

French Republic's rule of law. While ensuing debates would from then on focus solely on the scope of judicial intervention, the content of these debates reflects a persistent unease with the very imposition of judicial review in proceedings which the police were at one time free to implement on their own. To what extent may judges censure the actions of the police? Must the judges comply with practical requirements of the police's execution of deportation orders? These questions are posed in different ways with each subsequent reform of the deportation system.

Without retracing these debates in detail, I will outline their main arguments and the concrete effects they have had. The intervention of liberty and detention judges has been openly questioned, most notably by officials from the Ministry of the Interior, in the name of efficiency. From their point of view, the existence of judicial review represents above all an undue cost for the administrations in enforcing deportations: foreigners must be brought from detention centers to the courthouse, which in turn requires a police escort and vehicles for transportation. In light of these costs, the deportation procedure has in effect been streamlined, with hearings conducted via video conference, courtrooms set up in detention centers, and emergency provisions aimed at reducing time required by the hearings. Held on short notice, these hearings consist primarily of an oral debate in which the missing elements of the case can be presented in real time by the foreigner or his or her lawyer. To limit the autonomy of judges, successive reforms have likewise toughened the procedural framework for their decisions and allowed the prosecution to neutralize them with appeals that suspend their execution.

Although the administrative courts have not borne the brunt of these attacks, they have experienced comparable procedural adaptations. These changes are all the more significant given the fact that the administrative courts were established in 1953 to investigate cases that obviously had little to do with the repression of undocumented immigration. Their main purpose was to rule on cases involving "technical" disputes over, for example, tax law or the issuance of building permits. The entirely written procedure of these courts reflects their highly technical nature: it favors lengthy collegial debates among the judges—who discuss the cases behind closed doors based on the evidence presented to them—over the immediate and more readily emotional dimension of a public hearing. While this procedure does still exist for some deportation measures, it has for the most part succumbed to the urgency imposed by other cases. The deportations are thus examined by a single judge during a public hearing, at the end of which a decision is quickly handed down.

In the face of these changes, defenders of judicial intervention—whether they be union organizers or NGO leaders—see the judges as the last bastion of the rule of law in the deportation process, since they are the only ones able to protect the foreign defendant and to implement the safeguards afforded him or her as such. Yet the arguments put forth by those in favor of judicial intervention show that it is not only a question of defending foreigners. By affirming their right to a fair trial, it is the idea of a justice "worthy of a democratic state" that is upheld. Fighting for the rights of foreign defendants is therefore no different from fighting for the rights of French ones (an idea often stated in NGO press releases), justice being in a democracy a public "good" whose moral value is non-negotiable.

The tension between the repression of undocumented immigrants and so-called "frauds" and the protection of their fundamental rights has therefore pervaded both types of courts—liberty and detention, and administrative—since their creation. What remains to be seen is how the actors in the field position themselves with respect to these issues. This positioning is a matter of personal values and professional ethics, but it also depends on the particular configuration of each court, that is to say, on all the actors involved, on the networks of interdependence, and on the areas of specific interaction which unite them. The moral economy of immigration judgments can therefore be found in the convergence of the institution as "history materialized" such as it has just been presented and the way in which the officials who populate the institution accommodate it individually. The moral subjectivities of these actors interpret the official definition of their roles and the systems created for their implementation differently, but these systems also influence the moral subjectivities in return. These individual and collective rationales will now be presented, starting with the particularly illuminating case of liberty and detention judges.

Liberty and Detention Judges

Liberty and detention judges review the cases of foreigners who are to be deported and those who are detained at the French border. As the only judges who intervene in deportation proceedings, they are said to be "isolated." Their position is rather complicated, since the issues discussed during the hearings are marked by a high degree of uncertainty regarding the status of the foreigners who appear in court, even though their decisions can have a decisive impact on their fate. Foreigners detained at the border are migrants whose status is in theory undefined. They were arrested by immigration officers upon entering the country for failing to present necessary documentation, for example, a passport with a valid visa for the entire Schengen Zone. If they are thus suspected of trying to enter the country illegally, the very principle of a hearing nevertheless puts that suspicion to the test. Is the foreigner's trip actually suspect, or is the foreigner, as the lawyer frequently asserts, a tourist or a businessperson whose situation was misinterpreted by the police, or is he or she an asylum seeker whose hasty departure from his or her country of origin prevented him or her from complying with the rules?

Such are the issues raised during immigration hearings, and such are the issues that liberty and detention judges must rule on. Their decisions have an immediate effect on the fate of the immigrants whose detention in the waiting zone may be extended for up to eight days, after which their case must once again be reviewed. The magistrate may upon review decide to extend the detention a second time, or allow the immigrant to enter French territory. Each case and each solution therefore carries its own moral issues, embodied at times by the emotional tension which often characterizes the hearings.[11] Analyzing these hearings means first describing their material organization and understanding the isolated position of the judge at the center of the deportation system. The close professional relations among the actors will then be discussed, with particular attention paid to the individual and professional position of the judges and the impact of this position on their legal assessment in each individual case.

Producing a Negotiated Order in Detention Hearings

The agents involved in detention hearings are bound by the rules of a particular social configuration. A sign of the marginal position of liberty and detention judges within the process, the room where the hearings are held is a rather cramped one, spatially separated from the other rooms in the courthouse. Poorly signed, this square room is only recognizable by the ten or so people—relatives of the persons being judged—stationed at the door several hours before the commencement of the hearing and often forced to wait outside the room until "their" defendant appears before the magistrate. Inside, seats are at a premium: there are about thirty chairs on the left side of the room and some twenty more on the right. Priority is given to those who will appear before the judge: they take their seats next to their police escorts, waiting for their case to be heard. Only a dozen or so seats in the first row on the right side of the room are reserved for members of the public, who therefore sit just a few inches from the individuals brought from the detention center and their police escorts in the second row. Recesses in the hearings often become improvised visiting hours during which the two groups exchange family news, handshakes, and when police officers allow it, cell phones or bags of food. Some three feet away from these rows of seats, the lawyers for both parties take their places. Since the hearings are civil proceedings and not criminal ones, the lawyers for the foreigners sit behind a small desk opposite their colleagues who defend the interests of the prefecture. The former frequently get up to argue alongside their clients, who sit at a table in the center of the room, to meet with their families seated in the gallery, or to have a conversation with their opposing colleague.

The proximity of the various actors here is not only spatial; it is also embodied in the morally charged relationships that the professionals involved in these hearings have with one another. They share a high degree of legal specialization: in the court where I conducted my field research, a small number of judges (five in total, all women) assisted by two clerks heard the cases on a rotating basis, while an equally limited number of lawyers specialized in immigration law regularly found themselves opposing one another. Detention hearings are thus conducted by a small number of recurrent actors composing, to quote Niklas Luhmann, a "system of contact" soldered together locally by practical interdependencies and mutual trust. As a result of these relationships, a negotiated order is established throughout the hearings, the product of mutual expectations vested not only with values but also with emotions. This order is established in interaction with the procedure which from the outset assigns the actors in the hearing their roles and codifies their arguments. The necessity to adhere to these roles and their corresponding formats of discourse—the defense speech, for example—in theory requires that the legal practitioners control the expression of their judgments in court. Their familiarity with one another, however, authorizes a series of adjustments which allow for the alleviation of procedural constraints by simplifying hearings, but at the same time gives greater weight to the reciprocal moral demands and even on occasion causes outbursts of emotion during the hearings. It is a question of knowing and sufficiently respecting one's interlocutor in order to "feel that the other could accept the requirements and know where the limit lies beyond which the persons concerned will lose control of themselves."[12]

The daily routine of the debates highlights this local configuration among actors who have sometimes known one another for quite a long time. It is embodied primarily in the multiple signs of complicity among lawyers who, while opponents at trial, frequently socialize with one another due to their specialization in immigration law, even though they may not belong to the same bar association. In the few minutes before the hearings and during recesses, signs of complicity are common. For instance, one lawyer complained to his colleague on the opposing side about a case that he had lost in another court a few days earlier—even as he tried in the hearing that followed to inflict a series of defeats on each case examined. The humor between colleagues is likewise indicative of the distancing imposed by the procedure and the roles assigned.[13] The moral dimension underlying these tacit exchanges conversely manifests itself when the negotiated order of the hearing is challenged, causing the actors to judge the behavior of their colleagues in light of confrontations that are sometimes emotionally charged. This is what happened between two attorneys, one of whom was supposed to have "crossed the line" by abusing his position to the point of disproportionately deviating from his prescribed role. A verbal altercation broke out during the hearing over a procedural point. When the lawyer for the prefecture began to insult her colleague, an incensed magistrate suspended the hearing and walked out of the room, leaving the two lawyers to their shouting match.

Though the lawyers are not as familiar with the judges, on account of the latter's legal position of authority, their relative closeness is nevertheless revealed in their mutual knowledge and ability to anticipate their tactics. Magistrates would readily comment on a lawyer's command of the arguments or case law. And due to this game, judges felt authorized to ask lawyers not to make arguments that everyone involved knew no magistrate would accept and would instead insist that they come up with more "innovative" pleas. This adaptability is based once again on multiple signs of familiarity that emphasize the mutual understanding of all actors and define how far they are tacitly permitted to go when deviating from their official roles. Among the regulars at the hearings, several lawyers are thus frequently teased by the judges for the length of their arguments (one magistrate quipped during a recess: "We're not done yet—X is going to plead for another two hours!"). But exceeding the "limit" suggested by Luhmann typically ended in confrontation, as when one of the "regular" lawyers challenged the judge about a particular case.[14]

Though the objection was legally sound, the fact that it came from a lawyer known for his drawn-out arguments and that it occurred in an already difficult hearing resulted in a mutual challenge. The magistrate noted the objection, suspended the hearing, but then resumed the argument outside the courtroom in a particularly sharp tone of voice: "No, counselor, that's unfair, that's unfair, quit your antics!"

The court hearing is therefore not just a confined physical space. A specific economy is established through the interactions of its usual actors: the exchanges are of course organized by the procedure, but they are also regulated by the moral expectations that define the attitudes and arguments valued, and those which are on the other hand deemed unacceptable. In this restricted social realm, the positioning of the judges and their specific professional ethos nevertheless have a significant influence on the outcome of the discussions.

Between Police Suspicion and the Defense of Fundamental Rights

Within the hearings just described, the judges obviously occupy a special position. Guiding the debates and ruling on each case presented to them, they ultimately mediate the core tension at stake: whether to detain the immigrants and potentially deport them, or to release them in order to protect their rights. While the determination depends on the texts, procedures, and arguments developed, they are also inscribed within a local social order which bears equal influence on them. I will now analyze the important role of personal beliefs and professional ethos in the decisions produced by the magistrates. In the configuration as described above, they must take multiple positions. A product of their professional background, their professional ethics leads them to define their specific role in relation to actors who willingly call into question their involvement—whether the police or lawyers, or more generally political and government leaders who have over the years sought to limit the scope of liberty and detention judges. This stance with regard to their mission is closely linked to their personal beliefs and individual values regarding deportation policies and the treatment of immigrants.

On a professional level, the diversity of backgrounds and perspectives on justice is strong among these judges due to the way in which they are recruited. Statutorily vice president of the court, they only exercise this function after having occupied other positions in the judiciary, meaning an equal number of distinct professional socializations. The five judges observed over the course of our investigation, three of whom were interviewed,[15] attest to the heterogeneity of the professional backgrounds, which had a direct impact on their own perceptions of their role within immigration control. Their professional stance was therefore realized on two levels: in opposition to an immigration control policy in which their intervention was seen as marginal, if not incongruous, and in opposition to the Border Police, whose actions they judged as much as they judged the situations of the foreigners arrested. This stance was largely due to the way the magistrates understood and invested themselves in their professional role. Two of them who had more "technical" approaches cited the specificity of judicial work as justification for the distance which they placed between immigration policies and the officials who implement them.

The first magistrate, Jeanne Simon,[16] a criminal lawyer by training who had served as a judge on the National Court of Asylum, stated that she did not intervene in immigration control, but was there to "ensure that the individuals do not experience any violation of their rights, even if it will later have an impact on immigration policies. I do not intervene in the control." In addition to this refusal to contribute to immigration control, she distanced herself from the actions of the police, whose sometimes questionable "hunches" for making arrests she contrasted with the role of magistrates who do not have to rule on cases that are legally cut and dried, where the immigrants possess the necessary documentation and were arrested on mere suspicion. She also mentioned the "pressure" of the escort officers who attend the hearings, describing it as a paradoxical situation of role reversal—they were the ones who in turn judged her: "They are still there, and they react, they comment, they grumble, I hear them every time I make a decision."

The second magistrate, Marianne Prost, a former lawyer who had also held positions in prison administration, similarly stressed the importance of her intervention, seeing herself as the guardian of freedoms in a police procedure, but she also recognized that the inherent evaluation power of her office was necessarily exercised "to the detriment of the effectiveness of immigration control policies," a disconnect which made her feel "uncomfortable." She then went on to make a clear distinction between her work and that of the police, once again in contrast to police hunches:

> My role is not that of a police officer. When a police officer says on a hunch that the person wants to immigrate illegally, he is playing his role. It is not the role of the liberty and detention judge to say, "Uh no, that's not true, he's lying to us." That sort of thing is based on impressions, on hunches, and a judge, in my opinion, does not work like that. A judge has evidence, a judge has statutes, and a judge applies them. So there you have it: we judge according to the law, not according to a hunch.

The construction of a relationship with the institution thus distinguishes between justice and the deportation system in general. Affiliation with the institution is seen as being synonymous with judicial independence and the defense of individual rights. As such, it is contrasted with the procedure of deportation, referring to immigration policies which judges would prefer not to represent and to an ethos of suspicion inherent in the "hunches" of the police. This same opposition was evident in the radical rejection or support of police work of two other magistrates.

Claire Villet was eager to distance herself from the judiciary and the role of the liberty and detention judge. A senior university lecturer in secondment, she had occupied the function for only a year, after having spent the previous six fulfilling her academic duties as well as those of magistrate. She did not, however, rule out the possibility of returning to the academic world. This distancing with respect to her role was closely linked to the hostility that she showed towards the police—she claimed to be "anti-border police to the core."[17] In fact, the hearings she presided over frequently resulted in the release of the foreigner.

Adrienne Plart was almost diametrically opposed to this perspective. She emphasized her relationship with the institution: she showed a strong commitment to the role of judge, but did not oppose the work of the police and immigration controls that they implement. On the contrary, as she often repeated at hearings, she had been an examining magistrate before becoming a liberty and detention judge and displayed an affinity for, if not virtual complicity with, the police—an attitude consistent with the cooperation that is needed between an examining magistrate and investigators for there to be a case. The various comments that she made to the foreign defendants were evidence of a relationship based on two forms of support: for the state, which she saw herself as protecting against immigrants who try to enter the country illegally, and for the judiciary, again supposedly jeopardized by migrants. She frequently evoked her fear of seeing a foreigner deliberately lie in order to "manipulate the court" and readily justified her decisions by asserting that she was only "stating the law" and demonstrating an autonomy which guaranteed the separation of powers. This oft-stated ethos also corresponded to a specific mode of conduct during a hearing: the foreigner was frequently subject to a sustained interrogation, and the judge would systematically exploit the contradictions in the defendant's story in a manner not unlike that of a police interrogator. The moral significance she invested in her function thus revolved around the dual preservation of the integrity of the bench and the integrity of the state through the policing of borders and the suspicion cast a priori on the immigrants and their justifications. Again, this perspective was clearly reflected in the decisions made at the end of the hearings, which more often than not resulted in the foreigner's prolonged detention.

The question of the position of justice within the police deportation system is thus one that affects the individual magistrates, influencing their conceptions of legal practice and their actual decisions. At the same time, this representation of the judge's work is underpinned by specific values, both individual and specific to a professional ethos. However, these individual value systems are also part of the social dynamics of the hearings. The values described above—trust, esteem, or duplicity—freely circulate within those dynamics and are redistributed according to the judges, their relationship with the other actors in the hearing, and finally the specific attributes of each defendant.

The Offender, the Victim, and the Tourist: A Moral Scale for Judging Foreigners

The sentence is therefore the combination of each judge's individual background—itself tied to their professional ethos and their position on deportations and the police officers who enforce them—and the negotiated order of the courtroom.

From this junction emerge common standards by which foreigners are evaluated morally.[18] These standards can be defined through three relevant categories that recur throughout the various judgments.

The first category is that of offender, grouping together in the broadest sense not only foreigners who have been held or detained and those convicted of criminal offenses, but also those whose narrative or attitude during the hearing are suggestive of an affiliation with the criminal world. Breaking the law is logically the first criterion for inclusion in this category. As Claire Villet, who among the judges we interviewed was the most liberal and most distanced with respect to her role, indicated: "A foreigner guilty of an offense, I'm not saying I blame him, but I'm certainly not going to cry over him. It doesn't elicit feelings of injustice among us judges." However, this distanced assessment changes according to the attitude of the individual at the hearing, the moment that he or she abandons the passive role assigned to him or her as a foreigner and offender. This was what occurred when the same magistrate heard the case of an undocumented Tunisian convicted of running a red light. She reproached him for being in the country for five years but "doing nothing" to legalize his situation, and then declared: "And to add insult to injury, you ran a red light." The detainee tried to protest, stating that he was not responsible for the offense, which only further angered the judge: "No, you listen to me. You were found guilty, and what's more, running a red light is a serious offense. Legally and morally, you have the right to get yourself killed but not the person in the car opposite you!" The deviation from the norm—that is to say, the defendant had abandoned the passive role of remaining quiet throughout the trial and being "spoken for" by his lawyer and documents describing his situation—led to the moral evaluation of the detainee in a register that was much more emotional since his undocumented status doubled the moral stigma: he had committed an offense which put others in immediate danger, and moreover he refused to take responsibility for it.

The second category, that of victim, is the radical opposite of offender. In these instances—including cases involving unaccompanied children or asylum seekers—defendants are likewise assigned a role of total passivity, which in itself bears a positive connotation: they must be protected precisely because they are only enduring their fate, that is, the act of immigration itself, whether it be imposed by persecution in the case of asylum seekers or by parents or criminal networks in the case of minors when neither type of defendant can be held legally or morally accountable. In the latter case, there is a true "compassionate anchoring"[19] of the court proceedings: the perception of children and adolescents as a priori passive and innocent, possibly manipulated by others but hardly blameworthy themselves, precludes the use of certain stigmatizing arguments against them and on the contrary makes explanations that would have been rejected in the case of an adult acceptable.

This was what happened in the case of a 17-year-old Chilean who appeared in court assisted by a representative of the French Red Cross. He had applied for asylum upon arrival in the country, an act seemingly inconsistent with his originally stated reason for visiting: tourism. The representative stated that his family was waiting for him in Spain, but "given the lack of money, entering this way [with a tourist visa] was the only way. It is not very honest, but it was the only solution." She also added that the asylum application was filed "as delay tactic: there was a flight already scheduled [for his return to Latin America] … This is not something the Red Cross usually does, but there was no alternative …." The judge—in this case, Jeanne Simon who had previously served as a judge on the National Court of Asylum—released the teenager. The two irregularities in his immigration status could have been potentially stigmatizing: on the one hand, abusing the process by entering as a tourist even though in this case it was really a family reunion, a situation for which there is another, more restrictive procedure, and on the other hand, applying for asylum, done with the express purpose of strategically avoiding deportation and yet without any legal basis. This double irregularity is nevertheless accepted and does not prevent the minor's release, due in special part to the intervention in the debates of a representative[20]—a specific actor, the only other individual besides the lawyer to have interviewed the minor in the waiting zone and who could therefore claim an emotional proximity to him—who gave weight to the moral justification, attributing her abuse of the system to an urgent need to avoid the adolescent's expulsion.

Presenting individuals as victims who are to be seen in a purely compassionate light does at times come into conflict with competing qualifications, especially that of "offender" when the age and narrative of the minors can cast doubt on their "innocence" and the true reason for their visit. This was the case when, for example, a 16-year-old Cameroonian girl appeared before Adrienne Plart, the harshest among the judges and the one who shared the police's ethics of suspicion most closely. The teenager's real age was uncertain—which could imply that she had intended to remain in the county illegally and was hiding her true intentions—because the passport she had been carrying when checked at immigration control was that of an adult. This element was sufficient enough for the judge to suspect her of having lied about her age. The magistrate was also skeptical of the reason given as to why she had fled her home: she had sought to escape a prostitution ring. The particular ethos of the judge contributed to the adolescent's passing from the status of victim to that of guilty or at least suspect and to her further detention.

This same tension is at work in the third and final category, that of tourist. In cases involving tourists, the qualification itself is at stake: the foreigners state that they have come to France or Europe to sightsee or to visit family members who live there. However, for the officers who check their papers, these foreigners lack the documentation needed to enter the country and provide no valid explanation for this lack, which is why their visits are reclassified as attempts to enter the Schengen Zone illegally. The examination of such cases at a hearing is therefore a test of truth in which these two qualifications—tourist or undocumented immigrant—are weighed. It is also in such situations that the tension at the root of this contribution can be directly observed: the issue is indeed whether foreigners belong to "floating populations" and are thus stigmatized as "police targets" or whether they are migrants legitimately exercising their right to enter the country and who would be both respectable and outrageously offended by the suspicion placed on them. Again, the background and stance of the magistrates combine with the situation of the immigrants to provide a specific solution to each case. Adrienne Plart, the most repressive of the judges, thus examined the case of an Ivorian whom she methodically questioned: he stated that he was an importer of used vehicles in Côte d'Ivoire, buying cars in Europe from his home in Abidjan that are transported to Africa via Antwerp. He had intended to stop over in Paris because one of his intermediaries was located in Saint-Denis. The judge was doubtful: "You know that ninety percent of the cars passing through Antwerp are either stolen or tampered with, don't you? I speak as a former examining magistrate, nine out of every ten cars are stolen cars, and pass through Antwerp with fake documents ...." The counsel for the prefecture was surprised that the businessman's passport listed teacher as his profession, to which the defendant replied that he was indeed a mathematics teacher but had quit his job to start a business. The judge asked for evidence of this: "I have a tax ID number, I am registered ...." "Yes, but I want to see a business license to prove it! Well, to do business in France, you need a business license. I know in Africa you can have five or six jobs, but in France, that's not how it works." He was further detained in the waiting zone.

The judge's particular background serves as an explicit point of reference which allows for the Ivorian's harmless job change to be transformed not just into evidence of illegal entry into the country, but into a near-criminal enterprise in the trafficking of stolen goods. In addition to this transformation, there was a racialized representation of the seriousness of how one presents oneself professionally, contrasting a "here" in France where professions are stable or certified, with an "elsewhere" in Africa where professional identities are on the contrary fluid and lacking in credibility. This double stigma confirmed in the eyes of the judge that the foreigner was "unvouched for" and therefore could not be allowed to enter the country. It is also in this type of case that the moral qualification of the evidence and the concrete social networks that foreigners possess in the country are the most decisive. This was true for an Angolan arrested at the airport while en route to Belgium: the French police had considered the visa in his passport to be fake. His lawyer cast doubt on their assessment and pointed out that the man had an aunt in France who could host him if he were released. A lady was in fact present in the gallery with an ID proving that she was his aunt. Jeanne Simon, the more moderate judge, heard the case around two in the afternoon, deliberated on the matter, and then handed down her decision at the end of the session around ten in the evening. Speaking to the aunt, she said: "Well, I am not in a position to determine the authenticity of the visa, but I do note that the woman who signed the proof of accommodation, even though domiciled in Grenoble, is still present in the room. Which proves that you are, I wouldn't say obstinate, but determined ...." She released the young man.

The material organization of the hearings allows here for an extended evaluation of the case, based not only on the credibility of the defendant, but also of his principal contacts in the country. To seem "determined" is literally to affirm the strength of the immigrant's family ties and the veracity of his or her alleged story in contrast to the supposed indiscipline of undocumented foreigners. Significantly, in the eyes of the judge, this assessment took precedence over the material and objective issues regarding the authenticity of the visa, de facto difficult to determine and de jure disregarded in the final decision. This hesitation between the "respectable foreigner" and the foreigner who is not is reproduced in the case of administrative courts. But while individual values, professional ethos, and material conditions of the judgment are still involved, it is nevertheless in a different configuration.

Administrative Judges

Administrative judges have a distinct role since they examine the legality of deportation orders. While the procedures and professional statutes of the two benches differ, administrative judges face the same public as liberty and detention judges: undocumented immigrants who are subject to deportation. As magistrates, they too must intervene in the way the police handle this population. They too take both an individual and a collective stance with regard to a specific proceeding in which their recent intervention is not obvious, neither for the other actors nor for the judges themselves, even though it takes up an increasing part of their time. In the case of administrative tribunals, cases involving foreigners actually saw its greatest increase (48 percent) between 1999 and 2006, representing 26 percent of cases recorded in 2006. At the court I observed, they represented 49 percent of the cases adjudicated in 2009, far more than the second most common type of case, those involving local administration (17 percent).[21]

The response of administrative judges to this massive influx of cases involving a population of inhabitual defendants is particular. Reactions depend on the makeup of the court, the specific professional ethos of the judges, again combined with their individual ethics. The specificity of administrative courts is what makes them most interesting: magistrates exhibit professional backgrounds and individual values that differ greatly from those of their colleagues in criminal courts. This difference is accentuated by the influence of local configurations of judgment, again specific to the administrative courts. While oral hearings do exist in cases involving foreigners, the tradition of a collegial and almost completely written review of the cases specific to these courts also modifies the way in which moral judgments of the immigrants, most notably in their emotional dimension, are collectively produced by the judges.

Between Legal Work and "Human Problems"

Although they have the status of judge and review deportation orders, administrative judges differ sharply from liberty and detention judges. The primary difference lies in their formation and professional backgrounds: they either hold a degree from the National School of Administration (*École Nationale d'Administration* or ENA) or, if they are already civil servants or lawyers, go through an "external" recruitment process after passing an additional exam.[22] In all cases, the judges have had experience in government administration or at least have worked closely with the administration, particularly at the higher level.[23] This proximity is made apparent in their practice of law since administrative proceedings most often revolve around highly technical legal issues, from building permits to the awarding of public contracts. These are examined through written reviews, leaving no room for the orality of public trials and their readily theatrical dimension.[24]

Due to the conditions of their socialization in law—their individual background, their professional role, the type of law they practice, and the interlocutors whom they encounter—administrative judges are a lot like the "state nobility" described by Pierre Bourdieu.[25] This collective perception of their professional role influences the disdain administrative judges have for deportation cases. As already highlighted by several studies, this type of case is met with reluctance.[26] While liberty and detention judges are greatly invested in their role as defenders of freedom or take a stance on immigration policies, administrative judges instead see themselves mainly as technicians of French administrative law who guarantee its consistency and its force, and they use this representation of their professional responsibilities in order to distance themselves from the tension between the protection and the repression of foreigners. They rarely invoke the rights of the individuals or, vice versa, the need to suppress illegal immigration. For them, it is first and foremost a question of law and the legal quality of judicial work, and they readily dismiss the "moral" and "political" issues in interviews.

This insistence of administrative judges on the technical dimension of their job nevertheless conveys a series of moral evaluations not only of foreigners, but also of those who deport them and those who support them. It also covers a range of different moral positions, each related to the professional background or personal biography of the judges and the way they invest their institutional role as "technicians of the law" and guarantors of the rigor of each case's review.

The first stance is one of radically rejecting immigration proceedings as "fake law"—a position underpinned by the moral devaluation of the actors in the proceedings. It is primarily a generational issue. One of the judges defending this position, a 56-year-old, had joined the administrative court in 1988, a year before these tribunals began to review deportation orders and well before another deportation measure, the so-called "obligation to leave the territory" (*obligation de quitter le territoire*), was created in 2007, which came with its own administrative trial.[27] Formerly attached to a ministry's central administration, he was originally in charge of preparing his administration's legal defense in court, notably in matters of urban development law—an initial socialization to legal issues that led him to become a judge himself. He believed that he had been deceived and that the job had been misrepresented: when he first joined the court, "immigration trials were very noble affairs about extraditions or high-level law enforcement: they weren't trials about denied residence permits, let alone deportation trials." He claimed that he would have thought twice about becoming a magistrate if he had known that there would be an influx of such cases and argued that they probably act as a deterrent for current candidates. He saw the trials as being repetitive in nature, continually raising the same legal problems, the potential interest of which was offset by the handling of the cases:

> I just had one that was particularly relevant, because the man was a de facto polygamist. The minister of the interior made it a hobbyhorse of his, and so the position of the prefecture was a purely moral one and not at all legal. As a result, the deportation order was of course riddled with legal errors, but the only real legal issue raised by the case was never brought up. I would have loved to write a decision saying that de facto polygamy did not preclude the issuance of a residency permit when the family life, albeit de facto, was fine here. The moral positions of the judges are going to interfere in this case. Especially in this one, the court commissioner who was in charge shared the prefecture's moral standards and had the same approach: he argued that we can't give a residence permit to a woman who is cohabiting with a man who has no residence permit but has eight children and a wife at home. Maybe this woman didn't know the more intimate details of her partner's life, and so her family situation, moral standards notwithstanding, could have indeed been in France. But more important, a decision should not be based on moral grounds, but on a legal issue. That was not the case.

The representation of what constitutes here the judge's duties is built around the integrity of the legal work, undermined by the "moral" dimension and the politicized nature of the case. The same judge's opinion on the evolution of judicial practice demonstrates the moral position underlying this professional stance. If immigration cases were once more "noble" matters in the image of other administrative cases, judicial intervention in deportation proceedings constitutes a literal regression from "high" to "low" policing in which the practical and little formalized management of "dominated illegalities" and what was called at the beginning of this chapter "floating populations" predominates. Yet the moral stigma does not weigh primarily on the foreigners, but rather on the legal professionals— prefects or court commissioners—who handle their cases, and whose work seems "contaminated" by the triviality of the matter: their control of the legal instrument replaces the law and therefore the very possibility of a "good judgment" with moral positions and immigration policies.

Most judges exhibited this distancing with respect to immigration cases and their actors. This general position does, however, leave room for strong nuances, the first of which is generational. Young judges more recently appointed to the administrative courts have essentially dealt with immigration cases since their training, and see this matter as an integral part of judicial practice: a newly recruited judge who had studied history in college and received a degree in political science before passing the civil service exam in 2005, described deportation cases as routine and rarely problematic. Another 26-year-old judge with a similar background was more explicit in stating that he was used to such assembly-line legal proceedings, which were already a reality by the time he began his studies in political science. His appointment to the administrative court in April 2010 was his first since passing the civil service exam: after graduating, he had served as a clerk for the Council of State. But this inclusion of immigration trials into their legal work does not signal an end to the distancing previously mentioned: in both cases, the magistrates noted the monotony of deportation cases, justifying accordingly the procedural simplifications which allowed them to judge weak cases or presenting the same legal issues more quickly. They also displayed a similar moral distancing with respect to the actors in the case: the lawyers who are stigmatized for their incompetence and propensity to raise emotional or political arguments rather than legal ones in their pleadings, and the community activists who are belittled for their inconsistency in choosing the cases they will defend, fighting indefensible ones while ignoring, as the magistrate said, "cases that deserve support."

Predicated on a demand for quality legal work, a demand that the expulsion of foreigners cannot sufficiently comply with, this distancing ultimately conveys a moral evaluation not so much of the foreigners themselves as it does of the restricted circle of actors that forms around deportation cases: lawyers with questionable legal skills, community activists with too radical an agenda to allow for a meaningful assessment of the cases, officials from the prefecture whose evaluation is sometimes seen as not very legal. While these judgments about the social dimension of the trials characterize the professional distance of the administrative judges, they do not prevent the tension between the repression and the protection of foreigners from being reproduced when it is a question of assessing individual cases. Judges—especially those most recently appointed— stress the "human" dimension and its interest for a court where technical issues dominate precisely because deportation trials are not well-defined legally.[28] This judgment is above all formulated in cases of "escort to the border" (*reconduite à la frontière*) which involve a single judge who issues a ruling at hearings following an oral and face-to-face investigation. In these cases, the emotional dimension plays a more important role. As the young judge mentioned above noted, this dimension nevertheless also exists in completely written "obligation to leave the territory" cases, either because the judges may have an individual empathy for a foreigner whose request they cannot accept from a legal standpoint or, as in the case of seriously ill foreigners who face deportation, because the vagueness of the law they enforce makes them hesitate. Yet this hesitation manifested itself in a very particular configuration: it surfaced only when the judges met behind closed doors to review cases. It is the effect of this particular environment on the production of legal judgments that will be examined in the final section, for, although the professional and individual values of the judges still manage to be expressed, they are apperceived in the collective dynamic of producing—and negotiating—decisions made among peers. During these meetings, the local manifestation of the moral economy of immigration judgments deviated from the individual assessments of the liberty and detention judges described in the previous section. I will conclude by analyzing this difference.

A Writing Culture or the Collective Control of Emotions

Deportation cases follow a regular administrative procedure: the review is almost entirely written and takes place primarily behind closed doors among specialized judges. What is of interest here is this relative isolation of the review itself. If the organization of the court, including its material make up, is the "institution made thing," then it physically reinforces the moral distance separating the judge-technicians of the law and their public of deportable immigrants. This separation is moreover reinforced by the procedural filters necessary for the composition of the cases. They are initially sorted by court clerks responsible for dismissing manifestly ungrounded cases, after which the cases languish for several months at the court's administrative service as they wait to be rounded out by memos drafted by both the foreigner's counsel and the lawyer for the prefecture, as well as by various supporting documents. This series of intermediate steps greatly reduces the potential influence of outside actors on the review. Once the investigation is complete, cases are examined in investigatory review sessions—veritable legal marathons during which up to six judges discuss 45 cases in quick succession over the course of a half-day. Scheduled a month later, the hearing is merely informational, for it is then that both parties learn of the court's decision.

The analysis of each case is thus tied to the rationales of a professional community. It brings the court's judges together, but more specifically it brings together the members of each chamber, depending on their assigned specialties, which may likewise be tied to certain attitudes with regard to deportation cases: a court clerk indicated, for example, that the court specializing in tax law had a "more relaxed" vision of deportation proceedings than the one that focused specifically on immigration law. Thus, the work is immediately shared: conversations are frequent among the magistrates with those who have a particular command of a certain specialty serving as resource persons.[29]

In contrast to the individual approach of the liberty and detention judges, it is this logic of collective action behind closed doors which makes the investigatory review sessions interesting: for the administrative judges who are bound together by common skill sets and more broadly by daily routines that gradually become internalized, these sessions are an opportunity for the collective handling of the moral tension between the repression and the protection of foreigners. As was already noted, this handling is organized primarily around the law and its consistency. In this sense, investigatory review sessions reaffirm the common sense collectively shared by the magistrates on the legitimate uses of the law for issuing a ruling on an actual case. The importance of the "hesitation" and the "human" in immigration cases nevertheless implies that a moral evaluation of the foreigner's situation as well as of the government officials who ordered the deportation enters into this legal assessment. Judges use the discretionary power afforded to them to arrive at decisions that are just as moral as they are legal.[30] Because the tension between protection and repression is negotiated on a local scale, final decisions are influenced by the individual backgrounds of the judges, as well as by the social logic of closed-door hearings which allow the judges to "waver" over each case.[31]

Gathered in an office around a table where the day's 45 cases are piled, the four magistrates initially assume roles that have been specifically codified. The chairperson calls each case successively while two other judges take turns acting as the rapporteur. A third judge performs the function of court commissioner, in charge of analyzing all the cases independently and proposing his or her own legal solution that his or her colleagues will be free to accept or reject. If a negotiated order is once again established among these professionals, it has the effect of monitoring and controlling the emotional reactions and legal assessments that are morally legitimate for each case—even though no lawyer or defendant is present to oppose the judges.

Cases involving foreigners suffering from serious illnesses are particularly revealing of this logic. Sick foreigners cannot be forced to leave the country when the severity of their condition and lack of access to medical care in their country of origin are certified by a medical inspector from the public health department. As one young judge noted, the difficulty of assessing the medical condition of the immigrants and above all, the state of the health care system in their country of origin, leaves even greater room for the individual moral positions of judges in the evaluation of the cases, but it also allows for their collective framing during the discussions. Take, for example, a case involving a 64-year-old Moroccan woman with severe kidney failure. The court commissioner immediately stated that "clearly there is no disputing the fact that this requires a lot of treatment and that she is seriously ill." She also happened to have a sister who lived in poverty in Morocco, who had "no vehicle and lives 93 miles from a medical center. So there is a lack of access to care in this case." There was, however, sparse evidence to suggest that the family in Morocco was indeed poor, as the prefecture highlighted in its memo. The rapporteur therefore concluded: "I boldly propose that we stop the deportation proceedings on some other legal ground." The rapporteur noted that the debate essentially only focused on access to care, but added that "she is seriously ill." One of his colleagues opined: "She has no resources, she says she has no health insurance in Morocco, she is 93 miles from the hospital, and the prefecture says: 'We don't care, it's irrelevant.' For me, that still poses a problem ... I don't know if we can rely on the manifest error of the assessment ...." The president concluded:

> The Council of State has said that it is the prefect who assesses; our review is only to ensure consistency. And above all, to respond to the arguments made. The severity of the disease is not mentioned here. She is responding to what is brought against her. They talked to her about access to care and her sister in Morocco, so she responds, it makes sense. So we move to cancel? Good.

The moral basis of the debate—ultimately leading to the court's decision to cancel the deportation—clearly appears over the course of the conversation. The morally problematic dimension of the case is the subject of general agreement, facilitated by the indisputable nature of the disease's severity. If access to medical care is the real issue of the discussion, then the moral preconception favorable to the applicant—the one which causes the judges to rule that the prefect's position is problematic—guides the search for a legal means to settle the case. At issue is the assurance that the moral appraisal of the situation translates into a legally sound solution,[32] a task leading the judges to reframe the legal perspective they adopt on the case multiple times: the weak evidence of the applicant's indigence encourages them to find a more solid "ground," but to establish the evidence of a manifest error of the assessment (a legal argument that would enable judges to cancel the decision of the prefecture because its agents had misjudged the actual situation of the foreigner) proves legally impractical. So the chairperson's final intervention concludes the debate by reminding those present of the procedural rules—respond only to those issues raised in the case's memos—while at the same time validating the collective will to cancel the deportation. At the hearing two days later, the public rapporteur would insist on the access to care, but this time he would accuse the prefecture of not having convincingly proved that access was possible in Morocco.

Legal rigor is never abandoned in favor of a purely humanitarian assessment of the case. It is rather a translation of moral evaluations into legal terms with reference to the codified categories which become both a resource and a constraint for the judges.[33] If the rigor of the legal framework is gradually strengthened in the course of the conversation, the underlying moral evaluation remains apparent, and it is organized according to more or less consensual standards, rating cases from those most likely to attract the leniency of the judges to those which will be the most poorly received. This moral hierarchy is even more evident because, apart from those who are sick, the legal categories that determine which foreigners will have their status regularized and which ones will instead be deported are the immediate retranslation of a moral perspective on their stay in France: the parents of French children or spouses of French citizens are especially protected, provided that the parents actually attend to the needs of the child or that the spouses still live together, as are students so long as they are successful in their studies. Undeportable "good foreigners" are also good parents, good spouses, or good students, a portrayal that clearly influences the discussions during investigatory review sessions.

The evaluation was thus favorable in the case of an Armenian woman who had resided in France legally for twelve years, studying music until 2009, but whose residence permit the prefecture refused to renew when she enrolled in the university to study Russian: for the case's rapporteur, she is "exemplary" due to her study of music and job as a piano teacher, not to mention her volunteering with the Red Cross. Overruling the obvious error in judgment, the judges agree in the end to cancel the deportation. While the role that the individual backgrounds of the judges play is more difficult to discern in this configuration, it is worth noting the particular insistence of one of the magistrates, a former employee of a large public company who stressed his family ties to Central and Eastern Europe and his ability to read Russian. Demonstrating his partiality for the applicant and her situation, his intervention significantly bolstered her legitimacy: "In my opinion, she is someone who studied music in Yerevan and came to perfect her skills in France." However, it was this same judge who voiced disagreement with his colleagues in the case of an Ivorian appealing a deportation order on the grounds that he is the parent of a French child and already entitled to a residence permit. The rapporteur for the case notes that he "no longer cares for the child," but that he has lived in France for eleven years, arriving in the country with his family as a minor. He therefore proposes to annul the ruling on the basis of the European Convention on Human Rights (the agreement guarantees the right to lead a normal family life), a solution approved by the court commissioner: "He lived here between the ages of 16 and 26, and those are important years." The other judge interjects: "But he still abandoned his son!" The president admitted that "he is not a nice guy." The court commissioner likewise acknowledged that he was "not a model father," but noted that he had a child with a French woman and had essentially spent most of his life in France, where, the president pointed out, his entire family lived. The "reluctant" judge then remarked that the French child had conveniently come when he was an adult, thereby enabling him to obtain a residence permit, a comment which elicited smiles from his colleagues. Despite the reservations of their colleague, the magistrates concluded that the deportation would be cancelled. The tension at work in this case opposes two definitions of "normal family life," a legal concept with obvious moral content: the duty to be a good parent, which the foreigner on trial here had failed to be, is eventually supplanted by the importance for an individual to remain in the country where he or she had grown up. The tension pitting the "reluctant" judge against his colleagues is reduced through the same collective dynamics: once an agreement has been reached about the excessive nature of the deportation, the dissenting opinion can in the end be brushed aside with smiles to whitewash the point of contention.

Conclusion

The collective logic of administrative courts contrasts with the individual stance of liberty and detention judges. Certainly these two configurations present a common logic of variation within the local forms of the two courts and within the moral tension between repression and the protection of foreigners. Privileged places of formal debate and resolution of this tension, the judicial institutions analyzed here highlight, however, the important differences between the immigration and administrative courts and how these differences are dealt with on a local level. The moral economy of managing foreigners finds itself expressed in distinct ways, due to the particular moral subjectivities of the judges and their professional ethos: based on their professional background and their individual moral or political commitments, they differ in how they are invested in their role which in turn differs in its institutional definition according to its judiciary and administrative forms. To this subjective dimension are added the established systems—legal categories, codified procedures, or structures—and the negotiated local forms with which they are combined.

The judicial treatment of foreigners is thus determined in a complex institutional logic that cannot be reduced to the simple opposition between a purely retributive and a purely indulgent justice for foreigners without morally devaluing this particular population. As in the past, the figure of the "bad immigrant" is closely tied to the "floating" aspect of immigration.

Notes

1 By immigration trial, we mean a case heard in court.
2 On this point, see Lagroye and Offerlé (2011).
3 The field studies we describe here were conducted between July 2009 and February 2010 for the criminal court, and between March 2010 and July 2010 for the administrative court. Details on these two jurisdictions will be provided later. Similarly, the interviews took place between December 2009 and March 2010 for the liberty and detention judges at the criminal court, and in June and July 2010 for the administrative judges.
4 For examples, see Blanc-Chaléard et al. (2001).
5 According to the analysis of Emmanuel Blanchard (2011: 188).
6 See for example Jobard (2010).
7 See this now classic analysis in Noiriel (2007).
8 On this point, see Bernardot (2008).
9 See Noiriel (1988).
10 This is what Didier Bigo notably shows (1996).
11 On the intersection of value judgments, emotions, and their control by the institution, see Graham (2002).
12 These are the terms of Niklas Luhmann (2001: 70).
13 A few minutes before the start of a hearing, two opposing lawyers converse in a joking manner. One of the two concludes the conversation with the following remark accompanied by laughs: "G ... is arguing with me today, he'll eat you alive!"
14 Following a change in the schedule of the hearings, this judge was in fact presiding in place of a colleague that day. She was therefore reexamining a case she had reviewed two weeks before—a questionable legal situation which the rotation of magistrates would have normally avoided.
15 Data concerning the fourth judge were collected in the course of our observations.
16 Out of concern for confidentiality, the real identities of the persons have been replaced with fictitious ones.
17 Reference to the Border Police which control the travelers entering French territory.
18 For a similar analysis of the assessment of foreigners by officials (in this case, in the United States), see Heyman (2000).
19 According to the expression used by Janine Barbot and Nicolas Dodier (2012).
20 Ad hoc representatives are responsible for representing (legally incompetent) unaccompanied minors in court. At the court in question, most were women volunteers from two organizations (the French Red Cross and Family Assistance).
21 These numbers are based on a study by Barré and Aubusson de Cavarlay (2008) and on the court's own data (2010).

22 This exam is open to holders of degrees required for admission to the ENA, to senior civil servants working for at least seven years in a public function, and finally to criminal court judges.

23 For a sociography of administrative judges, see Colera (2001).

24 More precisely, two types of deportation measures will be considered here: so-called "escort to the border" (*reconduite à la frontière*), a deportation measure for which the trial is completely oral and differs from administrative procedure, and so-called "obligation to leave the territory" (*obligation de quitter le territoire*), a more recent measure for which the trial follows the ordinary process. More precisions will be given later on this last measure.

25 See Bourdieu (1998 [1989]).

26 On this point, see El Qadim (2008) and Cohen (2009).

27 Legally speaking, the obligation to leave the territory is not a simple deportation, but an administrative response from the prefect to a foreigner having requested a residence permit: it signifies both the rejection of the foreigner's request and the obligation to leave France in less than one month under penalty of forced deportation after this date. It is a combination of two decisions. The objective of its creators was to simplify the work of officials and judges responsible for examining the appeals of foreigners. This measure has nevertheless created even more litigation for the administrative courts.

28 We agree with the conclusions of Cohen (2009).

29 On this logic of collective action among peers, see Lazega (1999).

30 On this point, see Spire (2008).

31 On the importance of "hesitation" in the work of administrative courts, see Latour (2002).

32 On legal means, see Latour (2002).

33 On this point, see Latour (2002).

CHAPTER THREE

In Search of Truth
How Asylum Applications
Are Adjudicated

Carolina Kobelinsky

The asylum seeker had just delivered a five-minute-long monologue in fluent, well-spoken French when he was interrupted by the judge. "Sir," said the magistrate in a stern voice, waving his hand in frustration, "please just tell us the truth. I find your story very hard to believe!" The young Congolese man seemed annoyed, but the judge did not give him enough time to respond before adding: "Calm down, don't take it the wrong way, we are here to determine your sincerity, so please be sincere!" This exchange between an asylum seeker and a judge during a hearing at the National Court of Asylum (*Cour nationale du droit d'asile*, CNDA)—an administrative court responsible for assessing appeals from applicants whose requests have been turned down by the French Office for the Protection of Refugees and Stateless Persons (*Office français pour les réfugiés et apatrides*, OFPRA) —was hardly unusual. In fact, the use of terms belonging to the lexical field of truth during such hearings as well as in conversations with the various actors of the court is quite common.

The judiciary world is by definition structured around the search for truth. The courts in the French as well as English tradition employ numerous procedures— both formal and informal—that are designed to insist on sincerity.[1] But the omnipresence of truth here must also be viewed in light of the particular types of claims handled by this court, asylum, as discourses on this topic are characterized by the dichotomy between "real" and "fake" refugees. In fact, over the past thirty years, the mistrust towards asylum seekers, who are regarded as potential "fake refugees" has pervaded the public discourse in many countries, including France.[2] The majority of the applicants are no longer considered to be political exiles as was the case in the past, but economic migrants who abuse the protection provided by states—in accordance with international conventions—to those persecuted in their countries of origin. Thus, in the court, the judiciary search for truth is combined with a questioning of what asylum seekers, who are suspected of being profiteers, say and write.

The study of the court's decision-making process through an ethnographic investigation conducted over the course of two years[3] reveals the central role which suspicion—understood as an attitude of distrust or disbelief towards asylum requests—plays in the development of intuitions, feelings, and preconceived notions. Constructed in response to the political discourse and at the same time participating in its construction, the suspicion at work in the adjudication process has not always been at the core of asylum policies and representations. For nearly thirty years, since the establishment of the OFPRA and the Refugee Appeals Commission (recently renamed the CNDA) in 1952, most foreigners who sought the protection of France as refugees received it. Since then, the situation has reversed, and most candidates see their applications successively rejected by these two institutions.

For a long time, asylum seekers were not considered "applicants." Those in the process of being granted the status and those who had already obtained it were both simply known as refugees. It was only in the 1980s that the term "asylum seeker" entered the public discourse, becoming an administrative category in 1991 when a ministerial memo de facto prohibited individuals from working while in the process of applying for asylum. It was during this period that asylum claims started to be construed as abusive and that institutional practices implemented led to drastic reductions in admission rates. Today, the observation of public hearings and private deliberations, as well as interviews conducted with the various agents of the court, reveal an attitude of distrust towards applicants who are often viewed as stereotypes and to whom little credit is given. Conversely, applicants with claims considered too outlandish are similarly regarded with suspicion.

Here, I wish to examine, on the one hand, how suspicion has become a fundamental prism through which asylum seekers are perceived and treated and, on the other hand, how it affects the daily work of the agents at the court. Analyzing adjudication practices allows us to understand how the meaning attributed to the notion of truth—in other words, what a "true asylum claim" is—and the value ascribed by court officials to asylum as an institution relate to each other. First, I will approach asylum from a socio-historical perspective, tracing the status back to the late nineteenth century and focusing both on the construction of a system designed to protect refugees and on the recent creation of a specific bureaucracy which accords such protection. This brief historical summary will shed light on the challenges of accommodating this population, as well as the way in which truth-telling practices are implemented. Next, I will use the ethnographic material to explore how applications are evaluated, analyzing the way in which rapporteurs examine the cases before arriving at a recommendation, focusing on the interaction between the applicants and the judges during the hearing, and the deliberations of the latter afterwards. In each case, I will consider the frames of reference used to assess the applications as well as the place and role of suspicion in the daily work of the agents. Finally, still using an ethnographic method, I will concentrate on the importance which the strong ties established in the course of the hearings between the emotions of the judges and the veracity of the applications place on truth. Of particular interest is the relationship between the decision-making process and the conception of asylum held by court officials.

The Social History of Asylum

In this section, I will briefly trace the origin of refugee as a modern administrative category, the legal system built to assure the safety of this population, and the institutions created in France to grant refugee status. This short history of asylum shows how economic concerns are quickly intertwined with the project of protecting refugees. In times of crisis, the willingness of the state to provide protection to exiles clashes with a desire to secure borders, and truth-telling practices are put in place to weed out those wishing to benefit from the welfare state. Although these administrative practices have existed since the nineteenth century, we will see how, in the past decades, they have been overwhelmed by distrust toward asylum seekers.

Asylum before the Creation of Refugee Status

The modern concept of refugee is a product of the League of Nations, which in 1921 decided to appoint a High Commissioner for Refugees responsible for distributing aid provided by several countries and humanitarian organizations to those displaced by the Great War and the Russian Revolution.

In France, however, the history of refugee status can be traced back even further. Article 120 of the 1793 Constitution, for example, proclaimed that "the French people grant asylum to foreigners banished from their homeland for the cause of freedom." It was at this time that the ancient religious practice of granting sanctuary to strangers being pursued, a concept which was gradually codified by Christianity in the Middle Ages and further developed by the monarchy before the French Revolution, was endowed with a new secular meaning. However, as historian Gérard Noiriel shows, the right of asylum was quickly jeopardized by the tension between two principles: the generous welcome extended to persecuted foreigners and the exclusive defense of citizens.[4] This opposition resulted in a parliamentary debate on the differences between the two categories: should they enjoy the same benefits? Could they have the same rights? In the 1830s, another issue came to the fore in the discussions surrounding refugees: what was the definition of a refugee? In the absence of a specific legal status, those seeking asylum were not all treated in the same way. A system to identify and monitor "subsidized refugees," that is, those receiving state aid, was set up, allowing the government to control the movements of these foreigners through the assistance it provided.[5] But in return for the subsidies, the public authorities became increasingly demanding with regard to the identity of refugees and the evidence of their persecution. Seeking corroboration, they turned to the embassies of the states the refugees had fled, in order to verify the accuracy of their claims, but they quickly realized that this could prevent them from extending protection to opponents being sought after. The authorities then insisted on the authenticity of the documents produced, scrutinizing them carefully in order to identify possible fraud. Thus, the divergence between the centrality of the oral narrative of the exiles and the growing importance given to the written documents provided as evidence progressively took shape, and suspicion increasingly permeated the administrative practices related to asylum.

Shortly after World War I, the Norwegian explorer and scientist Frithjof Nansen was appointed by the League of Nations to oversee the repatriation of prisoners of war. He was also responsible for directing the High Commission for Russian Refugees, later expanding its purview to include Armenian refugees. They were soon joined by Italians fleeing fascism, Greeks, Bulgarians, Turks, etc. Asylum became an international legal problem. The Convention relating to the International Status of Refugees of 1933 considered that asylum applied to any person "who does not have or no longer enjoys the protection of his country," but the qualification was still based on specific groups of refugees defined according to their national origin (Russian, Turkish, Armenian, Syrian, etc.), each group being successively added to the list in accordance with international events. It further affirmed the impossibility of returning a refugee to his or her country of origin, which is now known as the principle of *non-refoulement*. However, the economic crisis put a damper on the acceptance of refugees in countries like France, which had had a great need for labor in the 1920s. The debates at the 1938 Evian Conference which was organized to facilitate the emigration of German and Austrian Jews trying to escape Nazism are emblematic of this tension between economic considerations and the willingness to protect the refugees. The new definition of refugee which emerged from the meeting nevertheless constituted an important step forward, as the conference adopted a universal criterion which transcended categorization according to specific groups: the fear of persecution. However, as Noiriel points out on the basis of archival work, no European state felt compelled to adhere to the provisions of the conference. In this sense, it is worth noting that expulsion orders greatly increased during the 1930s and that the Commission for the Protection of French Labor demanded that the government systematically oppose the hiring of any new refugee. Despite this reaction, the Popular Front established for the first time a clear distinction between "economic" immigrants and "political" refugees, exempting the latter from obtaining a visa issued by the Ministry of Labor.

The Definition of a Legal Framework

While the modern legal concept of a refugee was born in the aftermath of World War I, it was World War II which marked a real turning point in the conception and practice of asylum. Indeed, since the signing of the Geneva Convention in 1951, systems intended to recognize and protect refugees have been set up in each signatory country through the creation of specialized institutions.

In the wake of World War II, the tension between the will to protect human rights and the need to control the flow of transient populations was extreme. At a conference held in Geneva in 1951 under the auspices of the United Nations, 26 states, reprising certain aspects of previous conventions, agreed to define a refugee as a person who owing to a well-founded fear of being persecuted for reasons of race, religion, nationality, membership of a particular social group or political opinion, is outside the country of his nationality and is unable, or owing to such fear, is unwilling to avail himself of the protection of that country, or, not having a nationality and being outside the country of his former habitual residence as a result of such events, is unable or, owing to such fear, is unwilling to return to it.[6]

There were two opposing interpretations regarding the scope of this definition: one advocated limiting this definition in place and in time to the events which occurred in Europe prior to January 1, 1951; the other proposed a broader definition without any such restrictions. As a result of the French delegation's support for the first position throughout the negotiation process, two versions of the agreement were available at the time of ratification, and it was up to each state to choose between the two definitions. There were at the time an estimated 20–30 million displaced persons on European territory.[7] France had to repopulate the country and rebuild its industry, but it did not want to let more foreigners than necessary enter. For the states party to the agreement, it was one thing to designate humanitarian assistance as a universal value, but another to accept these refugees in their respective territories. Due to the reluctance of officials at the French Ministry of Labor who feared that they would be unable to protect their domestic workforce, it was not until September 1954 that the provisions of the Geneva Convention went into effect in France with the spatio-temporal restrictions.

In 1952, two institutions were created: the OFPRA and the Refugee Appeals Commission. Those who fell under the mandate of the UN High Commissioner for Refugees, those who met the definition of the Geneva Convention, and those designated refugees under earlier agreements were thereafter recognized as refugees. The applications were evaluated by protection officers, who numbered around twenty in 1954, with the vast majority of asylum seekers receiving approval. As a result, the Commission heard very few cases, but it did set the precedent for so-called "family unity," extending the status to spouses, minor children, and dependent parents of the refugee. The rejection of appeals was generally based on the temporal and spatial boundaries of the Convention or on the fact that the agents of persecution were not public authorities of the country of origin. Whereas the 1950s were characterized by the establishment of the asylum system and the management of large influxes of refugees from Europe, the next decade saw a decline in the number of applications. In 1971, France ratified the New York Protocol which lifted the restrictions placed on the Geneva definition, making it possible for a refugee to come from any part of the world. However, the consequences of this evolution in terms of the volume of applications was not immediate.

When labor migration was suspended in July 1974, applicants for refugee status continued to be admitted to the country. At the time, the number of asylum applications totaled 1,373 for 1973 and the rate of recognition exceeded 85 percent. Thirty years later, the number of requests totaled 54,429, while the rate of acceptance after initial examination was only 9.8 percent and barely reached 14.8 percent after appeal.[8] The increase in the number of requests in that period has often been interpreted as a sign of attempts at circumventing the closure of borders to labor migration.[9] Nevertheless, this interpretation ignores two important explanatory factors: the lifting of temporal and spatial restrictions of the Geneva Convention, and the fact that until the formal interruption of labor immigration in 1974 it was easier to obtain a work permit than refugee status. As a result, many potential applicants for refugee status under the Convention did not claim for asylum, as they already had legal residence in France.[10]

It is the conception of asylum applications as being baseless and exploitative that in fact allows successive governments to justify the growing number of rejections. This interpretation is reflected in political speeches and parliamentary debates at national and European levels. The implementation of the Eurodac computer system to compare the fingerprints of asylum seekers across the European Union is one example. Eurodac was allegedly created to facilitate the enactment of the provisions of the Dublin Convention,[11] but during debates in the European Parliament, the rapporteur of the commission overseeing the creation of the system admitted that it also served "to prevent the filing of concomitant applications and thus put an end to abuses."[12] The debate swung back and forth between members of Parliament stigmatizing the problem posed by the "so-called refugees" and the few voices denouncing the risk of reinforcing "Fortress Europe." However, the vote resulted in the creation of the file, which became operational in 2003.

The discourse associating asylum applicants with profiteers of the system also cropped up in the debates surrounding the recent reforms of immigration law. In 2003, the Minister of Foreign Affairs stated in Parliament that people who are "truly persecuted are far from representing the majority of asylum seekers," mentioning statistics from the OFPRA which granted refugee status to less than 13 percent of all applicants. Even more explicit, he explained that "many foreigners solicit our asylum system not to obtain our country's protection, but to remain here as long as possible, their motivation being economic in nature."[13] It is with this reform, which substantially altered the asylum procedure, that the notions of "manifestly unfounded claims" and "safe country of origin" appeared in the public sphere, allowing for many applications to be rejected before even being considered by the OFPRA. Thus, the image of the "bogus refugee"[14] served as a tool allowing the states to reject most asylum seekers while apparently remaining faithful to the principles of the Geneva Convention.

The Bureaucracy of Asylum

In order to screen for applications perceived as unfounded, OFPRA and the Appeals Commission saw both their budget and structure grow. This evolution was made apparent in efforts to adapt to the increase in the number of asylum applications, in the prioritization of administrative performance, and in the harmonization of procedures at the European level.

Since its inception in 1952, OFPRA's mission was to grant protection to refugees and stateless persons under the terms of the Geneva Convention. Following the passage of the law of December 10, 2003, it also afforded both "constitutional asylum" to "anyone persecuted for his action in favor of freedom" in accordance with the preamble of the 1946 Constitution and "subsidiary protection," a system of protection for persons not eligible for asylum who can demonstrate that they are subject to serious threats in their country.[15]

In its early years, the organization operated with 69 employees, more than half of whom were foreigners, including refugees, hired on renewable contracts. At the time, a large share of the work was devoted to documenting the identities of the 350,000 refugees registered in France between 1920 and 1950. After a period of stabilization, asylum applications began to increase in the 1970s with the arrival of Latin Americans fleeing dictatorships and victims of communism from Southeast Asia, followed by applicants from Africa. According to a brochure on the history of the institution, in the early 1980s, OFPRA noted "for the first time wide-spread fraud"[16] in the form of multiple applications for the same person under different identities and nationalities. From then on, the asylum seeker's sincerity began to be called into question. In 1983, the staff at OFPRA totaled 150 agents. By 2005, the number of employees had grown to 890. These new human resources—and the technical means which developed in parallel with the computerization of the service—allowed for cases to be studied more closely and for the time taken to process them to be greatly reduced, notably through the systematic implementation of interviews with the asylum seekers. Determining who the "real" refugees were became a more painstaking task because, as stated in a brochure put out by the institution, "many people want to settle in Europe for economic reasons and seek refugee status." The institution was thus considered a stakeholder in the fight against illegal immigration which was "a priority not only for economic reasons, but also for safety reasons."[17] The rate of admission dropped drastically, reaching its lowest level in 2006 at 7.8 percent or twelve times less than thirty years before. Suspicion seemed to be the primary attitude adopted toward asylum seekers.

Since its creation, the Appeals Commission has been responsible for examining appeals of OFPRA decisions submitted by applicants. During the first decades of its existence, it only had to deal with a very small number of cases. It was members of the Council of State (*Conseil d'État*) who handled them. But beginning in the 1980s, the growth in the number of applications and rejections by OFPRA converged in a very significant increase in the number of appeals. The Appeals Commission had to change its proceedings. Cases were from then on to be assessed twice: first by a rapporteur who examines the case, then by three asylum judges (*formation de jugement*) who issue a ruling after a public hearing in the presence of the applicant.

Currently the court, which has replaced the Appeals Commission, employs approximately 120 rapporteurs, half of whom are civil servants, the other half of whom work on a contractual basis. Most of the rapporteurs are young, between the ages of 25 and 40, and a large proportion of them are women. For some this is their first professional job. Each hearing is led by three asylum judges: 1) a chairperson who is a magistrate from the Council of State, the Court of Audit (*Cour des comptes*), or any administrative or judiciary court; 2) a French citizen appointed by the UN High Commissioner for Refugees (UNHCR), and 3) a qualified person appointed by the vice president of the Council of State at the suggestion of OFPRA's Board of Directors. Until 2009, the 160 judges were all temporary appointees who convened only a few times each month.

As with OFPRA, the changes in the court led to a significant decrease in the admission rate. While nearly half of the appeals made in the 1970s resulted in reversals of OFPRA decisions and the granting of refugee status, in the 1980s, less than one in ten applications were approved. This trend would continue until the early 2000s, with the Appeals Commission almost always upholding the decisions of the institution on which it depends administratively and financially: throughout the 2000s, agents of the Appeals Commission and members of NGOs adamantly denounced the consequences of this lack of independence. The creation of the National Court of Asylum in 2007 resolved this conflict by granting this body complete autonomy from OFPRA, since it is placed under the authority of the Council of State. The reform enacted by the law of November 20, 2007 served to reduce the number of temporary magistrates recruiting ten permanent judges who would be responsible for about 40 percent of the caseload. The goal was to address the inadequate coordination among the decision-making bodies and to work toward the standardization of case law, thereby reducing the disparities in decisions—according to unofficial data circulating in the institution, the admission rate was between one in every twenty cases and one in every two depending on the chair. After the establishment of the Court, the institution's permanent staff rose to 237, including more than a hundred rapporteurs, ten division heads, secretaries, interpreters, and experts at the Geopolitical and Legal Advisory Committees.[18]

In addition to these institutional transformations, two other changes—one in the law and one in the reception of refugees—would impact the court's work. Since December 1, 2008, access to legal aid has been permitted for all applicants—not just those who entered France legally—who cannot afford a lawyer to prepare their appeals and be present at their hearings. Moreover, the increase in the number of reception centers for asylum seekers since the mid-2000s has allowed for a greater number of applicants to obtain not only accommodation but also social and legal support. Both means contribute to raising the chances of obtaining asylum. Whereas the reversal rate was only 10 percent in 2000, the figure rose ten years later to 22.1 percent, a fact which the reforms undertaken over the past decade certainly explain in part. However, two other elements must also be taken into account. On the one hand, this percentage does not include rejections issued under the so-called "new rulings," which are not considered to present "serious claims" and are not sent to a rapporteur to be examined before being denied: one out of every five or six appeals is thus rejected without a hearing and therefore does not appear in the statistics. On the other hand, the fact that almost a third of all admissions by the court in 2010 are for applicants from Sri Lanka must be taken into account: this stems from the decision of the president of the court to grant, under certain conditions, subsidiary protection to nationals of that country during the most intense moments of its civil war which corresponds to a very specific circumstance. However, despite this increase in the reversal rate, the court continued to reject applications en masse, denying four out of every five appeals filed in that same year. Indeed, the truth of the claims made by the asylum seekers continues to be systematically questioned, with suspicion being the predominant attitude of the rapporteurs and judges.

Ethnography of Suspicion

To explore this attitude, I will analyze how the cases are examined and decided based on my observations of hearings as well as deliberations. I will show in particular how the tools used by the rapporteurs to produce a recommendation are guided by a particular conception of what is a true story and how the inner conviction[19] of the judges is based on their feelings toward the applicants, which convey a particular vision of what constitutes sincerity.

The Expertise of the Rapporteurs

Rapporteurs are tasked with preparing a report on the appeals submitted by the applicants; the report ends with a recommendation. They are also involved in the drafting of the decisions made by the judges. To ensure good performance, in 2010 the court set the number of cases each rapporteur must handle every year to 403. Not counting the time that it takes to draft the decisions and the time spent at hearings, this leaves them on average with little more than half a day to prepare each report. In 2012, after a series of collective protests, the number of cases to be handled each year was reduced to 387. The investigation consists in the examination of the documents which make up the applicant's file: the story, the summary of the interview with the asylum officer, the argument justifying the appeal, and any supplementary documents supporting the applicant's story, like membership cards to a political party, excerpts from articles, legal documents, medical certificates, etc. The rapporteurs complete their investigation with an Internet search on the situation in the applicant's country and sometimes with a request to the Geopolitical Advisory Center to evaluate how closely the stated facts and findings align, or to the Legal Advisory Center to consult on possible specific issues. The rapporteurs must then produce a text which summarizes the facts stated by the asylum seeker, as well as the arguments made by OFPRA when the application was first rejected. They conclude it with a recommendation which can take one of three forms: reversing the original decision, which means the granting of either conventional asylum or subsidiary protection; rejecting the appeal; and finally, reserving judgment usually based on the need for more information due to a lack of convincing evidence.

For rapporteurs, there are several elements which come together when they formulate their recommendations. From conversations with some of them and in the light of the reports read at the hearings, four elements of evaluation combine in distinct ways depending on the approach of the rapporteur. Aside from legal aspects in the strict sense—that is, the application of the Geneva Convention, of subsidiary protection, and of specific rules established by the Court and the Council of State—they evaluate: 1) the coherence of the story, which stems from its internal logic as well as from possible discrepancies between the initial narrative and the answers provided during the interview with OFPRA; 2) the external logic of the story, its plausibility in the light of the broader geopolitical context; 3) the accuracy of the answers, the perception of spontaneity having a significant positive value; 4) the analysis of the supplementary documents in the file. Several studies have reported on the ethnocentric bias of these evaluative frames of reference, which, without being formally systematized, are used by most decision makers in Europe and North America and which are also found in the procedural guide developed by the UN High Commissioner for Refugees in 1992.[20] A study influenced by behavioral psychology on the presuppositions of British judges who rule on asylum cases shows that behind the construction of a true story is the belief that truth is consistent and detailed and that traumatic events are never forgotten.[21] Similarly, the ability to tell the same story repeatedly seems essential for the truth of the story to be accepted.

Nevertheless, the four criteria appear to be the technical means by which an opinion on an application is formed. Thus, one rapporteur called a Congolese applicant's story "incomplete and underdeveloped" because it did not detail what made her join the Movement for the Liberation of the Congo to which she claimed to belong. Rereading the summary of the interview with the OFPRA officer, the rapporteur also believed that "the comments concerning the specific activities of the applicant in this movement are not spontaneous." He also noted that there were contradictions concerning the dates of attacks that the applicant claimed to have suffered between the initial account and the interview at OFPRA. In the end, the rapporteur determined that "the statements are not supported by any documentary evidence," and proposed that the appeal be rejected due to unsubstantiated facts. This was a fairly common conclusion because most recommendations were in favor of rejecting applications based on the vagueness of the story and the lack of supporting evidence. In fact, the technical expertise almost systematically led to casting doubt on the applications, which rarely presented the elements expected by the rapporteurs. This technical argument, which is part of the set of dispositions which the rapporteurs acquire when they arrive at the court and which constitutes their "professional ethos,"[22] also allows them to distance themselves from the stories in a form of "moral detachment"[23] shielding them from the constant exposure to the misfortunes and giving them the impression of being "objective."

Rapporteurs rely on these tools to form a recommendation. The texts they produce are generally similar in the expressions used and the meaning of the findings, but they do not organize these different elements in the same way. Although I initially assumed that to be either permanent or contractual would have an impact on how invested the rapporteurs were in reviewing the cases, my observation of their day-to-day routines refutes this interpretation. Rather than being based a priori on their type of employment contract, the differences among the rapporteurs seem instead to be linked to their backgrounds. Thus, it is possible to distinguish three ideal-typical forms based on the rapporteur's background and approach to the case.

The first category—"geopoliticians"—includes rapporteurs with a background generally in political science or international relations, who attach great importance to the geopolitical context of the applicant's country of origin and insist that the unique, personal experience described matches this context. One such rapporteur explained his way of dealing with the cases: "I read the story carefully and then OFPRA's report. I check online about the political developments in the region, looking for reports and any other information to help understand the situation." He explained further: "For some countries, since there are a lot of applicants, you know the situation, Sri Lanka, for example, but in this case the problem is that all the stories are the same. If I have a Chadian or Sudanese case, I will spend more time verifying certain information." The second group—"legalists"—consists of rapporteurs with a background in law, who are particularly attached to certain legal aspects like jurisprudence. "I immediately review the substance of the report, read the account, and see if it falls under the Convention or subsidiary protection. It's the legal implications that seem really important to me. I will then read the transcript of the oral statements and do some research to verify everything," explained one of them who had been working at the court for several years. The third set—"humanists"— is mainly composed of rapporteurs who have ties to NGOs defending the right to asylum or immigrants. They are former employees, volunteers, or members of these groups. They have a global approach to cases, often marked by certain empathy for the applicants. One rapporteur who had worked for a foreign aid organization thus commented: "At first I said, that's cool, I'll suggest that everyone's decision be overturned, but I quickly realized that it's not possible."

Regarding their political orientations, from the informal discussions I had with them, it seems that "geopoliticians" have more conservative opinions, that the "legalists" are more liberal in their thinking, and that the "humanists" sit on the left end of the political spectrum. But contrary to what one might think, the differences among the categories of rapporteurs do not lead to large differences in the outcomes of their work. In other words, despite their differences, rapporteurs for the most part propose at the conclusion of their reports that the appeal be rejected. In a sample of 395 cases, only eight rapporteurs suggested to reverse the decision and granting refugee status, corresponding to just 2 percent of all claims.[24] And not all of them were "humanists."

The Ethics of Doubt

While I did not notice significant differences with respect to the categories of rapporteurs in either the reports or the final recommendations that they issued, there was some variation regarding decisions to reserve judgment. In the hearings observed, such recommendations were almost exclusively issued by rapporteurs who fell under the category of "humanists." Although the decision to reserve judgment is not an official part of the hearing, it nevertheless represents what some rapporteurs considered to be a "fair" solution in the following three scenarios.

First, the technical aspects may not be sufficient to confirm the merits of the appeal, but the rapporteur still believes that it may be justified. For example, after reviewing the file submitted by a Tamil applicant from Sri Lanka, one rapporteur decided to reserve judgment because a note issued by the Geopolitical Advisory Center a few days earlier indicated that the situation in that country no longer justified a more systematic allocation of protection. But a medical certificate produced by the Medical Committee for Exiles, an NGO providing health care to asylum seekers and included in the file as supplementary documentation attested to significant scars on various parts of the applicant's body. According to the rapporteur, if the applicant was forced to return to his country, he could be subject to mistreatment by Sri Lankan authorities at the airport in Colombo. His concern, based on medical evidence and knowledge of the political situation in the region which he had gleaned from various other reports, led the rapporteur to reserve judgment.

Second, the rapporteur may lean toward recommending that the decision be overturned but knows that the judges might not agree in light of the applicant's nationality or the type of application in question. After reading a file, one rapporteur admitted to me that she was convinced by the story of a Kurdish applicant from Turkey who claimed to be involved in the struggle for the recognition of this minority's civil rights, but decided to reserve judgment because the judge who chaired the hearing and with whom she had worked several times before was "not very sympathetic to the Kurdish cause."

Finally, the rapporteur may wish to recommend that the decision be overturned but may not have strong enough evidence to justify doing so and instead prefers to maintain his or her reputation vis-à-vis the judges and other rapporteurs. This was often the case when one of them was supposedly too lenient. For instance, one rapporteur we met decided to reserve judgment on the appeal of a Coptic Egyptian who alleged persecution by the authorities due to his belonging to this religious minority. According to the rapporteur, the account was not detailed enough and there were no additional supporting documents, but the situation described did correspond to what was known about the treatment of Copts in the region. Knowing that the judge was familiar with the hardships experienced by this minority and "empathetic," the rapporteur decided to reserve judgment.

A young female rapporteur who had worked at the court for three years said during a recess in one hearing that such recommendations made some judges "think twice," encouraging them to be more attentive to the details of the account and the explanations of the applicants at the hearing, and that this was precisely the case with the magistrate who was presiding that day. For her, reserving judgment was the "fairer" thing to do, but she also noted that for some judges, doing so was pointless and a waste of everyone's time. In these instances, it was clear from the start that this type of recommendation would only complicate the interaction with the decision-making body, and she would often declare herself in favor of rejecting the appeal, sometimes adding a phrase such as "with hesitation." Rapporteurs thus make a sort of tactical calculation based on different variables: their inner conviction with regard to the case, the characteristics of the judges, and their reputation among colleagues. This calculation is the result of their assessment of when it is appropriate to comply with the rules of their work as well as of the amount of room that exists for maneuvering and negotiation. Thus, for rapporteurs, learning when to make such recommendations means learning about the ethos of their profession.

Reserving judgment provides some of them with the means to escape the daily routine of rejecting applications. In this respect, it can be considered a veiled form of commitment on the part of "humanists" who in doing so also leave room for doubt. This doubt is symmetrical with the suspicion prevalent in the court: it is not an attitude of distrust allowing asylum seekers to be labeled as either "real" or "fake," but is instead a hesitation opening up the possibility for admission. It can thus be regarded as an ethical position toward the applicants as well as the institution of asylum itself. Moreover, unlike suspicion, it will probably benefit the asylum seeker because, according to the data collected in the course of my study, these cases were more likely to result in a favorable decision for the applicant: out of the 121 cases analyzed, 16 percent resulted in reservations of judgment identified, two thirds of which resulted in the applicant being granted refugee status.

While reserving judgment may have been the more "fair" recommendation for the young "humanist" rapporteur mentioned earlier, all of the rapporteurs attached great importance to the notion of justice. They insisted that their evaluation of a case was carried out according to standardized criteria that gave them the impression of being "objective." In addition, they also expressed belief in a broader form of justice tied to the respect for asylum as an institution, implying that they protected it from abuse and defended those who genuinely deserved refugee status. Justice thus appeared to be a constituent value of the professional ethos of rapporteurs.

The Importance of the Encounter

Judges encounter the applicants at the court's public hearings. Thirteen cases are scheduled for each session, but most of the time, not all of them are heard. Requests for review made by the lawyers or, less often, postponements due to interpretation problems reduce their number. The president of the court has become increasingly strict about the need to reduce the review rate in an attempt to ensure better institutional performance. The judges constitute a very heterogeneous group due to significant differences in terms of professional training, personal backgrounds, and stances with respect to asylum. From the observation of hearings and informal conversations with them, it is possible to distinguish schematically three categories of judges chairing the hearing.

"Empathetic" magistrates consider themselves and are considered by others to be very accommodating to applicants. Their leniency stems from a sense of humanity toward the suffering of asylum seekers. Sometimes they are also critical of immigration policies which they deem too restrictive. "In any jurisdiction," one of them told me, "there are differences which depend on the personal discretion of the immigration judge. This happens in any court, but in ours, the applicant's life is at stake, that's why I take my time. Above all, I try to understand."

"Circumspect" magistrates are attentive to the details of the facts stated and look for any contradictions, either internal within an applicant's account or external in relation to known political events. One "circumspect" chair admitted to me in an interview: "The one big doubt I have is: Am I sometimes making a mistake? Did I understand what they told me? Am I making the right decision in ruling this way?" To alleviate this doubt, the judge said that he read each case carefully before its hearing and that he was attentive to the coherence between what he read and what occurred when he met face-to-face with the applicant.

"Hardline" magistrates are convinced that most asylum seekers are "cheating" the system. They believe that they must be severe if they are to avoid such abuse. They may seek to unnerve the applicant during the hearing or ask questions requiring a precise answer. For example, one of them, after commenting that the story of an asylum seeker was "not credible," asked if the man knew whether there were any women in the prison where he claimed to have been kept. The applicant said that he did not know but in the section where he was held, there were no women. The judge told him, like a teacher to a student who has just given the wrong answer: "Well, there are about three hundred women there." He later added: "You can see that it doesn't hold up," thereby affirming his belief in the unfounded nature of the application.

Although this tripartite typology concerns only the chairpersons, it became clear in the deliberation process that the positions of the other judges converged. For the eight to eleven cases discussed after the hearings, the process seldom lasted more than thirty minutes and very often resulted in unanimous decisions. Unlike rapporteurs whose individual approaches did not lead to significant discrepancies in their recommendations, judges were clearly differentiated in their decisions: "empathetic" judges were more willing to grant refugee status than "circumspect" ones, who were in turn more accommodating than "hardline" ones.

Whatever the attitude or approach of the judges, assessing an appeal always involves questioning the asylum seeker, in addition to scrutinizing the recommendations made by the rapporteur and statements from a lawyer. The hearing therefore has a performative dimension tied to the rituality of the legal world,[25] where speech acts are organized and codified and the body language and discourse of the applicant[26] play an important role. The hearing is when the judges first meet with the asylum seeker and learn about the case. Legal aspects, documentary evidence, arrangements of objects, the bodily *hexis* of the applicant and his or her language skills, the knowledge and prejudices concerning the country of origin will coalesce over the course of the hearing to form the judges' inner conviction about the application and the applicant.

Consider the case of a 37-year-old Kurdish applicant from Turkey, who arrived at his hearing wearing a brown suit and a patterned shirt without a tie and carrying a black suitcase. The judges were three men who had worked together before. The chairperson and the judge representing the administration were both in their sixties, while the one for the UNHCR was in his thirties. When the case was called, the applicant sat opposite the judges between his lawyer and an interpreter. To his left, sitting sideways, was the court clerk. To the right of the applicant, also sitting sideways, was the rapporteur who summarized the case. The applicant claimed to be a Kurdish activist and wanted by the authorities for his actions. The rapporteur indicated that it was the second time that the man had appeared in court and that he did seem admissible but concluded by proposing that the man's appeal be rejected, due to unsubstantiated fears in the event of his return.[27] The chairperson then gave the floor to the applicant's lawyer, a familiar face at the court. The lawyer insisted on the admissibility of the applicant, citing case law. He reminded the court that his client was on the verge of being expelled from French territory, but that a decision by the administrative court had stayed the deportation proceedings because the man was wanted in his country and feared inhumane and degrading treatment. Finally, he asked the judges if the applicant could show an excerpt from a visual document. The judges agreed and the applicant brought a laptop over to their desk to show them a brief clip of an interview on French television in which he explains his work to raise awareness about the situation of the Kurds through cultural activities. He also hands them a folder with articles about himself from Kurdish magazines and excerpts from Turkish newspapers illustrating the repression of the Kurds. The judges demonstrated their interest in the documents, and the chairperson asked the man how he had procured them. The applicant listened to the translation and then replied that most of the newspapers can be purchased in France. The chair next inquired about his knowledge of the French language. Without waiting for the translation, the applicant answered in French: "Yes, I speak a little, sir." The chair checked whether the other judges had any further questions. The young magistrate for the UNHCR asked the applicant about his perception of the recent openness of the Turkish government regarding the Kurdish question. The applicant thanked him for this question, which gave him the opportunity, he said, to explain to the court that the rhetoric served only to cast Turkey in a more positive light. There were no further questions.

Two-and-a-half hours later, the judges were deliberating. This case turned out to be the only one to receive a favorable decision. The magistrates highlighted the applicant's "earnestness" as well as the video images which he had shown them. The judge representing the administration underlined the man's "sincerity." The chairperson concurred, adding: "This guy's sincere, he's good." The rapporteur then indicated that in drafting the decision he would reiterate the cases cited by the lawyer, to which the judge for the UNHCR replied: "Yes, of course, especially since the case is being reopened." Two elements seemingly came together here to demonstrate the sincerity of the applicant and therefore the authenticity of what he had said: first, his language skills since he understood and spoke French and showed respect to the judges by thanking them for their questions and addressing them politely; and second, the documentary evidence in support of the application. And when it came time to draft the ruling overturning the deportation, a third legal element was put forward: the administrative court's argument that he would have reason to fear for his safety and well-being in the event of his return, a decision highlighted by the lawyer in his statement.

Obviously, most applicants are unable to muster as many documents or to exhibit the same skills as this asylum seeker. Over the course of my observations, the inequality of what applicants have at their disposal depended on their social class, educational level, and understanding of what was at stake during the hearing. Most of the time, the applicants had no documentation or very little to support their accounts. Their lawyers often did not raise new legal points and instead simply reiterated the previously stated facts. And the judges usually showed no sign of emotion or feelings. Comments such as "we know this story" and "this is the tenth time I've heard the same thing," which they would make either publicly during a hearing or during deliberations, reflect a form of jadedness with regard to applications that "are always the same." The repetitive nature of the cases and the routinization of the decision-making processes led to a kind of erosion of affects.[28] The resultant indifference of the agents was often consistent with the moral economy of suspicion: stories that are similar are assumed to be fake.[29]

The Semantics of Truth

The meaning of the idea of truth such as it is conceived and circulated in the court deserves special attention. We will see how the emotions of judges, though infrequent, are central both in the adjudication process and in the conception of what is a real asylum claim. On the one hand, moral sentiments like compassion or admiration reduce suspicion toward applicants. On the other hand, they reveal the value attached to asylum.

The Force of Emotions

Occasionally face-to-face encounters with the applicant may stir emotions. We attended a hearing where the judges were outraged by the flippancy of several applicants who were seen as callously perverting reality and "mocking" the judicial process, so much so that what they said was deemed "fake and caricatural," according to the remarks made by one judge afterward. In another hearing, the story of a Russian couple angered one of the judges, who questioned them incisively on the corruption for which the man, a senior ministerial official, was sentenced in his country and for which Russia had requested his extradition. The chairperson was astounded and commented in an aside, but loud enough for us to hear from the seats in the gallery: "This is the first time I have seen a judge for the UNHCR act like an immigration officer." During the deliberations, which resulted in the unanimous decision to dismiss the appeal, the judge explained his indignation, saying that the applicant was "very unlikable." He went on to say: "This guy was up to something. He lined his pockets. He wasn't taking a political stance. He was corrupt. How can he ask for asylum?" In other hearings, the magistrates were embarrassed by the "intimate" nature of the cases being heard, including ones in which the grounds for the appeal were based on female circumcision or sexual orientation. While I did not observe any hearings in which the judges showed some form of repugnance or disgust toward applicants for refugee status, as is sometimes the case in the criminal courts dealing with cases of rape, voluntary homicide or war crimes,[30] it can still be assumed that these negative emotions are sometimes produced in the court when applications made by persons known or strongly suspected of having committed crimes against humanity, most notably the so-called "Rwandan cases." Conversely, I observed hearings in which positive emotions came to light. In these instances, recommendations by rapporteurs that the appeal be rejected were overlooked and the original deportation decisions were overturned.

For every judge I spoke with, the encounter with the asylum seeker was a crucial moment. The manner in which the applicants talked, looked, and moved were all very important to the way in which the magistrates regarded them. When the latter mentioned cases that left a lasting impression on them, it was also these perceptions which they cited to account for their belief in the merits of the applications.

A young, rather slender Congolese woman dressed in jeans and a long black sweater, her long hair straightened and pulled back with a headband, sat trembling on a bench in the hearing room when the court clerk called her forward. According to the report, her brother belonged to the paramilitary group known as the Ninjas and an enemy group called the Cobras wanted to exact their revenge on her. She had been repeatedly threatened and assaulted before leaving the country. Her remarks were vague and not very developed. In support of her application, the applicant produced a medical certificate from a physician. In his conclusions, the rapporteur invited the asylum seeker to revisit the attacks she had endured and to explain what fears she had should she return, but he proposed that the appeal be rejected for unsubstantiated facts. The lawyer then made a statement in her defense, emphasizing the paramilitary activities of her brother and violence in the village where the applicant resided; he stressed "her physical and psychological fragility." The chairperson turned to the applicant and said softly: "We will not ask you many questions." He then asked the other magistrates if they had any questions. The judge for the UNHCR asked her about her fears in the event that she should return to her country. The applicant replied that she was afraid of being raped and killed. This was the only question. The hearing lasted just 22 minutes. During the deliberations, when the case was in turn discussed, the chairperson asked: "What do you think? I couldn't bear to let this girl [he stopped as if the rest of the sentence was obvious] ... but how to draft the decision?" The judges all agreed that the case should be overturned: "She looks confused, helpless," said one of them. All nodded, including the rapporteur.

In this case, the attitude of the asylum seeker seems fundamental when it came time to making a decision. She was perceived as a fragile young woman, devastated by events that, in the words of one of the judges, "no one will probably ever know," implying that something even more dramatic might have happened—perhaps sexual assault—which she did not share in her written account. Her body language became an indicator, if not of the sincerity of her remarks, then at least of the truth of her suffering. Her young age—19—and the lost look on her face seemed to arouse a feeling of compassion in the "empathetic" chairperson as well as in the other judges, who were both used to sitting with him. The emotion which they felt and their desire to help this young woman allowed them to overlook the weakness of the case as noted in the report. But "empathetic" magistrates are not the only ones to show affects which lead to the granting of asylum. The tears of a Sudanese applicant from Darfur, whose entire family had been murdered, stirred the emotions of the whole room and led the magistrates headed by a judge deemed "circumspect" to grant him refugee status. The words of a Guinean applicant on what motivated him to get involved in politics commanded the respect and admiration of another group of judges whose chair could also be classified as "circumspect," paving the way for a favorable decision. One of the judges even commented after the hearing: "This young man is exemplary," by which he perhaps meant that he perfectly embodied the image of a political refugee.

These cases demonstrate that the face-to-face interaction which takes place at the hearing represents a moment of truth during which asylum applicants are expected to play a role consistent with their condition—suffering victims, seasoned activists, in a word: refugees. They also show that the inner conviction of the judges is formed, at least in part, by the perceptions and feelings produced during the hearing. Affective reactions of course depend on the dispositions of the judges towards emotion, rooted in their personal backgrounds and their distinctive social characteristics. By virtue of their history, their political ideas, and their various identities—social, sexual, gender, etc.—some judges were more sympathetic than others to the case of a gay Kosovar, or the case of a Turkish political activist, to cite only two examples. But these reactions also depend in part on the ability of applicants to elicit emotion. Those who have the support of NGOs, the lawyers who frequently argue in the court, and the individuals familiar with the bureaucratic world of asylum all know that during the hearing, as one applicant told me, "you have to be convincing," which also implied moving. This suggests that applicants sometimes implement strategies to elicit emotional responses that predispose those who experience them to support the cause being defended.[31]

The manifestation of moral sentiments like compassion or admiration is, however, not the norm. Indifference is, as previously noted, the predominant attitude of judges and rapporteurs in their daily work. And perhaps it is because their routines do not encompass visible affects that, when the latter do arise, they weigh heavily on the decision, allowing for misgivings about the veracity of an account to be put aside and for a rapporteur's recommendation of rejection to be transformed into a decision by the judges to grant asylum. Compassion permitted, in the case of the young Congolese applicant, for the vague nature of her account, an issue raised by the rapporteur, to be overlooked and, in the case of the applicant from Darfur, for the lack of documentation to be disregarded. Nevertheless, the rallying of emotions has an ambivalent and paradoxical character.[32] It gives the magistrates a sense of gratification which comes from sometimes being able to assist the victims of the world's violence. But emotions also reinforce the distinction between those who are regarded as real refugees and those who are believed to exploit the system, as the affective reactions of the judges become an indicator of the sincerity of the applicants. And because these expressions remain infrequent, it can be said that the majority of the latter—those who do not stir up emotions—are not real refugees just as is the case for those who do not present additional documents or who do not have the requisite language skills.

The Value of Asylum

In the judicial world, the truth is what can be proven. In the field of asylum, evidence in support of a story is by definition very difficult, if not impossible to obtain. Judges and rapporteurs, most of whom have studied law, must face a contradiction between what they have learned during their training—truth tied to actual evidence—and the reality of asylum, which often defies this axiom. The granting of refugee status is based on the narrative which the applicant gives. Magistrates must therefore assess whether it is trustworthy. Trust can thus be thought of, in Georg Simmel's terms, as a hypothesis about the conduct of the other. "Do you believe that?" was the question often asked by the chairperson to the two other judges during the deliberations. This was also the question rapporteurs asked themselves when they finished reading a file. Truth in the court is thus what one believes, whom one trusts.

Rapporteurs and judges implement a set of techniques and practices to form an opinion and to arrive at what they consider to be the truth of the applications.[33] By virtue of the way in which they work, the tools used, and the recommendations which they formulate, the rapporteurs seem to have a particular vision of what a real asylum application is. It is, as we have seen, a chronological narrative which is relatively precise and abundant in detail, one that is consistent with the political context of the country or region in question, an account whose versions are similar and present no contradictions, a narrative which is supported by official, medical, or journalistic documents. Errors in dates of events recounted or confused remarks are seen not as signs of amnesia or trauma but as indicators of insincerity or deception. They lead the rapporteurs to question the "truth of the statements" or to deem the facts of the narrative "not credible." Judges themselves also rely on this conception of a real application in so far as they base their work on that of the rapporteur, who in the end is the only one who has read and analyzed the entire file. But magistrates attach great importance to the encounter with the asylum seeker. This is where their specificity (beyond their decision-making authority) lies: they compare the file to the individual, the analysis of documents they have read to the impressions that the person produces when they listen to and see him or her. If, for them, a true story is one that is told in an articulate and precise manner, it is also one that does not leave them indifferent when they face the applicant. Whether they talk about credibility, truthfulness, or sincerity, they base their work on this definition of a real application for asylum.

But their work also rests on the conception of asylum. For all those who work at the court and who spoke to me, whether "empathetic" or "hardline" judges, "humanist" or "geopolitician" rapporteurs, whether liberal or conservative, asylum is an institution to be protected. One judge who was considered "circumspect" emphasized during in an informal conversation: "We must guarantee this possibility to receive people who cannot live in peace in their country because they chose a different lifestyle or because they defend a different ideology. It is our duty to protect this right." In the same vein, one "empathetic" magistrate asserted: "People make stuff up, and we try to find out what lies closest to reality in order to help the people who really need it. We need to help those who have been persecuted, and we must also uphold the Geneva Convention." Both judges use almost the same words to account for their willingness to assist refugees as well as to protect the right of asylum. This was also evident in the comments made by a "geopolitician" rapporteur who declared in an interview: "We have a long tradition in France of protecting the persecuted, it is something very important, and our job is to contribute to that."

The emphasis on the protective dimension of the court's actions—and therefore of the state—is often propounded by judges and rapporteurs whenever they discuss the way in which they see their work. Also often apparent in their discourse is a reference to a tradition of refugee protection which they must continue. One chairperson admitted at the end of one hearing in which no case had been overturned: "You can't flout the principles of asylum, you can't grant the status to just anyone, you must respect these principles handed down to us from after the war." In every case, asylum is presented as endowed with a powerful moral burden and value which must be defended. The demanding criteria for granting protection therefore leads to the disqualification of most of those who apply because the more asylum becomes an idealized entity, the harder it is to establish connections among actual stories, real individuals, and this abstract institution.

Conclusion

Refugees only exist as a category by virtue of an international system that remedies the misdeeds of one state through the protection of another. Practices and discourses regarding the granting of refugee status by the French National Court today reflect the tension between the protective purpose of the asylum principle and the restrictive norms of the institutions that govern it. While it is true that asylum has always clashed with economic concerns and the desire to regulate the influx of immigrants into the country, since the late 1970s, public discourse has conveyed the idea that the institution itself was under threat, subverted by applicants who no longer seek protection due to political persecution, but are simply looking to qualify for a residence permit. Asylum is now deemed a vector of immigration, and the institutional practices are made more and more stringent in order to avoid abuse and to select "real" persecuted individuals. This discourse delegitimizing asylum applicants influences the judgment practices of the court, which is increasingly guided by suspicion.

Caught between the expectations of the authorities and the demands of the principles of asylum judges and rapporteurs are faced on a daily basis with the tensions which pervade the institution. Ethnography allows us to measure the effects of the ethical and political commitments of certain actors who sometimes displace the prevailing institutional logic, replacing the attitude of suspicion toward the applicants with the benefit of the doubt. Suspicion is likewise dispensed with when the face-to-face meeting with the applicant during the hearing elicits positive emotions from the judges. Although most of the time, indifference prevails, these rare cases nevertheless account for the centrality, as much by their presence as by their absence, of moral sentiments in the decision-making process. When empathy arises, it helps to affirm the truth of a claim. When it fails to be elicited, as is more often the case, it is tantamount to determining that an application is unfounded in nature.

The main objective of any court of justice is to dissociate the true from the false, and the National Court of Asylum is no exception. The political discourse which delegitimizes asylum seekers calls truth into question because it participates in the institutional logic of rigorous selection. In the end, for judges and rapporteurs, truth is also a value. They consider asylum to be not only a right or a political institution, but also a moral principle to which they must attest.

Notes

1 This is what sociologist John Barnes (1994) notes in his study on lying, a sizeable part of which is devoted to the legal world. Over the past few decades, North American legal anthropology has taken great interest in this question, relying on Michel Foucault's ideas of judicial practices as the origin of forms of truth. See, for example, the works of Susan Bibler Coutin at the intersection between legal anthropology and migration studies, in particular her article on the production of judicial truth in which she shows that the decision-making authority derives more from the procedures which validate them than from their potential tie with reality as conceived by the philosophical theory of correspondence, according to which truth is identical to the real (Coutin 1995).

2 Many authors have studied the suspicion surrounding this population in the United States and in several western European countries. Among these studies, see Daniel and Knudsen (1995), Bohmer and Shuman (2008), Valluy (2009), and d'Halluin (2012).

3 The ethnographic work my analysis is based on was conducted over the course of 13 months at the CNDA. I observed hearings, deliberations when allowed by the judges,

and case investigations. I also conducted formal interviews and had numerous informal conversations with the rapporteurs, the judges, the lawyers, and the interpreters. This ethnography was complemented by the study of sixty rulings made by the court over the last ten years concerning applications based on the sexual orientation of the asylum seeker (Kobelinsky 2012).

4 See the chapter "L'impossible définition" in Gérard Noiriel's work (1991) on asylum law in Europe between the end of the eighteenth century and the end of the twentieth century.

5 At the time, the movement of French nationals was also controlled. They were supposed to request an "internal passport" if they wanted to leave their department. Managing the movement of populations was fundamental because "it is the number of combatants in a given place which determines the outcome of challenges to power in a world in which the Bastilles and the Winter Palaces have yet to be taken in the literal sense of the word" (Noiriel 1991: 51–2).

6 Convention Relating to the Status of Refugees, chapter 1, article 1, A2: http://www.unhcr.org/3b66c2aa10.html.

7 These numbers come from Gil Loescher (1993: 46).

8 See OFPRA's 2003 annual report: www.ofpra.gouv.fr/index.html?xml_id=269&dtd_id=10.

9 See Karen Akoka's article (2011) on what she calls the "dreamed archetype of the refugee": www.gisti.org/spip.php?article2441.

10 See Alexis Spire's article (2004) on refugees as laborers.

11 The Dublin Convention, subsequently replaced by the Dublin Regulation, stipulates that the first country an asylum seeker enters is tasked with evaluating the application. Eurodac was operational beginning January 15, 2003.

12 Address by Austrian Hubert Pirker, a member of the European People's Party, during a debate on November 18, 1999 in Strasbourg: www.europarl.europa.eu/sides/getDoc.do?pubRef=-//EP//TEXT+CRE+19991118+ITEM-005+DOC+XML+V0//FR.

13 Taken from the *Comptes rendus des séances de l'Assemblée nationale*, June 6, 2003: 4590: http://www.assemblee-nationale.fr/12/cri/2002-2003/20030230.asp.

14 According to Cécile Rousseau and Patricia Foxen (2006).

15 Two clarifications about these different forms of protection: 1) the status of stateless person is rarely asked for and given; 2) territorial asylum which no longer exists as such was a protection created by a 1998 law granted not by OFPRA but by the Ministry of the Interior and was subject to annual reevaluation. It was a special form of asylum granted based on the advice of the Ministry of Foreign Affairs in cases where life or liberty was threatened, or where the applicant would be subject to inhumane or degrading treatment upon return to his or her country of origin.

16 OFPRA historical brochure: 24: www.ofpra.gouv.fr/documents/Brochure_historique_Ofpra_BD.pdf.

17 Ibid.: 34.

18 Placing the National Court of Asylum under the Council of State opened the door for staff (especially rapporteurs) to be transferred or promoted to other institutions.

19 "*Intime conviction*" (inner belief or conviction) is the term employed by the judges. Although I will not discuss it here, I will simply note that the notion appears in the French Code of Criminal Procedure, based on the idea of "moral proof" that arose in the eighteenth century. While it does not exactly correspond with the standards of proof used in common law, the two are similar. The term does not appear in any asylum legislation concerning asylum, but judges and rapporteurs use it on a frequent basis.

20 This has been analyzed by several authors. Among others, see works by Carol Bohmer and Amy Shuman (2008), Estelle d'Halluin (2012), and Anthony Good (2007).

21 A study by Herlihy et al. (2010), the results of which were published in the journal *International Journal of Refugee Law*.

22 We use the concept as it was defined by Bernard Zarca (2009) in his work on mathematicians.

23 Concept borrowed from Everett Hughes (1971).

24 Half of these proposed cancellations concerned Sri Lankans who benefited from this protection as a result of an internal memo at the CNDA. For a statistical analysis of the data, see the article by Fassin and Kobelinsky (2012).

25 As analyzed by Antoine Garapon (1997).

26 See works written from a linguistic anthropological perspective by Conley and O'Barr (1998).

27 Once the case is dismissed by the CNDA, the applicant can request that it be reopened if he or she possesses new evidence. If the prefecture allows for the case to be reexamined, it is sent to the Office, and if it is rejected again, the applicant can appeal to the CNDA.

28 See Didier Fassin's work (2001) on the distribution of emergency social funds.

29 According to Michael Herzfeld (1992), modern bureaucracy is based on the social production of indifference on account of the imperative of procedural rationality.

30 For an analysis of disgust in the judicial process, see the article by Kathryn Abrams (2002).

31 I am borrowing ideas developed by Christophe Traïni (2010: 350) in his work on commitment to animal causes.

32 In the first works on the anthropology of emotions from the 1980s, scholars already noted the ambivalent and ambiguous nature that feelings can have. See the article by Catherine Lutz (1986).

33 See Didier Fassin's analysis (2013b) on the "precarious" truth of asylum.

Part II
Repressing

CHAPTER FOUR

Maintaining Order
The Moral Justifications for Police Practices

Didier Fassin

"Obviously they'll just blame it on the police again." Bored and bitter, the police officers would often make such comments, voicing their opinions on the events reported in the news that implicated law enforcement agents in outbursts of violence or disorder as they cruised around low-income neighborhoods in their vehicles. Such predictions would almost inevitably prove correct because they were usually made in connection to acts for which the responsibility did indeed lie with the police, resulting in internal investigations and even lawsuits, developments which served to reinforce their sense of being the scapegoats of society, even though it is rare for a police officer to be convicted for abusive practices. These jaded remarks, readily fed by personal anecdotes about situations in which they found themselves accused by citizens or by their superiors, often concluded with a formula that summed up their disillusionment: "If I had known it was going to be like this, I wouldn't have chosen to become a cop." Such words not only highlight the gap between their expectations when they entered the profession and the realities of the job they have experienced in the field, but also suggest a moral discord between the evaluation of their actions by society or their superiors and the justifications which they provide for themselves: they are always unjustly accused.

The choice of the word "moral" may be unexpected. It is certainly not the adjective most commonly associated with the idea of law enforcement, either in its general sense or within the social sciences. Not because the police are presumed to be immoral or amoral, but because other associations lend themselves more readily to the task—power, order, security, repression, control, investigation, file, in other words, registers that seem to demand the political, the administrative, the technical, or even the plain physical. Yet there has been long-standing interest in the moral dimension of the profession if one considers, for example, that the first major sociological study of the police carried out in the United States, namely William Westley's dissertation which he defended in 1950, bore the subtitle "A Sociological Study of Law, Custom, and Morality." Following in the footsteps of Georg Simmel, the author maintained that the regulation of human behavior in general and that of the police in particular is carried out by law at the societal level, by habit at the group level, and by morality at the individual level.[1] In the ensuing decades, this interest proved a consistent feature of research conducted in North America, beginning notably with the pioneering work of political scientist Jerome Skolnick on the professional culture of the police, *Justice Without Trial*, which was published in 1966 at the height of Civil Rights Movement.[2] More recently, this time within the context of the debates sparked by the police's brutal treatment of Rodney King, the geographer Steve Herbert rightly stated that "police officers, for example, drink regularly from the fount of morality and replenish their internal esprit de corps by invoking a larger virtue that their actions serve," concluding that "any efforts to reform the police must be attentive to their morally created world-view and to the ways it shapes their everyday practice."[3] Despite these various initiatives, criminologists have little explored the moral dimension of law enforcement, preferring to explain police activity through the legal framework of their intervention and the characteristics of their public.[4] As a result, they limit their understanding of both the reasons for police deviance (how law enforcement agents account for them) and the variations observed among the officers (why their behaviors differ in the field). This is the path that I wish to take as I analyze the moral framework of police intervention in order to deepen the comprehension of their deviations.

In this perspective, I will defend and illustrate the idea that it is impossible to understand what law enforcement agents do without taking into consideration the moral framework of their actions or relating that moral framework to its political dimension. Institutions are governed by rules and procedures as well as values and emotions. In addition to the legal and organizational rationalities usually invoked to account for their activity, there also exist judgments and feelings which underlie them. The police are no exception. The work of law enforcement agents is inscribed within a moral economy, rests on moral arguments, constructs moral communities, engages moral subjectivities, and provokes moral conflicts—all elements that are indispensable when considering how to make sense not only of what is standard practice in their interactions with their public, but also the forms of deviance like brutality or cruelty, racism or discrimination.

To address this moral universe, I conducted a study in a large police station in the Paris region, focusing in particular on the patrol work done in the district. There were two reasons for this: patrol work is the main activity of the majority of police officers, and it is the most common way that they interact with the public. Those observed belong either to a public safety unit consisting of uniformed officers patrolling in marked police vehicles or to a unit of the anti-crime squad whose plainclothes officers ride in unmarked cars. With several large housing projects in the area, the conurbation which these squads patrol is characterized by a certain degree of social diversity, but the unemployment rate, the proportion of immigrant households, and the level of recorded crime are well above the regional average. For the officers, it was a "tough" district, one that they did not like being posted to. Unlike the large statistical surveys carried out in France, which have relied on questionnaires to understand the work of law enforcement agents,[5] the research presented here is an ethnography, meaning that it is essentially based on observations of the daily routines of the police officers.[6] While the quantitative approach may rely on the representativeness of the sample, the qualitative approach allows for a deeper understanding of the situations: the former permits generalizations about the entire population to be extrapolated from the results; the latter grasps the generality of the phenomena by exploring their mechanisms and processes. The norm is better captured by statistics, the deviation from that norm by ethnography.

But before reconstructing this moral universe of law enforcement agents, it is important to situate it within a historical or rather genealogical perspective, which will allow for a better understanding of the contemporary political issues. It will then be possible to grasp, first, the moral economy of repression, that is, the values and affects that underlie the work of law enforcement agents, and, second, the moral subjectivity of the police officers based on the observed differences in those values and feelings and the manner in which the officers cope with them. In this way, it will be possible to account for both the general rationale at work within the institution and the unique experiences of agents who comprise that institution. To do this, I will privilege mundane scenes, ones that are a far cry from the more or less violent headlines that feed representations of the police within the news media and film industry, thus emphasizing what can be qualified as the ordinary.

A National Body and Exceptional Practices

While we may not have great difficulty understanding the word "police" today, the meaning we are familiar with, namely that of the institution responsible for maintaining public order and ensuring public safety, is the result of a gradual narrowing of its semantic field.[7] In the first few centuries of the modern era, policing designated a very wide range of notions, including the form of government (monarchy, democracy, etc.) and multiple prerogatives of power (taxation, market, etc.). While there are certainly differences between the French meaning of "police" as denoted by Nicolas Delamare in the early eighteenth century and the German meaning of "Polizei" which Johann Heinrich Gottlob von Justi proffered a few decades later,[8] in both cases, the notion of police includes a variety of heterogeneous concerns faced by cities and states. What unites these definitions is the principle of monitoring for the supposed welfare of the population, if not its prosperity. Thus, according to the definition in the *Encyclopédie*, "the concerns of the police may relate to eleven main objects: religion, discipline of mores, health, food, security and public order, roads, the sciences and liberal arts, commerce, manufacturing and the mechanical arts, domestic servants, workers, and the poor."[9] And it is only in the course of the last two centuries that the meaning of the word has gradually been restricted to its contemporary use, giving rise to the birth of a particular rationality, institution, and profession. However, this consolidation around issues of public order and security, which is especially evident in France since it is accompanied by the formation of a national state police, and the parallel development of special forces aiming to divide an entity that is potentially threatening to the power or considered as such until recently and implement specific forms of repression against people and territories represented as dangerous, are not mutually exclusive. The analysis of these contradictory trends and their place within the evolution of French society allows us to grasp some of the present issues.

The Implications of a National Police

The Parlement's registration of the royal edict promulgated by Louis XIV establishing the Lieutenancy of Police in Paris in 1667 is generally regarded as the birth of modern policing.[10] Indeed, it marks a move towards greater autonomy for the function of order and security in relation to the judicial and the military. It also emphasizes the king's will to establish a centralized state apparatus for the control of society. Although this institution was abolished in 1789 by the French Revolution, during which a Ministry of National Police responsible for exercising control over the municipal police was established, it rose from its ashes eleven years later in the form of the Prefecture of Police in Paris, which Napoleon created to cope with a ministry deemed too powerful and which was destined to last for more than two centuries as a counterweight. Throughout the nineteenth century, the pendulum swung from phases of decentralization, granting major cities police powers, and recentralization, restoring state control over the municipal police with the exception of the capital. Three systems thus persisted in a permanent imbalance of power: the Ministry of the Interior, reinforced by the creation of the Directorate of General Security in 1903 in an attempt to assume the role of a national institution; the municipal police whose autonomy the state would suppress in 1940 with the establishment of the Vichy regime; and finally the Prefecture of Police in Paris, whose powers were even more sweeping since the capital had no mayor until the election of Jacques Chirac in 1977. This configuration is further complicated by the existence of a gendarmerie, which as heir to the Ancien Régime's constabulary and considered an elite corps is part of the military. It was not until 1966 that the National Police was finally created, harmonizing the statutes of the various bodies, but with no real authority over the Prefecture of Police and always complementary in terms of jurisdiction with what would become the National Gendarmerie. The municipal police were from that point on marginalized, often relegated to secondary roles and rarely coordinating with the National Police.

Notwithstanding the vicissitudes of the organization of the police institution and the laborious process of building a single edifice, which as it so happens remains unfinished, one body has emerged, covering all urban areas: the National Police—the gendarmerie retaining, for the sake of simplicity, control of the rural areas. The state organization, comparable to what exists in Spain or Italy, differs from that of countries such as Britain or the United States, where law enforcement is essentially the domain of local authorities. These structural differences have important implications for the work of the police, most notably in terms of recruitment and accountability.

The recruitment of French police officers—like that of other civil servants such as school teachers—takes place at the national level. This means that there is very little chance for young police officers to be assigned to districts they are familiar with. In fact, the very opposite is true: the new recruits start working in areas that are completely foreign to them. Statistics show that more than four-fifths of the police come from rural areas or small to medium-sized provincial towns, while just over a tenth of them come from the Paris suburbs where most will end up working.[11] As for those assigned to the Île-de-France region, most officers originate from the Nord-Pas-de-Calais region, an area affected by de-industrialization and high unemployment, where the prospect of a stable government job is valued. At the end of their training, recruits choose their assignment based on their experience and their class rank, which almost inevitably results in their being posted to districts little valued by their more experienced colleagues, namely the banlieues. They thus have no empirical knowledge of these areas, which have been presented to them as dangerous, or of the residents, which they tend to see as enemies, sometimes adding to this picture a racial connotation. Although they are themselves often from the same blue-collar background as the public they will deal with, the young officers differ greatly from the latter by their origin, by their skin color, and perhaps more decisively by the environment in which they have been socialized: the few who have lived in the projects often prove less confused in their understanding of the urban context and less inclined to make derogatory generalizations about the residents.

At the same time, the establishment of state control over the police also has the effect of instilling within law enforcement agents a sense of responsibility to the state rather than one of serving the public. When the police fall under the authority of a local elected official, they are essentially held accountable to that official and thus take into account the public, which can always complain to the municipality in the event of an abuse of police power. Conversely, when they fall under the sole authority of the central government, they feel no particular obligation to the public.[12] This statist approach reflects both a concern on the part of technocrats to distance enforcement activities from the leadership as well as a desire that the political control of the repressive apparatus remain beyond the reach of citizens. This has, however, been justified in more neutral terms. Whereas police under the authority of a local government might find themselves swept up in games of political patronage, those under the aegis of the state escape such politicization. But developments over the past three decades have nevertheless demonstrated the opposite. The police, far from being an impartial institution (which of course it never has been), have increasingly become a means to gain or to maintain power as potential presidential candidates now consider the Ministry of the Interior as a springboard for their careers. The manipulation of both crime and police performance statistics by the government as well as by opposition parties highlights this trend. Such a development, which makes law enforcement agents a communication tool for those in power and their opponents, can only be understood in light of the evolution of the public debate on issues of law and order. Following the victory of the left in 1981 and the rise of the Front National, a defeated and weakened traditional right believed that the only way to return to power was to adopt the themes that had made the far right so successful, namely immigration and insecurity. This strategy has paid off for conservatives who have won three successive presidential elections with campaigns based mainly on these two themes. The centrality of the law-and-order issue, despite a context of declines in the crime rate, particularly that of serious crime, makes the situation in France stand out in comparison to most other major western democracies where it is essentially a local issue, rarely discussed on a national level.

The Avatars of Exception

In most countries, the pragmatism which generally prevails in the management of law enforcement has at times led to the creation of special measures for specific problems and above all for marginal populations. Such policies correspond to moments of targeted repression for which the authorities believe that the existing structures fail to meet the needs of law and order, but the policies also derive from a performative approach which aims to create an exception while at the same time justifying it: the implementation of this type of measure is evident within the public space, demonstrating the concerns of the authorities while conceivably encouraging the outbursts that are meant to be contained. Although there is not necessarily any continuity between these various measures in a given national space, there are similarities that can be likened to historical homotheties: relations between the authorities, the police, and the groups perceived as dangerous derive from the same type of rationale and give rise to practices that are similar in nature.

The colonial period thus lends itself to the exploration of one of the most remarkable cases of policing exception, namely the treatment of people of North African origin living in France. Founded in 1925 as a part of the Service for the Surveillance and Protection of North African Natives, which brought together a group of institutions designed more to "monitor" than to "protect" these "colonial subjects," the North African Brigade's mission was to control and suppress the nationalist tendencies of some, as well as the undesirable presence of others. After the Liberation in 1945, accusations of racism and violence lodged against the group and evidence of its complicity with the occupying Germans led to its dissolution when the brutal repression of protests in the Algerian town of Sétif forced the colonial power to make concessions, including the recognition of the status of "French Muslims of Algeria." However, the demise of this structure did not imply the disappearance of the corresponding practices for, as Emmanuel Blanchard shows, the Prefecture of Police picked up where the North African Brigade left off, adopting much of the language of suspicion and disqualification, the culturalist and xenophobic prejudices, and above all the arbitrary raids, imprisonment, and registration requirements.[13] As concerns raised by the increasing separatist claims of the Movement for the Triumph of Democratic Liberties grew, this masked exception no longer sufficed and the Assault and Violence Brigade was created in 1953 following clashes on July 14 during which police fired on protesters, killing seven people. The new unit became a feared instrument of repression, performing numerous stops each night. Most of these stops were nothing more than simple identity checks so long as the residency and employment papers of those questioned were in order, but their ultimate function—surveillance and intimidation—proved very effective. The institution was transformed a few years later with the twin creation in 1958 of the Technical Assistance Service for French Muslims from Algeria, which integrated different administrative, social, and policing activities supposed to thwart the work of Algerian nationalists, and in 1959 of the auxiliary police force, often referred to as the "Harkis of Paris" and composed of soldiers recruited in Algeria to fight against the National Liberation Front. All these structures would disappear after the Evian agreements in 1962, but they nevertheless reveal the decades-long continuity of exceptional practices in special units tasked with repressing those deemed undesirable as well as in the ordinary police.

Without wanting to equate the residents of the banlieues with colonial subjects or to confuse the various squads active during the colonial period with the special units deployed today, the parallels are nevertheless interesting. They reveal the permanence of questions and doubts about the need for special institutions for specific territories and populations. Over the past thirty years, low-income individuals chiefly of immigrant backgrounds have become concentrated in housing projects, particularly in what are often called in administrative speak "sensitive urban zones," even though they form only a part of these neighborhoods which have been deemed a priority for government assistance. Public housing, which in the 1960s had helped to reduce the precarity represented by urban slums and emergency settlements, did maintain some social and ethnic diversity until the 1970s with the presence of low-income households of European origin often in the process of climbing the job ladder and awaiting the means to achieve homeownership. Since the economic restructuring and rising unemployment of the 1980s mainly affected poor families of immigrant origin, public housing has become less and less diverse, retaining more and more of the latter group. It was during this period that a new social question was raised, one marked by social segregation and urban violence.[14] The state's response to this twofold problem consisted, on the one hand, in the implementation of the "*politique de la ville*," a modest urban policy in favor of poor neighborhoods, and, on the other, in the deployment of a targeted policy of repression combining legislative action and police practices.

The urban policy attempted to bridge the growing gap between these relegated territories and the rest of the country:[15] the administrative mapping of 751 sensitive urban zones pinpointed the areas where aid was needed, and made it possible to present the socio-demographic evolution of the deficits afflicting these neighborhoods in statistical terms. City contracts aimed to better coordinate the various public services. Operations of urban development involved the demolition or rehabilitation of dilapidated housing; supportive measures, including tax exemptions and the promotion of business and other services, were introduced; and finally, legislation imposed a proportion of at least 20 percent of public housing in cities with more than 3,500 inhabitants. However, this list should not obscure the fact that, first, urban policy has always been considered more obedient to a performative logic of symbolically affirming the government's interest for these disadvantaged populations than it has been willing to rethink the inequalities among urban areas and, second, that its evolution has led to gradual disarray as the repressive component prevails over the social response to the growing inequalities. Indeed, the reinforcement of repressive policies comes at the same time as issues of law and order begin to take center stage in the public sphere:[16] the scope of delinquency is widened to include many new offenses such as loitering in the lobbies of apartment buildings; the criminal responsibility of minors is gradually expanded, with the lowering of the age one can be held in custody to ten years of age, while the practice of incarceration becomes widespread starting at the age of 13; penalties become stiffer, and above all, in contradiction with the principle of individualization, mandatory minimum sentences are enacted into law for repeat offenders; the executive exerts greater pressure on the judiciary in the fight against the alleged leniency of judges, even if the court statistics do not support the assertion; the number of law enforcement agents increases (at least until recently), with the deployment of new intervention in the banlieues; the prerogatives of the police are expanded, most notably in terms of identity checks, which according to administrative procedure no longer require the notion of suspicion of having committed or intending to commit an offense; police officers are encouraged to make greater use of their power to arrest for insulting and resisting an officer of the law. Although in theory this repressive trend could affect all categories of the population, the intention of its designers and the reality of the practices concern above all disadvantaged neighborhoods and their inhabitants as well as certain other groups like immigrants and Roma.

A significant element of this was the creation of special units assigned to these areas, the most feared being the anti-crime squad. Founded in 1994 under the leadership of the Minister of the Interior Charles Pasqua, their main priority was to respond to urban disorder and juvenile delinquency, the two phenomena often being conflated. Given the relative scarcity of the former, it was the prevalence of the latter which allowed the government to justify maintaining standing forces specifically dedicated to so-called "tough neighborhoods." Their presence has since gradually expanded into small towns, not because of increased urban disorder or juvenile delinquency, but because of a political will to manifest the government's effectiveness at a time when public order and security has been deemed a political priority. The anti-crime squads are composed of police almost always in plain clothes and driving in unmarked vehicles. Their concentration in banlieues considered problematic, their avowed specialization in catching criminals in the act, their selection among the supposedly toughest elements, and the tolerance which they enjoy from their superiors make these police officers feared by the populace, but also the objects of ambivalent assessments from their colleagues and superiors. Assuming the role of "bad cop," they are, in the words of a commissioner, a "necessary evil."[17] As explained by a senior official from the Ministry of the Interior, on the one hand they are needed because "they bring in business," but on the other hand it is a well-known fact that that "they often cause more problems than they solve." It is true that their practices often fall outside of the law. And the manner in which they provoke the inhabitants of housing projects often creates tensions which sometimes lead to protests and even riots. That these special units have been deployed to intervene in areas today inhabited mainly by "French Muslims," sometimes the descendants of those from North Africa, is certainly not enough to justify the comparison with the brigades of the colonial era (although some advisors of the Ministry of the Interior refer explicitly to the war in Algeria to interpret the contemporary urban unrest and justify their strategies to control it).[18] Yet because these two populations are viewed as alien and because they are considered threatening, the institution implements exceptional procedures and practices in terms of both its functioning as well as the legality of its intervention in order to handle them. It is these exceptional practices and procedures which call for structural comparisons.

The Moral Economy of Repression

According to Weber's famous definition, the state holds a monopoly on the use of legitimate violence. It is this monopoly that the state delegates to law enforcement as well as other professional bodies, for instance, prison guards, and as Egon Bittner has shown, what ultimately unites the police despite the diversity of their missions and assignments is their ability to use force.[19] As a result, there is an important tension in the practice of policing between the deployment of force in the name of a higher principle of order on the one hand, and the respect for the rule of law and the rights of citizens on the other. In fact, this tension is manifested and resolved simultaneously in what for over a half-century of social science research on law enforcement has been called "police discretion,"[20] namely the possibility to decide spontaneously how to behave when conducting identity checks or arrests as well as the attitudes and demeanor to adopt during these operations: police officers may or may not bring a drug user in, and they may or may not subject an individual being arrested to brutality. In the first case, the law requires them to do so, and in the second case, it forbids them. But in reality, the officers choose to follow or to disregard the law based on a broader and more personal assessment of the situation and its protagonists.

Yet this discretionary power, which must be understood to work in both directions—leniency or severity—cannot be attributed to a sort of irrational arbitrariness. On the contrary, it stems from rationales that are possible to identify and reconstruct both empirically and theoretically. First, this power is socially differentiated, and the police thus do not behave in the same way with respect to all categories of power. Second, this power is morally based, and the police explicitly or implicitly justify whatever their behavior. This combination of the social and the moral, of inequality and justification is one of the most remarkable dimensions of police work.

The Right Order

Consider the following scene which occurred during a routine patrol. An anti-crime squad was cruising around downtown as night fell. The early hours of the evening were oddly free of any episodes. The officers drove slowly so that they could scrutinize their surroundings for any sort of suspicious situation or behavior. Coming across a van, the leader in the car ordered his colleague at the wheel to turn around, which was done with a squeal of tires. On went the lights and sirens. The vehicle pulled over. The police surrounded it. One of the officers asked the occupants, two Turkish men, for their papers. The driver handed over his residence permit, but after a few failed attempts at an explanation, the passenger eventually admitted that he did not have one. His friend begged the officials to let him go, saying that he had "just come to find some work," that he "didn't do anything," that he "didn't steal." Unmoved, the squad leader soberly replied: "I'm not here to discuss the law, I'm just here to enforce it." The undocumented immigrant was taken to the station in handcuffs to be held in custody pending his transfer to an immigration detention center and possible deportation. During the ride back, the police made fun of him, his accent, and his origin, pretending not to know where Turkey was on a map and asking if it was located in Europe, an obvious allusion to the political controversy at the time of the country's possible entry into the European Union. When the group returned to the police station, the sergeant welcomed their arrival with a few sarcastic remarks about their petty arrest, "So the anti-crime squad's now hauling in illegals?" To which the squad leader proudly retorted, "I'm defending my country," adding, to make his point: "I always complain that there are too many illegals. So whenever I can arrest one, I do." In reality, his "complaints" were not just limited to undocumented persons, and while out on patrol, he never ceased to express his disdain for all immigrants and minorities in terms that left no doubt about the extent of his xenophobia.

This scene, both common with regard to the daily activities of the police and trivial compared to other more tense, if not more violent activities—although it is certainly not insignificant for the individual concerned—is interesting in several ways. First, it reveals a contradiction, of which the police officers were probably unaware, since in affirming the rule of law, they were at the same time violating it: the identity check, even in the most generous interpretation provided by the Law of August 10, 1993 is not legal when there is no argument to support a "risk to public order," as the Constitutional Council (*Conseil Constitutionnel*) and several other courts have stated. In this instance, the squad leader ordered his colleague to turn around and pull them over only after he had considered the physical appearance of the vehicle's occupants, which ordinarily qualifies as "profiling." Second, the sneering remarks of the sergeant highlight the gap between the mission of these special units which had been created to restore public order in the banlieues by catching crimes in the act and their actual practice as they were reduced to stopping vehicles like traffic cops. As far as delinquency is concerned, the squad had to be content with "illegals" who are far from being the primary concern of citizens when it comes to security. "It's too easy. All you have to do is go down to the immigrant hostels and make arrests," commented one of the members of the anti-crime squad later, annoyed. Beyond these observations, the scene allows one to consider how law enforcement policy manages to avoid the alternative of a top-down or bottom-up approach. To understand the significance of this arrest, it is indeed necessary to analyze how in the same act the government and the autonomy of the officers come together to reveal the moral economy of repression.

On the one hand, the arrest of the undocumented man fits into the political framework manifested by the public stigmatization of this category of immigrants, the setting of quotas for deportation, the reduction of the powers of judges to review the legality of the conditions of detention, and the lengthening of authorized stays in administrative detention centers. But this practice also belongs to the broader context of implementing a new form of managing public action which in the field of security became known as the "politics of numbers" and translates into a quantification of the results to be achieved. The two indicators for measuring police action insofar as patrol work is concerned are the number of arrests and the clearance rate. Since the chances of catching crime in the act are slim, the goals set are almost impossible to reach. The police can only attain them by using what they call "adjustment variables," of which there are two types: immigration violations and drug offenses. Both are, in their own words, relatively easy to "do": the first by targeting individuals whose physical appearance suggests that they might be immigrants either systematically in transit hubs like train stations, or by frisking individuals and searching vehicles usually during identity checks of youths in the public areas of housing projects. In addition, the two not only allow for the artificial inflation of arrest numbers, but also offer the prospect of improving the clearance rate, as each arrest of an individual equals another case solved. Under these conditions, the anti-crime squad's departure from its mission to hunt for "illegals and potheads" to use the expression of the police, is only a departure insofar as it diverges from the official definition of this mission since, on the contrary, the latter is unofficially redefined through the politics of numbers.

On the other hand, however, law enforcement agents still have room to maneuver. While some more skilled and resourceful agents may prove more efficient in their arrests of "real criminals," most keep the option to make up for their shortfalls by substituting either of the two offenses. As one police officer explained, complaining of the "hypocrisy" of his superiors when they denied the existence of quotas, these offenses were to be used "when needed," that is to say always, but he and his colleagues were inclined to use one or the other in accordance with their individual ideological affinities. In the recounted scene, the squad leader explicitly justified his arrest as done in defense of his country, which he felt was threatened by the presence not only of undocumented immigrants but of immigrants in general, whom he considered undesirable. Other law enforcement agents, less prone to xenophobia, stated that they believed their role not to be one of "stopping poor people who haven't done anything and aren't bothering anyone" and preferred to take on cannabis users because "at least they're screwing up." Thus, two visions of order emerge: one based on identity and another based on security, underpinned by two different political perspectives since governmental injunctions serve to legitimize an ideological inclination and practice fully claimed in the first case, while in the second, they become a constraint to which one adapts in an effort to make it more consistent with a certain sense of fairness. In either case, however, the right order of the police officers is an uneven order. Immigration violations concern only foreigners who are identified by their appearance, which implies a racialized order. Drug offenses focus on youths from the projects, the only ones systematically subjected to searches, which suggests a social order not devoid of an ethnic dimension.

Political repression is therefore defined simultaneously from above, in government and parliamentary assemblies, and from below, in the work of law enforcement agents and the framework of their hierarchy. Or rather it is manifested in the act which inseparably combines the expectations of the authorities and the intentions of the police. Actually, the public discourse serves to legitimize the work of law enforcement agents (the stigmatization and criminalization of immigrants and young people at the national level make their designation as the preferred clients of the police almost natural) while the work of the agents in turn sets the tone of public discourse (the controversy regarding the over-representation of immigrants and minorities in crime is fed by police statistics which justify the disqualification to which the authorities subject these groups).[21] Public order, which one claims to defend, and social, if not racial order, which one helps to produce and reproduce, are thus understood by the agents to be a just order. Special police forces—or ordinary police acting in a special capacity—can therefore inscribe their actions within a moral economy of repression, providing a reason for their acts—even when they deviate from professional norms.

The Justification of Practices

This is what the next scene illustrates. A young man of North African origin was pulled over as he waited at a traffic light. The anti-crime squad officers recognized him as one of those whose name appeared on a list of wanted persons. In fact, the man was one of the tens of thousands of people in France who have been given suspended sentences.[22] These are often short sentences for prior offenses, which, when they "fall," involve individuals who have turned their lives around, have a job and a family, and have thus put their delinquent past behind them. In this case, the man had several convictions that resulted in prison sentences, initially suspended, but then enforced a few years ago. He, however, thought that he had paid his debt to society. Upon learning of this old sentence and the prospect of returning to prison, he loudly expressed his distress in the small, fetid, transparent holding cell located next to the guard post where suspects are kept before interrogation and, if necessary, their detention. Desperate, banging against the Plexiglas walls like a caged animal, he shouted repeatedly: "I'm not doing another five months! I swear on my mother's life, I'm not going back to jail!" The police around him either made themselves look busy or chatted with one another. Some ignored him, others laughed from a distance, still others walked up and taunted him. It was rather troubling to see the broken man being detained in the confined space and subjected to taunts and provocations in front of everyone. Two members of the anti-crime squad who did not know the man and had only learned of his presence upon their arrival at the police station entered the holding cell for no apparent reason and stood in front of him. The first stood three feet from the detainee, eyeing him in silence, waiting for his litany to end only to set him off again with a scathing remark about his upcoming incarceration. The second, more talkative, tried in vain to attract the attention of the man with sarcastic comments even though the man, in his anxiety, was paying no attention to him. After a while, the second approached the man and began to threaten him, but seeing that his efforts were not met with any further success, he eventually walked out of the room, shouting to one of his colleagues: "I was this close to hitting him." Witnesses to the scene, which lasted several minutes, the other officers seemed to enjoy the distraction that it provided while they waited at the station for an unlikely call from a resident.

The viciousness shown by the police officers toward the demoralized and powerless man might seem a form of gratuitous, almost irrational sadism. Indeed, their excitement at that moment reveals an irrepressible pleasure in seeing the suspect suffer. Yet this also fits within a network of justifications that, from their point of view, legitimize their attitude. This network has two main dimensions: one concerning their public, the other their profession.

First, in order to treat a man with whom they had no prior contact and for whom they therefore cannot foster any personal antipathy, he must be integrated into a social group whose members are the object of generic hostility. As criminologists have long established, the police see themselves as operating in a generally hostile environment, and that feeling plays an important role in explaining their practices.[23] The sense of secrecy, the solidarity within the group, and the rejection of critics find if not their source, then at least their rationalization in this representation of their relationship with the public. Moreover, the alleged hostility of the population against law enforcement officers allows them to express their own hostility without too many scruples in return. But this antipathy is very socially differentiated. Some categories are subject to particular rejection, starting with youths from housing projects, who are seen not only as criminals but as enemies. On the one hand, they are delinquents, and officers struggle to distinguish "the thugs from the honest ones," as one commissioner stated, or to imagine that a "young black guy in a hoodie could be a masters or PhD student" as the mayor of the city put it. On the other hand, they are enemies in a belligerent relationship which the martial language of the government refers to as a "war on crime" to describe public action in housing projects and "urban guerrilla warfare" to describe the relationship of residents with the police. Under these conditions, some practices which would be inconceivable with respect to the majority of citizens become possible when targeting these categories.

Second, in order to give meaning to the cruelty which the police officers show toward a suspect who they know will be sent to prison to serve his time and for whom they see just how trying this prospect is, one must take into account their vision of how justice is dispensed. Most of them are convinced that the magistrates are too lax. "We arrest the suspects and then the next day the judges release them. It makes you wonder why we even bother," they often complained. The leniency of magistrates is yet another aspect of the discourse encountered in many studies conducted in other countries on law enforcement and reflects the complex relationship between the two professional bodies involved in the punishment of crimes and offenses.[24] In reality, as a squad leader remarked to his colleagues who complained about the clemency of judges, the problem is mainly that the latter can only convict the suspect when there is enough conclusive evidence to establish guilt. But without an airtight crime report or the undeniable identification of the perpetrator, judges can only acknowledge the contentious nature of the facts and the flimsiness of the evidence. The brigadier concluded that the cases brought before a judge had to be "impeccable, otherwise they won't stick" and that "because there had been too much abuse on the part of the police," judges no longer trust them. So he called for more rigor and more integrity in the work of law enforcement agents. However, few of his colleagues heeded his advice. The disqualification of justice had its function: it legitimized the justice rendered by the police in the field, that is to say, in the street and at the police station.

The two justifications that allow the police to account for their actions—the stigmatization of the public and the denunciation of the judges—echoed within the public discourse at the highest levels of the state. The disqualification of housing projects and their residents, of immigrants and minorities was part of the regular rhetoric of political actors: thus, the then Minister of the Interior Nicolas Sarkozy described youths from housing projects as "scum" and claimed that he would "power wash" the projects. Similarly, the leniency of magistrates was a hackneyed theme repeatedly used by the government: the executive branch's pressure on the judiciary had become commonplace at the time. That public hostility is contradicted by public opinion polls[25] and the indulgence of judges disproved by statistical studies[26] in the end weighs little in relation to the dissemination of stereotypes without empirical foundation, but legitimized by political authorities and legitimizing punitive practices.

The punishment of suspects thus finds its moral justification because if they are presumed innocent when they appear before the judge, they are assumed guilty when they are arrested by the police. To inflict punishment that is sometimes physical, but more often moral, taking the form of humiliation, is to restore a moral order thought to be poorly defended by the judiciary. But justice in the field may also be exercised in the absence of the alleged perpetrator, akin to blind retaliation against an individual or a community. On the one hand, it can take the form of random punishment: a youth, for example, is arrested and made to "pay" for others when a stone seen coming from a group is thrown and it is difficult to make out the members. Often, this youth is not entirely chosen at random, and sociological studies as well as statements gathered from officials show that they tend to punish an individual "already known to police," as the saying goes, or with whom they have a personal score to settle, having decided to impose a suspended sentence which they found too lenient. Unable to find the ideal suspect, however, they can make do by proxy with any person with similar social, ethnic, and residential qualities, in other words, a youth from a low-income background, belonging to a minority, and living in the projects. On the other hand, punitive operations may be launched: the police hold a stairwell, the wing of a building, or more rarely an entire neighborhood "hostage." This is the principle of collective punishment: all people are exposed to the repressive action. The search for a suspect is generally used as a pretext to break down the door of one or more dwellings, to throw around or even destroy furniture, to shove or mistreat the people present, most of whom have no connection to the alleged offense. These two models—random punishment and punitive operations—correspond to military practices used in wartime. Although the punishments meted out in the suburbs are certainly milder forms of such, there is nevertheless a sort of common matrix of intervention.

The work of the police in disadvantaged areas is therefore inscribed within a moral economy that allows for the understanding that some acts which many would qualify as deviant or perverse, or simply improper, if not illegal, have in the eyes of those who commit them a moral justification.[27] Construing the population as hostile gives basis to the resentment which the police show toward that population and the resulting various forms of abuse. Portraying the judiciary as being lenient authorizes their punitive practices by turning them into vigilantes working for the common good. This is certainly not to suggest that law enforcement officers always abuse their power, but to understand how, when they do abuse it, they can justify such actions for themselves, their colleagues, and their superiors by mobilizing shared affects (resentment) and values (justice).

The Moral Subjectivity of the Police

How then can we grasp the differentiations that exist within law enforcement practices? While there are general rationales that underlie these discrepancies and common justifications that legitimize them even when they diverge from the usually accepted norm, it is also clear that not all police officers behave in the same way or experience the constraints that their activity imposes on them in the same manner. Criminologists have mostly focused their analysis on the rationales and justifications common to what characterizes the police as a whole and what is readily described as a "culture."[28] But it has also appeared necessary to account for the variations observed in the field among the agents to establish typologies distinguishing different "styles" of patrolling depending on one's propensity to value order, the law, or negotiation.[29] Besides the ideal types of policing, the moral approach to police practices should identify two transversal elements: the moral criteria by which they are differentiated, and the moral conflicts which arise from differences between these criteria and the actual practices.

These two elements allow for moral subjectivities to be described in a double register: the identification of criteria outlines the distinct moral configurations found among the police while an analysis of the conflict explores the moral dynamics at play. In discussing moral subjectivities, I obviously seek to avoid investigating the psyche of the police and simply wish to expose the modalities by which they are constructed as a social subject through moral evaluations and conducts.

Ethics and Deontology

Born in a village near the large city where he worked, the head of the anti-crime squad had been in charge for more than 15 years. Knowing everything and everyone, he had become a local potentate in the police station but also a kind of celebrity dreaded in the neighborhoods where the young people referred to him by his first name. As is customary in these special units, he enjoyed considerable autonomy in relation to the hierarchy of the institution in terms of recruitment as well as oversight of his men. The practice of self-selection in hiring practices guaranteed the homogeneity of the group which was of only one gender (there had never been a woman in the squad) and of one background (no person of color had been admitted), but also the homogeneity of the group's ethos (most members shared certain dispositions, from a desire for action to the rejection of immigrants). Socialization within the different squads further reinforced the collective mindset (the rookies had to show how tough they were by demonstrating their adherence to standards that were more or less implicitly imposed). Conversations over coffee or in the squad car often had racist or xenophobic overtones to them, and when it came to political issues, allusions to affinities for the far right were not uncommon. "The Polish, the Portuguese, I've got no problems with them. No, it's the Blacks and the Arabs I've got problems with," stated the squad leader in all seriousness, who also liked to say whenever he drove past a group of youths of North African or sub-Saharan origin: "Those bastards don't like us. And we don't like them." Whenever he stopped and frisked one of these youths, he would put his money where his mouth was and insult and abuse the individual in the expectation of provoking a verbal or physical reaction that could lead to an arrest for insulting and resisting an officer. He was often called before the local board of discipline, had received several reprimands without obvious consequences, and ended up being transferred from the night shift to the day shift as a result of the violence he had committed, a punishment he hardly respected.

Towards the middle of my investigation, two officers whose ethos differed significantly from the dominant ethos joined the unit. The first was a young policeman originally from a low-income neighborhood of a large city in northern France. A reserved person, he did not express opinions about the residents or politics. An athletic man, he proved more effective than anyone else when in pursuit of an offender due to his speed as well as his intuition in the field. During identity checks, he was firm but not aggressive. The second, an officer in his forties hailing from the Seine-Saint-Denis department, had worked in other professions, including plumbing, before joining the police. He stated that he had no problem with people of color because while growing up in the projects he had had black and Arab friends with whom he would play soccer, and in his previous assignment, his closest colleague was of North African origin. In his interactions with youths or immigrants, he remained courteous, sometimes even mixing in a bit of humor. The presence of these two squad leaders gave a more peaceful tone to the proceedings of patrols. While feelings of solidarity prevailed in the relationship of authority between them and their colleagues, the latter two did not feel supported in their most deviant practices. The head of the anti-crime squad, who understood what separated him ideologically from the two officers, nevertheless seemed to appreciate them, one for his performance in terms of arrests, the other because they were of the same generation. Unlike the majority of their colleagues in the police force, the two officers had experiences quite similar to those of the urban teenagers and young adults whom they dealt with, and this was certainly a key factor in explaining their behavior toward them, notably their capacity for discernment, but other factors were probably also at play, including a certain conception of their mission that could be equated with a sense of professionalism.

It is possible to distinguish two dimensions in the characterization of moral subjectivities. We can call them ethics and deontology. The ethical dimension concerns the moral community which, by their words and deeds, the police constitute on a daily basis. By moral community, I mean all people, real or imaginary, with whom one envisages sharing the same human condition. So there are two possibilities. Either this community is inclusive and comprises a priori all individuals, even if a revision of this assessment must be made a posteriori about a given individual, when it is discovered that he or she has committed a heinous act. Or this community is exclusive and therefore discards certain categories a priori, this rejection being generally based on ethnic or racial criteria which can be validated a posteriori by the assertion that the individual in question deserved the indignity he or she had experienced. The deontological dimension entails the moral obligation that the police feel with respect to their job and a set of norms that are associated with it, including the use of force and the exercise of discretionary power. Once again, there is an alternative. Either this obligation serves as a more or less implicit reference in their professional activity, imposing a twofold respect for the law as a general principle for assessing the legality of their actions as well as for rights in so far as they are attached to the people they deal with. Or this obligation is minimized, leading to an unjustified or disproportionate use of force and a misappropriation of authority in an abuse of power, whether or not the deviant behavior is subject to sanctions. Ethics is thus revelatory of the relationship with the public and more generally with the world, while deontology constitutes the relationship to the profession and more generally the rules.

These two principles which organize the legal subjectivities of the police seem better able to grasp the latter in their generality than previously proposed criteria.[30] The political scientist William Kerr Muir was the first to attempt to characterize the morality of law enforcement agents: "A policeman becomes a good policeman to the extent that he develops two virtues. Intellectually, he has to grasp the nature of human suffering. Morally, he has to resolve the contradiction of achieving just ends with coercive means." He calls this first virtue "tragic sense" and the second one "moral equanimity."[31] However, this interesting model raises two issues. First, by involving a form of compassion, which is in reality less an intellectual virtue than a moral sentiment, one confers an excessive pathos on police activity. While they can certainly be exposed to distress, the police more often face situations that do not involve this dimension, be it responding to a victim of mobile phone theft or stopping and frisking an individual. So it is preferable to try to understand more comprehensively how the police view their public and, to put it more simply, those for whom they are likely to feel sympathy. Second, by situating the tension in between just ends and coercive means, one remains stuck in a definition of the profession which, on the one hand, is idealized because, as we have shown, the question of the justice of the acts is not seen the same way by the police as it is by the rest of society and, on the other hand, is essentialized through the use of force even though there exist other dimensions to police practice, like the quality of the investigative work or service to the public. It is therefore desirable to have a more systematic approach to the way in which law enforcement agents situate themselves in relation to the norms of their profession.

The combination of these ethical and deontological dimensions presents four theoretical possibilities: inclusive community and strong obligation; inclusive community and weak obligation; exclusive community and strong obligation, and exclusive community and weak obligation. In reality, the moral dissociations of the second and third categories are relatively rare. It is certainly possible to find officers who are rather sympathetic toward the public but unconcerned with the rules or, conversely, racist and xenophobic officers who are inclined to respect the codes of their profession, thus highlighting the fact that attitudes do not necessarily intersect with practices.[32] But for the vast majority of them, the police officers in my study belonged to the fourth category, while a few others like the two new officers corresponded to the first. In this instance, three groups were excluded a priori from their moral community, namely, in ascending order of rejection: immigrants, Roma, and youths of North African or sub-Saharan origin. The most xenophobic, such as the head of the unit and some of his colleagues who did not hesitate to display signs of their sympathy for the far right aggressively resent immigrants. The Roma are despised for their lifestyle but appreciated for their submissiveness to authority; often the discourse concerning them conveyed the idea of an uncontrollable invasion. Youths from housing projects, called "bastards," were the most disparaged because the delinquent and provocative behavior of a few is readily generalized to characterize the group as a whole. But in addition to their potential deviance, it was their very presence that was considered illegitimate and problematic as is suggested by their designation. This exclusion from the moral community on the part of the police has consequences for their behavior towards these publics, whether it be physical violence or more frequently alleged bullying whose public nature—in front of neighbors, friends, a girlfriend, family—renders the humiliation even more stinging. Because the moral condemnation surrounding this group concerns both their supposed origin and their association with delinquency, youths from low-income neighborhoods suffer the most aggressive and the most demeaning treatment.

The model we have just briefly presented should, however, not be considered set in stone. Categories are unstable and fluid. This is what certain trajectories reveal.

Conflicts and Resolutions

Despite its obvious limitations, the night shift is generally favored by the police for several reasons: the work is less intense because there are fewer calls from residents and fewer potential suspects out on the streets; the officers receive longer breaks, allowing them to spend time with their families; supervision is less noticeable due to the absence of hierarchy on site, which further increases the already high degree of the anti-crime squad's autonomy. Two of its members who nevertheless chose to forgo those benefits and join the day shift explained their decision as being a rejection of their colleagues' conduct: "We couldn't stand what was happening at night anymore, all that crap we heard and everything we saw." In fact, their intolerance of an atmosphere they deemed detrimental did not manifest itself immediately: "In the beginning, we thought like everyone else, we really went for it, we tried to be team players." It was only after two or three years that the words and actions of their fellow squad members began take their toll: "We couldn't take it anymore. We were sick and tired of listening to racist, xenophobic, and anti-Semitic colleagues all night long. We were sick and tired of seeing things and being forced to keep quiet." This frustration, however, remained for a long time hidden: "Even if you don't agree with what's being said or done, you can't let anyone else know. So you just keep quiet and live in your own little world. You don't want any trouble." So when they were offered the chance to switch shifts after several years, they did not think twice. While it is certainly possible that other causes may have led to their leaving the night shift, including poor relations with the head of the unit or some of their colleagues, it is no less likely that the difference in mindset and style of intervention played a key role in the tensions they experienced: less self-assured and less belligerent than most of their night-time colleagues, despite their best efforts, the two did not fit the image of manhood that the squad wanted to project to its public.

It is rare for police officers to criticize their peers in front of strangers. Their sense of solidarity and the risk of retribution prevent them from doing so. And as it so happened, they did not agree to individual interviews to talk more specifically about their disappointments and difficulties, not wanting, as they said, "to tarnish the image of the police." Having distanced themselves from practices they considered unethical, they nevertheless chose not to repudiate a certain deontology which demands that they not criticize their profession. Such an approach would come at a high cost in the various cases I was aware of. Media interviews are severely punished by the institution except when given by spokespersons for the police unions. Even internal disputes are subject to retaliation from colleagues and retribution from the hierarchy. Confronted with the deviance and abuse one has witnessed, the only viable solution is to keep quiet. And when the opportunity presents itself, it is then possible to distance oneself without denouncing what one has heard or seen, by switching shifts, units, stations, or even resigning from the police force altogether, as some confided they were tempted to do. Thus, in the triptych that Albert Hirschman proposes to account for attitudes expressed by agents who are not satisfied with the performance of an organization, speaking out (voice) proved too risky to be seriously considered a possibility, leaving only an alternative between renunciation (loyalty)—behaving as if nothing had happened—and defection—disavowal by individually withdrawing (exit).[33] The two police officers went through three stages. First, they adhered to the values of the group or at least did everything they could to convince themselves to adhere to them and thus fit in with the group at the cost of ethical contortions. Next, they experienced moral dilemmas due to the contradiction between their principles and their participation in the group's activities, making them in fact complicit with what they were incapable of preventing or challenging. Finally, they resolved their moral conflict by leaving the group, even if they knew that what they disapproved of would continue. Thus, their dissent remained secret: they repudiated in silence. But they were not alone: their superiors and colleagues in other units did the same.

This sequence is as logical as it is ubiquitous. It reflects the strength of the institution and its ability to reproduce itself. Within the squad, recruitment occurs through the self-selection of those who conform the most with the local ethos; socialization perpetuates the learning of the group's norms; and marginalization punishes attempts at resistance. In fact, the anticipation of retaliation makes these attempts highly unlikely. When a moral conflict arises because the contradictions become too great, withdrawal appears to be the only possible option. Even if withdrawal is not an ethical solution, since the silence of those who experience this moral conflict still signals their complicity, then it is at least a partly deontological solution, since those who withdraw continue to maintain group cohesion. Ultimately, only those elements farthest removed from the values that are supposed to characterize police professionalism remain in the unit. In the hierarchy, nothing is done to change this rationale, since only the most serious and in particular the most visible faults are penalized. Essentially, the commanding officers and above all, the commissioners, caught between the injunctions of the policy and the recriminations from the rank and file, prefer not to confront their men, especially when they are only doing what the authorities expect them to do. It was the Ministry of the Interior which set these special units up and which supported them even in instances of deviance that were re-inscribed within a moral order in the fight against crime. This entire system, the reproduction of which seems perfectly assured from the squads all the way up to the highest echelons of the state, essentially concerns certain areas and certain populations. What would be unimaginable in residential neighborhoods or rural areas and among the middle and upper classes, because the deviations from the law or code of ethics would be denounced by the citizens, is here viewed as normal—it is a policy of exception.

But no social world ever functions on the principle of a perfect reproduction. There is the possibility for flexibility in the seemingly intractable logic we have just described. In the field, atypical elements can find themselves inserted into the system, such as the two squad leaders whose attitudes are neither of "voice," nor of "loyalty," nor of "exit": they modestly changed the ethos of the squad through their practices. Similarly, the arrival of a new team to the departmental executive for security or a new commissioner at the head of a district can cause the practices of law enforcement agents to evolve thanks to supervision, evaluation, and punishment, as was reported to me by high-level officials. Finally, a change in the political orientation of the government and more specifically in the Ministry of the Interior can affect the mechanisms through modes of recruitment, training, coordination, and definition of assignments for law enforcement agents. However, these possibilities are limited: the forms of moral justification of police deviance that we analyzed are inscribed within structural rationales. This is why they are found, admittedly with significant variations, wherever the police are responsible for exercising control over the social order in the name of public safety which as a result implies extensive powers, flexible norms, and tolerance with respect to abuses.

Conclusion

"We have nothing to hide. There are no crooked cops here," replied the commissioner when asked why he had authorized my investigation at a time when the Ministry of the Interior had made researchers' access to the field of police work almost impossible. His response was significant and the scandal sparked by the discovery of ties to the underworld within the anti-crime squad in the northern neighborhoods of Marseilles a few years later confirmed his intention: moral deviance for police and for society in general resides mainly in corruption because it involves both the illegal obtainment of personal benefits as well as an unacceptable complicity with criminals. Nevertheless, these practices are probably marginal. Conversely, the facts that I have described, whether it be the abuse or the humiliation, the racism or the discrimination, are part of a tolerated daily routine.

Society delegates to the police not only the legitimate use of force to defend law and order; it also entrusts them with the exercise of forms of power that they deem necessary in areas and populations considered dangerous or simply unwanted by creating special units like anti-crime squads and developing specific forms of intervention like the proliferation of identity checks and friskings, among other things. Residents of disadvantaged neighborhoods, especially youths but also immigrants and Roma constitute in France the bulk of the categories so administered. The police have even greater discretionary power with respect to them because they know that the state will pay little attention to their deviant practices. Except in extreme instances, these practices are likewise not considered deviant by law enforcement agents in so far as they find justifications in both the disqualification of these categories seen as hostile and the suspicion towards judges considered too lenient. Superiors may be even less likely to intervene and regulate these practices because to do so would be to run counter to national policy and public discourse, thus undermining their authority. Disciplinary boards are permissive partly out of collegial solidarity. Prosecutors prove understanding, citing the difficulties of urban policy. In the end, the conditions of production and reproduction of practices specific to certain areas and certain populations come together. Under these conditions, the police's sense of ethics and their respect for professionalism turn out to be fragile resources for those who wish to defend a certain conception of their profession.

Notes

1 The dissertation was only published twenty years later with a preface updating the findings of the initial study (Westley 1970).
2 The work's third chapter is devoted to the "working personality" of a police officer, a term which in fact designates the officer's professional culture (Skolnick 1994).
3 The study was conducted on the Los Angeles Police Department (LAPD) which was implicated in the Rodney King affair (Herbert 1996).
4 In the only French study devoted to police brutality (Jobard 2002), the author, while maintaining his distance from their reality (he questions "the reliability of the accounts given by those claiming to be victims of violence" and "the credibility of the facts for which the proof is often only the memory of the individual or even a deceptive imagination"), concentrates on the "social and judicial conditions of the acting out" rather than on the acts themselves and their justification (Jobard 2002: 183).
5 One is reminded of the following remarkable surveys: "Interface" by the Ministry of the Interior in 1982, "Cohorte" by Dominique Montjardet and Catherine Gorgeon from 1992 to 2002, and "Sociodémographie des conditions de vie et d'emploi des policiers" by Geneviève Pruvost, Philippe Coulangeon, and Ionela Roharik in 2003 (Alain and Pruvost 2011).
6 The fieldwork consisted primarily of "ride-alongs" during the day and at night with uniformed police officers or more often with the anti-crime squad. The work was carried out from May 2005 to June 2007 with an interruption of ten or so months. This time period is thus practically bookended by the riots sparked by the deaths of two adolescents in Clichy-sous-Bois and the disorder that followed the deaths of two youths

run over by a police car in Villiers-le-Bel. The research has been presented in a book (Fassin 2013a [2011]).

7 For a genealogical approach to the police inspired by a Foucauldian viewpoint, see the enlightening article by Hélène l'Heuillet (2002).

8 For a discussion of the significance of the police in the modern era as well as national differences, read Paolo Napoli's book (2003).

9 As the author of the article points out, "security and public order are the sixth object of the police," aiming to prevent "violence, homicide, theft, larceny, and other crimes of this nature" as well as "illicit gatherings, the distribution of seditious, scandalous, and defamatory writings and all dangerous books." The ten other "objects" concern domains which would today be considered outside the purview of the police (Boucher d'Argis 1751–80).

10 There are several recently published histories of the police, notably works by Michel Aubouin, Arnaud Teyssier, and Jean Tulard (2005), Jean-Marc Berlière and René Lévy (2011), and Christian Chevandier (2012).

11 According to the study conducted by Geneviève Pruvost, Philippe Coulangeon, and Ionela Roharik (2004), 39 percent of police officers stated that they grew up in rural areas and 40 percent in a small or medium-sized provincial town. In addition, 28 percent of police officers stated that their fathers were blue-collar workers and 19 percent low-level office workers.

12 Attributing this fact to the nationalization of the police during the Vichy Regime, Christian Mouhanna (2011: 24) speaks of a "non-democratic model of management."

13 According to Emmanuel Blanchard (2004) whose work on the police and the Algerians fostered the subsequent developments, the question which dominated the public debates at the time is the following: "Does the presence of tens of thousands of Algerians in the Seine department require the creation of a police force with specific prerogatives or does the march toward judicial and social assimilation of this population imply ordinary police treatment?"

14 The expression "new social question" appears in works by Robert Castel (1995) and Pierre Rosanvallon (1995). It is significant that at the time the fact that this new social question concerned the immigrant and minority populations proportionally more than it did the populations of European origin was absent from the public debate and for the most part from the intellectual field (Fassin 2002).

15 On urban policies, see the analysis by Jean-Marie Delarue (1991) who as an interministerial delegate for cities and social urban development was one of the principal architects of these policies, as well as the analysis by Jacques Donzelot (2006), who was a privileged observer leading the research conducted by this delegation.

16 On the repressive trend, see Denis Salas's essay (2007) which refers to a "penal populism," as well as the collective work on the "security frenzy" edited by Laurent Mucchielli (2008).

17 Since Carl Klockars's eponymous article (1980), the character "Dirty Harry" played by Clint Eastwood in Don Siegel's 1971 eponymous film serves as a paradigm for the police officer who uses questionable means to achieve admirable ends. The parallel with the anti-crime squad is, however, limited by the fact that its members rarely claim to work for the common good or even for good at all.

18 Mathieu Rigouste's study (2009) sheds light on the continuities and the memories between the colonial police and the contemporary police.

19 This is the famous definition according to which "the capacity to use force [is] the core of the police role" (Bittner 1980: 36).

20 The theme of "police discretion" has been a mainstay of criminological literature for the past fifty years. A recent study (Sekhon 2012) shows that rather than thinking of the discretionary power of police officers in terms of individual choices, it is essential

to understand it as inscribed within the discretionary policies of the police force—to which one could add the Ministry of the Interior.

21 Thus, the policy of repression delimits what John Alan Lee (2010) rightly calls "police property," that is to say, populations whose public authorities delegate control to law enforcement agencies entirely.

22 An official report published two years prior to this episode takes stock of the 82,000 individuals awaiting the execution of sentences, 90 percent of whom have sentences of less than one year (Inspection générale des services judiciaires 2009).

23 The study carried out by John Van Maanen (1978) on the training and socialization of police officers allows for the dynamic behind the acquisition of these portrayals to be grasped.

24 As Albert Reiss writes (1971: 137), "Patrol officers commonly regard juveniles as the most difficult class of citizens to police and the most leniently handled in the system of justice."

25 An opinion poll shows that 73 percent of persons belonging to the "ethnic majority" and 59 percent of those belonging to the "ethnic minority" claim to have confidence in the police. These numbers reach 79 percent and 66 percent respectively when the question concerns confidence in the local police where those polled live (Roux et al. 2011).

26 A study conducted on immediate appearance trials which constitute the usual way in which offences committed by youths from low-income neighborhoods are dealt with shows that harsh prison sentences are handed down in two-thirds of the cases, well above the number handed down in normal criminal trials, that orders of committal or detention make up three-quarters of these cases while they remain the exception in ordinary proceedings, and that the length of the sentences has quickly and significantly increased (Conseil Lyonnais pour le respect des droits 2008).

27 In order to discuss this justice rendered in the field, Jerome Skolnick and James Fyfe (1993) speak of "vigilante justice," in other words the justice rendered by self-defense militias.

28 A detailed description of this can be found in Robert Reiner's book (2000), which lists a series of characteristics like a sense of mission, valorization of the action, cynicism, pessimism, conservatism, or male chauvinism.

29 An example of this can be found in James Q. Wilson's monograph (1968) based on a study conducted in eight US states.

30 It is interesting to note that in his study of the "professional culture of the police," Dominique Montjardet (1994) indicates two major issues at stake: the "relationship with the other" and the "relationship with the law." The former indicator concerns "the avowed opinions with respect to the adversaries which are the municipal police and private security firms," but also "the relationship with non-police (citizens, elected officials, authorities)." The latter includes two elements: "legalism" and "comprehension of the law." Montjardet's work is therefore more an analysis of the organization rather than the morality of the institution.

31 William Kerr Muir's pioneering study (1977: 3–4) is implicitly reliant on an Aristotelian approach in terms of the ethics of virtue.

32 That is what P.A.J. Waddington demonstrates when in his classic text (1999) he highlights the importance of not inferring from the discussions at the police station in the context of "canteen subculture" what practices prove effective on the streets.

33 The formula "exit, voice, loyalty" refers to withdrawing, speaking out, and accepting the situation (Hirschman 1970).

CHAPTER FIVE

Sanctioning Behind Bars
The Humanization of Retribution in Prison

Fabrice Fernandez

"We're not here to change Jean-Pierre or Mohamed. They're already in prison. It's already a big deal for them, it's complicated. But to try and change them? Are they supposed to be some sort of material that we can shape, like modeling clay that we can mold? No, they're not. And this is not a reeducation camp. The nuance is difficult to grasp because we always want to turn prisons into reeducation camps." These comments were made by the deputy director of a prison in the Paris region at the end of a disciplinary board he had just chaired. If the goal of prison discipline is not to shape bodies and minds, then what is the meaning of disciplinary punishment and what outcome do we have in mind when we punish inmates who are already in prison? Is it solely to punish and/or prevent misbehavior? In any act of punishment, what part reflects a straightforward concern to maintain order and what part stems from a moral action grounded in the desire to transform inmates in the more or less long term?

In prison, disciplinary boards represent a particular form of justice whose aim is to punish behaviors that disrupt prison order. As part of their primary responsibility to maintain order and security, prison and other detention center administrators have the ability to decide on their own whether or not to punish inmates who have broken internal prison rules.[1] Punishing individuals who have already been convicted by a court or who are being held in custody pending trial is no easy task. This type of judgment calls into question the ability of prison authorities to demonstrate a sense of fairness without slipping into arbitrariness and discretion.

The word "discipline" comes from the Latin *disciplina*, itself derived from *discipulus*, "disciple." Etymologically, discipline thus implies the ability to transform an individual through the integration of values and principles to which that individual must submit. While disciplinary action refers to the punishment itself,[2] it also signals moral opprobrium and serves as a warning, forcing the prisoner to respect the values considered fundamental to communal life behind bars in the future. Yet the move to humanize life in prison, a move that gradually took hold in France in the years following the end of World War II, has at the same time asserted that the inmate is to be considered a moral agent capable of modifying his or her own behavior.[3]

The concept of moral economy captures the art of managing or handling populations in a legitimate fashion through the production, circulation, and appropriation of norms and values, affects and moral sentiments in a particular social space at a given point in time.[4] Today, the moral economy of prison is so dominated by the meaning of the sentence that it has in fact become the main focus of contemporary debates regarding punishment in prison and its usefulness. My subsequent analysis of the emotional and moral content of disciplinary judgment practices relies on the understanding of disciplinary sanctions as both a punishment and a moral affliction. I seek to explain how consensus and self-evident morals have come to be imposed on the attitudes adopted toward inmates who have committed infractions in prison, in other words, efforts "to treat them well", and to demonstrate fairness in the punishments handed down. How do prison administrators attempt to hold these prisoners accountable for their behavior so that they do not re-offend? As for prisoners, what forms of dispute, negotiation, or approval do these punishments and reprimands give rise to?

While the two central elements of discipline have always been to maintain order in the prison and to support correctional officers, beginning in the early 2000s, a series of internal and external factors fundamentally changed it. First, a continuous increase in the number of reported incidents in prison (including physical and verbal assault) led prison administrators to make adjustments in discipline procedures. The aim of these changes was to punish a greater number of inmates in a shorter amount of time in an attempt to show active support for prison staff who often bear the brunt of reported offenses. Second, on a legislative level, the introduction of an adversarial system within disciplinary commissions (the possibility for the inmate to be represented by a lawyer) and the right to appeal a punishment confer on the disciplinary system the apparent technical quality of criminal law. But the European Prison Rules (EPR), which France has ratified, recommend that these commissions be used as a last resort when softer forms of sub-disciplinary practices have failed. Administering discipline is therefore subject to two opposing rationales: the intent to lower the threshold for tolerance of inmate misconduct through the establishment of standard responses (namely, in the form of incident reports), which reflects a bureaucratic management of discipline, and the formal recognition of the rights of prisoners, which, among other things, is indicative of the application of European rules and the legal formalization of a number of moral values (notably, fairness, and equality). In this context, how are administrators of discipline able to reconcile the management of incidents and acts of violence with the newly introduced right to a defense acquired by inmates, as well as European recommendations that offenses be regulated on a sub-disciplinary level? How and on what basis is the proper punishment evaluated? What form does this so-called "humanized" sentencing take today?

Through an ethnographic study conducted over a period of ten months in a prison in the Paris region,[5] I will show how the exercise of prison discipline is in fact a space of negotiation. Subject to relationships of power, the prison administration is forced to deal with agents (lawyers, guards, inmates) who are often in disagreement as to the solutions to be adopted and the punishments to be handed down. In an increasingly complex context affected by organizational changes, how does the institution manage to maintain a minimum of discipline? Order cannot merely be explained by the respect for the formal rules of an organization or by a community of interests which unites the agents, whether they be professional or not. It is not simply the result of a structural determination, but a complex set of processes in which each agent participates in the representation of the situation that he or she is involved in. In this sense, the sequence of interactions which take place during a disciplinary board is never static but constantly adapted, reinvested, negotiated; it is the product of know-how, conflicts, divergent interests, emotional and moral tensions, and personal and collective beliefs about the work which these professionals perform, but it is also about their training, their place within the hierarchy, etc.

To highlight the political and moral issues specific to the management of misbehavior in prison, I will develop a dual perspective: socio-historical and ethnographic. I will first examine the role of prison discipline through the historical transformations that have affected the moral economy of punishment. I will then show the tensions at work today in sanctioning faults allegedly committed by inmates through the discrepancies that exist between the moral order of offenses and the pragmatic use of punishments. I will then proceed to show how judgment practices are determined by certain expectations (docility, sincerity, acknowledgement of guilt, etc.) and evaluative criteria (dangerousness, responsibility, and vulnerability). Finally, I will compare these expectations and criteria to the attitudes of prisoners who appear before the disciplinary boards. Analyzing the interactions during a disciplinary board hearing will allow us to reveal the way in which inmates not only re-appropriate, but also oppose and resist the moral economy of punishment, as well as the different expectations and demands that are associated with it.

Changes in the Moral Economy of Punishment

Prison may be "omni-disciplinary,"[6] but its discipline remains one of the most salient aspects of a correctional officer's work and an arcane process that has long symbolized the opacity and arbitrariness of the institution. While prison discipline had for years been exercised outside the law, various changes in its regulations since the end of World War II have emerged under the growing influence of European law.[7]

In this section, I will present a brief outline of the genesis of carceral discipline from the Middle Ages to the aftermath of the French Revolution, when prisons started to be designed as places where prisoners could be punished as well as reformed. Next, I will analyze the gradual transformation of disciplinary punishment in prisons brought about by a policy of humanizing living conditions in prison. Then, I will examine how the disciplinary procedure has been framed legally by a set of laws guaranteeing inmates certain rights since the mid-1990s. Finally, I will show the forms in which this moral economy of punishment is actualized today within the context of European standardization leading to the transformation of both professional practices and the meaning of the disciplinary procedure itself.

Before Penal Prisons

A legacy of the nineteenth century, prison disciplinary proceedings are closely linked to the history of prison itself. In the Middle Ages, such measures were non-existent in ordinary prisons where those awaiting trial were held,[8] in forts which were royal prisons where criminals were often locked up for indeterminate amounts of time, and in Inquisition jails where heretics were tortured for years until they confessed, after which they were sentenced to isolation before they either recanted or were burned at the stake. The unruly, those who escaped, and those who refused to confess were not judged, but thrown into dungeons where they were chained up without trial. As for the poor, the needy, and the homeless who had been hounded since the fourteenth century, they were placed in general hospitals starting in the early eighteenth century, then in poorhouses,[9] where they underwent a form of moral rehabilitation until they were "rendered fit to earn a living with their hands."[10] It was not until the late seventeenth century that extensive reflection on imprisonment by the clergy and the laity alike would call these practices into question.[11] The philosophers of the Enlightenment in particular seized upon the issue to denounce the abuses and the arbitrariness of justice.

It was only with the discontinuation of public executions in the early nineteenth century that punishment underwent a veritable metamorphosis[12] and shifted from a physical suffering inflicted on the body of the condemned to an emotional suffering. During the Revolution, torture was abolished, and the 1789 Declaration of the Rights of Man and of the Citizen proclaimed that "no man can be accused, arrested, or detained except in cases determined by law and in the manner the law has prescribed." In 1791, the first criminal code was adopted, giving confinement a central role in the judicial system.[13] By the end of the eighteenth century, the use of deprivation of liberty as a punishment had become increasingly widespread, but both the death penalty and forced labor were still enforced. Prisons, both central (for long sentences) and departmental (for short sentences and those awaiting trial) were thought to be places of punishment as well as places of reform which was to be achieved through work and education. In 1810, France's second criminal code favored several other forms of punishment in addition to incarceration: ball and chain for forced laborers and branding with a hot iron. In 1839, the internal rulebooks of central prisons were toughened, followed by those of jails: from then on, it was forbidden to speak, smoke, or drink wine, and convicts were required to work and wear prison uniforms.

The tribunal (*prétoire*), an ancestor of the disciplinary board, came into being in 1842.[14] This marked the beginning of solitary confinement as the main form of disciplinary punishment in prison. Reforming prisoners was thought to be closely tied to the prerequisite adherence to strict prison rules: by subjecting inmates to this harsh discipline, it was believed that they would continue to practice it after their release. In this sense, prison discipline was related to the moral reform of prisoners, to their "moral regeneration."[15]

Humanizing Punishment after World War II

Although the General Assembly of the League of Nations adopted basic rules for the treatment of prisoners in 1935, it was not until the 1945 Amor Reform that the French prison system underwent a thorough revision with the implementation of 14 basic principles that drastically transformed prison discipline by placing greater focus on reforming convicts and rehabilitating them socially via humane treatment.[16] Such a method involved not only correcting the behavior of prisoners but also attempting to rehabilitate them, to humanize them somehow. Following the Amor Reform, the "discipline room" and "facing the wall" (1947), the revoking of visiting and mail privileges (1948), the systematic head shaving, the compulsory wearing of wooden clogs (1954), and the wearing of chains at night (1954) were one after the other eliminated. Suspended punishments made an appearance, and fines were limited to reparations. Little by little, disciplinary procedures in prison came to be legally regulated in an effort to conform to the provisions of the 1948 Universal Declaration of Human Rights.[17]

In 1969, the maximum period of detention in a disciplinary cell was lowered from 90 to 45 days, and aggravating measures (the removal of sleeping material, the covering up of windows, etc.) were proscribed. Dietary restrictions and mandatory silence were then abandoned. Finally, in 1975, disciplinary punishments were reclassified as disciplinary penalties. This semantic change is symptomatic of the slow emergence of a new moral economy of punishment that no longer focused solely on suffering but involved a more educational and reparative approach.[18] Whereas punishment connotes a legal order, penalties suggest instead a moral one. They are intended to provoke a sense of responsibility in the person guilty of wrong-doing and are meant to result in reparations for the prejudices caused. They seek to restore order, to prevent relapses, and to better inmates. But despite these reforms, disciplinary sanctions continued to fall short of the criminal justice system's requirements since there existed no legal recourse to challenge the decisions.

Access to Rights and Controlling Disciplinary Measures

Alongside this process of humanization developed a legal framework governing the use of discipline within prisons. A 1995 ruling by the Council of State (the Marie Decision) deemed disciplinary confinement a measure that could be challenged on appeal, the legal grounds for which lay in laws preventing the abuse of power. A subsequent decree issued by the government on April 2, 1996 conferred a strict regulatory framework on disciplinary proceedings with the notable introduction of inquests designed to investigate charges against inmates. As a result, disciplinary punishment lost its status as a measure of internal order decided at the sole discretion of prison administrators and became instead a measure subject to appeal. In addition, 36 disciplinary offenses were listed according to three degrees of severity. The intended goal was to frame prison discipline with a legal standard which would limit its reliance on discretion.[19]

More recently, inmates have gained important guarantees of their right to a defense[20] (including the possibility to access the files of the proceeding and to receive the assistance of a lawyer or any other authorized representative of their choosing when appearing before a disciplinary board[21]). Despite this process of prison judicialization and the new rights which inmates have at their disposal,[22] the disciplinary board continues to fall short of the guarantees of fairness found in a criminal trial (in terms of the parity of the trial body, the inability to call witnesses, the limited time to prepare a defense, etc.).

The Move toward European Standardization

Since November 2006, prison authorities in France have decided to make adherence to the European Prison Rules (EPRs) a guiding principle for its policy of modernization and its improvement of professional practices. The objective of the EPRs is to provide member states with guidelines on basic rules relating to life in prison. These 108 rules concern the human rights of inmates as well as the system of detention, health, security, prison staff, inspections, and prison oversight.

By integrating certain important precepts with explicit references to the European Convention on Human Rights, the jurisprudence of the European Court of Human Rights, and the work of the European Board for the Prevention of Torture, the EPRs are a "catalogue" of "good practices" proposed to national authorities with the intent that each member state might at its own pace improve living conditions in European prisons in accordance with a wider "humanizing" trend of such institutions. In particular, these rules address issues of discipline by attempting to strike a permanent balance between the imperative of maintaining prison order and the obligation to treat all inmates humanely and to respect their inherent dignity as human beings (rules 49 and 50). If the goal is to transform inmates into moral agents, then prison guards are in turn expected to exercise restraint by favoring sub-disciplinary warnings as much as possible over the reporting of incidents (rules 56.1 and 56.2). The moral economy of punishment hence refers to a way of managing and handling unruly inmates both lawfully and humanely. Through the circulation of norms, values, and affects, it promotes sub-disciplinary responses and measured penalties which are undoubtedly involved in maintaining prison order but also encourage inmates to take responsibility for themselves and to implement their own moral rectification.[23]

With regard to prison staff, the EPRs indicate that they must act with impartiality, humaneness, and fairness toward inmates and must possess a clear sense of the purpose of the prison system—which involves not only security but also preparing inmates for their eventual reintegration. This objective is emphasized to future prison guards during training at the National School of Penitentiary Administration (École nationale de l'administration pénitentiaire ENAP). And it is to this end the Prisons Act of 2009 sought to reform the correctional officer profession by establishing a code of conduct which reinforces their moral authority through an oath of office and an ethic of *care*. Yet this moral authority remains problematic in a professional environment where the value of virility prevails.[24] Privately, prison guards readily internalize this view of their responsibilities by stressing the human nature of their work and their sense of justice. In doing so, they participate in the revaluation of the somewhat negative image of their profession of "prison guard" and attempt to distance themselves from stereotypical representations that associate their work with plain disciplinary enforcement or the subaltern role of "turnkey."

But in conjunction with these gradual changes in the duties of correctional officers, there has been a growing complexification of these same duties as a result of policies meant to combat violence. These policies place the work of prison guards at the heart of measures taken to prevent and control violence. And while there have been reductions in the maximum duration of placement in security housing units (SHU) from 45 days to 20 days—30 days in cases of physical violence—in accordance with the Prisons Act of 2009 and European standards, prison violence seems to have increased, according to figures from the prison administration.[25] Given these circumstances, how do prison administrators handle incidents of violence locally and how do they punish the offenders?

The Moral Tensions in Administering Discipline

We have seen how the influences of a policy which favors humanizing the sentence, the establishment of a more precise legal framework, and a move toward European standardization have all gradually come to shape prison discipline. If the moral economy of sentencing affects both the management of prison order by mitigating the implementation of the penalty (sub-discipline) and the content of the practices of prison officers, how is this disciplinary procedure implemented and what moral tensions now pervade it? I will first illustrate the way in which the disciplinary procedure is carried out, then I will analyze how offenses and reports of disciplinary incidents in prison reflect a certain moral order, which I will afterward compare with the use of the penalties imposed.

The Sequence of Disciplinary Proceedings

Generally speaking, the disciplinary board hearing is a quick procedure (between 20 and 30 minutes long for each case) which always follows the same sequence of events: after a debriefing among the members of the board about the case, the accused is brought in, assisted if he wishes by a lawyer; the director who is the presiding member of the board then explains the charges by reading the incident report and the conclusions of the investigation; the chair next asks the accused to present his version of the events. A discussion ensues among the director, the two prison guards, and the inmate. When a lawyer represents the latter, he or she may provide background information for the context in which the offense took place. The chair then asks the accused and the accused's lawyer to leave the room so that he or she can deliberate for five to ten minutes with his or her associates. Finally, the accused is brought back in and the sentence is read. He must then sign the decision and is informed that he may appeal the decision within 15 days by writing to the inter-regional director of the prison administration.[26]

Paolo, a Brazilian inmate in his twenties, appeared before the board: a cell phone had been found in his cell. After the charges were explained by the chair, the inmate immediately admitted to everything he was accused of: "They gave me a phone to call my family. I don't get any visitors, because my family doesn't have papers …." The president asked: "What are you in here for?" "Papers," he replied. He attempted to explain his situation in limited French, and his lawyer was quick to add: "He was convicted for presenting false documents. In addition, he is in France illegally. His parents and his girlfriend are here illegally. He needs to communicate with his family. I ask for leniency from you. This is a difficult situation, he has no visiting rights." The chair turned once again to Paolo: "Did you appeal your two-month sentence?" "No …." "Why doesn't anyone come to see you?" "No papers … My girlfriend is Brazilian like me."

During the deliberation, it was clear that no one believed his story, starting with the chair: "His story doesn't sound true. It's a ruse!" The comment was then followed by one from the prison guard serving on the board: "He's new, he's the fall guy. He'll admit to anything. Maybe we shouldn't throw him in the hole [solitary confinement], but there's no space for him in ordinary confinement." For this prison guard, there was no doubt that the prisoner was a "fall guy," that is to say, a victim of a prison gang, who agrees to admit to offenses that he did not commit either for money or more probably out of fear of reprisals. The chair then steered the discussion toward deciding on the sentence that would be imposed: "No, we should put him in the hole … Pfff … How many spots do we have?" "Four," answered the other prison guard serving on the board. "We can put him in there for ten days. In any case, he ought to be punished!" concluded the chair. He then asked the guards to bring the inmate and his lawyer back in for the verdict: "Twenty days in the hole, ten of which are suspended. Do you understand?" "Yeah," he replied without much expression. "You have 15 days to appeal … Sign here." After signing the verdict, Paolo did not forget to show his manners: "Thank you, goodbye."

Members of disciplinary boards often find themselves in tricky situations when faced with inmates who are considered vulnerable, that is to say, weakened by certain problematic social situations (drug users, homosexuals, suicidal individuals, homeless persons, undocumented immigrants, those with disabilities, illiterate persons, etc.). On the one hand, they do not have the means to question the confession of someone who takes the fall for someone else, especially when the defense lawyer backs up the defendant's story. On the other hand, this type of offense cannot go unpunished, even if the inmate is innocent and risks another appearance in court. Aware of Paolo's vulnerability as a victim of a prison gang forced to confess in order to protect himself from retaliation, the members of the disciplinary board resolved to place him in the Security housing unit (SHU) due to a lack of space in ordinary confinement and adjusted his penalty by giving him a partial suspension.

No one denies that these vulnerable individuals are susceptible to abuse or that they can be easily manipulated. In order to avoid this type of situation, they are singled out upon their arrival in detention[27] because the prison administration feels obligated to protect them (which can be achieved by putting them in ordinary confinement cells). Of course, each prison has its specificities which influence the disciplinary procedures in place and the resulting penalties.[28]

Conversely, disciplinary hearings can be somewhat expedited when they concern an inmate who is considered dangerous, who requires special supervision, and who has already been placed in the security housing unit as a preventative measure. Preventative disciplinary confinement that is intended as a response to an urgent situation, is a legally recognized exception.[29] At one board meeting, before the accused was even brought in, the chairperson presented a difficult case: a prisoner set fire to his mattress in his cell and assaulted the prison guards when they tried to remove him. Following this incident, the prisoner was taken to the hospital to undergo tests. He took advantage of the situation to try to escape by punching two policemen and evading a third. Finally arrested by anti-crime squad officers and brought back to prison, he appeared before the board, his arm in a cast, for assaulting the prison guards. In this context, interaction was kept to a minimum: after the charges were read, the prisoner, surrounded by six guards, was given the chance to speak, but had nothing to say and did not seek the assistance of a lawyer. He was then escorted out of the room during the deliberations and quickly brought back in to be placed for the maximum amount of time in solitary confinement.

In theory, any inmate appearing before the disciplinary board may be represented by a lawyer, yet, during our observations, nearly a quarter of prisoners were not. Sometimes, lawyers did not show up on the day of the hearing. Other times, the inmates themselves waived their right to representation. Moreover, not every inmate was automatically offered legal assistance on the day of the hearing: inmates who display a lack of respect to prison officials and/or guards might not be offered assistance. One chair freely admitted: "When the appointed lawyer doesn't show up and the inmate mouths off to me, or when the inmate's a lowlife, I don't offer him an appointed attorney." It should be emphasized, however, that when lawyers are appointed on the same day as the disciplinary hearing, they find themselves defending inmates whose cases they have only read a few minutes beforehand.

Although the assistance of a lawyer is a right, many inmates do not avail themselves of it in an attempt to elicit a more lenient response by admitting to all charges without searching for excuses or appearing litigious. This attitude facilitates the board's work by speeding up the process, but also by allowing its members, freed from the presence of a lawyer, more leeway in their decisions and more directness in their tone. Indeed, the absence of a lawyer may also in some cases elicit a more lenient response from the board because it reflects a desire on the part of the inmate not to contest routine offenses or slow down the proceedings.

At the prison where I carried out my fieldwork, numerous disciplinary proceedings had been pending for weeks, if not months, which, according to some prison guards and officials, weakens the effect of the penalty handed down long after the alleged offenses has been committed—and this when the number of hearings had almost doubled in a single year (from three to five per week). Three deputy directors who serve as rotating chair of the board sometimes commented on the difficulty of repeatedly having to hand down penalties: "I calculated that in ten years I had handed down 120 years in the SHU," admitted one chair. Another criticized the situation: "What's difficult is the repetition without any possibility of change in the disciplinary hearings. It's really hard getting up at 8:00 and immediately starting to punish guys for acts that happened three weeks ago, for which there is little evidence, with guys who always give you the same spiel ...." To speed things up, the director tried to establish a "guilty plea" (which also included a letter of apology, repayment of civil parties if necessary, etc.), But "we had to get rid of it because we were told that it was not adversarial enough," he added. Other solutions were being considered at the time. For instance, one head guard proposed listing the prisoners who did not want a lawyer so that they could appear together in order to save time and minimize delays.

The Moral Order of Offenses

Faced with the multiplicity of offenses listed in the Code of Criminal Procedure[30] and the internal rules of their institution, prison guards make choices according to the perceived seriousness of the incident.[31] The incident report is itself an issue. During hearings, some lawyers denounced the ensuing disciplinary proceedings which they believed to be more closely related to the offender's personal background than the evidence of their offense: "You only reported him based on his previous history and personal background" fumed one of them in a hearing.

What's more, the terms used in the incident report may or may not facilitate the proceedings. For example, when a guard asked: "Should we put down that it's hash or a brown substance in the incident report?" the deputy director quickly replied "You've got to put down that it's hash. If the lawyer questions whether or not it really was hash, you can say to him: 'OK, fine, but prove that it wasn't. You can pay for your own expert opinion!'" With the inclusion of lawyers in disciplinary hearings, the characterization of the misconduct has become an important issue, and the prison administration must now guard against the possibility that the charges brought against the inmate might be challenged.

Following an incident report, an investigation is conducted by a senior officer to verify that the inmate committed the acts he is accused of and to explain the circumstances in which the events occurred. To that end, the senior officer interviews the persons concerned and, if necessary, any witnesses, and transcribes their statements. For his part, the inmate may also provide written statements. In the course of the investigation, the senior officer will also consult the file on the inmate kept by the institution's administration as well as the online database in which authorized persons (namely prison guards and probation officers) record their observations regarding each prisoner. The senior officer can thus check, for example, if the inmate has had any prior disciplinary incidents. From the moment each inmate enters prison, his behavior is in fact recorded in this digital database with prison guards noting their slightest impressions: "We record his nervousness, if he appears agitated, aggressive, if he doesn't pay attention to what he's being told. And most of the time we're not wrong, we can tell," said one senior prison guard in charge of intake.

Once all this information is synthesized, the senior officer submits the findings of his or her investigation to the director as well as the inmate. The chairperson of the disciplinary board then decides on the merits of the hearing. Accused inmates may for their part take steps to make amends (by writing a letter of apology or offering compensation). During this phase, they are subject to moral evaluations and observations, particularly in terms of their attitude toward any victims that might allow for their punishments to be adjusted. Conversely, if a new disciplinary infraction is noted, even if it is the subject of a separate incident, a more severe punishment may be incurred.

The reporting of an offense by a prison guard remains problematic when he or she is young, inexperienced, and due to the recruitment process forced to live in an urban environment that can be very unfamiliar. One deputy director acknowledged: "We have a problem with all these guards who come from the Caribbean or small towns and aren't accustomed to city life, who are intimidated by inmates who know a lot of people in the area." Reporting depends on the subjective assessment of what is acceptable or unacceptable, especially given the fact that certain incidents like insults and threats are a routine part of a prison guard's experience. In this context, amicable arrangements and efforts to make amends on the part of the inmate are sometimes preferred, especially given the fact that this type of approach is explicitly recommended by the European Prison Rules.[32] But such arrangements may also give the impression to prison administrators that the incidents are downplayed.

Another problem concerns inmates already in isolation cells: why write an incident report in this situation? Administrators acknowledge that prison guards are tempted to ignore the actions of some inmates in order to preserve their own safety or to avoid more work for themselves. Every Monday morning in the meeting room of the administrative area of the prison, the director, his deputies, the guards responsible for different areas of the facility, the head of Probation and Reentry Services, and a representative of the medical staff reviewed the problems that had occurred over the course of the previous week. One day, after the round-up, the director presented the case of an inmate who committed a disciplinary offense for which there was no incident report. Already in isolation, this inmate splashed urine on a guard, who was given 15 days' paid leave. After explaining that this was not the first time it had occurred and that the man was a "particularly perverse inmate," the director was surprised that there was no statement or incident report. One senior officer retorted: "Because he's in isolation, the guards feel that it's pointless." He explained that, given the situation, guards do not want to report a new incident which might increase their workload without resulting in a dissuasive penalty since the inmate is already in isolation. One of the deputy directors then spoke: "The problem isn't whether or not things were done by the book. It's that nobody showed the prisoner what's what. That's the real failure. Even if everything was done by the book, who the hell cares about the rules! The problem is that nobody showed him what's what."

Besides hearings and possible penalties, administering discipline in prison also involves restoring order. And this lies at the heart of how prison life is moralized: someone should have reprimanded the inmate, should have taught him a lesson. Prison discipline is therefore subject to a formal regulatory process (rendering justice during a disciplinary hearing) and different forms of informal control (rendering justice for oneself) that guards are encouraged to implement with restraint and discretion in order to maintain their authority.

If the priorities of the prison administration regarding incident reports are clearly stated (assault, then insults and threats), what tools does the administration have to put an end to this situation?

The Pragmatic Use of Penalties

The disciplinary board has several penalties at its disposal (it is exceptional for a case to be dismissed): a warning, community service for less severe offenses, solitary confinement in a regular cell or in the security unit for the more serious ones. These last two options are the equivalent of a new sentence during the sentence. Conversely, isolation has an entire procedure unto itself, the decision ultimately resting with the director.[33] The measure is intended to protect the most vulnerable due to their mental state, their suicidal tendencies, the nature of their offense (in cases of sexual abuse), their former activity in connection with the police (informants), or their former profession (for instance, a police officer or a prison guard). But it is also intended to isolate the most dangerous inmates for the sake of prison order, deemed as such by their criminal activities (organized crime, terrorism, escape), or their perceived violent personalities (aggression against oneself, against prison guards, or against fellow prisoners).

Contrary to this measure, confinement in a regular cell or the security unit are two penalties aimed at punishing misconduct in prison. While they both consist in individual confinement, they differ in their degree of severity. There are greater consequences on the conditions of prison life for being sent to the security unit.[34] According to my observations, the main and most widely imposed measure remained sending an inmate to the latter. The reasons can only be assumed:

overcrowding makes it difficult to find ordinary prison cells that can be used for the confinement of a single inmate. Therefore, sending an inmate to the security unit becomes the preferred measure, even if it means rotating the punished inmates in and out of the block more quickly.

So disciplinary board chairs must anticipate the post-penalty and consider not only the availability of cells, but also any problems a punished prisoner might create with respect to the guard who reported the incident or other inmates who are involved. In this context, being judged by one chair or another is an important factor in the severity of penalties. Despite the rules and regulations in place, the rotation of deputy directors as chair of the disciplinary board seemed to create a lack of consistency in the penalties, which prompted one of them to declare, ironically, during an interview: "I think we should have two disciplinary boards, one mean and one nice, and we'd sort through those who get to go to one and those who go to the other."

Moreover, the penalty can be adjusted according to the activities and classes that the inmates participate in, as evidenced by the chair of this board: "When they're in the SHU, they miss their classes, so if I don't really want to punish them, I send them there over the weekend. I split their time up." But this back and forth to the security unit is much more work for the guards. When too many inmates were sent to the disciplinary cell block, the director was sometimes forced to shorten the sentences: "When there are too many cases, we let the prisoners out of solitary sooner."

In this particular prison, the main incidents reported are insulting a guard, violence between prisoners, and the possession of either a cell phone or drugs. Although there exists a gradation in the seriousness of the acts in theory—violence or insulting an agent are considered more serious offenses—in fact, it is the possession of drugs or of a cell phone that is the most severely punished because either of these two offenses is subject to a triple punishment: placement in a disciplinary cell, the loss of the possibility of getting time off for good behavior,[35] and a new court trial. In the prison system, the moral order of the offenses differs from the official scale of the penalties.

The Moral Issues and Content of Disciplinary Judgment Practices

Administering discipline in prison, from the initial incident report to the sanction itself, thus cannot be reduced to the simple application of legal texts, general guidelines of prison policies, or even the moral order of offenses that the administration attempts to impose. The pragmatic use of penalties suggests on the contrary a flexible interpretation of the texts and a use of morality which is potentially controversial among the actors who are at times in disagreement over the nature of what is fair and what is unfair. So it is worth taking a closer look at the emotional and moral issues and content of judgment practices such as they exist. How is the moral economy of punishment actualized during these judgments? I will first observe what contextual factors may be taken into account during the hearings, then I will examine the various criteria for evaluating unruly prisoners morally, before finally analyzing the role that disclosures regarding the personality and character of those guilty of misconduct has on influencing the outcome of disciplinary judgments.

Evaluating the Severity of Offenses within Their Context

In general, the chair takes into account various parameters when determining penalties. He or she must of course follow external guidelines (national and supra-national) but must also take into account the local context of his or her facility: overcrowding, location in a sensitive urban zone, organizational constraints, etc. He or she must also consider the expectations of the staff who call for more security and guarantees of protection through their unions. Prison guards expect that their incident reports are followed by penalties especially in situations in which a guard has been allegedly insulted, threatened, or physically attacked. Administrators cannot allow guards to feel like their complaint has been ignored or, as I heard in the prison hallways, that "it's always about the inmates" without responding.

The chair then evaluates the circumstances of the offense. Many verbal altercations were attributed to having a bad day. During hearings, some guards tried to downplay the seriousness of incidents in order to reduce the inmate's penalty: "We don't usually hear that from him, he just got off on the wrong foot ...." Infractions related to difficult personal situations (for example, the loss of visiting privileges or the fact of having just spent a lengthy amount of time in isolation, etc.) can result in greater leniency. When the lawyer is familiar with the details of the case, he or she may attempt to provide background information on the inmate's life which might transform the circumstances surrounding the offense into explanations in the inmate's defense:

> It is true that the defendant has a real problem in the morning, but that does not justify what he did. He left solitary on December 24, but still had another 30 days of confinement. He says that he could not control himself after such a long period of isolation and frustration. Over the past three months, he has only been housed with the rest of the prison population for just two weeks. He has not seen his son who was born recently. He has taken a number of steps to find a job. If he goes back to solitary, he'll have nothing left.

The Values and Emotions at the Heart of Evaluations

Informally, members of the board hold different criteria for moral evaluation. Discretion, obedience, submissiveness, the relationship between inmates, and the offenses they are suspected of having committed are all taken into account. Their acknowledgement of the infraction, their sincerity, their potential remorse, if not feelings of guilt, are also highlighted. The same offense (for example, insulting a prison guard after refusing to clean up from breakfast which was eaten in the cell) may be punished with a sentence of ten or twenty days in solitary confinement with the possibility for a suspended sentence depending on whether or not the prisoner acknowledges the facts. Moreover, when the events are compounded by threats, but the inmate is said to be usually calm in detention, has acknowledged what occurred, and is thought to have "played the game," he might receive ten days with a suspension even though death threats can be penalized by up to twenty days in confinement. Thus, in the case of an inmate who acknowledged having insulted and having threatened to kill a prison guard, one of the board members felt during the deliberations that the inmate "played the game, he admitted to everything, and he did not use a lawyer—that makes our work easier," prompting laughter from the other members of the commission.

The interpretation of the explanation given by the inmate for his actions may influence just how seriously the offense is perceived or portrayed. For example, although taking one's time when returning from exercise can seem a minor offense, it may also be regarded as a challenge to the authority of the staff. Ultimately, the personal beliefs of the board members tip the scale towards a penalty that is either more or less harsh depending on the intention they purportedly detect in the offender.

Interactions during a disciplinary hearing are often more than simple official warnings reminding inmates of the facility's internal rules because they are also opportunities for reprimands. These reprimands, often condescending and infantilizing, are delivered by the chair or other members of the board and frequently make use of school, military, or professional analogies. So in the case of prisoners who take their time returning to their cell block after exercise: "When you are told that rec time is over, you have to return inside. That's how it was when you were in school! What kind of school did you go to?" Or, faced with an inmate who wants a paid job in prison but has repeatedly insulted the prison guards: "If on the outside you insult your future boss, don't be surprised if you lose your job, OK?" Another chair confronted an inmate who viewed the insults and expletives he uttered on a daily basis as a normal form of communication, reminding him of the rules of community life: "That's not what living in a society is about. Society doesn't adapt to you, to your truth."

It is possible to reconstruct the moral criteria that prison administrators use to evaluate what is a good inmate. Of course, discretion and submissiveness are the initial factors in the evaluation of an inmate: "We never heard a word from that guy," or "He doesn't usually give us problems" were informal observations made in favor of clemency during deliberations. Correlated with this expectation, compliance with the rules of prison life as well as the "minimum courtesy"[36] shown towards prison officials may likewise influence the board's assessment. More generally, these traits are in line with what a "good inmate" or at least one considered capable of taking responsibility for himself should look like.[37]

Indeed, making inmates accountable for their actions means submitting them to prison order while at the same time viewing them as actors in their own rehabilitation, their own reformation, if not their own care. This accountability is stated in Article 1 of the Prisons Act of 2009.[38] One of the deputy directors explained the philosophy behind Article 1 by relating it to what he saw as a form of humanism:

> Inmates must feel that they are able to exercise a choice in order to test their responsibility. They are deprived of their freedom, and that is the perfect time for them to demonstrate responsibility and thus their personal choice, and if in the end it does not work out, then too bad! Utilitarianism pushes us to give meaning to everything, but I don't believe in utilitarianism. I think we should tell the inmates: "Take responsibility for your actions, make your own decisions about what your life should be! And if you disagree, if you want to continue leading a life of crime, then fine! In that case, you'll be punished, just like always." I think that's how you show humanism. In any case, that's my vision of humanism: respect the other insofar as the other is able to exercise choice.

By tying prison humanism to the notion of individual responsibility, it is the inmate's ability to choose that is highlighted, encouraging him to demonstrate the qualities of a moral agent, if not setting him on the path to moral reform. Thus, during one hearing, Rachid, an inmate in his twenties who made racist insults to a correctional officer, admitted: "As soon as I get angry, whatever comes out of my mouth isn't right … That's my problem. I want help for that!" The chair of the board then explicitly urged him to change his behavior, to put an end to his verbal and emotional transgressions, and to rectify the situation by making amends for the offenses he has committed: "That's what prison is for, making amends. But it's not the racist insult! You know, you can change overnight if you want." "I did it, I apologized. I am a man now. I've stopped." "Being a man means knowing when to control yourself!" retorted the chair, with the prison guard on the board clarifying: "What we are asking for first is for you to listen. Learn how to observe and listen!"

The question of managing emotions is essential to understanding the interactions that take place during a disciplinary hearing. If prison administrators explicitly ask inmates to work on their emotions,[39] their expression leads them to treat different inmates differently. It is difficult to determine the extent to which embarrassment, fear, anger, contempt, resentment, or shame may or may not impact their decisions. While research has shown that individuals are more often deemed "disturbed and dangerous" when they show inappropriate emotional behavior and prove themselves to be emotionally deviant,[40] it seems that angry and aggressive behaviors are subject to swifter disciplinary action whereas emotional control on the part of an inmate leads to a calmer, lengthier deliberation and often a more understanding outcome. Rachid implicitly recognized the need for psychological help in learning to control himself all the while believing that he had taken responsibility for his offense by apologizing for his insulting words. Many others are likely to comprehend the moral rules by which they are judged and are therefore also in a position to "game" the system (while Rachid did recognize that he had a need for psychological help, he also knew that it was in his best interest to say so). The penal institution's main objective is to ensure that prisoners have sufficiently internalized the order it imposes so that it is not necessary (for its representatives) to remind inmates in a systematic fashion of the rules and to punish them when they fail to comply; consequently what is at stake during a disciplinary hearing is bringing the inmate to display a capacity for change through tangible arguments regarding his offense, not simply to justify or excuse it.

Those who do not accept this logic of assuming responsibility reduce their chances for leniency. Inmates find themselves faced with the demand that they acknowledge what they do, why they do it, and what the consequences are for it. But, as we have seen for Paolo, the assessment of their vulnerability also comes into play during deliberations and moderates the goal of having them assume responsibility.

Uncovering the Personality of the Undisciplined

As with criminal trials,[41] hearings also seek to explore the personality of the defendant, particularly on the basis of his disciplinary record. When deciding sentences, prison authorities may take into consideration the behavioral background of inmates: those who have shown adequately compliant conduct will be favored over recurring offenders. But whereas there may be a consensus on the qualities of a good inmate, prison officials struggle to describe bad inmates. One board chair nevertheless admitted:

> I have met some truly bad inmates in prison, evil in the truest sense of the word. It's frightening to see evil embodied in someone. These are people capable of manipulation and perversion so sophisticated and so ingrained—from their criminal cases to their behavior in prison—that it sends shivers down your spine. We always think that these people must be crazy or irrational, but I don't think so. I think that's the easy way out.

The prisoners deemed to have such evil attributes (cold, calculating, seductive, manipulative, lying) are believed to be inherently dangerous and incurable. As a result, the prison staff set out to detect the signs of this type of personality beneath the apparent normality of the inmates to justify their isolation.[42] Of course, in their discourse, prison staff and administrators gradated the supposed dangerousness of prisoners—from "evil" to "low-life" by way of "nut job." This informal ranking underscores the difficulty of untangling what is attributed to the strict management of prison order from other psychiatric and criminological concerns.

Moreover, assessing dangerousness remains a relatively complex task because not all breaches of discipline are indicative of danger. For example, prison personnel experience threats on a daily basis, and not all of these threats can be truly regarded as a sign of real peril. Thus, in spite of the principles prison administrators seek to enforce, writing an incident report depends on the judgment of the guard who determines which incidents call for official action, sometimes by drawing a distinction between one-off incidents and those attributable to an inmate's recurrent behavior. At the end of his argument, one lawyer asked if the administration would transfer cases of threats to the prosecutor, to which the chair replied: "No, we only submit cases of real threats to the prosecutor because it's so easy to make threats in here." The assessment of what constitutes a "real threat" nevertheless remains very subjective. It is based in part on knowledge of the inmate's criminal record and of his network as well as on the opinions of the guards who work alongside him every day. Although threats are common, they cannot be trivialized by prison administrators as they can pose a real risk to these guards who are easy targets both inside and outside of the prison, as one deputy director highlighted: "We had a problem with an assault just outside the prison gate. He was a good officer, good at finding cell phones. They followed him when he left the facility. Four of them jumped him in the center of town. Their faces were not even covered. They had baseball bats. It was a close call."

If, upon the arrival of an inmate, the prison administration also tries to assess the potential menace that he may represent with respect to the safety of personnel and users of the prison, then this dangerousness becomes de facto one of the informal criteria for assessing penalties. During the deliberations over the case of an inmate who violently assaulted one of his fellow inmates, the criminal background of the former had an impact on the judgment. "He's no nice guy," admitted a guard on the disciplinary board, "he has a laundry list of convictions and he's in here for assault which he has been convicted of before. His disciplinary file weighs a ton." And before sentencing him to 30 days in the SHU, 15 of which were to be served, the chair acknowledged: "For him, reintegration is pointless, he was in a halfway house and did so much stupid shit that he was sent back to prison." This dangerousness, which is based on the overall assessment of the inmate and his behavior since his incarceration, actively contributes to the harsher penalization of those who are deemed a threat to the internal order of the prison facility.

The Attitudes of Inmates toward Penalties

Judgment practices are thus dominated by various expectations (compliance, sincerity, recognition of fault, etc.) which shape the penalties handed down within a space of negotiation in which the values and emotions of the members of the disciplinary board combine with an assessment of the seriousness of the offense in its context and the personality of the undisciplined inmate.

But to understand more precisely what is at play in the interactions during hearings, we must now examine the attitudes of the prisoners. Any interaction is based on respect for conventions and on the definition assigned to a situation. The bedrock of evidence on which our intersubjectivity is founded can be shaken, and everyone implements an interpretative framework in order to guide the beliefs, convictions, and perceptions of their interlocutor about the course of events.[43] During disciplinary hearings, the inmate attempts to influence the interpretation of the acts he is suspected of having committed. Here I present the five main attitudes of inmates facing punishment that I observed: submission, rebellion, supplication, apology, and denunciation.

Submission

Submission to the penalty (or acceptance) is an attitude expected by the members of the board. It reflects what they consider to be responsible behavior in contrast to the reported infraction. In fact, it facilitates and expedites the disciplinary procedure (since it does not lead to conflict when the verdict is announced or lengthy exchanges among the inmate, his lawyer, and board members). The inmate may adopt this attitude to emphasize his overall good behavior and his acknowledgement of the rules on prison life imposed by the administration. He can, for example, recognize that the penalty is the best solution for him. Thus, Paul, who appeared before the board without a lawyer after insulting a prison officer and breaking a door in the infirmary, acknowledged his offenses and the legitimacy of the penalty. Paul stated that he was feeling "down," that he felt he had been the "victim of a conspiracy." Because he did not want to "leave prison feet first," he swore that he would "cut the stupid shit out." "From now on, I'm going to keep my mouth shut," he concluded.

But submission can also participate in a form of self-protection and self-preservation. Inmates deemed vulnerable are the most likely to adopt this attitude. In admitting responsibility for an offense that they did not commit, they undoubtedly hope, as we have seen in the example of Paolo, to make the threats against them stop. This attitude may also include a request on their part that they be placed or kept in isolation. The offense in itself may reflect a desire to be separated from other inmates considered harmful, if not hostile. Isolation is then perceived as a form of protection: "It's better for me. I don't want to get into a mix-up with other inmates over some stupid shit," admitted one inmate.

Rebellion

Rebellion can take many forms, including threatening or blackmailing members of the prison administration. As it so happened, incidents of rebellion were relatively rare in my study. Nevertheless, some inmates did threaten to take their own lives if they were sent to the security unit. This was the case for an inmate accused of assaulting a guard following the discovery of a SIM card in his cell. When the verdict was read (30 days in confinement), he became indignant: "You're talking to me like that? Nobody talks to me like that! I'm not going to spend 30 days in there; I'm going to slit my wrists!" Here revolt takes the form of moral indignation with regard to the verdict which the inmate considers both unfair and infantilizing. The threat of suicide[44] can be interpreted as a form of resistance to the institution, the main concern of which is to keep the inmate alive.[45] Suicide attempts or hunger strikes are in that sense a last resort aimed at challenging the prison administration in the hope of mitigating the sanction.

Threatening to take their own lives when the verdict is read is also a chance for the inmates to try to effect a change in their relationship with the prison staff: from affective neutrality to emotional involvement through pity, remorse, or compassion. However, when one lawyer confirmed the suicidal intentions of his client, the chair responded sternly: "That's his choice." Yet despite this apparent distancing, the suicide of inmates remains a major concern for prison administrators,[46] especially given the fact that the Ministry of Justice has implemented a prevention program in response to a highly publicized wave of suicides in 2008 for which the prison administration was strongly criticized.[47]

Supplication

Inmates appearing before the board often combine internal and external reasons in their statements to account for their behavior. Some talked about their personal problems in an attempt to make the board members feel sorry for them. Another acknowledged having participated in a fight but begged for mercy: "I'll do anything you want, just please don't put me in solitary," or "It's a matter of life or death, my wife is Polish, she could run off at any time. I'm going nuts in here." Although the excuses invoked before the board were reinforced by pleas from the inmate in anticipation of an excessively harsh punishment, according to one of the three chairs, they had little impact on the verdict. "That's the story of your life, you're always going nuts," he concluded when he sentenced the inmate to time in solitary confinement.

These pleas are often over-determined by a discourse bearing all the hallmarks of psychology. The multiple psychiatric treatments have shaped the way in which many inmates narrate their experience. They are involved in a process of subjectivation that allows them not only to divorce the image they have of themselves from the image of themselves that they present to others, but also to dissociate acceptable social behavior from some of their actions which they have the greatest difficulty in explaining. For example, an inmate who called a prison guard a "dirty Jew" stated: "I apologize, I had just spent 30 days in confinement. I have major issues, I'm working on it ...." But the pleas were not always heard: "You're always saying, 'I'm working on it, I have a major problem.' It's amazing how a 22-year-old knows how to say just what we want to hear, using the language of psychologists. Keep that crap to yourself! Here, you are asked to be a gentleman." During deliberations, the chair categorically stated: "I can't deal with these permanent victims anymore. I suggest we put him in the hole for four days!" In response to these arguments, some board members therefore criticize what they perceive as a form of hyper-adaptation to prison environment. In doing so, they refuse to look with compassion on these inmates, substituting instead an accusatory tone by reminding the inmates of their responsibility.

Excuse

In opposition to the discourse of assuming responsibility which they are confronted by, inmates can invoke a number of excuses which consist primarily of erasing or distorting certain events that might discredit them, if not attributing the cause of their behavior to external conditions beyond their control. As with revolt, by soliciting an affective response from their interlocutors, inmates seek to influence the judgment by exploiting emotions. But excuses can be interpreted as attempts to minimize the gravity of the misconduct and thus to create more room to maneuver. It may involve redefining the role that they played in the alleged acts by invoking external conditions and personal explanations, for example, in the case of an inmate who insulted a guard who had informed him that it was too late to go for a walk. The inmate insisted: "I hadn't gone out and it was hot that day, my brain was fried. I was pissed. Honestly, it was all starting to add up … I'm seeing a psychologist. I'm impulsive, I'm not dangerous." The inmate thus tried to situate his behavior on a moral scale: his nervousness was not only placed in its proper context (that of isolation, loneliness, heat), but it was also relativized by comparison to a real danger that he thought he did not pose. In the case of an inmate who first did not get out of bed to collect his bread for breakfast when the guard passed by, and then insulted and threatened him, the argument was: "Put yourself in my place, I didn't have anything in my stomach, I wasn't thinking about what I was saying."

Denunciation

Prisoners may adopt attitudes considered more aggressive, especially when they implicate prison guards in the alleged misconduct. They denounce the perceived excessive power of prison officers in the same discourse of victimization and domination. "Sometimes the guards push us around a little. Sometimes they talk to me like I'm a dog. They should understand that you don't talk to a 30-year-old man like you talk to a 15-year-old boy," said an inmate who had insulted and threatened the guard assigned to his floor. In these narratives, the guards are not only accused of demeaning inmates, but also of being biased, of abusing their power by threatening to withhold the right to take a shower, to exercise, to eat, to sleep. They are also suspected of writing false incident reports or of toying with the nerves and emotions of prisoners. Similarly, probation officers are sometimes accused of speeding up or slowing down the process at will. Some inmates who have racked up numerous appearances before the board think that they are therefore victims of a conspiracy or even dramatically compare the prison to a concentration camp. "I'm here for nothing. What do you want? Do you want me to salute you? Heil Hitler!" said one inmate accused of insulting a probation and reentry counselor as well as a prison guard.

On a tactical level, what is at play here is a form of intimidation that allows the inmate to avoid questioning his background or his actions by displacing his aggressiveness onto the administration. Playing on the indignation felt with regard to living conditions and social relations in prison does not always take an aggressive form. Thus, when they appear before the board, some inmates switch from denunciation to supplication, while others limit themselves to excuses.

The attitudes of the inmates when facing their sentence demonstrate how they must learn to adapt their lives in prison, which often means smoothing over the rough edges to project a more favorable image of themselves, but also in sensitizing, impressing, intimidating, or destabilizing their interlocutors. These attitudes constitute an emotional staging[48] in which various moral components are deployed. In this context, inmates as well as members of the board display their emotions in a manner that is measured and tailored according to what is said and done by the other actors present at the hearing. In other words, they produce an emotional and moral performance.

Conclusion

Using the moral economy of punishment as an optic for studying how discipline is administered, as well as how it is received, allows for a better understanding of how the implementation of new rights opens the door to new modes of regulation through the enactment of norms and values against which the normality of inmates or their willingness to abandon a behavior considered deviant is judged. Contemporary prison discipline is no longer that put forward by Michel Foucault in *Discipline and Punish*, a discipline whose intent was to educate and correct offenders. Today's discipline is relatively superficial in nature and less directly connected to the idea of redeeming, reforming, or bettering; it has instead been increasingly reduced to a simple tool used not only for maintaining order in prison,[49] but also and above all for reprimanding undisciplined inmates in order to remind them that it is their responsibility to undertake their own moral rectification. Although the moral content of disciplinary practices has gradually lost sight of this shaping of bodies and minds in the name of humanizing the treatment of inmates, the fact remains that respect for the humanity of prisoners can paradoxically go hand-in-hand with new forms of domination and symbolic violence through infantilization, accountability, and moral rectification.

Of course, in addition to this process of humanization and the moral sentiments that accompany it (notably the compassionate aspect), the goal of reforming disciplinary procedures in prison, of redesigning the scale of sanctions, of allowing for the presence of a lawyer at the hearings is to introduce more justice and more rights in prison by regulating discipline. Yet despite the moral values underlying these reforms (notably a concern for fairness as well as for the respect of the rights of the inmates), the prison disciplinary hearing has only the appearance of a fair trial. The social uses of morals are instead reconfigured during these hearings. The moral economy of punishment consists primarily in establishing a hierarchy of the humanity of prisoners by differentiating between those who are recognized as moral agents capable of modifying their behavior and those considered more dangerous, or those deemed unable to take responsibility for themselves, if not completely irredeemable. While morals contribute to the collective regulation of relationships with others through general principles and values, they also serve to define the active components of an inmate's personality and character, from their rationality to their humanity. In this context, the disciplinary boards aim to reintegrate those inmates who are viewed as behaving in accordance with the generally held idea of what a responsible and reformable person is into the moral community: those who are able to acknowledge their fault, to correct themselves, and to develop a sense of their own dignity.

In addition, administrative memos and European policies reveal the intolerable nature of the impersonal treatment of incarcerated persons and advocate for a more respectful manner of acting toward them. But humanizing the very heart of prison, that is to say, its disciplinary process, nevertheless means retaining its core principle—punishment—while at the same time softening its methods, reinforcing the moral authority of guards, and granting moral recognition to the inmates.[50] Through the attitudes that they adopt toward the penalty incurred, inmates illustrate how they try to address this increased attention, reflecting the prison administration's contradictory imperatives: penalizing in order to maintain order, humanizing in order to alleviate prison conditions. Tensions arise as a result of the different moral conceptions that are staged during these hearings.

Between a moral economy that tends to humanize prison conditions and a professional ethos that primarily consists of ensuring safety, correctional officers develop a conception of justice as a legitimate penalty that takes into account not only the professional imperative to maintain order, but also their own interpersonal relationship with the accused inmate as well as his sense of responsibility, his perceived dangerousness, or his supposed vulnerability. What is remarkable in the interactions, given the seriousness of the alleged acts, is the indexing of the scale of penalties according to a hierarchy of the inmates' moral sense. For example, one need only highlight the good behavior of an inmate to diminish the gravity of the act of which he is accused.

The conception of justice held by the inmates is more focused on their need to have their sentence recognized as moral suffering, as well as a demand that the emotional work they perform on themselves in order to endure life in prison be acknowledged. Perhaps what characterizes the conduct of inmates appearing before disciplinary boards is not so much the transgression of a normative system than the weakening of its reach. In the interactions during the hearings, prisoners attempt to shift the debate from the dangerousness of their behavior to the seriousness of their social situation, their prison conditions, and their mental suffering.

In the course of their interactions with administrators and prison guards, it is expected—often implicitly, sometimes explicitly—that prisoners exercise their freedom to consent to proceedings that are primarily intended to constrain them.[51] They must present a different image of themselves, even if that means glossing over events that could discredit them again. The impossibility of escaping ascriptions and pressures which weigh on them invites them to change the meaning of the interactions during disciplinary hearings. Without really being able to escape the imposed framework or the normative expectations associated with it, inmates may try to introduce a new interpretative framework interfering with the one the prison administration tries to force on them. Through submission, rebellion, supplication, excuses, or denunciation, they of course attempt to shift blame and to insert distance between them and the acts they committed, the roles they played or allegedly played. But in doing so, they contribute to this moral economy of punishment, reappropriating or challenging it depending on the needs of their own construction as moral subjects.[52]

Notes

1 The disciplinary board is chaired by the director of the facility (or by delegation a deputy director or a high-ranking prison guard), who is assisted by two other committee members chosen from among the correctional officers. Since June 2011, a civilian may also become a member of the committee in place of a prison guard. The chair of the committee alone retains the power to issue a verdict; the other committee members are present only in a consultative capacity.

2 See, in particular, Kellens (2000).

3 I use the third-person singular pronoun "he" and possessive adjective "his" because all inmates in this prison were male.

4 On this point, see Fassin (2009).

5 The study was based on the observation of 21 disciplinary boards (corresponding to the judgment of 81 prisoners in total, from hearing to deliberation). The boards were chaired by one of three deputy directors at the facility and also included the presence of two other prison guard members (and sometimes a lawyer). I recorded 29 hearings relative to insulting or threatening a prison guard, 15 for possession of drugs, twelve for assaulting a prison guard, eight for refusing to return to a cell, eight for fighting with other prisoners, eight for possession of a cell phone, and one for returning in a state of intoxication. They resulted in 1,468 days in solitary confinement (of which 460 were suspended), 90 days of confinement, 60 hours of community service, eight warnings, one withdrawal of permission to leave, and eight acquittals on the benefit of the doubt, which in proportion to the rest of the year corresponds to the numbers provided by the facility's administration. These ethnographic observations were complemented by ten semi-structured interviews with the correctional officers and the administration as well as in a more informal manner by conversations with the inmates and the other prison staff. In addition, observations were made during other hearings upon which disciplinary penalties could have further consequences.

6 Prison can also be qualified as an omni-disciplinary institution insofar as the coercive forms it implements are multiple and diffuse, as Michel Foucault highlights (1979 [1975]: 238).

7 On this point, see the works of Céré (1999).

8 See Petit et al. (1991).

9 See Vimont (2004).

10 Imperial Decree of July 5, 1808.

11 See Pédron (1995).

12 On this point, see Foucault (1979 [1975]).

13 See Lascoumes et al. (1989).

14 Known as *prétoire* in French, the term stems from Roman law to designate the place where justice is handed down by a *prætor*. Today, the word designates the room where a tribunal takes place, and it is still used by old inmates and officers to designate the disciplinary board in prison.

15 On this point, see O'Brien (1988: 56)

16 The first principles of this reform stipulate that "the deprivation of liberty has for a main goal the reform and social reclassification of the convict" and that "the treatment inflicted on the prisoner outside of all corrupting promiscuity must be humane, free from any humiliation, and focus principally on his general or professional instruction and on his improvement," quoted in Céré (2001: 23).

17 The latter stipulates that "No one shall be subjected to torture or to cruel, inhuman or degrading treatment or punishment" (art. 5) and assumes that "Everyone has the right to recognition everywhere as a person before the law" (art. 6). The International Covenant on Civil and Political Rights adopted by the UN General Assembly on December 10, 1966 specifies that any person deprived of liberty must be treated with humaneness and with respect for the dignity inherent as a person before the law (art. 16).

18 These same changes can be found in the supervision of delinquent youth.

19 On this topic, see in particular works by Liebling (2000).

20 Law of April 12, 2000 on the relationship between administrators and users.

21 In the hearings observed, this representative was always a lawyer either chosen by the inmate or appointed by the committee.

22 See Rostaing (2007).

23 As Heyman writes (2000: 636): "Some moral action simply affirms existing social arrangements, but, in rectification, action is intended to change the social situation, of oneself or of others, to conform with moral ideals."

24 Marie-Hélène Lechien shows how the introduction of feminine values in the prison guard staff, whose virility was constitutive of their image "destabilizes the already blurry lines of the job of prison guard, a law enforcement profession involving rarely asserted layman's psychology associated with femininity" (Lechien 2001: 26).

25 In 2011, there were 833 collective actions (occupation of walkways, refusal to return to cells, etc.) compared to 769 in 2009; 3,230 attacks on staff, of which 109 resulted in the affected staff member's paid leave, compared to 2,825 in 2009, of which 113 resulted in paid leave; 7,825 attacks on other inmates compared to 7,590 in 2009, and four homicides compared to two in 2009 (source: www.justice.gouv.fr/art_pix/chiffres_cles_2011.pdf). In the prison where my study was conducted, a similar change in the number of procedures is noticeable, with 844 disciplinary committee hearings in 2008 (compared to 704 in 2007), 268 of which were disciplinary infractions for threatening or insulting a staff member (compared to 262) and 82 acts of violence committed against a staff member (compared to 45).

26 In this prison, 0.2 percent of disciplinary hearing committees were subject to appeal in 2009.

27 During interviews with new inmates, the head of detention is armed with a questionnaire entitled "Checklist for Assessing Dangerousness and Vulnerability." This checklist is structured around six themes based on specific categories of risk (tied to conviction, prevention, previous legal or penal history, behavioral problems, previous history of self-harm) and elements relative to the inmate's social and personal environment.

28 Constructed in the 1990s as part of a program to build 13,000 new places, the mixed-management prison (a public-private partnership) where I conducted my study presents the characteristics of a prison located in the Paris banlieue affected by violence and an underground economy. Since the prison had a capacity of 600 inmates but at the time housed approximately 800, the reasons for an inmate's presence in the prison were a faithful reflection of what was encountered within the region itself, with a strong

predominance of theft (25 percent) and drug offenses (20 percent). Specifically, there were 844 appearances before the disciplinary commission in this prison in 2008 which led to 669 sentences to solitary confinement (compared to 525 in 2007), 57 confinements in cell, and 69 acquittals. Of the 1,062 disciplinary infractions counted (not including the confiscation of cell phones, which numbered around 200), an increase in acts of physical or verbal violence was noted with 268 infractions for threatening or insulting a staff member (compared to 262 in 2007), 82 acts of violence committed against a staff member (compared to 45 in 2007), 80 for acts of violence committed against or fighting with another inmate (compared to 76 in 2007). Of the 1,545 confiscations of drugs that year, only 174 appearances before the disciplinary committed were noted. This last point reveals the difficulty in determining to whom the drugs belong during prison or cell searches, as well as a pragmatic tolerance of products which may nevertheless be considered as contributing to a certain social peace in prison. However, this argument is qualified when acts of violence between inmates can be linked to the traffic or consumption of these products (Fernandez 2010).

29 Article D. 250-3 of the Penal Procedure Code allows the head of the facility to place an inmate in solitary confinement as a preventive measure for acts that constitute a first- or second-degree offense when this measure appears to be the only means to preserving the facility's internal order.

30 First-degree offenses, which are considered the most serious (Penal Procedure Code, art. D. 249-1), include acts of violence, destructions of the facility's property, premises, and equipment, the possession or trafficking of drugs as well as attempts to escape. These infractions are also behaviors subject to possible further criminal prosecution (art. 222-7). Second-degree offenses include behaviors disturbing the facility's operations (art. D. 249-2), that is to say, insulting or threatening a staff member, participating in a collective action which disturbs the internal order, theft or fraudulent use of another's property (or attempts thereof), the deliberate destruction of the facility's property, premises, or equipment, but less serious than acts targeted in first-degree offenses, obscene acts, or acts liable to offend decency, etc. Third-degree offenses which are deemed the least serious but nevertheless provoke deliberate disturbances (art. D. 249-3) include written insults or threats directed at administrative authorities, insults or threats directed at the authorities or staff made to a third party, insults or threats made to a fellow inmate, refusal to obey or non-compliance with internal rules, etc.

31 As Chauvenet et al. have shown in their report on prison violence (2005), while the low number of recorded acts of violence between inmates may undoubtedly be attributed to "no snitching" codes, the staff's lack of motivation to report these types of infractions should not be underestimated.

32 Of course, prison guards are also liable to trump up charges (by "overstating" what occurred in incident reports, for example) in the hope that the offender will thus be punished more severely. In an aside, one administrator admitted to such: "We know that guards sometimes lie in their reports, and we know that each time it's a moral dilemma … It's annoying, annoying because each time we have to re-explain to them what prison is."

33 This measure is governed by articles D 283-1 through D 283-4-1 of the Penal Procedure Code. It can be renewed every three months. It is not properly speaking a disciplinary measure, but subjects an inmate out of concern for his protection or security to individual confinement, excluding contact with other prisoners. This measure can last for up to three months and is renewable without limit either automatically or at the request of the inmate, by taking into account the personality of the inmate, his particular dangerousness or vulnerability, and his state of health.

34 A cell in the solitary confinement unit is equipped with a bed, a sink, a toilet, and a small table. The inmate may only leave the cell to take a shower and for one hour of exercise

which takes place in an individual courtyard. He remains in his cell for 23 out of 24 hours a day. The inmate may continue to read, write, and receive visits from chaplains and lawyers, but is no longer permitted to make purchases at the commissary outside of personal hygiene products, writing materials, and tobacco. In addition, visiting and telephone privileges are limited. The penalty of confinement consists in housing the inmate individually in an ordinary cell. He may only leave for exercise, visits, and religious services.

35 Being sent to solitary confinement (even if the penalty is suspended) automatically adds half the number of days of the penalty to the end of the inmate's detention.

36 During committee hearings, as in the more general context of detention, it is a question of "inventing a form of minimal courtesy which encourages the inmates not to insult the prison guards or do whatever," as one committee chair explained to me.

37 See Bosworth (2007).

38 Article 1 of the 2009 Prison Act specifies that "the system of executing a sentence of deprivation of liberty reconciles the protection of society, the penalty of the convict, and the interests of the victim with the necessity to prepare for the incarcerated person's integration or reintegration in order to allow said person to lead a responsible life and prevent the commission of new infractions."

39 On the notion of emotional work, see Hochschild (1983); for an application of this notion in the health and social field, see Fernandez et al. (2008).

40 On emotional deviance, see in particular Thoits (1985).

41 See Fernandez et al. (2010).

42 On this point, see Rhodes (2004).

43 Goffman (1986 [1974]) analyzed this aspect of interaction in his work on the organization of experience.

44 See Goffman (1968).

45 On this point, see works by Fernandez (2010).

46 The suicide rate in French prisons (in 2010, 18 per every 10,000 inmates) remains one of the highest in Europe (Duthé et al., 2009).

47 This program includes the training of prison staff in how to spot suicide risk, the implementation of a system to detect for this risk upon intake, and the removal of items in cells liable to be used to that end.

48 Such emotional scenes can also be found in non-institutional contexts; see, for example, works by Fernandez (2011) on drug users in the streets.

49 As Chauvenet, Benguigui and Orlic (1993) state: "We note a decline in the use of discipline as a means for learning, for reform, and for modification of the self with prisons adapting to society's mores and to its conceptions of education and a shift in the meaning of discipline as it is applied to the maintenance of order to the extent that discipline constitutes nothing more than a means which is itself also in decline."

50 On this aspect, see Fernandez and Lézé (2011).

51 On incarcerated drug users, see, for example, works by Marie-Sophie Devresse (2006).

52 On this aspect, see Foucault (1988: 557).

CHAPTER SIX

Assisting or Controlling?

When Social Workers Become Probation Officers

Yasmine Bouagga

"We're just going to end up doing it like they do in the United States, with our leather jackets, handguns, and badges. We'll just become probation officers. At least, I think that's their plan." That was how one probation and reentry counselor (*conseillère pénitentiaire d'insertion et de probation*) put it when she voiced her concerns about the reforms affecting her profession. She had joined the prison administration as a social worker, having felt a call to assist a particularly disadvantaged population. But she now suspected that the new duties assigned to her had negatively altered the nature of her profession, steering it toward control and repression. Indeed, a series of changes to the regulations between the years 2008 and 2011 have succeeded in rewriting the job description of probation and reentry counselors, defining their main role in relation to sentence execution and criminological assessments. While these institutional reforms have significantly improved their status within the penal system and have granted them recognition for the important role that they play, they have also brought about a shift in their activities from social assistance to the evaluation and prevention of security issues.

Prison social workers could once think of themselves as the administration's "left hand," charged with softening the system's brutality by providing social support and organizing cultural activities.[1] However, recent reforms have given them a central role in determining the modalities of a sentence's execution and in facilitating possible adjustments through various forms of parole. Today, they are expected to provide criminological assessments of the potential dangers that inmates may pose to society as well as ensure that the penal obligations imposed on them as guarantees of their good behavior are respected (therapy sessions, treatment for addiction, payment of compensation to victims, the securement of employment, vocational training, etc.). Such changes have transformed the relationship that probation and reentry counselors maintain with the authorities as well as the image that they have of their role. Studying their work thus sheds light on a poorly understood facet of the function of punishment within the prison system: individualizing the sentence, that is to say, evaluating, shaping, and modifying the constraints exerted on the inmates.

To understand the meaning of these changes, the activity of probation and reentry counselors should be situated within the political context of the reforms of their status and mission as well as the professional field in which they are active. Their moral position within the prison administration is essentially an ambivalent one. Whereas counselors were previously seen as empathic actors whose actions were merely peripheral to the system, they have today become an integral part of that system, contributing to the institution's repressive role. This shift has considerably transformed the moral dimension of the job. Of course, social work has never been tied solely to ideas of assistance, care, and compassion: in fact, many authors have already highlighted its controlling and normalizing functions. And security is no longer maintained exclusively through repression, exclusion, and violence: on the contrary, the individualization of sentences, the consideration for individual needs, and the humanization of carceral conditions are structural features of the contemporary prison system. But care and custody nevertheless structure the types of relationships that are forged with the inmates, and by redefining social work as probation, the latest reforms have as a result blurred the lines between these two poles.

Yet these transformations in the management of prisoners should not be viewed solely through the general and normative framework of penal policies, or, in other words, the moral economy of punishment. The practical re-appropriations of this framework, the value attached to its use among the agents in charge of implementing these policies, and more specifically the moral subjectivities that make it a social reality must also be considered. For several years, sociologists have studied how subaltern agents take ownership of their institutional framework, highlighting the "law in action," that is to say, the law such as it is practiced, implemented, and on occasion perverted.[2] Policies are interpreted and put into practice by agents who are confronted with concrete problems in their interactions with their public and their colleagues. The rationales for their action are therefore shaped not only by top-down requirements, but also by the relational positions in the organization of work, by the specific backgrounds and socializations, as well as by moral values. The ethnographic approach thus allows us to analyze the shift in the ethos of counselors which took place when they were redefined as probation or parole officers as well as to understand how individual moral subjectivities account for the re-appropriation of these changes or the resistance to them.[3]

Although the notion of contradictory demands has become a topos in the sociological analysis of work situations, particularly with regard to social work, it is difficult to escape this notion when it comes to probation and reentry counselors. The paradoxes become evident when these agents are forced to consider both the repressive penal policies which have led to an ever-growing number of people behind bars as well as the requirement that they develop methods which facilitate sentence adjustments: they find themselves pressured to "get the convicts out" as quickly as possible in order to free up space. This complexity is reflected in the statistics of the prison administration, which counted as of January 1, 2014 over 252,000 persons placed under its responsibility ("persons in the care of justice"), divided between those incarcerated in prisons and those supervised in the community. While the number of inmates increased from less than 48,000 in 2001 to nearly 68,000 in 2014, the number of persons under supervision in the community or under electronic surveillance grew from 135,000 to 184,000 during the same period. Yet a lack of public funding devoted to assisting those leaving prison means that the goal of reentry has at the same time been neglected. Even though the work of probation and reentry counselors is statutorily valued, it is thus simultaneously devalued as a simple task of "influx management," a task that nevertheless remains tricky, since it is accompanied by the increasing responsibility of the agents for the future behavior of the inmates. This sort of schizophrenia of the system is a fundamental element of a counselor's daily work and of uncertainties of his or her practice and ethical positions.

In this chapter I will first explore the public policy regarding the treatment of prisoners in their historicity and in their concrete implementation in the field through the study of the profession of probation and reentry counselor. I will then turn my focus to the practical contradictions these professionals face, to the values and affects which shape practices as well as are shaped by them. It will thus be shown that anxieties about the professional identity of the counselors shed light on the tensions and contradictions of contemporary liberal ethics regarding the prison system.

A Shift from the Social to the Judicial

Locating the origins of and transformations in the profession of prison counselor within the context of public policy can help to clarify the evolution that has taken place in the penal system and, more broadly, the action of the state. Heir to prison social work, this profession as it is officially defined also signals a break with a certain vision of assistance and intervention which favors partnerships and contractual logic. It is through the normative acts which govern the work of counselors that one aspect of the transformations in the welfare state can be grasped: being the product of a charitable activity that was gradually institutionalized within the prison socio-educational service, the probation and reentry service as it was set up in 1999 assumes a more judicial function aimed at individualizing the sentence.

From Relief to Rehabilitation

In the past, social intervention in prison was the work of private charity, its need being fulfilled by religious orders or other charitable support groups which aimed to provide both material (clothing, personal hygiene products) and spiritual assistance to prisoners. This intervention was inspired by a philanthropic vision of assisting those in distress which nourished the reform movements from the moment the prison was born. Driven by a humanitarian approach, this intervention was intended to mitigate the violence of the penal institution and promote the reentry of prisoners into society after their release.

This charitable and socio-educational action was initially directed at minors, with the monitoring of young offenders beginning as early as the mid-nineteenth century. But it was in 1912 that France, inspired by progressive reforms in the United States, enacted its first probation and parole law (*liberté surveillée*). Concerns with recidivism were a constant in the debates under the Third Republic, and those who voiced their opinions on the matter were preoccupied as much with penal policy as they were with the material conditions of detention.[4] Socio-educational support, which according to the reformists was meant to combat against criminogenic social conditions (poverty, ignorance, alcoholism), fit within this perspective of treatment and social prophylaxis.

The atrocities of World War II did much to cement the position of this correctional philosophy. Post-war France was generally distrusting of closed facilities and as such favored forms of social prophylaxis instead. As part of his plan for a comprehensive and somewhat ambitious overhaul of the penal system, Paul Amor, the post-war director of the prison administration, decided to create a prison social service whose goal was to facilitate the reentry of prisoners.[5] The philosophy underlying this reform is clearly stated in the text of a memo issued on June 29, 1945: "The essential aim of the custodial sentence is the reform or social rehabilitation of the convict," and this principle implied that "the convict not feel like an outcast whom society ignores and rejects, but someone 'punished' who nevertheless remains an object of concern for society and who must be prepared to reclaim his position therein." And within this new service, the caseworker (a professional licensed by the state) was given the task of embodying society's "concern" for the prisoner and managing the various voluntary initiatives.

While some facilities were set up for the sole purpose of facilitating the reentry of the inmate with security plans based on individual behavior ("tiered plans"), it was mainly the prison social service which introduced the innovative philosophies which reformers had been trying to inject within the prison administration. This philosophy was the so-called "new social defense" (*défense sociale nouvelle*), promoted in France by Marc Ancel and Pierre Cannat, judges who supported the idea that the defense of society against crime should not lead to the exclusion of the criminal, but rather to a benevolent action allowing him to find a place within the community.[6] The concept of reform (or "moral rehabilitation" under the terms of a 1952 decree formalizing the social service) no longer reflected simply the idea of repentance, but rather that of improving the socioeconomic condition of the prisoner. Indeed, the latter was assigned a positive social role through the external intervention he would receive in terms of training and job search. Under these principles, the penal institution itself had to ensure the social reentry of the offender, in particular by adapting the length of the sentence and the conditions of imprisonment according to his specific situation.

To accomplish this task, a new professional body was quickly created in addition to caseworkers: prison educators. While the former belonged to a professional field that was independent of the prison system (an identity asserted through a state-issued degree and a code of ethics), educators were specifically devoted to the world of prison.

They were often recruited at the high school level and received only brief training at the prison administration's school, which would later become the National School of Prison Administration (*École nationale d'administration pénitentiaire*, ENAP). Officially, their mission was to "monitor and reeducate inmates in preparation for social rehabilitation" (Decree of July 21, 1949): in reality, they informed the sentencing judge of the detainee's personality. These magistrates were a key element in the system of individualizing sentences, since they had the ability to decide on any adjustments to the penalty, such as furloughs or parole. However, the practical role of educator was less to assist the court than it was of facilitator. Close to the inmates, the prison educator was kept at a distance by caseworkers who were wary of penal agents not bound by professional confidentiality. Despite the differences in their training and their professional cultures, caseworkers and educators merged into a single socio-educational department in 1979 with the issuance of a memo designating them as "social workers of the prison administration."[7] From then on, they had three main duties: to take charge of the social and family problems in the lives of the inmates, to prevent physical and mental decay due to their isolation, and to prepare them for their eventual reentry into to society.

There are very few studies on prisons that mention the role of social workers.[8] Since their numbers are small in comparison to prison guards, they are viewed as only minor institutional actors. Jacques Faget, a lawyer and sociologist, maintains that until the 1990s,

> one cannot seriously speak of social work within a closed environment. One counts a few social workers here and there marginalized by the administration, not always well accepted by the prison guards, lacking any decent means to tackle their job, overwhelmed by the task.[9]

Despite this subaltern position, they enjoyed considerable autonomy and could even embody forms of counter-power in the prison, especially during the 1970s and 1980s, when the latter became a target of the anti-authoritarian critique.[10]

The Emergence of Probation

Because prison social work was seen as part of the post-prison context and closely tied to probation's goal of promoting the gradual transition between incarceration and freedom, these changes also grew out of simultaneous developments in community corrections. The supervision of parolees was not fully conceived of as an activity exclusive to the state, but one that was largely delegated to para-statal charities. In the 1960s, supervisory committees were formed to oversee probation and to offer assistance to released offenders. Placed under the authority of sentencing judges who decided on the post-penal supervision, probation, and parole of inmates, these committees were legacies of earlier philanthropic groups from the nineteenth century and were largely made up of volunteers rather than social workers.[11]

Increasing cooperation between prison social workers and their colleagues working in community corrections attached to the courts would eventually lead to the development of a state model of prisoner reentry and the creation of Probation and Reentry Services (*Services pénitentiaires d'insertion et de probation*, SPIP). This new institution merged the socio-educational services and the supervisory committees into a single department with its own organizational structure independent of both the heads of correctional facilities as well as sentencing judges. And while this merger was primarily intended to facilitate the continuity of the follow-up between prison and community, it also reflected a desire on the part of the state to professionalize the reentry component of its penal system by establishing a clearly identifiable professional domain. This evolution corresponds to the changes occurring at the same time in the field of social work more generally, with an increasing emphasis placed on the autonomy of the individual.[12] A Ministry of Justice memo from November 21, 2000 outlining the purpose of the reform stated:

> In correctional facilities, social workers have a role of supporting incarcerated persons. Although they play a part in solving the various family and material problems associated with incarceration, they also strive to ensure that the inmate develops a plan for the short, medium, or long term allowing him on the one hand to manage a portion of his time while in detention and on the other hand to consider the modalities of his return to freedom.

The focus placed on the contractualization of the aid relationship as a way to preserve the autonomy of the inmate and promote responsible behavior stems from a reflection within the field of social work on the pitfalls of intervening on behalf of others. The use of the term "counselor" rather than "social worker" or "prison educator" is thus a semantic indicator of a shift in the conception of institutional intervention. This qualification also signals a shift in the duties of the agents from mere assistance to a more legal dimension. Although social workers and prison educators were already working under a judicial mandate and were required to submit reports to sentencing judges, their role in evaluating inmates and developing recommendations was solidified by changes in the Code of Criminal Procedure in 1999.[13] The Probation and Reentry Services from then on had two main duties: one social and the other auxiliary to the judicial system. In Article D-460 of the code, it was tasked with preventing the desocializing effects of imprisonment, maintaining family ties, and preparing the inmate for reentry. In the subsequent article, it is stipulated that the professional opinions and reports of probation and reentry counselors are intended to "provide judicial authorities and administrators of correctional services with the elements that allow for a better individualized execution of each inmate's custodial measure." While the latter component is made compulsory, the former is in fact left to the discretion of the agent based on the "profile" of the person placed in the care of justice. Because of this prioritization, probation and reentry counselors became first and foremost advisers to administrative and judicial authorities rather than to the inmates assigned to them.

A Double-edged Modernization

Emphasizing a form of "colonization of the social by the judiciary,"[14] the first studies on the impact of these reforms described "probation" less as an aid to reentry than as a kind of guarantee of the judicial system's obligations. This same analysis can also be applied to correctional facilities: in prison, the Probation and Reentry Services are crucial to guide the decisions of a system in which sentence adjustment have become increasingly important. In fact, the establishment of this service is part of a greater movement to open prisons to the outside with the goal of allowing inmates access to ordinary public services (education, health, social organizations) and reflects a political desire on the part of the state to develop forms of penalties alternative to incarceration. The transformation of prison social workers into probation and reentry counselors has therefore taken place within the context of a policy aimed at humanizing the prison, which in turn has contributed to the redefinition of professional roles, the respective scopes of the agents, and their relations with their inmate "clients."

This redefinition also occurred at a time of a profound change in the socio-demographic makeup of the profession. Although the total staff of the Probation and Reentry Services increased from 1,175 in 1997 to 3,198 in 2010 at the national level, the proportion of caseworkers recruited decreased sharply, falling to nearly zero after 2008. Once a minority in socio-educational services like the former supervisory committees, caseworkers have continued their disappearing trend. Counselors now tend to be recruited among young professionals with law degrees. The proportion of women has increased from 66 percent in 1995 to 77 percent in 2007, while the proportion of university undergraduates, that is, with four years or more of higher education, has gone from 62 percent to 83 percent. The profession has thus become more feminine, but it has also become better qualified.[15] The predominance of counselors with a law degree has in the end reinforced the general trend of judicialization of their activity.

The changes in the duties of the job as well as in the recruitment process have also widened the generational divide separating the prison educators from the new counselors. Indeed, the latter have sought to set themselves apart by their professionalism, an effort that is reflected in the words of a 30-year-old department head who described educators as "permissive hippies." Conversely, a 58-year-old, who started out as an educator, criticized the excessive distance introduced by the new recruits who do not know how to handle face-to-face interaction with prisoners, who prefer hiding in their office where they write reports, and who are incapable of meeting the social needs of the inmates: she described them as "failed judges."

These antagonisms are not just generational. They also reflect in the opposing stances taken by the two main unions for correctional counselors. While CGT-

Pénitentiaire defends the social duties of the job against an exclusively penal approach to the person being monitored, SNEPAP instead favors the profession's annexation by the more prestigious "justice" sector of public service.[16] In a programmatic document, the latter union makes use of a manifestly humanist argument in order to explain its position: "The SNEPAP-FSU today rejects the definition of the probation and reentry counselor's professional identity as social workers, because this overly vague label encompasses a restrictive conception of crime and pigeonholes the offenders according to categories based on a reductive determinism."[17] Boasting a work ethic built on the recognition of the offender as a responsible citizen, the union bases its political position on a liberal morality, using the principle of personalized sentences to promote individual responsibility and the humanization of punishment.

Experts in Criminal Sentencing?

The principle of personalized sentences enshrined within the Criminal Code allows for significant adjustments in a sentence's duration in order to adapt the restrictive measures to the personal circumstances of the inmate. If the latter presents the promise of a successful reentry and a low risk of re-offending, he may be granted additional reductions in his sentence, furloughs to prepare for his parole, or other modifications of his sentence allowing for it to be served outside the prison (halfway houses, day release, electronic monitoring, etc.).[18] This principle of sentence personalization is based on an assessment of the individual's "profile," for which the responsibility falls largely on the probation and reentry counselors.

The March 19, 2008 memo on the tasks and methods of Probation and Reentry Services defined counselors as "in charge of the implementation of measures and sentences." Although this text does mention the socio-educational dimension of their action with regard to the employment, training, or "resocialization" needs of the inmate, it also specified their particular area of expertise: "concerning the criminological aspect, consideration must be focused on the criminal act [*passage à l'acte*], the identification and treatment of risk factors for recidivism, and on the interests of the victim." Counselors were deeply critical of the vocabulary used in the memo, seeing it as stressing the role of individual choice in the criminal act at the expense of its social context and fearing the increasing reference to criminology in their job description and training. In their view, the changes indicated a shift toward more standardized and positivist methods of assessing criminal behavior. Whereas the French model had long favored interviews, the experimental introduction of the "Diagnostic for Criminological Assessment" in 2010 was influential in promoting the use of checklists. Counselors resisted this evaluation tool. Although it was inspired by the European Penitentiary Rules rather than the actual checklists in use in the United States or Canada, French counselors felt that their responsibility in preventing recidivism had been transformed into risk management.[19] As evidenced in the quote at the beginning of this chapter, counselors felt that their role was shifting toward one of repression, resembling police work—with or without the accessories like the "badge" and "handgun" mentioned by the counselor who feared that the French system was sliding toward an "American" approach to probation.[20]

Professionals were also disapproving of what they saw as criminological assessment's tendency to rationalize the way in which they handled their clients. The "Diagnostic for Criminological Assessment" defined five categories or "segments" of the prisoner population, each of which differed in the degree of follow-up individuals within the group received from the counselor. As one counselor explained,

> There are five segments. Each prisoner has to fit in one segment. Segment 1 is for those who meet all the criteria for a successful reentry into society, while segment 5 is for those for whom nothing can be done: either he is in pre-trial detention or he is not fully cognizant because he is mentally ill … so nothing will be done for him. It's really scary!

Her comments are reminiscent of the criticism that sprung from the "new penology" of Malcom Feeley and Jonathan Simon. According to these authors, this nascent penal philosophy is less concerned with how the criminal is treated than it is with the production of techniques meant to identify, categorize, and manage dangerous groups. It is a form of governmentality which has been set up in order to manage systemic risks and which offers fewer services but more tools for modulating control. It is oriented less toward social engineering (the transformation of the individual, which was the main goal of penal welfarism) than it is toward punitive evaluation. This perspective thus not only corresponds to "technical choices" but also to "cultural and political choices" in line with a now dominant philosophy which proves less favorable to the transformative action of the state, to which is merely assigned a function of holding individuals accountable.[21]

The evolution of the activity of prison counselor thus reveals greater shifts in the transformation of state action. Individual attribution of responsibility and systemic risk management correspond to two features of the contemporary liberal state: an emphasis on responsibilitization and an emphasis on the rationalization of public intervention. They also reflect what has been described as "new public management," a process which entails the downsizing of staff in some areas, the refocusing on an exclusive "core business," and the controlling of action by means of indicators and performance targets.[22] For the agents, the two political orientations seem to pull them in opposite directions: individualization and mass management; reentry and essentialization of "risk." Reforms in the missions of prison counselors therefore fit into multiple rationales and reflect complex transformations in the welfare state. In these mutations, the position of street-level agents is rendered uncertain, if not uncomfortable. How do they reconcile demands to individualize the sentence with demands to manage the risks in their actual practices? How do they position themselves with regard to the inmates when their role is as much one of assistance as it is of control?

The Individualization of the Sentence in Action

One summer morning in 2009, a counselor with three years of seniority and a background in law was filling out the social forms for inmates who had arrived at the facility the day before. The inmate, a 26-year-old of North African descent, was already familiar with the facility: it was his third time there. The counselor asked him the questions listed on the form: marital status, family situation, health condition, personal background. The concern in her voice was evident. In the course of the interview, she offered to help the man contact his family and envisaged solutions for the period following this imprisonment. For his part, the inmate stated that he lived with his mother and worked as a stock boy at a local supermarket. Despite being a trained plumber, he had not been successful in finding a job in the field because he was not licensed. He did not explain the reason for his "relapse": "I don't know ... I've got family problems. I often just stay at a hotel. I'm in here for possession of stolen goods. I did have stolen goods in my possession, but the charge was actually reclassified as theft, and that's on top of other sentences for previous offenses." Due to the presence of these offenses on his record, the theft had incurred a mandatory minimum sentence as well as triggering the execution of his suspended sentences. As a result, he had in fact received a rather stiff sentence. Because of this, the inmate was considered a "bad client": he had no stable job and no permanent home since he was at odds with his parents. Because he had also been granted day release during a previous incarceration, his case was "complicated." The counselor explained: "Listen, you should pay attention because you're now a repeat offender. I don't want to lecture you, but you do run the risk of getting yourself in some serious trouble, and it's really not worth it." She concluded: "I suggest you take some time to think things over. Go see psych services." "Psych services?" responded the prisoner. "Yes, to focus a little," answered the counselor. The prisoner was doubtful, but said he would take the first step. At the end of the interview, the counselor told the prisoner that when he would be assigned to a specific counselor, he would be able to ask to take classes and put in a request that his sentences be served concurrently, but that it would take several weeks for this to happen.

As part of their duties to evaluate the needs of the inmates, to help them maintain family ties, and to steer them toward the adjustment of their sentences, probation and reentry counselors meet with every one of them at their arrival. European Prison Rules provide specific recommendations on the organization of dedicated spaces and services in prison facilities for incoming inmates. Having inherited the functions of prison social workers, counselors are assigned a key role in humanizing conditions of detention. It is an objective with vague boundaries related to consideration for both the physical and the psychological "welfare" of the prisoner.

The Caring Figure in Prison

Despite the evolution in the duties assigned, the fact that counselors are mostly women in a world still dominated by men contributes to their identification by their colleagues as a "maternal" center dedicated to the care of the inmates. One of the specific activities of counselors in prison is to conduct individual interviews with the inmates. While prison guards often described themselves as simple "turnkeys" who open and close doors without taking the time to build relationships with a public that is kept at bay for safety reasons, counselors enter into an intersubjective relationship with the inmates through this activity.

The difference in the role of counselors is marked on a daily basis by small gestures that reveal a distinct professional ethos. For example, whenever they meet with the inmates to interview them, counselors shake their hands, accepting through this courteous gesture a physical contact that is off limits for correctional officers (except in a situations of coercion). Counselors express their desire to build with the prisoners a relationship of trust that is distinct from the power dynamics which characterize the relationships between guards and inmates. When confronted with tensions in the prison, officers sometimes even call counselors, who thus embody protective values that mirror the custodial functions of prison guards. They comfort distressed prisoners, make contact with the family, check that inmates have access to basic items, and listen to their complaints. In doing so, they take on a traditionally feminine role in the gendered division of prison work. But increasingly prevalent within the discourse of counselors is an insistence on distinguishing themselves from caseworkers whom they denounce as being too lenient, too caring. Statements like "We are not nannies" or "We are not caseworkers" show how their role as caregiver is now enacted with some emotional distance.

In one instance, a counselor was called to intervene in a situation involving an inmate who according to the guards "had lost it" because he no longer had any visiting privileges, had not received an expected sentence reduction, and feared that his family would be evicted from their apartment for not paying the rent when the winter was over.[23] The counselor reminded him that if his sentence was extended and his visiting rights revoked, it was because his wife had smuggled in drugs to him during a visit, an infraction for which they were both convicted in immediate appearance trials and for which he had received an additional 15 days in detention and she a suspended sentence. The tension escalated; the inmate shouted: "I want to see my children, you've got to understand!" To which the counselor responded: "We do understand! We do have hearts, you know!" Upset, the inmate pounded against the wall. The counselor proposed a solution to appease the situation: another family member could bring the children to see him. She explained the procedure, filled out the paperwork, and ended the meeting. Privately, she explained that the inmate was "not really violent," just "very fragile." In fact, he had attempted to commit suicide the week before. Yet she also refused to take him too seriously, saying that he "was acting up" to get what he wanted, even if in reality "he's lost one too many brain cells" from doing drugs.

But anyone showing an empathetic stance is immediately suspected of naivety both by the prison guards as well as the counselors themselves. In the present case, the counselor made it clear that she did not want to be seen as a maternal figure for the prisoners: "A counselor is not here to make up excuses, but to put things back in their place, to talk with people who have made other choices or who find themselves having to make difficult choices, but no counselor-mom, no Sister St. Counselor!" Although she considered the caregiving responsibilities of her job as degrading in light of her professional qualifications, she nevertheless fulfilled her duties since the prison also has an obligation to protect persons under its care. But she did view her evaluative responsibilities as being more noble because they were associated with judicial decisions.

In her research on the impact of the health reform in prison, Marie-Hélène Lechien shows how an institutional demand to improve care for prisoners has "unthought of" consequences in terms of changing work situations and definitions of tasks, not only for the caregivers, but also for the other staff working in the prison, especially the guards. Tensions around the definition of work highlight "the sustained systems of opposition which structure the care for the most disadvantaged sections of the working class," that is, the opposition between security and more humaneness. At the same time, they also qualify these oppositions.[24] Thus, probation and reentry counselors try to distance themselves from the functions of care: "We're not social workers, we are judicial professionals" as one department head in prison put it.

Bureaucracy at Work

"The service which executes a sentence and decides on the modalities of its execution and its individualization is in fact the Probation and Reentry Services"; stated a SNEPAP union representative summarizing the actual work of the counselors. This valued aspect of the job consists in the writing of plans, reports, and opinions destined for sentencing judges to facilitate his or her decisions regarding the adjustment of sentences. The Prisons Act of 2009 expanded the powers of counselors in this matter, allowing them to propose inmates eligible for automatic sentence adjustments like electronic monitoring at the end of a sentence, or to circumvent the formal constraints of adversarial proceedings before a sentencing judge by using a simplified legal procedure to which the magistrate simply stamps his or her approval. These provisions in theory permit counselors to play a central role in separating those for whom imprisonment is necessary because they pose a danger to society from those who can be monitored outside. The final decision still rests with the sentencing judge, but he or she relies heavily on reports written by counselors, so much so that the supervisory staff of the Probation and Reentry Services believe they can eventually replace sentencing judges.

In theory, the counselor's inherent skill is to provide a response "tailored" to the individual, to implement individualized support, and to propose a relevant plan in relation to the specific circumstances of the inmate. For example, a counselor with two years' experience on the job and a background in social work met with a young, 22-year-old man of African descent who had been a professional soccer player for three years before his career was cut short by a conviction for several offenses. The man was seeking to be released under electronic surveillance. The counselor informed him that she did not support his request: "This is your first incarceration, and a lengthy one, and your soccer career is all but over, so it's better for you to come up with a more reasonable plan." She deemed the electronic monitoring inappropriate given the profile of the inmate, whose new career plan was to work for a cleaning business (his family had helped secure the job offer for him). She proposed a more restrictive measure which was to last longer than the remaining time of his sentence: day release. He would work during the day and return to the prison to sleep at night. "That way you'll be better trained, you'll get a fresh start," she explained. The counselor was required to devise a "sentence plan" that included any possible sentence modifications based on an assessment of the specific circumstances of the inmate. But as she explained to me, she was only able to come up with this solution because the prisoner had been incarcerated for more than a year already. For those serving shorter sentences, she did not have enough time to set up any reentry strategy.

The issue of time constraint is a recurring theme in the counselors' descriptions of their job. Each one of them was responsible for 80 to 120 prisoners. As one phrased it, "We are just doing population flow management. We can't deal with people individually. So what we do is decide whose case is more urgent, who should be prioritized. It's an everyday moral dilemma. But you have to do triage." However, counselors do not determine what is urgent completely on their own. Court appearances, parole hearings, commissions deciding whether or not to grant time off for good behavior or furlough—these judicial activities impose their own rhythm on the counselors who must also evaluate the needs of the prisoners according to this same rhythm. While counselors always felt overwhelmed by the number of reports they had to write, inmates tended to feel neglected or even abandoned. It is not uncommon in overpopulated prisons for a prisoner to wait weeks or even months before meeting with his counselor.

Although intended to be "tailored" specifically to the inmate, the work of individualizing sentences more often than not translates into the Taylorized management of influxes in the prison population, with counselors relying on a relatively superficial knowledge of the personal situation of each prisoner. In the day-to-day work, it is the "relationship on paper" that has superseded face-to-face time with the inmates. In most prisons, counselors' offices are located in the administrative section of the facility next to the accounting and management offices and away from the "detention" area where inmates are housed. The offices of the former are equipped with computers connected to the different databases used to manage the prison population. And the more the written work increases, the less contact there is with inmates. As a result, the interview serves as an adjustment variable in the amount of time worked. In the prisons studied, direct interaction with prisoners took up no more than one hour in the daily routines of the counselors. The importance attributed to written work only further distanced them from their public with whom direct familiarity was once the hallmark of a social worker's professional expertise. The individual one-on-one work with inmates was thus threatened by a trend toward bureaucratization.

Thus when counselors did not have enough time to meet with inmates who were requesting time off for good behavior, they would instead send them a questionnaire before drafting their reports for the request. Sometimes, the counselors would conduct brief 5 to 15-minute interviews during which the inmate would be asked if he had participated in any activity that would show evidence of his efforts at rehabilitation (academic classes, vocational training, prison work, therapy sessions, etc.). When the inmates had questions or asked for assistance, the counselor would postpone handling the matter until a later time.

On one occasion, a counselor met with an inmate who had been convicted of petty theft and entering the country illegally. The inmate's French was poor, but the counselor felt that he understood enough to fill out the questionnaire and did not call for an interpreter. She indicated that he would be released at the end of the month and that since the court had ordered that he be deported, he would be sent to an immigrant detention center pending his eventual deportation. Given the backlog in the system, she felt that she did not have the time to take care of his administrative situation and that Cimade, a non-governmental organization would, if need be, take care of him while he waited at the detention center after his release from prison. Having joined the prison administration after four years of studying economics and working in the private sector, this counselor seemed to have internalized official demands to develop objective methods for assessing the situations of the inmates more than any of her colleagues. In fact, she had been well reviewed by her superiors who deemed her working methods to be very effective: "To deal with cases more quickly," she explained, "I developed a clinical procedure: I identify the prisoner by the crime committed, his age, his work background, his family history, and that lets me sort them into categories." Her systematized forms of judgment are similar to the policies implemented by the prison administration in 2011: the prison population is sorted into "segments" according to the degree of staff-time required.

The priorities in terms of inmate supervision are defined according to the criteria for adjustment in the execution of sentences: those whose sentence is likely to be adjusted see their probation and reentry counselor more frequently than those who are not close to any legal deadline or who have not yet been convicted. In the facilities studied, those awaiting trial are not assigned a counselor and cannot meet with a social worker unless they submit a written request stating their reasons. In theory, criminological assessments must allow for adjustments in the amount of time and attention invested by the counselors in evaluating the dangerousness of the inmate. But public policies meant to prevent recidivism in dangerous individuals seem ill-suited for their actual clients. In fact, the inmates were rarely hardened criminals and were often locked up for non-violent offenses like theft, drug possession, or driving without a license. In light of the counselors' newly assigned responsibility of assessing criminological dangerousness, this public was seen as "not the good one."

Facing Precarity

In addition to these factors, there are also economic, social and legal issues. Most sentence adjustment measures require that the inmate show "promise of reentry" and in particular, a stable job and a place to live. But the prison population is composed mostly of young men who lack both stable jobs (they are either unemployed or work temporary jobs) and qualifications, and whose precarity stands in the way of having their sentences modified. While a majority live with their relatives, a significant portion of them do not even have a stable place to live. In reaction to a question on the equal treatment of inmates by the Probation and Reentry Services, a counselor stated: "Of course not everyone's treated equally. If the guy's homeless, there's definitely nothing we can do. If push comes to shove and the person works hard, we might be able to find a placement for him, but there aren't enough halfway houses and homeless shelters." The powerlessness in situations of social precarity is accepted and internalized by counselors who adapt accordingly in their involvement with inmates. This is the case for foreigners in particular. Despite an overall decline in incarcerations for immigration offenses, due to the fact that specific detention centers have been opened for them, the proportion of undocumented foreigners remains significant in correctional facilities located in the Paris region (about 30 percent). Lacking legal status in France and sometimes slapped with deportation orders, these prisoners do not have access to the tools of reentry and are therefore often sidelined by counselors, even though many will reenter French society after their release.

Far from being a borderline situation, the presence of particularly precarious publics on an economic, social, health, or administrative level is a central issue in the daily activities of counselors. At once deviant and vulnerable, these precarious publics lie at the heart of the practical problems faced by the institution and its agents, as well as the solutions proposed to circumvent these problems and the frustrations expressed in the field. Faced with a population for whom they lack resources to provide them access to employment, housing, or means of regularizing immigration status, the counselors implement practices that are de facto unequal in their treatment of precarious publics. Such differential management, born of pragmatic constraints, favors those among the inmates who enjoy stable social situations (employment, family, housing). These practices thus contribute to the perpetuation of the inequalities at work throughout the criminal justice system.

Frustration arising from this inability to resolve the social problems of the inmates explains in part the prevalence of professional grievances lodged with government regulators and the denunciation of the "lack of resources." Counselors have few tools at their disposal for reentry, be they internal (places in prison training programs or jobs are hard to obtain, and their allocation is the responsibility of a multidisciplinary committee on which, at many facilities, the detention personnel have the upper hand) or external (outside partners are essentially non-profit organizations whose activities are hampered by cuts in public subsidies).

Technicians without tools, counselors focus their efforts on developing a critical rather than supportive expertise. The aid relationship in practice becomes more complicated. Those among the inmates who are in need of the most assistance, who present problems that require a major effort are described as "difficult" cases, as "drags" who slow work down, or in the words of one young counselor, as "sea urchins": thorny cases in which the social disabilities and psychiatric troubles just pile up. Conversely, the (rare) "good clients" are those people who "get it together," who "take steps," who "get a move on," that is to say, inmates who do not have a passive relationship with their detention, who know how to "invest" their time in training programs, jobs, social and cultural activities, but who also have the necessary resources (in terms of professional skills and social networks) to "develop a release plan," to find a potential employer, and to secure housing.

The work of probation and reentry counselors is primarily seen as supporting inmates along their path toward autonomy: this support is defined in contrast to assistance, supposedly creating a relationship of dependency. This paradigm is common to all areas of social work, redefining the content of the activities performed by agents of social intervention. Tasked with "responsibilitizing" their publics, social workers have seen their duties shift more toward control rather than direct intervention.[25] Because the counselors open the door to rights guaranteed by the welfare state (like health insurance, help with finding employment, family allowances, etc.), their duties are more bureaucratic, if not more legal in nature— a change highlighted by the fact that their job is not strictly speaking related to "welfare" and that they function mainly as auxiliaries of justice.

Successive reforms of prison social work have caused a gradual shift in the profession from a relationship of providing assistance to the inmate to a duty of assessing his profile on behalf of the judge. Although there has been no abrupt break with the previous practices in use, the change is still visible in the organization of what is both judicial and bureaucratic work. Within the prison, counselors are poorly identified and occupy an uncomfortable position. They do not have a specific outfit that allows them to be easily distinguished by the inmates like the uniforms worn by correctional officers. They are part of the "prison staff," but fall under the purview of a hierarchy situated outside the facility. Moreover, their role is itself ill-defined. The ambivalence of their situation reflects a difficulty on their part in adjusting their professional ethos to changes in their missions. When they mention the difficulties of their job and the diversity of their responsibilities, they implicitly refer to conflicting loyalties—towards inmates and judges. This recurring theme is formulated in terms of uncertainty about their professional identity. The unease that they feel reflects their uncomfortable position in relationship to their work. In addition to their multiple duties, they are faced with two distinct moral demands. As one young counselor, who was trained in law with three years on the job, stated: "You're helping, showing empathy, listening and at the same time you're also evaluating and supervising." It was difficult for her to reconcile a response to the humanitarian demand that she alleviate the violence of the constraints related to the detention with the demand that her evaluations be individual and objective.

The Moral Work of Counselors

One day, a debate broke out in one of the Probation and Reentry Services offices. A counselor had received a call from a correctional officer troubled by an inmate who was about to be released, but said he did not know where to go and did not have enough to pay for a hotel room; the guard was surprised that no provisions had been made for the prisoner, a drug addict who was homeless and an undocumented immigrant. The counselor who had answered the call turned to the colleague who had been this inmate's caseworker, asking if she contacted an emergency shelter. The latter explained that she had recommended that he dial the homeless hotline when he would be released. This is what the guard in charge of discharge repeated to the inmate as he handed him some meal vouchers and public transportation tickets. In the office, the debate raged on between the counselors over whether or not this type of intervention was one of their duties. The one who had answered the phone believed that as prison social workers, counselors should intervene in situations of social distress whereas her colleague believed that the inmate who had spent the last days of his sentence in solitary confinement and had used all the money he had on his prison account to buy cigarettes did not deserve any special assistance.

Illustrating the divisions mentioned before about the different conceptions of the job that exist within the service, this scene draws attention to the moral work of counselors, both in terms of the specific form of intervention which requires inmates to adopt "good" behavior and of the way in which the relationship of the counselor to "obligations" and "duties" shapes her approach to her work. The place of morality and of moral sentiments in prison is complex. Although it seems obvious (since prison is about setting offenders on the straight and narrow), it is highly problematic for those whose job it is to manage prisoners. At the time prison social services were created, caseworkers had the role of ensuring the "moral reform" of an inmate, but this terminology disappeared in the 1980s in favor of the inmate's "reentry." Devalued by those who criticize the dominant morality and social work as a normalizing practice, the term "moral" gradually fell into disuse, disappearing from the professional vocabulary of intervention in prison. In interviews, probation and reentry counselors explained that they had learned during their training (either at school or as interns) to refrain from making moral judgments: by provoking subjective interference in their work, these judgments would taint their actions with the suspicion of amateurism.

Yet the observation of the practices of counselors reveals the importance of moral subjectivity in how they manage inmates on a daily basis: the exhibition of concern or disgust, listening to the prisoner, or deploying technical vocabulary to distance him or herself from the inmate differs depending on the situation. The practices reflect a sense of justice specific to the institutional context (which consists, as we have seen, in mitigating the violence of the punishment while at the same time emphasizing the responsibility of the person) as well as to the various interactions of the individuals. To understand how counselors appropriate or not the moral framework imposed on them by reforms in the penal system, it is interesting to examine their interactions with the inmates and the conflicts that may arise due to the uncertainties with respect to the professional obligations of the counselors: a duty to be loyal and a duty to assist.

Distance and Sentiment

The notion of social work is morally connoted as involving a form of sympathy with regard to the person being helped. The fact that counselors "side" with the inmates is considered commonplace in prisons, although such a position is far from systematic. Since they prepare requests for furloughs or for sentence reductions and then present them to the judges in meetings called "sentencing commissions," counselors find themselves playing the functional role of "attorney" for the inmate, while the role of society's defender is assumed by the prosecutor. In fact, counselors rarely oppose requests openly, preferring pre-situation avoidance strategies (like trying to dissuade a prisoner from making his request) or post-situation compromises (like suggesting a deferment rather than a rejection). The reports are therefore rarely unfavorable to the inmate. Yet this stance cannot be expressed too explicitly. The comments made by counselors in their reports are simple ("proper behavior in detention," "earnest release plan"); they do not "plead" in favor of the prisoners whom they supervise and the concern for "saving face" in front of the judges imposes a certain restraint in what they say.

Regarding the issue of the proper distance to maintain, the practices of the agents vary according to their professional socialization and the situation in which the interaction takes place. Generational differences among them in connection with the profound changes in their backgrounds and training is important. However, professional distance cannot be reduced to a distinction in terms of seniority. While a former educator may be used to working in a prison, to entering the cells of the inmates, and sometimes even having a cup of coffee with them, and a recently recruited counselor may tend to conduct a formal interview in an office, using the computer screen to distance herself from the inmate, other elements play a significant role and individual positions intersect with political sensibilities regarding the meaning of social work.

In the context of the discussions on the evolutions in the profession of probation and reentry counselor, the reference to social work serves either as a model or as a foil when staking out an ethical position with respect to the public of the prison. For example, the union SNEPAP advocates for a clear positioning of the job in the judicial field, out of "respect" for inmates. According to a representative of this union, who had five years' seniority and was a law school graduate, to say that a counselor fulfills a social function or is on the "good side" is hypocritical. Counselors "express their opinion to the sentencing judge regarding a request for a furlough or sentence adjustment": in this perspective, maintaining a relationship based primarily on assistance would reveal a lack of honesty and lack of clarity. For her, to claim to be a social worker would be to lie about the reality of her job. It would lead the prisoner to believe that she is on his side (on the non-repressive side) when at the same time she produces evaluations for the judge that are the determining factor in decisions about the sentence.

At the heart of these distinctions lies not only the question of the relationship with the inmate but also of the moral sentiments and their place in how the job is performed. Those who have a social vision of their function tend to defend a relationship in which feelings of compassion can exist, while those who believe it falls within the field of justice tend to dismiss such subjectivity, which they regard as unprofessional. The opposition between these two perspectives (casework vs. management) is formulated through the assertion of a particular relationship with the inmate—engaged or distanced.

Nevertheless, these oppositions must be nuanced. On the one hand, a number of law school graduates went into a profession which straddles the line between the "legal" and the "social" precisely to have "human contact." This was the case for the counselor cited earlier who valued empathy and listening. On the other hand, the line between the "legal" and the "social" is less clear than it would at first seem. Social professions have in general experienced transformations similar to those of probation and reentry counselors. So among the "new" generation, those who have degrees in social work demonstrate professional practices not very different from their law school colleagues. In fact, the relationship a counselor has with emotions and moral sentiments is tied to the different professional socializations, but also to personal history and experiences more or less favoring the expression of sympathy toward the inmates, the use of comforting words or humor, the maintaining of cordial relations with the family, and the recourse to small arrangements or adjustments to facilitate daily life in detention.

Lecturing or Preventing

Maintaining a more distanced relationship with the prisons also conforms to a certain philosophy of social work which, in the name of respecting the individual's autonomy, denounces the risk of moralization and privileges a relationship built on contracts. Although paradoxical in an institution as restrictive as prison, the vocabulary of contractual relationships has made great inroads into both the administration as well as the practices of the counselors. Inmates are encouraged to take ownership of the direction of their sentence through "sentence plans" and other contractual arrangements.[26] The new methodology of social work thus requires the "responsibilitization" of the inmate, his recognition as an equal on a statutory level, and a formal agreement in the perspective of his eventual reentry.

As a result, during follow-up interviews, counselors must work on the prevention of "acting out" and on encouraging a "sense of worth," that is to say, getting the inmate to reflect on his own responsibility and to accept his punishment. The counselors are also required to focus on the criminal offense when physical violence was involved, particularly in cases of sexual assault as their reports must indicate that the prisoner has "worked on his acts." Yet counselors often feel uncomfortable broaching the topic, claiming that they are poorly trained to address such psychological issues. For example, in the case of a prisoner convicted of rape who maintained that the sexual act had not been forced, the counselor showed signs of discomfort and ended the meeting by recommending that the inmate reflect on "signs of consent." The combination of legal and psychological vocabulary has thus replaced the discourse of morality. By focusing on "the acts," the inmate is made to reflect on the moment of his transgression.

But the composition of the prison population leaves them with little opportunity to "dig into" these acts, primarily because the workload entails a reduction in the amount of time spent face to face with the inmates, but also because the counselors do not spend much time focusing on acts such as theft, drug possession, driving drunk or without a license, which represent the majority of the offenses. In practice, counselors prefer to focus on preparing the prisoner for the difficulties he will face after release and on discussing solutions to prevent relapse.

Despite holding offenders accountable for their acts, "lecturing" them is perceived as improper, too intrusive, at odds with the liberal ethics that paradoxically pervade the prison. One counselor stated after an interview with an inmate convicted multiple times for theft and possession of stolen goods: "It's his job to do the lecturing!" She explained: "He's caught, he returns to prison. So I'm not going to waste my time pretending to be his mother. That would mean that I get too emotionally involved." Lecturing is identified here with a maternal practice, that is to say, both asymmetric and emotional. Such a rejection of the moral dimension of the work seems surprising in an institution for which moralization remains one of the major social functions. This discourse may, however, be understood if we compare it to the emphasis placed on the technical and legal aspects of handling inmates today. Characterized by detachment, formalness, and—paradoxically given their duties—a lack of moral qualification of the criminal acts being punished, this apparent indifference is also used by counselors as a way to protect themselves against the emotional strategies of the prisoners to avoid being "manipulated" by them (in the words of some counselors), or to skirt the issue of social distress for which they have little in the way of a response.[27]

However, there is another aspect to moral detachment. It allows counselors to implement evaluation practices. Thus, those who in their interactions with inmates adopt an attitude of neutrality and distance and favor using acronyms and legal jargon in their conversations rather than colloquial language are also those who have internalized to a greater degree official demands that they develop methods for the objective assessment of inmates and their individual situations. It is nevertheless worth wondering to what extent this apparent detachment effectively eliminates moral judgments on inmates. Isn't it instead a sign of rejection? After a follow-up interview with a young man of African descent who was applying to have his sentence modified and who had asked whether the counselor had received his promise of employment in time for the hearing before the judge, the latter justified her refusal to answer his question by explaining that he "would never be able to reintegrate into society." Although the meeting had been very cordial and the polite young man had handled himself well, she thus became aggressive, proceeding to explain to me: "He's domineering. He uses intimidation to get whatever he wants. He's that typical macho guy from the banlieue. But it's not going to work." Since this stigmatizing judgment was not based on the nature of the offense, which was only a theft, and since it was also accompanied by the counselor's visible display of indignation and disgust, it could be interpreted as an affective reaction of rejection, reinforced by the stigma tied to the social, ethnic, and gender background of the man. While resorting to a "clinical procedure" supposedly dispels emotion, her evoking of the stereotypical guy from the banlieue shows how social prejudices have a moral as well as affective dimension. Far from being neutral, legal technicality is in fact an instrument of moral work for counselors.

Alleviating or Contributing to the Punishment?

The assessment of the inmate's merit constitutes a stumbling block in the professional ethos of the counselors. While the measures described as falling under the "new penology" understood as differentiated risk management seem to leave little room for the moral evaluation of the individual, the logic behind the individualization of sentences is actually based on the incentivizing and rewarding of inmates. Thus, additional sentence reductions depend on an assessment of the merits of the convict (although the current conditions for examining applications tend to reduce the emphasis on moral reform) as do sentence adjustment (which is not granted when the convict "does not make sufficient efforts"). Counselors, who do not have the upper hand in decisions regarding work placement and training in the prison, must nevertheless assess the reentry efforts made by inmates and how they "get it together" to achieve this goal. A counselor explained that in evaluating the behavior of inmates, she was "not mean": she primarily took into account the work the inmate had done, the efforts he had made to "prepare for his release," but "the guy who doesn't care" will be described as undeserving. Between the moralization of the inmates and the justification of their abandonment, the use of "merit" is sometimes ambiguous and reflects different appropriations of conflicting discourses by pitting humanization against responsibilitization,[28] as was seen in the case of the prisoner who without a place to go upon release did not want to leave the prison and whose counselor felt that a lack of help constituted a just reward for his bad behavior.

In the end, is it a question of moralizing the inmate through a reminder of the norms or of moralizing the institution through forms of compassion? Some counselors maintain that they remain humane and sensitive to the individual fate of inmates. A counselor trained in law, who joined the profession out of a "social calling," explained:

> You see, this morning when the newcomers arrived, I had this kid, my poor little depressed boy. His case dated back to 2005. He said: "I don't understand why I'm here. I didn't get any summons." He told me: "This stuff's so old I don't even know what I did anymore!" So they put him in the slammer for two

months even though he's been out for six years! It doesn't make any sense. What's more, he was a minor at the time of the offense. All he could tell me was: "I'll kill myself if I have to stay here." So I put him in my cell block and give him a cellmate for support. I told him: "We'll see what we can do to get you out of here quickly. Just a little sentence adjustment, that's all."

Minimizing the responsibility of the inmate (a minor at the time the crime was committed and moreover psychologically fragile), the counselor embraced a feeling of empathy which was expressed in the affectionate way she referred to him ("my poor little depressed boy"). Her role as an auxiliary of justice serves to soften the effects of the punishment, to humanize it. The counselor's actions take on a political meaning, one of resisting the punitive tendencies, the absurdity of which she denounces (the executing of "old sentences"). But if the display of this form of compassion can be explained by the personal commitment of this counselor, it is not unrelated to institutional requirements that the agents be responsible for the inmates by reducing the violence of the institution and managing the suffering of the prisoners.

There are various meanings to the redefinition of the professional responsibilities of counselors which recent reforms have brought about. The scene of the prisoner at the prison gate shows how these reforms contribute to reconfigurations within the world of prisons, a world in which correctional officers traditionally confined to functions of security and repression increasingly assume the role of humanizing the institution, helping to blur the boundaries of professional fields and gendered expectations. But this scene also helps to shed light on a blind spot in current reforms of the job: the lack of a "left hand" as an appendage of the penal state capable of responding to the social distress concentrated in the prisons. The shift from casework to criminological assessment and recidivism prevention in the activity of the counselors ignores these social needs. Nevertheless, the actual practices of agents moderate the effects of the reforms, mobilizing other moral and legal demands at work within the institution.

Conclusion

The recent reform of the profession of probation and reentry counselor exemplifies the moral reconfigurations of the penal institution. It is inscribed within the longer history of social work in prison, which is characterized by the sedimentation of successive layers and progressive shifts from a form of compassion to a "liberal-repressive" combination that redefines the moral economy of the prison world. In charge of implementing the individualization of punishments, counselors are still assigned the charitable role of potentially softening penal restrictions, but they also have the harder task of assessing the risk of recidivism and the promise of reentry. From a relationship based on assisting the inmate, their primary mission has turned to advising the judge in a context of significant bureaucratization and standardization of procedures. The transformations in the activity of probation and reentry counselor uncover certain contemporary forms of moral treatment of the populations handled by state institutions. Combining a proclaimed respect for the person through the individualization of the sentence, a differential management of populations which confines the most precarious to a state of neglect, and a punitive enforcement of a principle of responsibility that contributes to the moral legitimacy of the institution, this handling is as much the product as it is the source of values and affects present in work situations. It is in the course of these situations that the agents re-appropriate the use of a predefined moral framework or sometimes circumvent it on behalf of other values of the institution—especially "humanization." By juxtaposing the reforms such as they were introduced by official texts and the daily practices of agents who implement them, the aim is not just to underline a disconnect, but also to show how institutions produce both categories of thought and categories of sentiments. As the main actors in the implementation of a liberal reform of the penal system, probation and reentry counselors shed light on the practice of punishment in France today as well as on the moral tensions which pervade the concrete actions of the state with regard to the precarious populations which it supervises while at the same time increasingly disburdening itself of their fate.

Notes

1　The term "left hand of the state" is used by Pierre Bourdieu in *The Weight of the World* to identify the agents in charge of social functions meant to compensate for the most intolerable effects and deficiencies of the logic of the market (Bourdieu 1999 [1993]). It is used here not in opposition to the logic of the market, but in contrast to the specific repressive and punitive functions of the state, the harshness of which prison social workers in part soften.

2　Studies on street-level bureaucrats in welfare services (Dubois 2012 [1999]), immigration administration (Spire 2008), or child protection agency (Serre 2009) highlight the forms of social and professional construction of legal norms when they are implemented by administrative agents. On this last point, Didier Fassin's ethnographic survey on the anti-crime squads (Fassin 2011) shows both the heterogeneity of practices and their inscription within a comprehensive moral and political framework which renders them intelligible.

3　This chapter is based on a survey conducted at two Probation and Reentry Services in prisons near Paris. At Dugnes, which houses more than 2,000 inmates, the agency has 24 probation and reentry agents, one director, and four administrative secretaries. At Broussis, which houses more than 900 prisoners, the service has ten agents, one director, and two administrative secretaries. Despite the difference in size, the offices were comparable in terms of their composition (mostly women under 35 years of age with less than five years on the job, a large number of trainees or newly hired staff) and the population supervised (men, mostly under the age of 30 from working-class backgrounds, awaiting trial or sentenced to less than 18 months for the most part). The work of the counselors was observed in situ for several months between 2009 and 2011 in various contexts: intake and monitoring of prisoners, sentencing commissions, relations with judges, prison guards, court clerks, and various members of the prison administration); observations were supplemented by in-depth interviews (Bouagga 2012).

4 The law on the banishment of repeat offenders to the colonies based on the presumption of "irrefutable incorrigibility" and the law on the conditional release of "reformable" inmates, both passed in 1885, attest to the importance of the discussions concerning the transformative effects of penal punishment. At the same time, debates on imprisonment in cells reflect the importance of concerns about the "contagion" of crime within the prison and the need for humane conditions of detention in order to promote the moral rehabilitation of convicts.

5 Some organizations (*Entraide Sociale*, St. Vincent de Paul societies, the French Red Cross, and Cimade) assumed an important role in daily life of prisons during the Occupation and during the purge which followed the Liberation. Prison social services were designed both to control and perpetuate the social involvement of these organizations.

6 This philosophy also influenced the reform of correctional procedures in immediate appearance trials.

7 On these differences in recruitment, social origin, and habitus, refer to a contemporary work on the phenomenon described here, which highlights the heterogeneity of jobs in the social field at a time when they saw a huge development in their functions of support, control, or prevention (Verdès-Leroux 1978); even today, social workers are professionals with diverse social backgrounds and qualifications (Ion and Ravon 2005). On the importance of personal commitment, of a "calling" in the biographical trajectory of educators, see *Le métier d'éducateur* (Muel-Dreyfus 1983).

8 Sources on the history of prison socio-educational services are scarce; one can refer to a few academic publications before 2000 (Faugeron and Le Boulaire 1988; Faget 1992). More recent reforms and debates about the redefinition of the job raised new enquiries in the institutional and professional sphere (Lhuilier 2007; Ferlay 2011) and in academic research (Larminat 2012; Bouagga 2013)

9 See Faget (1992).

10 Michel Foucault's major work *Discipline and Punish* (Foucault 1979 [1975]) epitomizes this anti-authoritarian critique: drawing an analogy between the school, hospital, and prison as disciplinary devices, it unveils the power techniques designed to impose standards on supervised populations. The text has exerted a considerable influence on how social interventions were conceived of in the 1970s. The work *Prévention et contrôle social* analyzes the development of the field of social work as an insidious extension of the control of disadvantaged populations (Lascoumes 1977).

11 For the 11,000 individuals incarcerated in 1963, there were only 124 social workers (36 educators and 88 certified counselors) who mostly worked part-time; they were assisted by more than 1,500 volunteers (Faget 1992).

12 See Astier (2007).

13 Decree modifying the Code of Criminal Procedure issued on April 13, 1999.

14 The expression is taken from an article analyzing the reconfigurations of social work in probation services "between the social and the legal" (Chauvenet et al. 2001); on the history of probation, see the timeline established on the Criminocorpus website (Renneville and Carlier 2008) as well as a recent dissertation (Larminat 2012).

15 The source of these statistics is the National School of Prison Administration (Gras 2008).

16 The CGT in CGT-Pénitentiaire stands for *Confédération générale du travail* or General Confederation of Labor. SNEPAP stands for *Syndicat national de l'ensemble des personnels de l'administration pénitentiaire* or the National Union of All Personnel in Prison Administration. Formed by prison educators, it represents the interests of the body of probation and reentry counselors and their supervisors.

17 Summary document of the union, entitled "PRC's Job: What the SNEPAP-FSU Is Defending" published on the website of SNEPAP-FSU: http://snepap.fsu.fr/spip.php?article202.

18 This risk is measured not only in a probabilistic manner, but also in terms of a representation of the seriousness of the offense. Thus, a study published by the prison administration shows that in terms of sexual assault or physical assault, while recidivism rates are low, consideration for the damage inflicted on the victims leads to judging the risk as high (Kensey and Benaouda 2011). On these uses of risk in the "government of crime," see Chantraine and Cauchie (2005).

19 Using empirical studies on crime as their starting point, software programs for standardized risk calculation have been developed most notably in the United States and Canada, and their use is spreading in Europe. Robert Castel had identified their use in public policy on mental health in the mid-1970s with the development of screening practices, the establishment of computer records, and the "construction of population flows" to which different social outcomes are assigned (see Castel 1983).

20 In the United States, which has experienced an unprecedented "punitive turn," (the American prison population grew from half a million in 1980 to 2.3 million in 2008), the status of probation officers is closer to that of a police officer than it is to that of a social worker and plays an important role in the growth of the prison population by sending those who do not respect the increasingly more demanding conditions of their supervision in the community back to prison (Lynch 1998).

21 On this "new penology," refer to the formative text by Malcolm Feeley and Jonathan Simon (1992) from which the quotes are taken. Stéphane Enguéléguélé (2010) studied the circulation of these new techniques of differential control of at-risk populations and their importation into France.

22 "New Public Management" refers in the French context to a reorganization of public administration toward performance and efficiency. It entails a redefinition of public policies and of working conditions for state agents (Froment and Kaluszynski 2011).

23 In France, evictions are not enforced during a what is called a "winter truce" from November to March.

24 The transformation in the roles within the penal institution following the reform of prison health care entrusting care to hospital personnel outside of the prison hierarchy is analyzed by Marie-Hélène Lechien (2001).

25 See, in particular, the works of Delphine Serre (2001; 2011) on the increase in legal procedures and methods of managerial leadership in social work. Working on the comptrollers of the family allowance fund, Vincent Dubois (2009) signals a more repressive shift in the warnings given to recipients of allowances they do not qualify for and who are held accountable.

26 The development of this contractual philosophy within the prison administration is discussed in the book La Part d'ombre de l'État de droit, which places them in the context of a statement of recognition of the rights of detainees (Salle 2009).

27 To compare with other street-level bureaucrats, see Vincent Dubois (2009, 2010).

28 This tension is discussed in an article on the "moral ambitions" of evangelical Christians engaged in charitable activities by implementing a requirement of compassion for persons in need and a demand for responsibilitization of these persons (Elisha 2008).

Part III
Supporting

CHAPTER SEVEN

Discipline and Educate
Contradictions Within the Juvenile Justice System

Sébastien Roux

"It's a tough job ... If I had to do it all over again, I'm not so sure I would. I don't think I could anymore."[1] It was impossible for this psychologist to forget the reasons why she had chosen her job, and yet at the same time she no longer knew how to fulfill her professional role. She had recently left her job at the Youth Protective Services (*Protection judiciaire de la jeunesse*, PJJ) and had started her own practice, getting involved in various forms of advocacy and working with various non-profit groups. As was often the case, she did not admit to these doubts during the formal interviews conducted as part of an ethnographic study of a Non-residential Education Unit (*Unité éducative de milieu ouvert*, UEMO) located in the banlieues of Paris: her confession came instead within the context of a casual conversation. Units such as these seek to leave minors who have judicial issues in their everyday environments without tearing them away from their families. These minors are supervised by professionals employed by the Ministry of Justice whose work is overseen by a juvenile court judge in the name of protecting a child in danger (in civil cases) or a child who demonstrates delinquent behavior (in criminal cases).

Some of these children have been abused or mistreated; others have committed minor offenses which have landed them in juvenile court (shoplifting, drug dealing, fighting, insulting an officer, etc.). Whether they are being supervised during the pre-trial phase or in the post-trial context of serving out a sentence, they rarely bypass this branch of the Youth Protective Services. They will be monitored for a few months or years by their counselor, their caseworker, or their psychologist, with whom they will form relatively close bonds and who will with varying degrees of success seek to "give these kids a second chance." The young people are mainly from the so-called "problem" neighborhoods, low-income areas generally comprised of housing projects. Most of these adolescents are boys (approximately 90 percent) between the ages of 13 and 18 who are either immigrants or the children of immigrants from North or sub-Saharan Africa, or are minorities from French Caribbean Islands. Some of them show the same defiance to the Youth Protective Services that they show to other institutions, especially the police. They are often loudmouthed teenagers whose intentionally aggressive and intransigent attitudes are meant to prove their masculinity. Others, however, are more reserved and more withdrawn, who sometimes do not speak during therapy sessions, do not respond to proposals from their counselors, and refuse to play sports or participate in activities, let alone make friends. They all have particular stories, ones that cannot be summed up by the clichés that pervade the public sphere. And it is these stories that, according to youth protection professionals, contain the reasons for their problems and might in part explain their delinquency or misbehavior. So it is up to the social workers to understand the motives and in collaboration with the judges to "give these youths the guidance" which they deem necessary.

Yet, as evidenced by the psychologist's admission, some professionals now believe that the purpose of their job has been turned on its head. A number of them recognize feeling somewhat uneasy about the recent changes in the Youth Protective Services. Both liberating and guilt-inducing, their confessions are often made outside the framework of formal conversation when no one else is listening. The majority of those who venture to speak their minds will later take back what they have said, rationalizing their mental anguish as the product of a particular point in time (they were "tired" or "stressed"), or a particular situation (it was the "hierarchy" or the "atmosphere" of the unit). But the recurrence of these admissions belies their subsequent justifications and encourages a look beyond the youth workers' temporary or personal circumstances to question why this institution's professionals claim in one way or another to have experienced a loss of meaning in their jobs, which in turn has caused them to doubt their vocation.

Many sociological studies that take a look at suffering in the workplace have rightly emphasized the practical effects which activities have on the psyche of the agents. Experienced differently depending on the social characteristics of the workers, the effects of some current forms of management can upset one's relationship with the world as well as with oneself.[2] This dynamic can also be seen at work in the Youth Protective Services, which is the Ministry of Justice department in charge of at-risk children and delinquent youths. The specific activities of the agents are in effect transformed by a gradual bureaucratization and standardization of their duties imposed by a series of administrative reforms. But in explaining the unease of these professionals, we cannot ignore the particular context in which it is expressed. In addition to the ways in which changes in the juvenile justice system have adulterated the integrative capacity of their work or have suddenly transformed their routines and work habits, most agents were deeply skeptical of the manner in which these changes have fundamentally affected the exercise of their profession.

These tensions are both political (insofar as they relate to the definition of the forms of government and the reactions which they produce) and moral (since they involve the definitions of what is good and what is just). When considering the unease of the institution and its agents, it is necessary to take a multi-layered approach. To adopt a compassionate interpretation of the suffering experienced by these professionals presumably runs the risk of creating a critical analysis that remains blind to the contradictions that pervade actions performed within a given historical and political context. Conversely, a grammatical approach based solely on the succession of discursive regimes runs the risk of underestimating the practical work of the agents, its effects on daily life within the institution, and, more generally, what it reveals about a particular period in time. Rather than contrast an ethnographic approach with a discursive analysis, I will instead combine the two in order to consider not only the difficulties faced by the main institution in charge of juvenile delinquency, but also the specific effects on the way its agents understand the populations for which it is responsible.

The judicial supervision of young people is a product of recent history, lying at the crossroads of the development of the prison and of social work. By briefly retracing the major dynamics that have shaped the French judicial system for minors, I will show how the treatment of children has grown increasingly more specific, singling them out over time as subjects with particular rights who as such demand unique responses from the penal system. This evolution has led to the emergence of a specific administration—initially known as Supervised Education (*Éducation surveillée*). Without limiting the activities of the Youth Protective Services to just these agents—who in reality work with other specialists—I will next focus on the norms and values underlying their actions in an attempt to define how these supervisory professionals think about their field and its evolution. Finally, by examining more specifically the moral dilemmas and ethical and political problems that these agents encounter in their daily work or in response to the changes in their activity, I will show how the moral economy of juvenile delinquency has been transformed and how this inversion calls into question contemporary transformations of the state.

A Contradictory Institution

As far as children are concerned, the law as well as judicial practice began to change in the late eighteenth century when the penal treatment of minors became both specified and specialized. To be sure, children have been subjects of particular rights since ancient times (as evidenced, for example, by Roman family law). But it was in the modern era that a set of specific legal technologies was strengthened and developed. The Youth Protective Services are a legacy of that evolution. If we look at the inconsistencies within (and oppositions to) penal responses to juvenile delinquency today, there seems to be general agreement that some form of justice specifically adapted to children is needed. Therefore, in order to understand the conflicts pervading the juvenile justice system, we must first situate the formulation and application of the principle of separation within the system's long history and grasp its consequences on the administrative and judicial management of children and their families.

Childhood and Justice

A brief genealogical review of the penal system's handling of minors and a reminder of its governing principles will highlight the profound contradictions at work within juvenile justice. Over the last two centuries, the criminal justice system at large has favored a series of systems designed to separate minors from adults, contributing to the modern definition of juvenile specificity based mainly on a lower capacity for discerning right from wrong. Newly defined, childhood came to be understood as a period in life requiring a special repressive technology. But at the same time, this dynamic also portrayed children as both vulnerable beings and adults in the making.[3] The contemporary juvenile justice system thus maintains a delicate balance between repression and compassion, the desire to punish and the desire to protect, a balance that has spanned the history of the penal system's handling of children.

While the idea of a differentiated responsibility dependent on age may have been enshrined in French law by the Criminal Code of 1810, the notion nevertheless represented the continuation of a trend begun under the Ancien Régime: in accordance with the code of 1791, the age at which one could be held criminally responsible was lowered to 16 and minors shown to have acted "without discernment" were to be acquitted. Legal recognition of the influence of age on the severity of the misconduct and on the capacity of the child to understand the charges laid against him or her served as the basis for the subsequent formalization of a defense. Starting with these early initiatives, the impulse to "humanize" sentences or to attempt to soften the violence of the penal response by distinguishing between minors and adults slowly gained momentum. Initial arguments focused on the need to separate them in prison in order to isolate them from a potentially corrupting environment. Directives issued on April 18 and September 29, 1814 established the first specific institutions (called "reform prisons", *prisons d'amendement*) for incarcerated children. In 1824, the Strasbourg Prison established the first section reserved for minors. In 1836, the Petite Roquette opened its doors. This dual dynamic (the sequestration of juveniles and the "humanization"[4] of sentences) was ushered in by a reformist wave popular among the educated middle class that championed a new political response to juvenile delinquency and vagrancy. One of the most famous examples of such philanthropy remains that of the Comte d'Argout, minister of commerce and public works under the July Monarchy. In 1832, he proposed that the prison administration institute apprenticeships in juvenile prisons. Although this highly contested proposal was in the end abandoned, it is nevertheless representative of a general desire to "reeducate," a desire which would soon take on a new dimension. The focus on minors continued to evolve, and other pedagogical experiments were conducted. In 1839, Auguste Demetz opened the first prison farm near Tours, operating on the premise that juvenile delinquents had to be removed from the vices of urban life and instilled with the moral, religious, and professional education that they lacked. In addition to prison farms, reform houses were also set up. According to Michelle Perrot, these houses counted 5,293 youths in 1840 and around 22,000 twenty years later.[5] While the private sector assumed responsibility for minors destined to be re-educated (particularly through prison farms), the public sector focused its efforts on those juveniles considered the most difficult. With the passage of two laws on

August 5 and 12, 1850, "incorrigible" children or those with sentences lasting more than two years were gradually steered toward specialized penal institutions called "correctional camps" (*colonies penitentiaires*). And in 1855, the first "penal colony for children" (*bagne d'enfants*) opened its doors in Ajaccio.

The nineteenth century is thus characterized by a progressive polarization of penal policies concerning minors. Two models of justice were established, and although they functioned more or less in unison, they were defined largely by their dialectical opposition. On the one hand was the retributive model with a judicial response focusing on the imposition of a penalty intended to be proportional to the crime; on the other hand was the rehabilitative model, which viewed the judicial response as more of a healing process. To be sure, these competing visions were held by agents who represented divergent political interests and clashed over broader opposing values (conservative vs. reformist, protecting society vs. moral education, etc.), but the two models were—in practice—intrinsically linked. It was the simultaneously repressive and integrative initiatives developed by disciplinary institutions (in keeping with the nature of the offense and the spirit of the times, of course) which initially brought these two models together. But both were largely based on the adoption of a belief in the uniqueness of children, who were from then on called "minors," that is to say, subjects with particular rights for whom special attention and dedicated institutions were required.

On July 24, 1889, the French legislature adopted the first law on the "protection of abandoned, neglected, or abused children." Complementing that law was another passed on April 19, 1898, the purpose of which was the "suppression of violence, assault, cruelty, and attacks against children." In the eyes of the law, a child was no longer simply a threat to be dealt with, but also an individual to be protected, even within the privacy of the home, which could no longer escape the state's reach.[6] These laws formalized institutions—the first and foremost being Public Assistance—which were tasked with the compulsory protection of children and which served as the foundation for the contemporary system of juvenile justice. By partially or completely replacing fathers, the state combined its juvenile justice system with its policy on children. The need to specify the particularity of minors, their diminished responsibility, their lower capacity for discernment, or their re-integrative potential (which certain pedagogical experiments sought to build upon) was no longer enough. The state now had a duty to protect children based on their constitutive vulnerability. And judges were thus in charge of defending society from uncontrollable children as well as protecting children from adult behavior.

Professionalizing Educators

During the twentieth century, this move toward specification continued to gain steam and increasingly relied on a body of educational professionals in the justice system. A law passed on July 22, 1912 provided for the establishment of juvenile courts. To aid the judges of these courts in their decisions, the system made use of inspections to ascertain the moral and material situation of the minor and his or her family ("should the child be the perpetrator of an act qualified as a felony or misdemeanor"). Provisions were also made for juvenile offenders to be left with their families and supervised by volunteers under the authority of the court. The tasks of inspecting and of supervising were gradually professionalized.[7] An August 17, 1938 directive ordered the prison administration to create a body of specialized professionals called "educational monitors" responsible for intervening in "houses of supervised education" (the official name for reformatories since 1927). On April 10, 1945, the position of "special educator" was created in compliance with an order dated a few months earlier, on February 2.

This order, issued by the Provisional Government of the French Republic, placed the courts, institutions, and professionals specializing in juvenile delinquency under the authority of a single magistrate: the juvenile court judge. Assisted by Supervised Education, a new division within the Ministry of Justice, the juvenile court judge lies at the heart of the state's juvenile justice policy. This order—albeit regularly amended since its adoption—is now recognized, praised, and even mythologized as the pivotal moment when the primacy of the educational over the repressive was finally affirmed. Enshrined in the text is the general presumption of criminal irresponsibility for any minor, signaling a break with previous judicial efforts which had tried to set such limits.[8] The juvenile justice system was restructured according to the principle that it is an educational undertaking with a mandate to protect in the name of national interest; indeed, the preamble to the ordinance states that

> France is not rich enough in children for it to have the right to neglect anything that can produce healthy beings. The draft regulation attests to the fact that the Provisional Government of the French Republic intends to protect minors and in particular delinquent minors effectively.

This change would profoundly transform the job of special educator by limiting its supervisory role and favoring an educational purpose that was itself in the process of being reinvented. By the late 1940s, Supervised Education was importing new pedagogical theories that revised what was understood about juvenile offenders at the time. New supervisory practices were put in place. Group activities, for example, like those practiced by the Boy Scouts, were promoted. In the 1950s, a training center was established in Vaucresson where specific theories about juvenile delinquency were formalized and professional expertise was imparted. On April 23, 1956, the profession of *educateur* was overhauled to emphasize the "relational" work with minors. It was soon redefined, with a greater focus placed on its capacity for pedagogical support. This process was bolstered by the Law of December 23, 1958 regarding the protection of children and adolescents at risk, which placed all minors in the care of the state under the protection of the juvenile court judge. From then on, the juvenile court judge and the Supervised Education had jurisdiction in both civil (children at risk) and criminal (juvenile delinquency) matters.

In the 1960s, Supervised Education grew and expanded its reach to include so-called "open environment" or non-residential structures which proliferated at the time. These structures made it possible for minors to remain with their families in their usual surroundings while at the same time allowing professionals to monitor them prior to trial or subsequent to their conviction. With guaranteed funding from the government to facilitate their mission, the Centers for Guidance and Educational Activities (*Centres d'orientation et d'action éducative*) came to play a central role in the work of the courts. They brought together multidisciplinary teams comprised of counselors, social workers, and psychologists (or on occasion psychiatrists who worked on a consulting basis). These structures would eventually become today's Non-residential Educational Units.

This institutional transformation was also accompanied by changes in the make up of the institution's agents. As was the case for many other branches of the civil service, those recruited by the Youth Protective Services in the 1970s and 1980s were increasingly female and increasingly college graduates. Supervised Education experienced what many agents today refer to as its "heyday." Little criticized and rarely debated in the public arena, it enjoyed a relatively high level of autonomy, allowing it to increase the number of non-coercive educational initiatives. More important, however, cooperation became the norm, and the multidisciplinary teams learned to work together—either within the institution or through partnerships forged with the private and non-profit sectors. Through the expansion of their activities and the reinforcement of their capacity for initiative, counselors were gradually able to free themselves from judicial oversight. Within the larger jurisdictions, the increasing autonomy of Supervised Education paved the way for the eventual separation of the counselors' investigative and supervisory roles from the act of judgment.

On February 21, 1990, Supervised Education was renamed Youth Protective Services. This name change represented an official endorsement of the evolution in the institution's mission from one of monitoring to one of protection, and also highlighted its aim to intervene in all situations where juvenile court judges had jurisdiction. Yet the agency's new moniker did not reflect the reality of its activities. If anything, the Youth Protective Services were gradually shifted their focus to the penal, leaving its civil cases (children at risk) to Child Welfare (*Aide sociale à l'enfance*) and other local structures. This institutional reform was accompanied by increased bureaucratization. A managing body was established in 1992, allowing for the external recruitment of the administrative elite. Above all, this change went hand in hand with a transformation in professional practices and the implementation of a more streamlined system of agent management. Long left to their own accountability, the units were reorganized under the supervision of a centralized administration. At the same moment that the government led by Michel Rocard (1988–91) was changing the institution's name and endorsing its protective mission, the Youth Protective Services—like other public institutions devoted to social work—initiated a period of reorganization which fundamentally changed administrative practices, making them more codified, centralized, and bureaucratic.

Thus, over the course of the twentieth century, Supervised Education was established as an administration in charge of educational work in relation with the justice system. Working closely with the juvenile court judges—but not under their direct authority—the institution became an indispensable agent of juvenile justice. Now a veritable administration for the education of children "in the care of justice," the Youth Protective Services today number some 8,618 agents, half of whom are special educators.

Contemporary Threats

Although the Youth Protective Services remain largely unknown to the general public and rarely find themselves in the media spotlight, they are nevertheless inextricably linked to contemporary issues surrounding juvenile delinquency, being positioned at the sometimes confusing juncture between two conflicting missions—education and punishment, in other words subjection and subjectivation. As such, it is regularly blamed for its alleged inefficiency and is often directly called into question by those who defend or promote a range of securitarian policies.

To be sure, juvenile delinquency has been considered a form of public nuisance since the development of the mainstream press. Pundits have bemoaned the rise of "Apaches," "hoodlums" (*loubards*), or "leather jackets" (*blousons noirs*) in opinion pieces since the beginning of the twentieth century, and while their labels may have in the meantime changed, the fears that they arouse are no different and operate according to a similar logic.[9] The image of the misbehaving teenager—typically a product of low-income families with an immigrant background (initially Europe, subsequently the Maghreb and sub-Saharan Africa)—combines the fear of the poor with that of the stranger. But in the last 15 years or so, society's preoccupation with juvenile delinquency has found greater resonance, and teenage misbehavior has become particularly visible and even more discussed.

Comprised for the most part by unionized educators who are politically attuned, but little prepared for the contentiousness of the debates surrounding juvenile delinquency over the past 15 years, the Youth Protective Services find themselves in a particularly challenging situation today. In an even more delicate position than judges and prosecutors—who are already strongly criticized by political authorities for their alleged leniency—the institution is frequently attacked by those in power who are concerned about its "inefficiency." The Youth Protective Services are also battered by administrative and budgetary decisions which accelerate their fall from grace and tend to confirm the belief in the need for the reform of the juvenile justice system. Thus, for example, child protection was the only Ministry of Justice program in 2011 to see its funding cut compared to the previous year (−2.1 percent), while the general budget of the Chancellery rose (+4.3 percent).

For many, the Youth Protective Services either operate inefficiently or respond inadequately to the supposed changes in its public—the two criticisms coincide in most cases. The conclusion is seemingly obvious: because it is unable to cope with its population, the juvenile justice system should be radically transformed.

Since the mid-1990s, supporters of this standpoint have grown even bolder in denouncing the alleged increase in juvenile delinquency rates and lamenting the ostensible debasement of the delinquent acts themselves, thus justifying the implementation of coercive and repressive measures deemed more adapted to the restoration of a faltering judicial authority. However, these discourses have been contradicted by sociological and statistical analyses that undermine the idea of an explosion in rates of juvenile delinquency as compared to adults, of a decline in the average age of juvenile offenders, of an increase in violent behavior by teenagers, or of the "laxity" of judicial authorities.[10] But such facts have been largely drowned out by the grandstanding.

The recurrent debates concerning the publication of official statistics—staged by the Ministry of the Interior during the 2000s—are in fact indicative both of the successive desires to reform penal policies and also of the resistance engendered by these intentions. In France, the debate has focused on either the reform or the preservation of the 1945 decree (and/or the principles that inspired it). This decree has today crystallized the opposition between two antagonistic visions of the judicial, political, and moral treatment of juvenile delinquency. Whether an obsolete legislative aberration (per its detractors) or the last line of defense against securitarian impulses (per its supporters), this text is now vested with particular symbolic weight; few are the speeches on juvenile delinquency that do not take a stance on the appropriateness of this legal provision. But it would be wrong to think that the centrality of this text in French debate is evidence of France's exceptionality. In reality, many countries have similar dynamics at play, of course in ways specific to each context. And extensive research into the law's handling of juvenile delinquency shows an increase in repressive efforts to the detriment of education policies, coupled with a loss of purpose for those traditional institutions in charge of non-coercive supervision.[11]

Nevertheless, the critical debate surrounding the current treatment of minors has had some rather concrete effects. In addition to the wave of legislative reforms, the moral economy of juvenile delinquency—or, more precisely, how it is handled by the institution—is now characterized by a vague sense of being threatened, by a shared (albeit variously experienced and variously interpreted) concern. The Youth Protective Services thus lie at the heart of these conflicting issues: as a public administration in charge of handling a threatening population, it is itself threatened by discourses which call its practices into question. Charged with a mission that its agents in part refuse to fulfill (while at the same time adhering to some of its objectives), the institution is experiencing a crisis in which the policy of the state remains at odds with the values of its staff.

Educating in the Care of Justice

According to the Ministry of Justice, there are 275 non-residential educative units (*unités éducatives en milieu ouvert*, UEMOs) in France, compared to 63 reinforced educational centers (*centres éducatifs renforcés*, CERs), 44 residential educational centers (*centres éducatifs fermés*, CEFs), three immediate placement centers (*centres de placement immediat*, CPIs) and six juvenile detention facilities (*établissements pénitentiaires pour mineurs*, EPMs).[12] Although 45 percent of special educators from the Youth Protective Services are assigned to non-custodial facilities where most of the supervision of minors is provided (social reports, educational assistance, legal supervision, etc.), these units receive far less attention in the media and academia than do the custodial ones.

Yet the public response to juvenile delinquency is built around this invisible administration of judicial pedagogy. Using data collected as part of an ethnographic study conducted at an UEMO, I will analyze how the agents of this institution organize their daily activities. By detailing practices which are fundamental to a particular professional ethos, the study seeks to grasp the underlying tensions within the juvenile justice system: the necessity to help as well as restrict, to empower as well as discipline. Special educators—faced with this dual requirement—perceive the inter-individual "relationship" as the time and place for the practical resolution of this ethical and political conflict.

Restrictive Assistance

A teenager and his father appeared before a juvenile magistrate for a hearing in her chambers. Although the 40-year-old judge had only been on the job for a couple of weeks, she was nevertheless familiar with the juvenile justice system, having previously worked as an examining magistrate handling cases that involved minors. Perhaps the years she had spent questioning witnesses explained the curt tone of her voice and the coldness in her demeanor, both of which served to command respect from the educators who appeared before her. The accused, a white teenager, had just turned 16, but his broad shoulders and thickset body hinted at the regular manual labor he performed. He looked just like his father. The two stood side by side, their backs hunched over, their fists clenched in the pockets of their pants, their faces devoid of expression. In the waiting room, the educator supervising the young man tried to strike up a conversation, but she struggled to keep it going. She knew from experience that hearings could be difficult for families, so she quietly distanced herself from the pair in order to give the father and his son some privacy before they entered the magistrate's chambers.

The judge sat behind an imposing, dark wooden desk. A clerk assisted her throughout the entire hearing without saying a single word. The young man and his father sat next to each other on folding chairs, facing the judge; the educator took her seat to their left. After a quick summary of the situation in which she regretted the "gentleman's lack of commitment to the educational process in place for his son," the magistrate invited the educator to speak. In a few sentences, she summed up the teenager's situation: the boy had missed school for the past two years, had psychological problems and trouble sleeping, and was "a reclusive teenager who stays at home and plays video games all day: that's not good." Turning toward the boy, she explained: "he needs help, he needs educational supervision." It was the father's turn to talk. He could hardly contain his anger as he addressed the judge before him:

FATHER: You say that I rarely showed up! But I had to take off from work! I made every appointment! I don't get why you're saying that! Besides, you in the justice system are always off work, always sick, always on vacation. I asked for help and I got nothing! It's been four years since my wife died. And now you're starting to piss me off!

JUDGE: Sir, watch your language!

FATHER: I'll talk how I want to talk, I'm French! I'm not some crook! And now you're just nitpicking.

JUDGE: [Raising her voice] You do realize, sir, that two years out of school is a very serious matter. You're the one who made the choice.

FATHER: I wanted help. I never heard anything about problems at school. I asked for help from the social worker, and for six months I got nothing ... But now Jeremy's 16. He'll find a job just like his brothers. That's how we do it in our family. We earn our own living. So you're the ones who are wrong! I got no help for six months!

JUDGE: Ah, so now we're responsible? Fine. I'll stop you right there. We're just going round in circles.

The tensions ran high in the magistrate's chambers. The door remained closed, as minors are tried *in camera*. Though the judge had a panic button hidden under her desk to call security in the event of a problem, she seemed used to managing confrontation and did not appear to be unsettled by the heated tone of the exchange. She turned to the teenager and continued in a calm, collected voice, but one which nevertheless betrayed her annoyance:

JUDGE: What do you have to say for yourself?

TEENAGER: Uh, nothing. [Silence.] I'm fine. I'll help out my brothers ... I'll take care of myself.

JUDGE: And where do you see yourself in the future?

TEENAGER: In construction—plumbing.

JUDGE: And you're ready to do an apprenticeship?

TEENAGER: Yes, of course.

JUDGE: Aren't you worried about the theoretical part of the apprenticeship?

TEENAGER: No.

JUDGE: Have you signed up at the Youth Employment Center?

TEENAGER: No.

JUDGE: So then how do you intend to go about achieving your goal?

TEENAGER: Maybe some guy will want to give me a chance.

JUDGE: And what about school?

TEENAGER: They told me that the hardest part was finding a boss.

The judge then ordered that the teenager's non-residential educational supervision be extended. She explained to the minor that the measure would help him "to see how things really are, to have a better chance of getting by, particularly with respect to these plans, to see what they actually entail." The supervision was thus extended. In a private conversation following the hearing, both the educator and the magistrate agreed on the need to "help" the family, to "continue the work" in the interest of the child.

The situation speaks to the distress of a family still reeling from the death of a wife and mother, but at the same time confronted with the violence of an institution which imposes the help it deems necessary. The racist remarks on the part of the father reflect his sudden indignation. He thinks himself "French," but the mention of his citizenship is an implicit reference to the color of his skin (to be "French" is to be "white," that is to say, neither "Black" nor "Arab") and to the rights that he associates with that color. He works and does not live off government subsidies ("we earn our own living"). The assistance he had demanded of the social worker was only received after a delay that he considered too long. His aggressive attitude reflected his sense of injustice, reinforced by the belief that his case was not being handled how it should be, and that the institution summoning him was not up to the task. And so he turned toward the educator in the course of the hearing and bitterly complained, his voice choking with rage, that he "works" while educators "are always on vacation" and that it is never possible to do anything for his son.

However, it is rare to observe situations as openly confrontational as this one, even though most professionals—from the courts or the Youth Protective Services—can attest to moments of particular difficulty. The situation described above, although specific to one case, reveals a tension that pervades the activities of the socio-educational system. If action is thought of as help—that is, given in accordance with the best interests of the child—it nonetheless remains a restrictive kind of help, one that attempts to articulate in actions the contradictory and complementary missions of the juvenile justice system. This supervisory work is underpinned by the norms and values of the agents (either implied or explicit), which in turn conform to the definition of a responsible subject these agents are supposed to correspond to. But such work also seeks to support, assist, educate, and make autonomous; to provide minors with greater skills, and families with new resources, and to address—in part—certain inequalities that primarily affect "at-risk" children. It is important to understand the weight of this desire—which is, of course, not without issues of power—on the general conception that the socio-judicial and judicial agents have of their work. To represent one's professional actions as altruistic is not necessarily to euphemize an act of domination that must remain hidden in order to exist and perpetuate itself. This conception of one's self and one's actions also produces concrete effects on the organization of one's work, on the judgments made about oneself and others, and on the policy implemented by the state.

The Legal Relationship

On December 3, 2008, Rachida Dati, then minister of justice, received an official report by André Varinard on the topic of juvenile justice system reforms. A law professor at the University of Lyon-III as well as a former superintendent of several school districts, the author had chaired a committee of 33 people responsible for proposing reforms to the 1945 decree. The committee brought together representatives (mostly from the right, which was at the time the majority party in the National Assembly and the Senate), lawyers, juvenile judges, counselors, and independent experts (a professor of adolescent psychiatry, a lieutenant-colonel of the gendarmerie, etc.). The 70 proposals issued by this committee called for a greater crackdown on juvenile delinquency, and to that end included an array of measures not limited to the creation of a specific penal code (proposition 1); the redefinition of the age of criminal responsibility to twelve (proposition 8); the classification of parents' failure to appear in court as an offense that carried the possible penalty of "parenting classes" (proposition 21); the possibility of accumulating sentences and educational sanctions (proposition 34); the creation of "weekend jail" sentences (proposition 40), etc. The report was harshly criticized at the time of its publication.

Without delving much further into the contents of this highly controversial report, I will focus my attention on Chapter 3, which lists possible solutions to a common problem in penal activity: delays in the judicial process. To its detractors, the juvenile justice system is too slow to be effective. Within the Non-residential Educative Units, agents repeatedly mentioned what they viewed as the negative effects of the pressure that they felt to reduce delays, a pressure stemming from both their supervisors and the judges. Contrary to bureaucratic or judicial logic, these agents claimed to value the educational relationship and its particular temporality. For those whom we encountered, questioning the length of their intervention and its practical modalities was tantamount to denying their professional expertise and also to devaluing the educational component of their work in favor of economic and bureaucratic rationales at odds with their own values.

As the relationship between a juvenile and his or her educator is particularly involved, the time necessary to form "ties" is also valued. Thus, for most educators, the temporality of supervisory work is indicative of its quality: a successful job is a long-term one, especially inasmuch as it serves not only as a condition of the euphemization of the state's violence (justifying their job), but also as a practical resolution of the tensions pervading the actions of the agents. The value placed on long-term work is based on a desire to soften the burden of the legal constraints placed on the minors and their families in favor of a necessary relationship of trust. The ethnographic investigation revealed just how often agents were obliged to accommodate missed appointments, postponed interviews, or hours lost in the corridors of the court. Although the professionals' day is governed by strict schedules, the time for their activities is fragmented and highly dependent on the cooperation of minors and their families. As one educator explained:

If the teen doesn't show up two or three times, then you try a home visit. You try to find out what's going on. And when you do home visits, it turns out the kid isn't there. Sometimes you lose track of the kid for six months. You wait for the hearing. I'm not gonna beat a dead horse. There was this one kid who didn't show up to two hearings, even with a bench warrant out on him ... When he doesn't show up, that's it for him. It's not so much the pressure from the judge, you can shield yourself from that. You send the summonses; you do what you can. But OK ... You're not the strong arm of the law.

Measures imposed by the juvenile court judges grant a high degree of autonomy to the counselors who alone determine—within regulatory limits—how they will implement the duties assigned to them. And while there may be some constraints on time, the period allotted to supervision often remains relatively malleable; for example, in pre-sentencing hearings, educational guidance investigations[13] are scheduled for a maximum of six months, but the agents tend to systematize their requests for extension on the grounds that the legal duration of the procedure is "too short even to begin to understand what happens in families."

The urgency imposed by judges or supervisors, which the educators often complain about, contrasts with the observation of lulls in their activities, periods of boredom, repeated breaks, and wasted hours. The particular temporality of socio-educational work contradicts the managerial logic that seeks to quantify the productivity of agents in order to monitor their work. The latter are aware of this and regularly complain of a reduction in the time allotted to minors, which has a negative effect on the creativity of the educational support provided and on the personalization of the supervision: "We can put together fewer plans," "We don't have the necessary perspective to do any real work with the teen," etc. However, bureaucratic time-saving measures are not that restrictive, and there is not that much demand for codification. Although supervisors seek to systematize educational supervision, the educators often refuse to cooperate. For example, forms standardizing the handling of minors are not filled out (but are made fun of), interviews are neither taped nor transcribed, and files often consist of barely legible handwritten notes.

Within the unit, one episode nevertheless elicited strong emotion and was cited as the epitome of the new bureaucratic controls being enacted to restrict the actions of agents. A minor already under the supervision of an educator for a previous offense was involved in the robbery of a jewelry store. Because the case had been highly publicized, the educator was forced to justify the steps he took toward facilitating the teenager's reintegration by producing written documentation of his actions for his supervisors. By granting responsibility to the minor (a re-offender despite the initiatives taken by the educator), the institution is partly exonerated. But the event only makes sense in terms of its exceptionality. The ire of the educator obliged to give a full accounting, the solidarity of his colleagues and immediate supervisors, and the team's shared belief that the attitude of management was proof of the loathsome evolution in their profession are indicative of a relative consensus surrounding the definition of a professional ethic centered on educational freedom. This freedom was perceived as being undermined by the management's request that the educator justify his actions, a request which was itself produced in a particular political context. But it is precisely this upheaval, this break with the profession's commonly held belief that educators may implement any initiative they deem necessary to do their work, which reveals the strength of the consensus uniting the agents and serving as the basis for their profession.

Because the tasks seem to require greater social skills and personal expertise than technical know-how, time becomes even more protracted. The few activities that are codified are little valued. Thus, for example, professionals place relatively low importance on written work or reports that they submit to the judges. In order to ensure efficient communication, these reports are sent to the court in a systematic fashion. The text is written by the educator and/or the psychologist and/or the social worker, then signed by the unit director before being passed on. The reports are generally written according to the same model: a presentation of the minor and his or her environment, often limited to a description of the family and succinct biographical elements (parents, siblings, place of birth, age); an account of his or her school situation; a psychological analysis; a review of actions taken during counseling; analyses of the minor's behavior and that of his or her family, which are evaluated based on their level of cooperation; a discussion of future plans; and, finally, recommendations. At the unit I observed, the director would correct spelling and grammar mistakes with a red pencil before the report was rewritten and would make sure that the information provided did not stray too far from the usual pattern. With few exceptions, the final recommendations generally requested that the adolescent's supervision be extended. These reports rarely included information on the social situation of the child and the child's family (standard of living, housing, income, etc.) and never mentioned information considered private (relationship status, sexuality, religious beliefs, etc.). Unlike the relationships that educators claim to have with minors, the written reports value a more clinical approach. It is understood that since the reports are submitted to the magistrates, they must remain "informative" without the agents ever questioning the nature of the information they provide or the effects produced by this neutralization within the judicial process.

Socio-educational work is thus granted more and more autonomy from a judicial authority that legitimates and oversees this work while at the same time (and somewhat paradoxically) obtaining its continuation and extension. Indeed, much of the activity conducted by the educators does not necessarily correspond to the expectations of the judges who direct them, nor can it be brought to their attention by the bureaucratic tools at hand (standard written formats, shorter interviews, limited conversations). This disconnect accentuates the de facto separation between the work of the judges and that of the counselors and also favors the use of a more administrative than judicial supervision of delinquency, whereby minors are monitored by multiple agents who are increasingly specialized and diversified and whose involvement is never explained to the minors or their families. Agents from Youth Protective Services come one after the other—educators first, then sports counselors, members of cultural associations, health professionals, psychologists, etc.—and can implement overlapping plans of care the meaning and purpose of which are not necessarily obvious. The initial offense therefore tends to be obfuscated, replaced by a polymorphic pedagogical action justified by the repeated diagnosis of a dysfunction that is sought—and found—in the private lives of the minors or their families. A teenager originally monitored after committing assault or theft can be supervised by agents for several years, while the pedagogical process is revealed in the relationship that professionals attempt to build and in the problems they are in charge of correcting (learning difficulties, psychological problems, family issues, desocialization, etc.). Educational assistance is thus often used to justify additional educational assistance. Therefore, it is not uncommon for special educators to admit in the course of informal conversations that they themselves question the length of their interventions and their "difficulty terminating care" as their socio-educational action becomes more easily adjustable and more easily justifiable when it remains indefinite.

Dilemmas and Ethical Subjectivities

Socio-legal agents are in part aware of the power dynamics in which they participate and which form the basis for their action. A number of them expressed a sense of contradiction—reinforced by the constant criticism the Youth Protective Services are subjected to from the public—in the values that guide their mission and reveal the delicate balance between the repressive and educational components of their work. By exploring the judgments they make about themselves and other professionals, the moral dilemmas they face, and the problems they may sometimes experience as they perform the duties of their job, it becomes possible to explain what is at issue in socio-judicial work, thus allowing us to examine through the practices of the agents the political and moral sense of the ethical tensions.

(Mis)understanding Young People

Knowing how to find the "right distance" is one of the skills most expected from Youth Protective Services professionals, especially from educators. The ideology underlying this normative definition of the relation to the self and others values a certain empathetic skill (knowing how "to listen," "to understand," "not to rush," "to take time," etc.) as well as an ability to give new meaning to the institutional hierarchy which justifies the intervention and supervises the interaction ("We're not 'big brothers,'" "We're not buddies with the kid," "I expect a minimum of courtesy," etc.).

An anecdote, which the professionals found hilarious, made the rounds in the unit. A minor was sent to a residence (an educational placement facility) for, among other things, drug dealing, an offense for which he had been previously convicted. He had already been to two educative centers managed by non-profits, but had left them because he could not stand being so far away from his family and friends. Soon after the boy's arrival, he ran away, returning to his mother. Upon learning this, one of the educators decided on his own initiative to pick up the teenager on a Sunday evening. He went by himself and had no legal authority to do so (this task is officially the responsibility of the police). Furthermore, he called before arriving to inform the boy and his mother that he was coming to their home. As he got out of the car, fifty or so teenagers tried to prevent him from leaving with the boy, who, aware of the risks and what was at stake (or simply playing the role of peacemaker) in turn attempted to defuse the quickly escalating situation. After a few minutes, the windows to the educator's car had been smashed and the contents of its trunk stolen. Upon returning to the facility, the agent complained that all the shopping he had done that day had been stolen—including a large flat-screen television—only to be met with laughter from his colleagues. One educator later commented: "You see, that's what annoys me about some colleagues. That, 'Yeah, I'm an educator' side. Hold on, you don't go pick up some runaway like that on a Sunday night … Telling yourself, 'It's fine, I have a relationship' … No, you can't do that." The official report drafted after the incident and sent to the juvenile court judge stated:

> Following the evasion, the educator on duty visited the home upon prior agreement with Mrs. X to collect the teenager and escort him back to the facility. The return was not without incident as the educator found himself ambushed by adolescents who sought to prevent him from leaving with the minor. But with the latter's help, the educator managed to prevail and was able to return to the facility the same evening.

Although the educator's overestimation of his social and professional skills is certainly amusing, the story is also indicative of a belief systematically shared by many agents. The humor in overplaying one's hand does not invalidate the game; being a good counselor means knowing how to forge not just "a relationship," but rather one that is sufficiently distant to benefit from the legitimacy of the function and to be able to maintain it. One must "prevail" or, in other words, embody an authority whose justice is vested in the agents, but which ultimately rests on their individual capacities, and to establish an educational relationship that walks the line between paternalism and camaraderie. Therefore, one hallmark of the educators' professionalism is their way of expressing empathy while at the same time distancing themselves from not only the juveniles and their families but also the other actors in the judiciary. At court, for example, their demeanor, their lack of robes, and their seat in the gallery are all indicators of a position that has been attributed to them, but also claimed by them. These negotiations about the right distance and the right relationship are particularly invested and are the object of constant vigilance. But while it is difficult for agents to quantify just how distant is too distant, there exists a general tendency to condemn excessive familiarity, which everyone agrees is pathogenic in nature. According to the educators, excessive closeness is potentially harmful in three ways: first, minors risk forgetting that they are in fact in legal trouble, consequently minimizing the "seriousness" of an act of which they are repeatedly reminded and failing to make any "progress" in their expected self-transformation.[14] Second, parents are forced to compete on an emotional and authoritative level, despite the institution's stated goal to consider parents as primary partners in the rehabilitation process. Third, educators who are perceived as being too invested in their supervision of some adolescents might be seen as discriminating against others and as growing emotionally attached, in conflict with their expected professional neutrality.

Trouble in Action

The arrangements that underpin and reinforce the identity of special educators also play a part in the formation of a professional solidarity which is needed to exist alongside others; their job—difficult to pin down—can be defined in negative terms as an activity distinct from that of other experts in juvenile delinquency (lawyers, police, "big brothers", "street counselors", etc.), whether or not they are professionals. As such, it is not uncommon to hear educators make disparaging comments about those responsible for judgment (prosecutors, defense lawyers, and above all, judges). While I never heard anything insulting or derogatory— the educators show the magistrates the same respect for judicial authority that they expect the minors and their families to demonstrate—they often mocked the distance (social, racial, and sexual) separating the judges from the minors. It was often said that the former "don't go to the projects." And educators regularly joked about how interesting it would be for the judges to go on a "banlieue safari." Of course, "going there" means learning about the area first-hand, smelling the stairwells, experiencing the grimy elevators and the dirty looks. It means being reminded of one's class, sex, or skin color, which as a member of the dominant majority one is allowed to forget. It means encountering the discomfort of "knowing your place" which the hushed corridors of the courthouse and the insularity of the judicial world hide from those who work in the field. Deriding the distance separating judges from minors and their families also means legitimizing and validating one's job as a go-between or intermediary.[15]

   This belief is based on the specificity of professional experience and is reinforced by the relative freedom available to agents to conduct their educational action. In September 2010, an educator decided to visit one of the teenagers he was in charge of, a 17-year-old boy of Ivoirian descent. The youth was being monitored in relation to a drug case and was just about to go on trial. After a 15-minute drive through an abandoned neighborhood on the outskirts of Paris, the educator parked in front of a medium-sized, early-1990s style building. According to him, the building had been a relatively nice place to live when it had first opened, but things had since then quickly deteriorated. Trash littered the ground in front of the entrance. The purpose of the "home visit" was to meet the minor in his daily environment, to assess how well he fit in to his surroundings, and to talk with him and his parents about his current difficulties and future plans. But neither the young man nor his family had been informed that the educator was coming. Not knowing the code to the building or the number to call, we waited for a few minutes until a neighbor opened the door for us.

We had to take the elevator to the sixth floor. The smell of urine was overwhelming; the floors in the hallways were black and sticky with grime. The educator rang the doorbell to the apartment, which he recognized from memory. A little black boy of about three opened the door. He remained silent for a few seconds until his mother arrived. She seemed weak and remained quiet. After the visit, the counselor explained that she had been suffering for the last ten years from the effects of a stroke, which had left her disabled. A somewhat apathetic teenager joined us on the doorstep; the counselor introduced himself to her and asked if the young man he was monitoring was there. The girl told us that the boy was not home, but that we should wait inside the apartment while she looked for the cell-phone number of one of his sisters.

The apartment emitted a strong musty odor mixed with the smell of food. We waited in the living room or what served as such. The small rectangular room was furnished with four single beds arranged along the four walls. In the center of the room, a coffee table was strewn with dirty bottles, crumbs, and leftovers. The room was dark, the curtains drawn. Electrical sockets were damaged and cords ran along the walls. Everything seemed decrepit, save for a huge flat-screen television that had been hung on one of the walls. The girl who had opened the door sat on one of the beds, turned to the television and stared at it blankly, wrapping herself in a blanket. The educator tried to strike up a conversation. The girl gave terse, sometimes curt replies, her eyes glued to the screen. She said she was the young man's stepsister. The man must have gone to sleep "at a friend's place," since "as you can see, there is no room here." He only came back to take a shower—maybe later in the day, but she was not sure. The educator handed the young woman an official juvenile court summons and asked her to give it to the young man. She mechanically grabbed it, her eyes still fixed on the television. As we were leaving the apartment, the three-year-old began to cry. No one returned our goodbyes.

Back in the street, the educator pointed out a nearby building where a 22-year-old had been killed two months earlier. He had been shot by one of his old friends, who had been involved in a drug case. The shooting victim had been "monitored" for several years by the Youth Protective Services. As he recalled the young man, the tears in the educator's eyes betrayed his emotion. Back in the car, a heavy silence set in. I asked if "something couldn't be done" for the three-year-old child. I hinted at reporting the family without daring to say so explicitly. The educator reacted angrily: "What did you have in mind? Reporting them? We're not going to call social services every time someone's poor. Otherwise, we'd get nowhere. And would it really be better for the kid to be removed?" A few weeks later, in the educator's report to the judge about the minor's situation, there was virtually no mention of the extremely difficult living conditions in which the adolescent was growing up. As often was the case, the educator preferred to focus on the academic behavior of the minor and above all on his efforts to enter the job market by seeking appropriate training.

Socio-judicial work thus produces paradoxical effects. Like the one just evoked, many educators refuse to detail the domestic conditions of the minors in reports or discussions with judges, obscuring the social dimension of their work. There are multiple reasons for this reluctance, some of which can be attributed to the history of the job and its organization: the increasing weight given to a psychological approach in social work, the analytical primacy of psychological causality in instances of "dysfunctional" behavior, the training of professionals who are not very open to the social sciences, the bureaucratic management of exchanges between the Youth Protective Services and the courts, etc. But the educators' reservations in characterizing the privations of their charges can also be attributed to a conception often exhibited in informal conversations: that "reducing the minor to where he's from does nothing to help him." Paradoxically, mentioning (and in particular writing about) certain domestic conditions—not just poverty, misery, social distress, but also sometimes color or religion—is often seen to contradict the image that educators have of their work. They fear endorsing a determinist interpretation which might harm the minors by suggesting, to use the infamous phrase, a "sociological excuse,"[16] which they know from experience that magistrates are unreceptive to. Above all, this silence is a response to the entrenched belief that the purpose of their intervention is to give a "second chance." However, social factors are seldom considered: "The minors we supervise are just like everyone else," "He's not going to be a plumber just because his father's one," "He can get himself out of the projects, there's a ton who already have," "He can do anything. He can take charge of his own life" are phrases often heard and repeated which tend to gloss over the particular social conditions of the minors whom the educators are supervising. Everyone mentions the heterogeneity of their audience—in terms of class, color, or ethnic background—in blatant contradiction with the objective reality of the cases they have to manage. Most have sordid stories about white upper- or middle-class individuals that they can draw from in order to prove, for example, that delinquency affects all segments of the population. When these agents try to convince themselves that the situations they encounter are in fact diverse, it is less because they are blind to class, color, or ethnic background than it is because they wish to deny the deterministic influence that social factors have over the fate of the minors in their care. It is as if they rejected in the name of equal opportunity and the expansion of possibilities the very reasons for their involvement. Paradoxically, the "respect" they wish to show the adolescents in their care entails a negation of who those adolescents are.

Divisions and Borders

The knowledge of teenagers so valued by counselors is based on professional expertise. Skills acquired by means other than training are systematically suspected of being in conflict with the purpose attributed to their job. Yet the sense of familiarity that counselors demonstrate in many situations can also come from personal experience.

Instances in which the desired neutrality of public agents is undermined seem particularly and especially revealing of latent anxieties about their intermediary position. This was notably the case when minors or their families unintentionally dragged educators into relationships that exceeded the socio-legal bounds of their involvement. Additionally, language often induced significant tensions in those who knew Arabic. Many Youth Protective Services agents are either immigrants themselves or come from immigrant backgrounds, particularly from the Maghreb. Their physical appearance, their names, and, for some, their accents are all clear indications of their origins. It was not uncommon for some families to try to switch into a language that is implicitly assumed to be shared. In the presence of the sociologist, the educators routinely refused to speak in a language other than French. Admittedly, this was in part to avoid excluding anyone from the conversation, but their embarrassed refusals were also indicative of the deeper political issues at play. For them, being an educator also means being an official representative of the French government, one whose duties are defined by a supposedly impartial justice. This means speaking in French, refusing to make accommodations for requests perceived as contrary to the secular nature of the state (the day of appointments, prayers, etc.), and reproducing the false neutrality of a state that claims not to recognize individual communities. And if, in practice, they continually adapt (for example, by agreeing after some discussion to respond in French to questions asked in Arabic), their situation is no less difficult. They often feel torn and make mention of the discomfort that they experience in this position. As educated civil servants, they do not completely belong to the world of the minors in their care. As Arabs and as Muslims, some are confronted however by a public that reminds them that they themselves are foreign to the institution that legitimizes their function (or that they, too, are members of the community targeted by the institution), and in turn participate in the violence of that state. Even though they value their role as intermediaries, educators may also be required to confront the fear of being stigmatized as a traitor.

Within the unit, the assignment of cases proved particularly revealing of these divisions in identity, for case assignment is an instance when function enters into conflict with experience. During the study, what was presented as routine procedure belied just how powerful these issues are. The director seemed to assign cases according to standardized bureaucratic criteria, making sure that each counselor was given an equal number of charges (between 11 and 25). And when educators were asked about the criteria that determined, on one side, the assignment of cases and, on the other, the acceptance or rejection of those cases, their responses inevitably attributed greater value to a certain democratic impartiality. The organization and frequency of meetings prevented me from observing whether or not there was any statistical significance to the distribution of cases. But following the study, the unit began to hold monthly meetings focusing on sociology. At a meeting on the topic of racial issues and discrimination, some agents present—the majority from immigrant backgrounds—wanted to reexamine these specific issues in greater detail. It quickly became clear that minors tended to be assigned to educators with similar backgrounds. The latter, however, were divided over whether or not minors should in fact be paired with them based on racial criteria. No one remained neutral when the question was asked if a youth with a North African background should be assigned to an agent of the "same background." The question was instead subject to constant debate. A seemingly random procedure, case assignment quickly proved to have political repercussions. Thus, the fear of racialization or conversely the defense of shared knowledge, demonstrate the extent to which an educator's imperative to maintain the "right distance" is not limited solely by the ethics of the educational relationship. In the Youth Protective Services as elsewhere, policies extend beyond the scope of their institutional function to become embedded in debates outside the profession. Ethical dilemmas and subjectivities are proof that an educator's social skills and practical knowledge are not the only components of their work. Educating means drawing boundaries, participating in a justice that is alert to class and color, and perpetuating discriminatory rationales, but it also means—whether counselors are conscious of it or not—resisting, coping, circumventing, and, in short, experiencing the distress caused by one's partial awareness of fragility.

Conclusion

On Friday, May 21, 2012, the National Union of Educators and Social Workers sent out an email with the subject line: "No guards in the residences!" The email was in response to a Youth Protective Services initiative to privatize night-time security in the residences, which had begun a few months before. During my fieldwork, the educators often brought up this proposal, which they almost unanimously considered as an affront to their profession. This position was widely shared by the staff in other units as well, including the regional directors. The pamphlet, written in a militant and combative tone, directly confronted management: "They dared …," "Youth Protective Services management has decided for the umpteenth time to force through," "We will not let them do this," etc. But in addition to its union rhetoric, the content of the email reveals a concern on the part of educators that their work is at risk of being depreciated. For example:

> In educational practice, this project would mean: more violence, more restrictions, more conflict, and more mistreatment for the staff and the youths. It also signals the immense contempt that management has for the qualifications and expertise of the staff. After closing Youth Protective Services units, they are now launching an attack on our ethics and our professional commitment! This proposal to put guards in the residences is yet another step in the denaturing of our jobs that our administrators wish to take.

Some private non-profit organizations already employ security guards, but the system was never implemented within the publicly run facilities of the Youth Protective Services. The proposed measure was an attempt to test a new means of securing minors and their supervisors, and also to rethink the (occasional) presence of law enforcement agents within residences. The initiative raised numerous concerns: professionals, for example, emphasized the loss of autonomy that the public administration would experience as duties became increasingly blurred. Above all, the proposal demonstrated the growing presence of security firms in public institutions, which now outsource some of the duties previously fulfilled by the institutions themselves. There are two dynamics at work in this partial privatization of institutions of social control: not only has the state lost its monopoly on legitimate symbolic violence, but it also appears to be the main instigator of its own weakening.

These dynamics have coincided with the establishment of new structures initially thought to provide a set of judicial "alternatives" to detention "adapted" to adolescents through the "humanization" of the penal process (prisons for minors, juvenile criminal courts). But successive legislative reforms have actually promoted the development of more restrictive facilities. These new institutions have grown increasingly similar to the model for which they were supposed to be a humanist alternative, enclosing non-custodial institutions more so than they have opened custodial ones. These new facilities are often private, and their integration into the socio-educational system has radically transformed the political management of juvenile delinquency. On the one hand, custodial duties have been gradually delegated to non-public organizations, which, even if they are officially non-profit, are no less market-driven: they receive a fixed amount per day and per youth housed which allows them to pay the salaries of their employees. On the other hand, some social duties, likewise delegated to other specialized institutions, are not only isolated from the system as a whole, and therefore made vulnerable, but also freed from the constraints of equality that the public sector is supposed to guarantee. The repressive becomes partially market-driven while the social becomes competitive. Finally, this trend emphasizes a de facto evolution in the job of Youth Protective Services educators: the professionalization and rationalization of its "educational" component has led to pedagogical responsibilities being managed separately from the repressive and social duties of judicial intervention. Reducing the work of educators to some indeterminate "educational" action, especially within a context that denies its scope, contributes to a loss of meaning in the job and a negation of those who exercise it.

But this change is not only the product of external constraints exerted against professionals for political, bureaucratic, or administrative reasons. These dynamics exist in and contribute to the transformation of the job of educator and the conditions in which it is exercised. This transformation is in turn inscribed within a restructuring of the duties of public service and exclusive state functions. The reflection of this situation within Youth Protective Services, however, reveals and highlights the contradictions inherent in socio-legal professions. The work of special educators, social workers, managers, and psychologists is being threatened not only by changes in the welfare state characterized by the ideological primacy of a repressive response to delinquency. These transformative dynamics are also reflected in the practices of the agents themselves and shed light on the internal tensions and contradictions in the exercise of socio-educational professions.

At a particular historical moment in which challenges to social policy intersect with the increased repression of juvenile delinquency, educators see their moral standards modified and their professional practice questioned: their knowledge of minors is not valued by the judicial process; their supervisory work (given their autonomy from the courts) has become increasingly methodized without being examined; their practical (and sometimes personal) experience struggles to find an institutional correspondence, etc. These dynamics weaken the professionals' work by questioning the basis of their job and the values that guide their duties. But above all, these developments have an impact on the vulnerable populations that are the intended objects of this socio-educational work. Children and teenagers are the ones directly affected by the consequences of decisions and actions made by an administration that struggles to supervise them. Their dilemma perpetuates both the challenges to and the criticism of the institution itself. Therefore, the historical dynamic which for nearly two centuries has helped to articulate within a single public policy both support and restraint, compassion and repression, education and punishment, is today called into question. Thus, the current disposition of the liberal state has profoundly transformed its socio-judicial institutions, troubling not only the professionals but also their public and—more broadly—disrupting the way vulnerable populations are managed politically and morally.

Notes

1 The author wishes to express his gratitude to Daniel Frazier for his attentive and thorough review of a first version of the English translation.

2 These new forms of management are indicative of the growing precarization of the wage system which, as Christian Baudelot and Michel Gollac (2003) have shown, has transformed as well as intensified suffering in the workplace.

3 Philippe Ariès has shown that parental attachment to children (which is tied to a decline in fertility rates) primarily developed at the end of the eighteenth century (Ariès 1960). His historical writings on the subject of family "mentality" greatly inspired Michel Foucault and sparked the philosopher's reflections on the connection between the socio-historical definition of age and the penal system's development of specific repressive and disciplinary technologies (Foucault 2003 [1999]). This approach illustrates the correlation—rather than the opposition—between sentiments and punishments in modern policies on youth.

4 It is difficult to speak of a "humanization" of sentences given the reality of detention. Thus, for example, "La Petite Roquette" used to incarcerate minors as young as seven years old, isolating them in cells for 23 hours a day in deplorable conditions. But this notion is used here less to qualify humanity with regard to the sentences imposed than it is to highlight that these initiatives—even though they may seem "inhuman" today—are

the product of a reform instituted with the expressed purpose of protecting of the child's best interest.

5 These data are taken from an article published in 1975 in which Michelle Perrot proposes one of the first critical historical analyses of judicial statistics (Perrot 1975).

6 For an analysis of the emergence of public policies on child protection in France, see Noiriel (2005) and Vigarello (2005). These approaches do not contribute to a radical analysis of child abuse as only a "social construct" (Hacking 2008), but on the contrary show the historical evolution of new moral imperatives in the political and judicial realms, including the subjection of paternal authority to that of the state (which is subsequently responsible for punishment as well as protection).

7 The investigative and supervisory duties bring to mind the "educator-observer" and "educator-scout" functions that Nicolas Sallée has distinguished based on a genealogy of the profession (2010). More generally, the relationship between look and action reflects both the different modes of control pervading the pair subjection/subjectivation and also their political and ethical effects on subjectivity (Faubion 2011). In fact, the act of supervision is not only a question of maintaining those minors in the care of the state—through surveillance—but also of "helping" them—through action—to become autonomous subjects of their own existence, that is to say, controlled individuals in whom the state has sought to instill an suitable and compliant ethic.

8 The 1945 decree reaffirms the abandonment of the notion of discernment, such as it was defined by the Law of July 27, 1942 on juvenile delinquency (Yvorel 2012). Nevertheless, the "advances" of the 1945 decree, a statute often depicted as the birth of the contemporary juvenile justice system, must be seen in relative terms. For although the text is today defended as a symbolic achievement—having anchored the contemporary juvenile justice system in the left hand of the state (the social) more so than in the right hand (the political, the repressive, and the economic) (Bourdieu 2012: 581)—the decree perpetuates as well as validates a vision of delinquency as an individual and social pathology which is possible to correct through the bolstering of authority (embodied by the figure of a juvenile court judge who is from then on more benevolent than repressive).

9 For an analysis of "gangs of youths" and the fears that they raise, see Mohammed and Mucchielli (2007). That certain stigmatizing rationales persist does not imply that the power dynamics at work are permanent. Thus, for example, when Claude Fossé-Polliak and Gérard Mauger look at "hoodlums" in 1983, they write: "The designation of so and so as a hoodlum, that is to say implicitly as a delinquent, is more often than not just a product of a class racism in which the fear of the 'working class' (which is also suspected of being 'dangerous'), or a petrifying fascination for the exoticism of the banlieues is clearly apparent" (Fossé-Poliak and Mauger 1983; 52). But more recent examinations of the subject show that "class racism" can be amended to include racism pure and simple, as the "gangs of youths" who are often the subject of contemporary media attention are today racialized and exoticized as well as discriminated for their physical, social, sexual, and generational attributes in their interactions with the police (Fassin 2013a) and with judicial authorities (Terrio 2009).

10 These debates over numbers are a reminder that statistical measures of delinquency are the subject of contradictory analyses, notably tied to political and media interests. In France, Laurent Mucchielli discussed a requirement to "achieve quotas" in the police and courts, a new "security management" tied to a culture focused on results (Mucchielli 2008). His work represents an updated version of a well-established sociological critique of crime statistics. Indeed, Aaron Cicourel had already highlighted the specific purpose of crime statistics in 1968: less an objective snapshot or inventory, these numbers serve more to shed light on the public policies which surround them (Cicourel 1968).

11 This repressive change in direction is tied to the liberal state. In their introduction to a special issue of *Déviance et société* devoted to the juvenile criminal justice system in Europe, Francis Bailleau, Yves Cartuyvels, and Dominique de Fraene thus write as part of an important comparative examination: "The juvenile justice system has by and large experienced a significant evolution over these past years in Europe rooted in the questioning of the 'protective' model generally associated with the ideals of the Welfare State under pressure from the generalization of a neoliberal approach to the social question" (Bailleau et al. 2009: 256).

12 Created in the 2000s, CERs, CEFs and CPIs are controversial institutions which seek—according to their own modalities—to break all ties between the minor and his or her original environment. While some of these facilities are run by the public sector, the majority belong to authorized non-profits. Not counted in these statistics are cell-blocks reserved for minors within adult prisons; on this particular institution, see Le Caisne (2008).

13 In the area studied, educational guidance investigations were at the time the investigative measure favored by juvenile court judges to help in their decisions. The Youth Protective Services might also be assigned to conduct other types of investigations: the gathering of socio-educational information, social reports, and most recently judicial measures for educational investigation. The variations depend on the professions involved (social workers, educators, psychologists, etc.), on the stage in the legal process, or on the nature of that process (civil/criminal). But even though the terminology is different, the techniques employed by the professionals to conduct their investigations are more or less equivalent.

14 A concept often used by the professionals, the notion of "progress" is a reminder that the expected subjective transformation—which must take place both in practice and in feeling (Roux 2012)—is akin to a secularized requirement of conversion. For an anthropological analysis of the ethical transformation produced by disciplinary practices in the religious sphere, see Mahmood (2009).

15 Yet these two worlds are not quite so impervious to each other. Some minors (and/or their parents) have a rather advanced knowledge of the judiciary world, albeit a more practical rather than theoretical knowledge. It is not uncommon for siblings to be monitored, for example, or for the most closely watched minors to have a long institutional career, the length of their supervision exceeding that ordered by the judges. This "hidden discourse" is a reminder that the ways subalterns resist judicial authority and preserve a capacity to act should be taken into consideration (Scott 1990).

16 Lionel Jospin, then prime minister, declared in an interview granted to *Le Monde* on January 7, 1999: "So long as we continue to accept sociological excuses and continue not to question individual responsibility, we will never resolve these issues [of juvenile delinquency]." The expression, which became a buzz-phrase in the media, signaled a radical distancing of the left, then in power, from a social interpretation of crime and the recognition of the liberal principle of responsibility.

CHAPTER EIGHT

Listening to Suffering
The Treatment of Mental Fragility at a Home for Adolescents

Isabelle Coutant and Jean-Sébastien Eideliman

"The issues are getting more and more complicated. You start to wonder which came first, the chicken or the egg," admitted a school social worker when asked about her work in a disadvantaged town near Paris in the spring of 2011. "The housing problems are now really shocking. Families have been broken up, the youngest living with a neighbor, the oldest with a friend, and the mother in a hotel. We have families with no papers, no money, no place to live. The children continue to grow up, they keep going to school, but everything around them is falling apart." According to her, these situations ultimately make the adolescents she sees "go nuts," causing them to act out in class or to skip school altogether. Like many professionals of her generation, she had internalized the criticism lodged against schools (notably by social scientists) and considered the institution to be "abusive," that is to say, "extremely violent and dismissive," but she also thought that the schools were themselves "abused," ordered to curb the effects of the growing precarization of their public. As part of her efforts to find solutions to complex situations combining both psychological disorders and social difficulties, she may, as is often the case in her field, reach out to a nearby youth center called a "Home for Adolescents" which lies at the confluence of the mental health and social work. In these new institutions, professionals from diverse backgrounds (psychiatrists, psychologists, nurses, social workers) work together to welcome, counsel, and monitor troubled teenagers and their families.

The increase in inequalities since the 1990s and the further deterioration of the economic and social situation since the early 2000s have done more than simply create individual problems. They have also undermined a number of institutions which support children and youths (the school system, Child Welfare, Youth Employment Centers), particularly in areas where the socioeconomic disadvantages continue to add up. The state thus struggles to impose its authority in some neighborhoods and, in Pierre Bourdieu's terms, to invest its representatives with the symbolic capital necessary for their legitimacy. The justice system and psychiatry are called upon to help restore the authority of institutions weakened by a public that is both difficult and in difficulty: this is done through the establishment of new local facilities which seek to create a network of professionals based on a so-called "house" or "home" model like the Houses of Justice[1] or the Homes for Adolescents we will be examining here. The proliferation of facilities which use either care or punishment as a basis for supervising young people signals both the state's concern regarding troublesome youths and a form of powerlessness to regulate behavior through classical educational institutions.

Alternating between compassion and repression,[2] the political responses of the last decade have placed greater emphasis on psychological explanations and the individual responsibilitization of troublemakers. These developments are part of a moral economy[3] of individual responsibility which manifests itself through punishment (chastising those who behave irresponsibly) and understanding (recognizing individual merits and taking personal plans seriously). As measures directed against juvenile delinquents have grown stricter, the notion of suffering has become more widely promoted and has been used to encourage the opening of numerous facilities which received the peculiar name "listening spaces" (lieux d'écoute) and of which the homes for adolescents form part. Two images of adolescence thus emerge from the state's recent policies regarding "problematic" youths: while the 1945 decree on juvenile delinquency represented it in terms of children who were also in danger (and therefore needed to be protected and educated), there is a growing tendency today to make a distinction between the troubled teenager and the teenager in trouble and to deal with them using separate systems.

Opposite these developments, the explanatory power of social factors and material conditions has been increasingly challenged in national debates. Yet critical discourse emanating from the social sciences has at the same time denounced the "psychologization" of social problems. Social scientists see this phenomenon as reinforcing social domination by making marginalized populations believe that their difficulties stem from themselves and not from collective and structural phenomena. The Weight of the World,[4] a collective work edited by Pierre Bourdieu, garnered the attention of the media in 1993 because it showed how poverty and suffering were the products of social and political conditions that had been denied and were therefore particularly powerful. The authors asserted that this new form of suffering affected the most disadvantaged ("situational poverty") as much as it did those most dominated even in favored spheres ("positional poverty"). They noted in particular that the agents in charge of dealing with those confronted with material difficulties were themselves facing difficult challenges because they were deprived of the resources necessary to carry out their work.

Our study, which was conducted from January 2010 to March 2011 at a Home for Adolescents in the banlieues, led to the discovery of the expression of a generalized form of suffering affecting not only the teenagers concerned, but also the various institutions responsible for handling youths as a result of a lack of resources, time, space, legitimacy, or recognition. Without adopting or supporting the language of suffering ourselves, we want to shed light on the origins and social functions of suffering by situating it within a more general moral economy of juvenile delinquency. In addition to the moral economy of individual responsibility highlighted above, there exists a tension on the part of the families between the imperative that teenagers blossom into autonomous subjects outside the family sphere[5] and the importance placed on family ties and the emotional bonds between parents and children. The primacy of family affection can also be found in the norms of childcare (for example, the monitoring of the maternal bond at birth), in new diagnostic categories for adolescent disorders ("emotional deprivation" having been promoted as a quasi-medical category), and in the emotional moralization of ordinary family ties. It imposes new constraints on those who do not have the resources (due to precarious housing or working conditions, for example) or are not accustomed (due to differing social or cultural norms) to functioning this way. Alternatives to being raised in a loving family have essentially become much less neutral than in previous decades: sending a child to boarding school as a means of upward social mobility for those from more modest backgrounds is not as common as it once was.

In the following pages, we will analyze the origins and the socially diversified appropriations of these moral economies. With the psychologization of social problems in mind, we will focus on the changes and practices of the institutions as well as the resulting reconfiguration of relations among professionals, families, and the state. However, the very idea of psychologization remains difficult to define since this extension of the mental health field produces the phenomena of both psychologization (through the popularization of psychological concepts and the growing use of experts with skills related to psychology) and de-psychologization (insofar as mental health professionals find themselves increasingly competing with other actors over their objects of interest).

As part of this extension of the field of mental health, Homes for Adolescents are of particular interest. Driven by new demands that professionals come together to form a network and that they listen to individual suffering, they appear as a sounding board for problems encountered by other institutions which turn to them in desperation: the school system which no longer knows how to handle disruptive students, Child Welfare which sometimes feels overwhelmed by the "cultural" issues of its users, or Youth Protective Services, which does not know what to do with those teenagers who get passed from institution to institution. The study, which was carried out in the Paris region, consisted in our regular participation in family counseling sessions at the facility, access to the files of the adolescents, and interviews with the staff, with the teenagers, and with their families, in their homes whenever possible. We tried to understand how the dialogue between the institution and its public is created, extended, or broken off within a context marked by the exacerbation of tensions between good and bad students, between French citizens and immigrants, between professionals and parents.

Compared with institutions which view themselves as liberating but are known to reinforce the domination of the existing social hierarchy (like, for instance, the school system), the professionals who work at Homes for Adolescents explicitly seek to de-stigmatize the most stigmatized, to resolve conflicts between families and institutions, to reconcile viewpoints that are at odds for social, cultural, or psychological reasons. Even if they use the psychological framework of the so-called "adolescent crisis" to analyze these problems, they are for the most part aware of the social determination of behavior and the role of living conditions in the onset of the problems for which their help has been requested. They obtain results which the parties involved often consider satisfactory, if sometimes unconvincing, but rarely negative. Does this mean that the psychologization of social problems is clinically effective? Does the process even run counter to certain forms of domination and social control, contrary to what is usually thought in sociology? Our study resulted in a more ambivalent assessment. On the one hand, the work these institutions carry out is performed within a moral economy whose reach is greater than that of the institutions themselves. In fact, this moral economy is the product of a long history which influences the perceived meaning of conversations among professionals, parents, and adolescents. On the other hand, the line between social and psychological determination is drawn a priori in favor of the latter, thereby minimizing the role of the former. Such a perspective results in the stigmatization of those the institutions seek to de-stigmatize. Far from simply reinforcing or on the contrary diminishing the institutional mechanisms of domination, Homes for Adolescents instead help to change the balance of power in a way that is not always anticipated by either side. We will thus describe the moves to reallocate symbolic capital (reputation, the image of each other) and their effects on institutions and their public by explaining the weight of these macrosocial changes as seen through the moral economy of juvenile delinquency as well as the professional positions and the social characteristics of those involved.

In the first part of this chapter, we revisit the medico-social management of juvenile delinquency using a socio-historical approach. In the second part, we focus on the role that Homes for Adolescents play in the contemporary institutional landscape in treating troubled youths. In the third part, we suggest that this complex configuration provokes misunderstandings with the families. In the final part, we show that teenagers can paradoxically, under certain conditions, benefit from them.

From Abnormal Childhood to Troubled Adolescence

The Medicalization and De-medicalization of Misbehavior in School

According to Michel Foucault, the medicalization of juvenile delinquency is part of a long history rooted in the transformation of power mechanisms in the nineteenth century: because the new penal system gave center stage to the question of the offender's comprehension of the crime, the involvement of psychiatrists became possible, if not obligatory.[6] This led to the "psychiatrization" of a whole series of behaviors in addition to delirium. Deviating from the rules of conformity became a symptom of a possible disease, and anything related to disorder, indiscipline, restlessness, or stubbornness could therefore be defined in psychiatric terms. This taxonomic craze signaled an end to the tendency more characteristic of previous centuries not to make any sort of distinction, a tendency which Michel Foucault analyzes through the paradigmatic example of the General Hospital in Paris. In the seventeenth century, the hospital housed vagabonds and other idlers considered dangerous in the same space without regard to whether they were sick, infirm, or simply poor outcasts. At the end of the nineteenth century when the children from the lowest segments of the working class began attending school in compliance with new compulsory education laws, two new figures of so-called "abnormal" children began to make an appearance: the "unstable" and the "retarded."

In a famous article that built upon Francine Muel's previous work,[7] Patrice Pinell and Markos Zafiropoulos revisit this medicalization of misbehavior in school.[8] According to them, teachers at the time were confronted by a public that fell far short of the institution's expectations. This cultural gap, manifested in the child's perceived misbehavior, was in turn pathologized. Academic instability therefore came to be interpreted as a sign of future delinquency, a prospect which was to be prevented through screening and reeducation. From 1909, when special classes for children with learning problems (classes de perfectionnement) were established, to the specialized education outside the purview of the school system developed under the Vichy regime in the 1940s, a wide range of institutions and systems emerged. Beginning in the late 1960s, psychoanalysts also took an interest in this misbehavior, reinterpreting it as a symptom of the child's suffering, which, they believed, was determined by the relationships within the family. As a result, some of the most unruly children who were thought treatable through psychotherapy were directed to newly created Medico-psycho-pedagogical centers (Centres medico-psycho-pédagogiques, CMPPs).

However, the interpretations of Francine Muel and of Patrice Pinell and Markos Zafiropoulos have, been called into question by Monique Vial, who attacks these representatives of Bourdieu's sociology for their readiness to denounce the cultural arbitrariness of school.[9] A historian, Vial shows via her archival work that the teachers were not the ones who complained about their new unruly students, but the psychologists (Alfred Binet and Theodore Simon in particular) who received permission to test in the classes their new hypotheses on students, which would lead a few decades later to the development of IQ scores. Yet this internal sociological debate should not obscure what was a fundamental result of the interaction between schools and mental health professionals: the sidelining of a significant number of students for medical reasons. Indeed, the gradual construction of the field of disability caused many children to be steered toward fully specialized institutions, and the vast majority of those "excluded" came from low-income backgrounds. The "medical" reasons given were often reduced to diagnostic approximations (mental retardation, school maladjustment, behavioral problems) which failed to explain exactly why these children were victims of academic underachievement. Despite the decline in the power of psychoanalysts who had long dominated the scene in France and the rise in the clout of neurologists which took place in the 1980s and 1990s, few if any questioned this interpretive approach. Hyperactivity and "dys" pathologies (dyslexia, dysgraphia, dyscalculia, etc.) replaced emotional deprivation and psychosis as reasons for directing a student toward special education or treating him or her through medication.

Yet, there were also new developments in the field at end of the twentieth century and the beginning of twenty-first century which were not in keeping with this overall movement. For instance, the development of the concept of school phobia no longer targeted children who disrupted school order, but instead those who had to be sent back to school out of fear that they might disrupt the social order by becoming offenders. Although this example of a pathological category remains relatively isolated, it is indicative of an overall dynamic that aims to keep children in school as long as possible all the while highlighting the crisis within an educational system which was itself described as rigid and ill-suited. Ushered in by the wave of mass education that began in the late 1970s, the movement resulted in numerous disappointments, especially in disadvantaged neighborhoods where significant investments in time and energy in the schools did not have the desired effects.[10] In this context, it seems necessary to nuance our thesis of a long-term medicalization of academic underachievement, especially given the fact that since the 1990s the field of mental health has expanded so much that the line between normality and pathology has been blurred. By addressing the psychological well-being of individuals and not just their medically identified pathologies, professionals in this new field now extend the inclusive power of medical categories which encompass a larger number of individuals previously ignored by health professionals. Among them are more students from low-income backgrounds rather than those from more affluent backgrounds, since parents of the latter category are more active in enforcing the line between an identified pathology and normality. This observation should be further qualified by distinguishing cases according to pathology, but more affluent parents seem quicker to search for a specific medical diagnosis to characterize behavioral problems, especially if those problems affect their children and expose them to academic underachievement. Among students from low-income backgrounds, behaviors labeled (often by the schools) as problematic are less often subject to specific designations. "Dys" pathologies in children from privileged backgrounds are the equivalent of behavioral disorders in children from more modest backgrounds, while school phobia corresponds with truancy and dyspraxia with learning difficulties in these respective social groups.

Facilities like Homes for Adolescents, particularly those located in disadvantaged neighborhoods, are precisely confronted by these indeterminate problems. Their work lies in the no man's land between normality and pathology. Whereas they refer children with defined disorders (notably psychoses) to medico-psychological centers (*centres médico-psychologiques*, CMPs), they concentrate their efforts on situations difficult to define, conveniently called "teen crises." Although psychiatrists and psychologists are present in these structures, they may be considered as part of a process of de-medicalization or para-medicalization, which involves shifting the focus away from pathology onto the adolescent's suffering or angst, while at the same time blurring the professional boundaries, since these facilities require social workers and mental health specialists to work together on these new categories of public action.

Troubled Adolescence: A Way to Access the Families

Because the focus on teenage suffering broadened the scope of possible interventions, it began to occupy an increasingly prominent position in the political agenda from the late 1980s on. Departmental guidelines insisted on the need for all sectors to devise "new approaches" for adolescents as well as a "specific reception." In the second half of the 1990s, the government started to encourage the establishment of "youth counseling centers," based on the premise that listening would help teenagers to sort out their problems. Such centers would spring up in the early 2000s around the same time that psychiatry saw its role expanded, with a shift in emphasis from the treatment of mental illness to the promotion of mental well-being. For those who initially conceived of these centers, they represented an opportunity to create places where the relief of psychological suffering no longer carried with it the stigma associated with insanity.[11] The goal was to establish at least one facility per department. This has yet to be achieved: in 2013, 74 of France's 101 departments had at least one such center up and running

These concerns stem in part from the noted increase in youth suicide rates. Since the late 1970s, the gap between senior citizen suicide rates and youth suicide rates has dramatically declined, a sign of the younger generation's social difficulties.[12] In addition, greater consideration has also been given to high-risk behaviors and addictions. Studies have shown, for example, that the use of cannabis does have an effect on the onset of some mental disorders. Over the years, eating disorders, school phobias, and addictions have led to the emergence of specialized hospitals and professionals.

When it comes to low-income youths in particular, demands that mental suffering be taken into account are not unrelated to the re-emergence of "urban violence." So-called "listening spaces" were encouraged to be set up out of fear that "troubled adolescents" might eventually become violent. In doing so, the role of social and spatial inequalities in determining behaviors and feelings was glossed over. Specifically moral issues (for example, the unacceptability of youth suicide) are thus combined with more specifically political issues (such as the management of public order) which track back to the socially differentiated populations: behavioral problems, which are always suspected of leading to delinquency, for the most part affect lower-income boys, whereas attempts at suicide are made by girls from diverse social backgrounds. The separation between victims and perpetrators encouraged by the repressive policies of the last decade has allowed for the surreptitious reintroduction of distinctions in gender and class, with boys from the banlieues more and more often being cast in the role of offender. However, in a moral economy that promotes the values of responsibility and autonomy, compassion and repression are so inextricably linked that the distinction between victim and perpetrator is often difficult to determine whenever concrete examples are considered.

Many other developments have contributed to this reinforcement of social control and surveillance, in relation with the individualization of social policies. But with this individualization, which was officially presented as the antithesis of a bureaucracy blind to the specificities of personal situations, come processes that are in some measure contradictory if interpreted only through the lens of social control. In the field of child protection, the Directive of December 23, 1958 on the protection of children and adolescents in danger laid the groundwork by instituting educational assistance measures that allowed social workers to act sooner with families in difficulty by seeking their cooperation rather than imposing their intervention. The scope of their involvement was gradually expanded, and the agreement of the families to participate in the work carried out has been increasingly sought after. The reasons for this development are inseparably economic and moral: the devaluation of institutionalization, the affirming of family ties, the criticism against bureaucratization go hand in hand with cost-cutting measures in public services and the process of transferring part of the financial costs from the institutions onto the families. The effects on the relationship between users and institutions are both numerous and ambivalent. As Delphine Serre shows, "whereas control has weakened, the scope of controllable has constantly grown."[13] In this area as in others, users have been granted new rights that give them some control over the institutions and professionals who work with them, but have also seen imposed upon them new constraints and new demands.

However, along with the individualization of social policies come particularities in the field of juvenile delinquency. More than a true individualization, it is a form of "familialization" that is witnessed, since the family is often seen as an actor in its own right. Of course, the interests of the child are considered the first priority, while their rights are increasingly invoked and recognized. But when the child is considered a delinquent, the parents return to the fore, and the family is analyzed in an attempt to find the core problem. While some believe they see the decline of this institution starting in the 1970s,[14] a body of studies from the 1990s onward show that the family did more than resist, it became the preferred value of the French. Social workers who deal with precarious populations are generally no exception to this rule and see the family as the building block of society which is to be protected and strengthened by all means at their disposal. Even though a number of families were severely affected by the fallout of the economic crisis of 2008, social workers are reluctant to separate children from their parents and break up the family unit. This validation is nevertheless a double-edged sword: on the one hand, working with the family tends to replace the work done on its members; on the other hand, those who stray from the ideal model are quickly suspected of causing the problems in their children and are duly warned. The resulting responsibilitization of the parents in recent years has taken more violent forms, with the threat of taking away family subsidies in cases of truancy or the implementation of parenting classes (as outlined by the Law of March 31, 2006, and bolstered by the Law of September 28, 2010).

These developments have coalesced in a new moral economy of juvenile delinquency. Closely tied to the rise of other values such as autonomy, the value of responsibility has since the mid-twentieth century become extremely important. It is possible to speak of a moral economy, because there exists a body of significations endowed with various moral connotations that the individuals are subjected to, but which they can also appropriate for themselves. First, the notion of responsibility refers to the current image of the ideal adult, master of his or her own actions, thoughts, and projected self-image.[15] Second, the responsibility is extended to those "irresponsible" persons for whom an individual is responsible: it is in this sense that parents are responsible for their children. The behavior of their children brings the reputation of the parents into play, and it is increasingly expected of the parents to contribute not only to the material needs of their children, but also to their harmonious development and their emotional growth. Mirroring this norm of pursuit of happiness for one's children, the notion of abuse has come to characterize situations in which parents stray from this standard. Third, the notion of responsibility refers to the possibility of attributing fault to an individual. In this sense, the notion of responsibility has experienced a rise parallel to the decline of structural explanations, especially from the social sciences, of social problems.

Today, the idea that the cause of a disorder is not to be found in a difficult socioeconomic context, but in an individual's immoral behavior, is well established. Context is no longer enough to excuse immoral behavior. Legitimate excuses for delinquent behavior are now found in a completely different way. The medical world has recently produced, as we have seen, a large number of new categories to mitigate—without going so far as to guarantee the "irresponsibility" in the legal sense—the most severe moral judgments. Specializing in treating teen angst on a temporary basis, Homes for Adolescents thus sit at the confluence of how social problems and psychological problems are managed. A legacy of both medico-social and psychiatric sector, but reliant on the new dynamic of individualized (or better yet, familialized) social policies, they are deeply rooted in contemporary moral economy of juvenile delinquency, which legitimizes institutional intervention through the relief of mental suffering, promotes individual responsibility, and seeks to safeguard family ties as much as possible. Conceived to deal with supposed teenage weakness and today a target of public intervention, they also aim to compensate for the weakness of other institutions dedicated to children, starting with the school system. However, Homes for Adolescents also find themselves in a difficult position due to a lack of stable funding and a push to de-compartmentalize professional fields and to create low-cost structures by redistributing existing resources and relying on regional governments, in particular that of the departments.

Homes for Adolescents: A Release Valve for Other Institutions

Created in the early 2000s and serving youths aged 12 to 21, the Home for Adolescents we studied was headed by a psychiatrist. It was intended for adolescents "with psychological or psychiatric problems or who are at risk," barring an acute crisis or psychiatric emergency. The "pathologies" listed in the handbook given to interns are varied: depression, attempted suicide, drug addictions, speech disorders, eating disorders, neurotic disorders, school phobias, school dropouts, family crisis situations, difficulties related to immigration status. The facility begins an initial welcome interview (there will be three on average) during which a team (often composed of a psychologist or psychiatrist and a social worker) assesses the situation. More detailed follow-ups may then be proposed: individual therapy, family therapy, relaxation therapy, workshops, in a general dynamic that privileges a psychoanalytic approach and/or transcultural psychiatry in the case of immigrant families, who are frequent visitors.

Referrals often come from other troubled institutions: the school system and, to a lesser extent, Child Welfare and Youth Protective Services. Even when the teenagers or parents contacted the institution themselves, they were often sent there by a professional. In the case of schools, several patterns can lead to referrals: the student may show evidence of learning difficulties (supposed cognitive problems), be disruptive in the classroom (behavioral problems), or exhibit conducts identified as symptomatic of suffering (self-mutilation, suicide attempts, repeated abortions). More recently, another pattern is regularly cited: truancy. Institutional management of the former has become increasingly codified: a database records absences hour by hour, and since 2006, the law requires that the superintendent of the district be notified after four half-days of unexcused absences in the course of a month. The regional superintendent (*recteur d'Académie*) is then free to decide whether to report the family and have its benefits suspended. Rather than reporting the families and exacerbating their situations, school social workers generally prefer using alternative measures like recourse to a Home for Adolescents. This development is in some ways part of the continuing medicalization of juvenile delinquency. The professionals we met were nevertheless relatively aware of the issues surrounding the reclassification of delinquency in terms of a "disorder," a requalification which they sought to resist.

Resisting Institutional Demand

Professionals at this facility sometimes felt that the teenagers suffered from what was primarily institutional mistreatment, whether it be the "failure" of social and educational services or the "violence" of the school system. School social workers were the first to subscribe to the idea that the educational system might mistreat adolescents on account of the symbolic domination that it exercises. In fact, the French school system is denounced in reports sponsored by the OECD (PISA, Program for International Student Assessment) as being particularly unequal. Although the methodology on which the surveys were based remains controversial, the results indicate in France a greater tendency for socio-cultural differences as well as particularly large gaps between high-performing and low-performing students, gaps which have grown worse since 2000. Home for Adolescents professionals are also concerned by high turnover rates in some schools. In their own way, they highlight what the sociology of education terms the "school effect": the degree of cohesion of the teaching staff is not without an impact on the results and involvement of students.

The psychiatrist in charge of the facility we studied claimed to be mindful of the risk that schools might exploit his service, which would only reinforce the stigma that the child already carries. An Algerian immigrant and descendant of marabouts who had fled the violence in his country in the 1990s, he was trained in transcultural psychiatry and was particularly attuned to the backgrounds and situations of immigrant families. He believed that the whole point of the institution was paradoxically to "de-medicalize this period of life." In order not to stigmatize the adolescents any more than they already had been, it was for him a question of partly resisting the demands of other institutions whenever they seemed inappropriate. It was also a question of working as much as possible with the parents. But again, in an effort to distance himself from intrusive social control, he was regularly reminded "not to put himself in the place of the families" and to avoid any judgment. Older professionals learned the ropes at a time when the power of doctors and social workers was being called into question, and their current practices bear the traces of this. A counselor in her fifties, a Portuguese immigrant from a modest background, explained: "You can't just say to families, 'Here's what I know.' You can say: 'I think that ...' but that's not the same as saying 'As a counselor who knows more than you do, I think that ....'" One psychologist with years of experience likewise stated: "There are very few bad parents. There are isolated families, there are parents who feel overwhelmed, who have trouble with their children. But they are not bad parents." When it came to immigrant families, he distanced himself with a purely culturalist reading: he believed that just like teens from wealthy families, teens from immigrant families suffered from a great deal of pressure placed on academic achievement, especially when a desire to climb the social ladder was the reason for immigrating in the first place. In these cases, parents may have unrealistic expectations regarding school, and their children may suffer from an inability to satisfy them.

The case of Hamidou[16] is particularly enlightening in this regard. The school social worker was the one who referred his parents to the Home for Adolescents on account of his "behavioral problems." The family of nine originally hailed from Guinea. Twelve-year-old Hamidou was the only boy. His father had pinned all his hopes for social mobility on him. Ever since starting middle school, which also coincided with his family's move from a suburban neighborhood to a housing project, Hamidou had been causing problems. With no brother to defend him and an outcast due to his recent arrival in the neighborhood, the short teen was the target of bullying to which he reacted violently. The father was called in several times to school and reacted angrily to what he perceived as humiliation. He threatened to send his son back to Guinea, worried that Hamidou might become a delinquent and that he would be held responsible in court. The psychiatrist in charge of the Home for Adolescents and handling the case was anxious not to make the stigma which Hamidou bore any worse either in the eyes of the school system or in the eyes of his father. He thought it best not "to rush into any sort of individual treatment." By meeting with the parents, he sought to defuse the anger of the father, to let him express his feeling of having been mistreated by the educational institution. During the consultation, he thus referred to what we imagine to be a disciplinary board: "I had the impression of being in court. They bad-mouthed me!" The psychiatrist legitimated these feelings. At the same time, playing on their common immigrant background, he tried to get the father to revise his aspirations for his son and to change the way in which he viewed his son by relating his behavior to the difficulties of being a teenager. He was nevertheless careful not to offend him even more by quickly adding: "You're the father. You're the one who gets to decide."

However, some professionals go even further in their analysis, arguing that the institutions which call upon them are sometimes themselves "mistreated." When gathered at the quarterly "network meetings" that took place during our study, these professionals spoke out against the processes which were destabilizing the institutions, be it recent layoffs and a lack of job security, or the new forms of performance evaluation they were being subjected to. Without delving any further into the analysis of these changes, which would require greater elaboration, it should be noted that institutions supervising youths are demanded to resolve issues for which they are not always equipped, at a time when their resources are being restricted even though the living conditions of the population continue to deteriorate. Institutions thus serve indirectly as a repository for the economic and social hardships of the areas where they are located. According to data from the INSEE, more than 50 percent of the housing in the municipality where we conducted our study was public housing. In 1999, 33 percent of its population came from countries other than France, 30 percent had not graduated from high school, 22 percent lived in single-parent families, and 38 percent were under the age of 25. According to income tax records from 2004, half of the households in the town did not earn enough to be taxed. In 2006, the unemployment rate hovered around 20 percent.[17] The professionals at the Home for Adolescents were therefore tasked with untangling complex situations in which family conflict, social (and sometimes legal) precarity, cultural distance, and academic underachievement can all blend together.

For her part, the social worker quoted at the beginning of this chapter felt that it is often the living conditions of the teenagers which make them "go nuts." She spoke of families "torn apart by precarity." The case of two girls from Haiti who entered France using fake identities illustrates the intricacies of these social issues in conjunction with mental suffering. Once again, it was the middle school (in the form of the school nurse and the school social worker) that requested the Home for Adolescents' help when the youngest expressed suicidal thoughts before telling her story. She and her sister had recently immigrated to join their mother who was also undocumented: they had been demoted in school (they were in fact older than the ages indicated on their fake papers) and were being exploited by the people who had smuggled them into France. The mother worked as a virtual slave for a well-to-do family in Paris. While the treatment of the girls and the steps taken to restore their identities did translate into quick improvements in their mental states, their material and legal precarity did little to relieve the anxiety of the mother and the eldest daughter, Gladys. The 2010 earthquake in Haiti only served to intensify their fears since the two youngest of the family had remained behind. The professionals questioned the point of their involvement when it appeared to them that objective life conditions were the source of their problems. Nevertheless, the eldest daughter insisted that they continue treatment, and the mother willingly attended the proposed monthly family counseling sessions.

The Internal Contradictions of Homes for Adolescents: Revealing the Ambivalences of the State

Questioning the meaning of their involvement is a recurrent theme among Home for Adolescents professionals. At this particular center, they sometimes opposed mental health specialists and social workers. Called upon to resolve tensions, the facility was itself riddled with conflict, as if it were somehow contaminated by its object. Its professionals experienced the ambiguity of their duties, which in principle were based on listening and support, but in practice were related to issues of social control. Psychiatrists regularly reminded us that their role was not to respond to what was primarily a social issue. So long as the material and administrative problems went unfixed, they considered it difficult to perform any therapeutic work properly, since the families had more pressing concerns on their minds. And therein lay the initial paradox: acutely aware of how inextricably linked social problems and psychological problems are, professionals nevertheless seek to untangle them in order to be able to work unhindered, that is to say, to focus on the psychological work. Social problems were seen as an obstacle to therapeutic work, and it was up to the social worker to try to improve the material situations of the families who used the center before she even attended a single family counseling session. During these sessions, she participated in the clinical work, sitting in the circle of psychologists, psychiatrists, counselors, nurses … and sometimes sociologists (since it was possible to observe these consultations provided we become "co-therapists"), who questioned the teenager and his or her family mainly about their family history.

In many cases, the importance of social problems makes professionals think twice before committing themselves to what they consider to be a real follow-up. This, for example, was what happened in the case of a North African family referred to the center by a school social worker. The two eldest sons, Omar and Yacine, aged 13 and 14, had stopped going to school for almost six months. The family had already been reported two years earlier due to the father's abuse without any sort of monitoring put in place on account of the willingness shown by the parents. The school social worker had been concerned: the father, who was known to have psychiatric problems, did not always follow his treatment plan, and the mother, who worked as a cashier, but had irregular hours, struggled to gain control of the situation. She noted that the family was "left on its own to manage the father's violence." Although she was theoretically required to report the truancy to the school district, the social worker, wary of exacerbating the family's already difficult situation, deferred reporting them. The Home for Adolescents' professionals were divided over how they should respond. The facility's counselor commented: "It's mostly a case of social distress. But the family really is in danger and they just keep getting passed around from institution to institution. The kids have been out of school for a while, but nobody says anything so that the family doesn't lose its benefits." The Youth Protective Services special educator collaborating with the center thought that this type of situation illustrated the contradictions present in educational intervention. He stressed the impact of new policies on child protection, which, in an attempt to divert youths from the justice system and avoid placing them in the foster system, could lead to unnecessary delays before anyone intervened. Following the passage of the Law of March 5, 2007, professionals who are concerned that a child may be in danger are in fact required to inform the departmental committee in charge of monitoring children at risk. In such situations, when the parents agree to cooperate and are not suspected of having committed any crime, the matter is no longer referred to the courts (except in cases when a family repeatedly fails to adhere to educational measures). In the case of Omar and Yacine, no interim placement order had been issued because a judge can only issue this ruling when the parents refuse to cooperate. The psychiatrist in charge of the unit wondered about the legitimacy and efficacy of an intervention in this type of situation: "The social and physical aspects are not our responsibility. We have to concentrate on what we can do: clinical work. Calming the kids down, sitting down and talking things over."

In difficult situations like these, when therapists feel powerless, the entire team sometimes finds itself in a difficult position, and the "flash" meetings during which new situations are discussed and decisions made can sometimes become quite heated. Since the professionals vary in their status and answer to different departments (hospital administration, medical hierarchy, external agencies such as Child Welfare or Youth Protective Services), the balance of power can be upset, especially given the fact that the most legitimate (psychiatrists) are not always the most experienced, because turnover is particularly high among therapists. One young psychiatrist commented: "We don't have much experience or oversight. Everyone is very young, and training is sometimes limited. There are many who find themselves in precarious situations, especially among the psychologists." The different legitimacies often clash with each other: some may tout their experience and their social and cultural proximity with the public (the majority of the team, like almost all the families who come to the center, are from foreign backgrounds) in order to devalue the degrees of the young psychiatrists, whose authority is occasionally challenged. The psychiatrist quoted above, the daughter of poor Italian immigrants, was in fact resented for her Parisian origins and her assumed status as a "native-born" French person, both of which supposedly hindered her understanding of situations whenever tensions ran high with hierarchically subordinate colleagues whose immigrant backgrounds were much more "obvious." It was as if the Homes for Adolescents were pervaded by the ambivalences of the state on the correct way to respond to the precarious immigrant populations.

These tensions were exacerbated by the lack of material and administrative resources which threatened the very existence of the team and the facility. After a period of enthusiasm in the 2000s, Homes for Adolescents began running into financial difficulties. For most, funding is not permanent. Some essentially depend on the departmental government, whose resources are not always stable enough to maintain the subsidies and which are themselves susceptible to political about-faces. As for those attached to hospitals, while they may in theory be more stable, they nevertheless experience other difficulties, subject as they are to cost-saving measures and managerial constraints that are specific to hospital administration. The push to quantify the amount of work done has led to a devaluation of the job's fundamental purpose: relational work, particularly for social workers who do not fall under the hospital administration and whose work goes largely unrecognized. They have to "turn a profit," to account for even the smallest of tasks (including the numerous phone calls they make) because their future funding is dependent on what is included in their evaluations.

Although Homes for Adolescents are expected to support other institutions, one of their paradoxes thus lies in their institutional instability. This instability raises questions about the contemporary features of the state and its difficulty in playing the role of "bank of symbolic capital,"[18] at least for some of its institutions. The questions of many professionals in this facility and in partner institutions, their occasional difficulties in enforcing their authority—or at least the fact that they feel as though they occasionally have to justify it—their doubts about the purpose of their position, the ethical concerns that they have regarding certain transformations in their jobs (as evidenced by the discussions surrounding the demands that there be more collaboration among institutions, more sharing of information, etc.) are all signs of the state's deficit in moral legitimacy in the eyes of its own agents in a number of situations. But while the state's ambivalence may prove troublesome for professionals, it is all the more pertinent when we turn our focus to the way in which the families perceive these interventions.

Institutions and Families in Disarray

Unheard Requests and Hard-to-find Answers

Because they were often referred to the Home for Adolescents by the schools or social services, the families we met were a priori submissive to institutions. However, the mental health professionals often found it difficult to get the families to make a "request" in therapeutic terms. For them, such a request ensured that the families take ownership of their own treatment. Yet the parents sometimes left the sessions that they attended with the impression that what they considered to be their real "request" had not been heard or at least that they did not get a real answer. Hamidou's father thus admitted that he felt ambivalent about the Home for Adolescents: he appreciated the fact that the professionals took the time to listen, acknowledged their kindness as well as their apparent lack of judgmental attitudes, but he afterwards questioned the point of the intervention. He would have preferred some advice, in particular about education, and used a rather evocative image to describe his experience: "In the end, this center was like a big blank book." With no writing, with no message, the reader is left confused.

In the case of Omar and Yacine, the disconnect that existed between the request expected by the institution and the actual request of the parents was especially noticeable. Despite their hesitation about how to handle the case, the professionals at the Home for Adolescents finally agreed to schedule welcome interviews. They met with the eldest son and his parents, both Algerian immigrants, for the first time in February 2010. During the meeting, the issue of the father's violent behavior was brought up. Also discussed was the story of the couple—they had had an arranged marriage. The son expressed feelings of worthlessness, particularly in school. He had failed sixth grade, but was nevertheless promoted to seventh grade because of his age (he had already repeated a grade in primary school). He admitted that he had trouble sleeping and spent hours playing video games. The mother explained that she was exhausted and that the irregular hours of her job as a cashier often meant that she did not get home before 9 p.m. She had just managed to reduce the number of hours that she worked (22 hours per week, down from 37) in order to be more present in the lives of her children. But the family's income also took a hit: she went from earning 1,050 euros a month to earning 620 euros a month. Her husband received 680 euros in disability benefits because of his mental disorder. The psychologist and the counselor noted in the file that they were "somewhat worried about this family." The son told the two when they met without the parents that he had not wanted to come, that he had wanted to sleep. He said that his father had been violent since he was ten years old. He also explained that he was bored. He was forced to stop playing soccer in order to pick up his younger brother from school since his father was not always capable of doing so. Moreover, once he turned ten, he was no longer able to participate in activities at the local recreation center, and there was no system in place to fill the subsequent void. In June, the family participated in a counseling session; it was devoted to the history of the father. Another appointment was scheduled for two months later. The morning of this meeting, the mother called to cancel because her son had refused to get out of bed. Asked to comment on this case a few months later, the psychiatrist in charge of the session noted the cancellation and wondered what to do in this sort of situation. He thought that there was no point in chasing down families all the time, that for therapeutic purposes they had to "find their own way," to take ownership of the first step. At the same time, he asked himself whether or not for some families, especially immigrant families, he should be more involved, more "supportive" since they did not necessarily seek out institutional help. But he never acted on his speculation.

We met the couple at their home in a housing project three months later. The mother was better able to explain her point of view. She did not at all correspond with the image that had emerged from reading the files. It was more difficult to follow what the father had to say since his thoughts were relatively incoherent. The mother immediately expressed her concern and her need for institutional help: "It's gotten worse over the last year or two. I can't figure anything out. I need outside assistance. That's why I agreed to let someone help me out, help me find a solution. I can't figure things out on my own." She described her children as being "held back" in their lives and as being "apathetic" since they started middle school; she thought that they were "out of shape" and was surprised that they "no longer wanted to go outside." In the file, the mother was presented as having given up, but a completely different picture emerged from the interview. She described in detail her unsuccessful attempts to rally her children:

> I showed him some pamphlet that said it was important to sleep. It's good for the morale; it helps you do well in school, to be right in the head. But he didn't care. I told him that the subsidy was not meant for buying video games, but for buying things for school. It's not OK with me if he uses it to buy X-box games. I tell him he's my responsibility.

Recently, the police found the two boys at the Charles de Gaulle Airport; they had tagged along with a friend who was skipping school: "That worries me. Anything could happen to them. I won't abandon them like that. They need supervision. They don't go to school, they don't do their homework, I'm not going to abandon them like that."

The mother had clearly asked the institutions for help, for guidance, and for information. But the institutions seemed in no hurry to respond to her "request." This mother had too much on her plate not to be suspected of wanting to pass some of her responsibilities on to institutions. At the same time, she was submissive enough for the children not to be seen as being truly "in danger." To a certain extent, she does not fit into any one category which would allow for more effective action. As for the Home for Adolescents' professionals, they did not respond to her request because it did not really fall within their responsibility and because they were expecting a different type of solicitation. As a result, they left her to face the situation on her own. And just like Hamidou's father, she did not know where to turn to:

> Right now, all they do is ask questions. I don't know what good that'll do. They don't propose any solutions. Sometimes I get discouraged. I need help, but I get the impression that all they're going to do is ask me questions. I'm waiting for them to tell me what's wrong with the kids, to tell me what I should do,

to tell me what they need, welfare, anything. What I should do and some outside help.

At the end of the interview, she wondered: "Who has to come up with the solution? Them or me?" To which she added pensively: "They say it's the parents who don't know how to control them ... Well, whatever it is, I can't figure it out."

Beyond the Institution: The Weight of Suspicion

In doing so, the mother points out the contradictions in the moral economy of the monitoring of low-income adolescents: absolving society of its responsibility, institutions demand more of the families even though their living conditions do not always allow them to do what is expected of them. Despite the reflexivity on the part of the professionals and their desire not to stigmatize the families any more than they already are, their involvement is thus caught up in more general developments which exceed the scope of their intervention and partly inscribe it within a logic of suspicion. The social and political context has led some parents to feel that they are suspected of being "bad" parents or at least of "not knowing how to handle their children." The powerlessness of policies to resolve the social question weighs first and foremost on them. In the case of Omar and Yacine, the support provided to them in the end ignored what from a sociological point of view seems crucial: besides the father's illness, what the adolescents were experiencing also had to do with, on the one hand, the mother's irregular schedule and exhaustion as well as their age discrepancy in school,[19] and on the other hand, the lack of supervisory institutions (the boys becoming too old for recreation center activities and their ensuing boredom) which left the family socially isolated. These elements were all highlighted during the initial interviews when the family's situation was assessed, but they seemed to fall by the wayside as the team went about building its case, zeroing in on the fear present in the family's history and the parenting arrangements.

The father's opinions, which at first seemed somewhat incoherent, in fact condensed, albeit in a very exacerbated way given his pathology, what pervades the majority of the interviews conducted with fathers outside the structure. More so than mothers, fathers seize upon the presence of investigators in reaction to the image of themselves that French society in the form of its institutions as well as through the representations and discourses conveyed by television reflects back on them.[20] The investigators who come to their home to discuss the problems caused by their children appear as representatives of French institutions and thus become the repository of the parent's attempts to resist these designations. Echoing his wife, the father insisted in a rambling manner on his willingness: "I've watched my son. Where's he going?" "He goes to school, he'll do well," "No drugs," "No hanging out with thugs." He brought up his accidents and commented: "I'm not a slacker, don't steal from the government, if you cheat, it's not good." For immigrant fathers, the relationship with France via its institutions can be particularly painful and threatening. Confronted with a delinquent child, they often have a binary understanding of the direction that their teen may take in life (the right path/the wrong path). And behaviors that might be tolerated or at least downplayed in other environments for them immediately take on worrying proportions.[21]

These fathers feel repudiated because their parenting methods are generally perceived by French institutions as violent, or as being in conflict with the norms of child protection. So they may cling to the prospect of sending their child back to their home country as a last resort. This was what drove Hamidou's father to say: "If he stays, then I'm going to have problems with the police and if they call me into the school again, I might become uncontrollable." The threat of sending his son back to Guinea is indicative of the confusion and humiliation that he felt when dealing with his son in France. In contrast, he was grateful to the professionals for not taking "the side of France or the side of Africa." The perception that he has of his son seems to have changed since their contact with the center: "My son's not a criminal, he's a troublemaker," he said, referring in addition to a "teen crisis" and "his need to exist." The situation in school also seemed to have calmed down according to the social worker. Despite everything, the father still seemed ill-equipped to handle his son, on whom he had pinned all his hopes for his family's success. "Today, at the dawn of a new millennium, it's hell raising a boy in France," he sighed as he compared his son with his daughters and their academic achievements.

If parents take offense to institutional intervention, then it is also because the professionals always wind up glossing over the way in which their living conditions affect their family balance. The professionals have no control over commuting times, work schedules, or housing conditions and thus allow these objective parameters to fall by the wayside, even though they can be specified at the outset. When they are brought up, they may make the parents feel guilty if no solution is proposed to address them. Hamidou's mother, for instance, had been offended by a psychologist who informed her that it was not good for him to sleep in the same bed as his little sister despite the fact that the nine-person family had to endure living in a three-room apartment after being forced to leave their larger house in a quieter neighborhood.

These misunderstandings between an institution that expects an adequate request and families that seek actionable responses show how words are connoted by the moral economy in which they are spoken. Yet the families were rarely angry with the Home for Adolescents. They often remained ambivalent instead, as was the case with Hamidou's parents. The effects of these conflicting discourses are very difficult to anticipate, especially since not all family members are affected in the same way by contact with the facility. In general, institutional action contributes to the destabilization of the internal balance in the family configuration, redistributing the symbolic capital within the family so that some adolescents may benefit, while others may react more or less strongly. This is also what came across in the interviews we will now analyze.

Teenagers: Between Resistance and Appropriation

Occasional Use and Halfhearted Commitment

Homes for Adolescents aim to be places where teens are able to drop in at any time for various problems without feeling stigmatized, as might be the case with medico-psychological centers which focus their attention on diagnosed pathologies. From their name (with the peculiar but significant reference to a home) to their choice of decor (the colors of the walls, the style of the furniture, the decorations all similar to what might be found in an individual's home), these facilities do everything they can to avoid the stigma of insanity that often looms over this type of institution, including hiring non-psychiatric professionals to welcome the teenagers. There are, however, a number of obstacles in the way of achieving this goal. In some departments, the facility is located in a hospital; in several places, psychiatrists and psychologists make up the majority of the team; elsewhere, the difficulty in finding the actual center reduces it to a simple telephone switchboard and a few mobile professionals. Beyond these key material issues, the desire to encourage the teenagers to come on their own initiative and to have the families make the request is rarely fulfilled, since the vast majority of the adolescents are referred from other institutions. Although it is difficult to know the underlying reasons why youths are willing to visit these centers, we can assume that the hope of finding professionals able to solve their problems and the desire to show the referring institutions their commitment jointly contribute to their willingness. There is no sanction for those who refuse the "invitation." For low-income families belonging to minorities, showing one's commitment to the institutions supervising them is a basic strategy and one that often pays off.[22]

The teenagers we interviewed had a rather positive opinion of the facility, even if there is obviously a selection bias in these interviews since reluctant ones do not visit the institution or cut short their monitoring before it is possible to hear their points of view. In most cases, this monitoring was relatively short, lasting only a few months. And, according to the various actors involved, the problems, although they are never really addressed, seemed to diminish. In the case of Karim, for example, the work done at the Home for Adolescents consisted in meeting with and listening to him and his parents separately. The latter were first alerted by the school after their son (the youngest of three) had skipped class several times. It was then that they realized that Karim spent a lot of time playing video games and had even stolen money from them to buy some. His mother worked mainly at night preparing meal trays for Air France and his father was often in Tunisia, where he was renovating the family home since he retired from his job as a runway worker. It was the school social worker who suggested that they visit the Home for Adolescents. It took some difficulty, however, persuading Karim: "You're wasting your time. I'm not crazy. I know what's wrong with me," he told his parents. The psychologist who helped them summarized the situation in the following way:

The family was worried because he was no longer doing well in school and spent all his time in front of his computer. So the family and the school said, "He's lying to us. He's not telling us what he's doing." You should have seen the mom. That was exactly what she said: "He's lying to us." There was something else: he had stolen money. But that wasn't very important. He played games online and had stolen money. There was the problem at school and that was a problem of poor guidance. He was placed in the vocational track and did not like it at all. He wanted to go back to general education. When he had to choose at the end of ninth grade, he made a choice or was pushed to make a choice that was not right for him. So he said: "I don't care what they make me do."

After a few sessions during which everyone told their version of the story, things settled down. Then summer vacation rolled around. They agreed to meet that following September, which never happened. As often is the case, school vacation brings with it an interruption in the monitoring process that is difficult to overcome, as if the Home for Adolescents were intimately linked to the academic calendar. The fighting had nevertheless stopped, explained Karim's father afterwards: "He went to a few sessions. He started doing better in school again. He still plays video games. He complains when we don't let him play, but he doesn't do any more online gambling. We keep an eye on him. Let's just say he's not a bad kid, but we still keep an eye on him." From Karim's point of view, a major change had occurred: his parents had come to realize that the vocational track was not right for him and after making a special request, he was able to return to the general education track after taking a placement exam. Such a situation is not exceptional: other teenagers who visited the center expressed similar feelings of unhappiness in their educational choices. They had been placed in devalued educational tracks because neither they nor their parents knew how to evaluate the options when it was time for them to make a decision.

Many things play upon the misunderstandings: Karim's father was afraid his son might be addicted to video games and left the center reassured by the benignity of this pathology. For the psychologist who treated the family, the problems stemmed from the difficult relationship between the father and his son, which he thought he had improved by making things seem less dramatic without really perceiving the father's concern about the disorder and the delinquency. For the son, he profited from his reluctant visit to the center in terms of symbolic capital: his academic reevaluation was accompanied by lesser supervision. In short, perhaps no one found exactly what he was looking for, but the new balance proved satisfactory for everyone.

When Teens Are Confronted with the Destabilization of Their Parents

One of the objectives of the system that could also be said to play a role in the case of Karim was to transfer as much as possible the burden of the intervention from the teenager to the parents who are thought to be stronger. In the context of family counseling, for example, only the parents are invited to speak, and in most cases they are asked to speak about their past, while the teenager is there to listen and if possible to reclaim some of his own past. It is only in certain specific sessions that adolescents were invited to speak about themselves after having been reminded that nothing would be repeated to their parents or teachers without their consent. As we saw earlier, this bias puts immense pressure on the parents, who are made to be "good parents," to expose themselves to their children and to an often impressive group of professionals. However, this process can also be violent for the teenagers when the breakdown of their parents proves too unbearable for them.

This was what happened, for example, to Gonzalo, who during a family counseling session lost his temper after his mother was asked a question he considered overly intrusive. The main therapist had inquired if the mother dreamed about anything important when she slept, to which she responded negatively. He then hinted that she might not want to discuss her dreams and told her to be ready to talk about her dreams the next time. He said that if she was afraid she might forget them, then all she had to do was to share them with Gonzalo who would remember them because "he has a very good memory." The boy dug in his heels: "No," he said curtly. The psychiatrist turned to him: "Oh?" Gonzalo raised his tone of voice; he became aggressive: "My mother's not going to tell you anything. If she wanted to say something, she would." As was his habit, the psychiatrist interrupted Gonzalo for a moment to name and to legitimize the emotions that the adolescent was feeling: "Are you angry right now?" Gonzalo reacted loudly again: "No! If I was really upset, I'd punch you!" The psychiatrist tried to calm him down: "You can say anything you want in here; it's a therapy session. Nothing's off limits. That's what a therapy session is about. There's medical confidentiality. That's how we make progress." Gonzalo became increasingly hostile: "But why do we have to make progress?" The mother then tried to calm her son down, patting him on the shoulder and talking to him tenderly. He would have none of it. The psychiatrist continued: "We're talking about complicated things. It's important to talk, to say what's on your mind. Why are you angry?" Gonzalo got up and tried to leave the room, but the door was locked. He became even angrier: "What's up with this?" The social worker sitting in on the session helped him to unlock the door and then ran after him to try to reason with him. He refused to go back into the room. The primary therapist, a little unsettled, commented that the teenager did not seem to be aware of how things worked, especially the group aspect of the session. The social worker admitted that she had not given him enough information: since she had a good relationship with the boy, she did not anticipate this kind of reaction from him. The only way the adolescent was able to extricate himself from the symbolic violence of the situation was by slamming the door. He could not stand the fact that his mother was the subject of an inquiry which he considered indecent, an uncomfortable situation for her, which he knew was due to his own misbehavior.

This atypical therapy session gives us greater insight into how family configurations are affected by the work done at Homes for Adolescents. With varying degrees of success, these institutions attempt to redistribute the symbolic capital within a family, especially between the parents and the children. Teenagers arrive at the Home for Adolescents lacking in legitimacy, particularly within their families. The attempt we just described may have turned into a fiasco, but other cases have more favorable outcomes. The efforts on the part of the professionals seem to allow the teenagers to get back in the saddle socially by making some sort of clean break with their families. However, the contemporary moral economy makes it more difficult to effect a social and geographical separation from one's family, since maintaining emotional ties has become implicitly moral, while upward social mobility is much less offset by monetary transfers from the children to the parents than it has been in the past. The ability to distance oneself from one's family presupposes certain conditions, conditions to which Homes for Adolescents can contribute, as two cases we will now discuss show.

Using the Institution to Climb the Social Ladder: A Gendered Trend

The youngest of five children, all of whom were born in Algeria except for her, 18-year-old Jennifer explained that she had felt that she was different from her siblings who were significantly older. She had started having anxiety attacks when she was a teen and had attempted suicide several times, which resulted in repeated visits to the emergency room where she met with professionals from the Home for Adolescents. Her parents, who lived in the same apartment even though they were in fact separated, were deeply worried about their daughter and agreed to participate in transcultural family counseling. Yet they soon distanced themselves from the institution. Jennifer was very attached to her individual back-to-back sessions first with a psychiatrist, then with a psychologist, and finally with a developmental therapist.

After a few sessions, the transcultural family therapist concluded that through her problems the girl was attempting to keep her parents together. Therapy would allow Jennifer to detach herself from her parents without fearing what the consequences would be for them. Without exploring the therapist's conclusion in greater detail, it should be noted that at the same time she began visiting the Home for Adolescents, Jennifer also began to distance herself from her family, not only on a geographic level (she had enrolled in a prestigious Paris college to study law), but also and more importantly on a social level. She was in fact the first in her family to graduate from high school. Her boyfriend was a sociology student at a different major university, which was why he had wanted to attend the interview. Jennifer explained her attachment to the institution: "For me, going to a psychologist was a lot easier than going to see a social worker." To which her companion added that there was no shame in seeing a psychologist because even the CEOs of major companies see psychologists whereas social workers were specialized in dealing with difficult social situations and could threaten the family unit if they reported anything. Although it is often thought that seeing a psychologist is something to be feared because it suggests mental instability, in this instance it was invested with a social value that casts psychological patients in a positive light.

At the Home for Adolescents, Jennifer found a type of relationship and a use of language much more in line with the practices of the sphere she aspired to join than those which prevailed in the world of her family. She said that she had "learned to think differently," that it had helped her to "grow." She had learned to "manage stress," which was invaluable to her when it came to exams (driver's test, finals). She "relativized," "de-dramatized," saw things "in a different light." The reflexive use of language is seen as a quintessential characteristic of the middle and upper classes, and Jennifer felt that she had made progress on this front at the Home for Adolescents. Thus, her appropriation of the institution— she said that it was "her own space" that she did not want anyone "encroaching" upon—highlights a number of differences with respect to her family: she was the youngest, belonging in fact to another generation, the only one to be born in France and therefore French from the start, the most Western in appearance, the only one to go on to higher education … and the only one prone to anxiety attacks. Jennifer was not just preparing herself for a psychologically difficult dissociation from her parents: she was also quietly preparing for a major social dissociation and found the tools she needed to ready herself for her future role at the Home for Adolescents.

This was not an isolated case. Gladys, the eldest of the two girls from Haiti, demonstrated a similar relationship with the institution. She had initially been referred by the nurse at her high school on account of her problems (insomnia, loss of appetite, difficulty concentrating) and her complex social situation (immigration under a false identity). Since then, Gladys had begun seeing a psychologist. She readily explained her reasoning when we interviewed her, which was in stark contrast with her diffident behavior during the family counseling sessions: "I wanted to see a psychologist, but in my mother's mind, a psychologist was for crazy people." This desire for psychological counseling particularly resonated because her immigration coincided, as in many similar cases, with high-flying social ambitions. She had told her mother when she arrived in France that she wanted to become a psychologist, but her mother was opposed to the idea. So she decided to study to become a nurse: "I told myself that I could do the same things as a nurse. That way I can help people who are in intensive care and are having operations. I want to help them accept the operation and make sure that everything goes well."

Gladys's disappointment at having to repeat several grades due to her false identity is therefore understandable. Exploited by the person who housed her, made to do household chores and to look after children, she failed to succeed academically and ended up studying for a vocational certificate rather than a high school diploma. But once her immigration status was regularized, she was placed back in the general education track and was able to study for the nursing exam. Like Jennifer, she too had developed a narrative that gave meaning to her past and the difficulties she had encountered. At first seen as a stigma within the family and in the eyes of her peers, the problems for which Gladys had originally sought treatment were transformed into a distinctive element of a coherent discourse. Gladys had learned to construct this discourse after resituating her problems within her own family and social history. She thus recounted how she had always thought that she was different from her siblings and that her extreme shyness made her very attentive to the stories and sufferings of others:

> Ever since I was a child, I never managed to make friends. I just sat in my corner all the time. I watched the others play because I have three sisters and two brothers. When I was little, I spent all my time with adults. I spoke more with adults than with kids my own age. They used to call me over when they had problems at home and I used to tell them what I thought. I liked how people would talk to me, how they would tell me their problems. It was like I had solved a problem.

This rather feminine-seeming "work of self-transformation" has many similarities with what Muriel Darmon[23] has described about anorexic girls who were themselves also in a process of using school to climb the social ladder, but in their case from middle class to upper class. This self-transformative work is also a moral work, which seeks to reverse the stigma attached to mental suffering and to manage feelings of guilt through the physical and symbolic distancing from one's family. It demonstrates how the institution is appropriated, complicating the idea that the adolescents and their families are completely divested of any domination or social control. Ready to dissociate themselves from their families for various reasons (generational gap, fragile sociability oriented towards adults, self-perception as "different"), Jennifer and Gladys relied on the Home for Adolescents to help them in their climb.

It is worth noting that it was girls who on the whole did well in school. It is also worth noting that the two interviews with these girls took place on local university campuses, a setting that is of course quieter but also gives a more positive image than their respective homes. We are a far cry from the representation of a minor in danger who risks becoming a delinquent. For girls, psychological fragility and academic success can go hand in hand, while this combination is rare among boys. Psychological strength may be more easily recognized in men,[24] but showing psychological weakness is more excusable in girls and the act of seeking mental help can be more easily overcome by them, if not used to their advantage. Therefore, when the welfare state today requires individuals to assume responsibility for themselves and to become autonomous actors, these demands may weigh more heavily on boys who do less well in school and have greater difficulty overcoming the inequality. Although male domination in general remains an undeniable reality, there are areas where women fare better than men, especially in times of economic crisis or social difficulty.[25] Hence the indignant remark made by Hamidou's father: "Today, at the dawn of a new millennium, it's hell raising a boy in France!"

Conclusion

Institutions at the confluence of social work and mental health established in the early 2000s, Homes for Adolescents, especially those in disadvantaged neighborhoods, are a repository of both the structural issues in society and the problems of other institutions in charge of youth. Our observation of the work being done and of the way in which both the professionals and the public envisage it exposes the state's ambivalence about its relationship with low-income families, particularly of immigrant background. This ambivalence is also reflected in the very status of these new institutions: their forms are poorly defined and vary from one department to another, while their status is precarious and their financing not guaranteed.

Although mental health professionals and social workers say that they are committed to resisting the possibility that they become instruments of social control, although they worry about the excessive medicalization of social problems, and although they are careful not to blame the parents, they are nevertheless caught up in social and political changes that are beyond their control and that in part influence how parents perceive their involvement. Both penal and social policies regarding children and adolescents are inscribed within a moral economy that, contrary to the prevailing post-war ideas, relates behavior to individuals rather than society. This often translates into shifting the responsibility onto the parents: forced to speak for themselves, they express how confused they are by an institution that listens to them without providing them with real solutions, especially since child protection policies tend to favor less intervention whenever the families are conciliatory. Immigrant parents feel particularly challenged by the state which suspects them of being bad parents who "do not know how to handle their children" when they cause problems.

No analysis of what the institution does would be complete without taking into account the perspectives of the adolescents, which are sometimes quite distinct from those of the parents. By playing on the categories of perception specific to families, institutional involvement potentially contributes to the redistribution of symbolic capital within the family. While some teenagers may be offended by this intrusion, others seem to take advantage of the situation with a view toward setting themselves apart, freeing themselves from their families, mustering the material, social, and cultural resources that the institution can provide. These two reactions do not seem to be randomly distributed: girls appear to grab at these opportunities more quickly than boys—in keeping with what the sociology of education has already shown regarding the relationship of low-income children with the educational institution.

Homes for Adolescents thus lie at the crossroads of the mental fragility of low-income teenagers belonging to minorities and the structural fragility of institutions meant to supervise them, both of which reflect more generally the processes of precarization and destructuration at work, at least in some neighborhoods. But it is precisely this well-known social issue which is quickly excised from analyses produced in spaces where social work has been progressively transformed into psychological work. The expression and analysis of suffering, shame, or guilt during therapy sessions quickly supplants that of inequality and injustice on the part of the professionals, as well as the teenagers themselves. However, this psychological approach produces effects that are sometimes sought after, but are more often unexpected, and most actors who intervene in the Homes for Adolescents adapt to them or even seize them as they are unable to act on the structural disparities that affect individual fates.

Notes

1 At Houses of Justice (*Maisons de la Justice et du Droit*), a portion of the complaints comes from institutional agents (teachers, counselors, gendarmes, police officers) who are asking for the justice system to reaffirm the authority of the institution to which they belong (Coutant 2005). This is part of a more general movement to externalize the handling of legal cases by institutions which ask the justice system to fill in for them.

2 This is what Didier Fassin (2005) shows concerning a group of policies affecting various sectors.

3 The notion of moral economy is used here in the sense described in the introduction of this book, which is distinctly different from that used by E.P. Thompson (Fassin and Eideliman 2012). Moral economy is organized around a question at a given moment and in a given society.

4 The text grouped together interviews—coupled with commentaries—conducted with low-income individuals and the institutional agents responsible for these populations (Bourdieu 1993).

5 The growth in power of the norms of autonomy and individual fulfillment since the second half of the twentieth century has been documented in various fields, in particular those of health (Ehrenberg 1998) and family (Singly 1996).

6 Foucault expounds upon this thesis in lectures given at the Collège de France in 1974–75, which were published posthumously under the title *Abnormal* (Foucault 2003).

7 In particular, her works on the invention of the abnormal childhood (Muel 1975).

8 See Pinell and Zafiropoulos (1978).

9 See Vial (1990).

10 This is illustrated in a study conducted by Stéphane Beaud (2002) in disadvantaged neighborhoods.

11 On this point, see the report by Marc Buisson and Francis Salles, "Les maisons des adolescents," Direction de l'hospitalisation et de l'organisation des soins, ministère de la Santé et des Sports, February 2009.

12 In France in 1950, those in the 65–74 age group were almost five times more likely to commit suicide than those in the 25–34 age group. By 1995, the likelihood had fallen to 1.5 (Baudelot and Establet 2006).

13 Delphine Serre (2009) uses her study of child endangerment reports made by social workers to demonstrate this twin movement (the extension and weakening of control).

14 See Roussel (1989).

15 This is what Robert Barrett (1998) shows when he explains how the schizophrenic was constructed in the twentieth century as the antithesis of the ideal adult.

16 First names have been changed in order to protect the anonymity of the individuals.

17 Data from http://www.insee.fr/fr/bases-de-donnees/default.asp?page=statistiques-locales.htm.

18 Pierre Bourdieu (2012) developed this analysis of the state as a bank of symbolic capital in a course devoted to the topic at the Collège de France from 1989 to 1992.

19 Because these teens have been promoted to the next grade without having attained the required level, they are completely lost and devalued in class, as Daniel Thin (1998) notes in numerous situations. The analysis of school dropouts that he and Mathias Millet (2005) propose also emphasizes the role of academic failure in their decision to leave school.

20 The television was often prominently displayed in the homes we visited, sometimes in stark contrast to the bareness of the apartments. The fact that the television was not always turned off during interviews hints at its routine importance in the life of the family (Schwartz 1990).

21 See Coutant (2005).

22 In cases where child endangerment has been reported, Delphine Serre (2009) has shown that social workers tend to be kinder toward the cooperative families than they are toward those that appear "evasive," "full of demands," or "aggressive."

23 Muriel Darmon (2009) proposes the notion of "self-transformation work" to account for the different stages of anorexia from beginning to end.

24 Olivier Schwartz (2010) studies these questions in his latest work.

25 For another illustration of this process, Florence Weber's study (2008) of a working-class town over twenty years is particularly illuminating. She shows how blue-collar pride in "side jobs" has largely given way to pride in working under the table and in nearby jobs which are filled mostly by women.

CHAPTER NINE

Profiling Job Seekers
The Counseling of Youths at an Employment Center

Sarah Mazouz

"That's what makes it even more of a paradox … We can't pick and choose our public, and yet despite the sociological characteristics of the youths we deal with, we still have to meet performance goals." That was how one counselor at a Youth Employment Center described the contradictory demands he faced as he went about his job each day assisting youths from the banlieues of Paris find jobs. He and many of his colleagues felt that newly assigned targets conflicted with their initial motivation for choosing the job, and during team meetings and coffee breaks they voiced their unease with these transformations.

Based on a principle of "unconditional welcome," the center provides counseling to any out-of-school youth between the ages of 16 and 25 who comes in and signs up for help in finding a job or training program. Those welcomed at the Youth Employment Center where the study was conducted lived in the low-income neighborhoods of the banlieues. The vast majority of them came from families that originally hailed from North Africa, sub-Saharan Africa, the Caribbean, or South East Asia. Many still lived with their parents. Some resided in foster homes because they had been abused or mistreated by their families. Others went from one temporary place to the next. Still others already had children and were either looking for housing or trying to keep the housing that they were already in. A number of them were also being supervised by other social agencies like Youth Protective Services or Child Welfare. And the staff at the center would often find out about prior convictions when the youths applied for jobs which required a clean criminal record. A few were being monitored by psychiatric services. Such factors explain why helping the youths has more to do with devising career plans than it does with immediate job placement. Counselors must presumably pay constant attention to the living conditions of those they assist, and a significant part of their job is dedicated to finding financial aid or other temporary relief measures in order to provide necessary stability in the young people's lives. As a result, the "unconditional welcome" counselors are supposed to offer comes into conflict with what is also demanded of them: finding jobs for as many youths as possible.

Funded mainly by local governments (the department and the municipalities), and the European Social Fund, Youth Employment Centers are a public service which plays the role of intermediary between the business world and job market as well as a hard-to-employ segment of the population whose role is similar to that of an "industrial reserve army" called up depending on the economic situation. Unlike the system in Germany where professional training is seen as the main means of responding to unemployment among unskilled youth,[1] or in the United States where there is no support and where employment agencies place young people with analogous social characteristics in precarious jobs,[2] the French system is made up not only of employers and people to be employed, but also intermediary public structures tasked with *making* these youths employable by providing social support and preparing them for their professional future. But while making these youths "employable" does involve providing them with social support, it also means adapting them to employers' demands by teaching them how to be responsible and to know how to present themselves.

This normative aspect and the moral component which lies within are reinforced by managerial changes in the focus of the Youth Employment Center's work. The funding the institution receives is dependent on the number of youths hired, and through a combination of control procedures, a counselor's performance is likewise subject to a statistical assessment which takes into consideration the number of youths "placed in a job," but ignores the "social dimension" of his or her work. Although the normative logic corresponds in part with the idea that counselors have of their work, the methods of evaluating their results call into question what for them are the "main responsibilities" of their job. The imposition of quantitative goals essentially replaces the social support that they once provided with the task of matching youths to jobs. Exposing the counselors to the difficulties experienced by the youths they assist, the new targets also demonstrate the limits of what the center can do as a social employment service.

The managerial reconfiguration of the Youth Employment Center therefore combines a normative logic tied in part to the supervisory practices defined by the counselors with an administrative logic based on a quantitative assessment that conflicts with the principle of social support. I will explore this tension in greater detail by focusing on the job searches I observed. On the one hand, I will analyze the way in which this managerial reconfiguration has been implemented. On the other hand, I will examine the practices of the counselors and attempt to see how it has become possible for them to fabricate and validate this configuration or conversely to try to correct it through their daily work.

Although the Youth Employment Center is a relatively recent institution, its creation is part of a longer history of ways in dealing with the "jobless." I will first retrace the evolution in the way work as a right has been constructed, analyzing how the question of this right has since the end of the post-war boom been progressively reformulated in terms of adapting the unemployed to the job market. I will then focus on the quantitative assessments insofar as they structure the practices of counselors, transforming not only their work methods and the moral representation that they have of their professional responsibilities, but also their understanding of what the youths they assist experience socially. Revolving around the question of employment status and the development of short-term contracts for counselors, the evaluation of their work also introduces a demand of responsibility and autonomy on their part. In this sense, while this contractualization does characterize programs which assist precarious populations,[3] it also determines the practices and positions of the counselors who must demonstrate their responsibility to the institution by selecting "employable" youths and who are only granted the autonomy to establish the criteria on which this selection is based. Finally, I will shift my attention to how the intermediary position of the counselors between employers and youths affects their practices. I will show how the counselors force the youths to adapt their behavior to the expectations of employers, even if it means condoning or perpetuating the unfair treatment and forms of labeling these youths are subject to.

The Metamorphosis of the Labor Question

Work as a Right

The question of work as a right dates to as far back as 1789, when the Constituent Assembly saw it as a major political issue affecting both the subsistence and the control of the working class.[4] Only a few months after the storming of the Bastille, public works (notably the construction of the Canal de l'Ourcq and the stabilization of the banks of the Seine) were launched and "relief workshops" set up in Paris as well as the rest of the country.

The French Constitution of 1793 declared in Article 21 that "Public relief is a sacred debt. Society owes maintenance to unfortunate citizens, either procuring work for them or in providing the means of existence for those who are unable to labor." The right to work is thus for the first time perceived as a responsibility of society to its members. Due to France's subsequent declaration of war, the Constitution of Year I was never enacted, and this question would be eclipsed by rivalries within the Committee of Public Safety and issues surrounding the regime's preservation against attack and the various attempts to restore the monarchy.

It was not until the establishment of the Second Republic in 1848 that the labor question returned to the fore in political and intellectual debates, most notably within the different schools of socialist thought. As a result of the events of February 1848, which called for the establishment of a social republic, the provisional government added the concept of fraternity to the motto of the Republic. On February 25, 1848, Louis Blanc, a member of the provisional government, unilaterally declared the people's right to work and demanded that a Ministry of Labor equipped with human as well as material resources be created. The other members of the government were concerned by this demand. They decided instead to convene a commission of economists, socialist theoreticians, and representatives of Paris workers tasked with devising a plan for the organization of labor; the group came to be known as the Luxembourg Palace Commission. The provisional government placed Louis Blanc at its head in an attempt to distance him from the decision-making process as well as in an effort to avert a possible rebellion among Parisians who viewed the refusal to create a Ministry of Labor as a betrayal of the principal demand of the events of February 1848: the establishment of a "generous republic."

Just two days after Blanc's declaration, "national workshops" were already being set up to accommodate out-of-work Parisians. However, these workshops were more similar to the "charitable workshops," which previous conservative regimes had created to deal with the problem of poverty, than they were to the "social workshops" or industrial cooperatives made up of workers without employers proposed by Blanc in his 1839 work *The Organization of Labor*.[5] Using the military as their model, the national workshops recruited unemployed workers by arrondissement and coordinated various tasks like the leveling of land and the construction of roads, railways, and buildings. The activity assigned did not always correspond to the skills possessed by the unemployed worker, which meant that the national workshops also became de facto training centers. Despite these reforms, the results of the first elections in which suffrage was extended to all male citizens gave considerable power to the rural areas, which voted overwhelmingly in favor of conservative deputies. The Assembly that was elected on April 23, 1848 was largely made up of previous monarchists who were late and opportunistic converts to republicanism. These deputies would declare open war on what was achieved under the provisional government. They considered the national workshops as both a money pit and a symbol of the February mindset. On May 16, 1848, the National Assembly abolished the Luxembourg Palace Commission and threatened Louis Blanc with prosecution. On June 20, the Assembly voted to close the national workshops; the very next day, the Executive Commission decided to enforce the May 24, 1848 decree requiring workers between the ages of 18 and 25 to enlist in the army and for all other workers to be prepared to be sent to work on public projects throughout the country.[6]

Given the state of near-universal employment in the decades that followed, the Second Empire and the government of "moral order" found it easy to keep the question of the right to work largely under wraps. However, the question did resurface just as the laws "entrenching" the republican form of government were being enacted. For instance, the organization of unions was first authorized by the Waldeck-Rousseau Act of March 21, 1884. Yet at the same time, proposals made by the Deputy François-Vincent Raspail between the years 1886 and 1892 to create a Ministry of Labor were rejected, and it was not until 1906 that a Ministry of Labor and Social Providence came into being under Clemenceau. So while the proposal to establish such a ministry was in 1848 perceived as a means to affirm each individual's right to work and society's responsibility for the unemployed, its creation in the early twentieth century brought to the fore the question of working conditions and retirement while at the same time avoiding the question of what to do with workers who were unemployed.

This reformulation—from the right to work to the rights of workers—nevertheless led to the transformation of the way in which inactivity was understood: the state of being unemployed was from then on dissociated from the question of poverty and the forms of supervising marginal populations.[7] Defined as an able-bodied worker deprived of employment, the unemployed worker was distinguished not only from the seasonal worker, but also from the poor. Thought of as being involuntary, his inactivity was no longer tied to his moral qualities (or more precisely his deficiencies), but instead to how the labor market was organized.[8] The notion of unemployment thus signified a problem—the lack of work—faced by society at a time when salaried jobs were becoming increasingly more common.

Work as the Basis for an Insurance System

In this way, the emergence of the concept of unemployment strengthened the demand for a right to work by tying it to campaigns in Great Britain, France, and the United States to reform the collective response to the issues raised by the existence of involuntarily unemployed workers. The idea of a society accountable for the unemployed coincided with the birth of a science, presenting the social as a force exerted on individuals, which allowed for inactivity to be thought of as a scourge or as a dysfunction extrinsic to the workers themselves. It also proceeds from a transformation of the state whose action has been "governmentalized."[9] Unlike the moral register employed by philanthropic movements to distinguish the "deserving poor" worthy of assistance from those left to their own devices, unemployment is considered in terms of the rights of the workers, collective accountability, and redistribution of resources.[10] More fundamentally, the problematization in terms of involuntary unemployment led to a distinction being made between insurance and assistance. It enshrined the idea of the insured unemployed worker who possesses social rights and cleared the way for the implementation of an unemployment compensation system. Yet even as the category of the unemployed worker was in the process of being formulated, newly revived images of its flip side were accompanied by condemnations of supposed inactivity.[11] For example, in France, the inactive who were undeserving of unemployment insurance were labeled as "vagrants" or "professional beggars."

The move taking shape was therefore twofold. Being unemployed was no longer considered as indicative of individual moral deficiencies. But by "demoralizing" the inactivity of certain workers, the status of being unemployed and the rights it entailed were at the same time moralized. Only those who wanted to work but were prevented from doing so were deserving of the status. By contrast, the contradictory categories of unemployed designated those persons who could work but refused to do so and lived on the kindness of others like the "able-bodied indigents" philanthropists sought to flush out. This suspicion persists today in the forms of control developed by the bodies in charge of distributing unemployment benefits in order to identify the "fake unemployed" and other fraudsters.[12]

On the eve of World War I, the category of unemployed designated any able-bodied person who was temporarily out of work and looking for a job. The solidification of this definition made it possible for the formulation of political proposals which, as in Great Britain, led to the creation of a mandatory unemployment insurance system and the opening of the first public employment centers. The rise in the number of unemployed due to the economic instability caused by the war prompted the belligerents to set up public structures, like the Committee to Combat Unemployment created in France in 1915, which were responsible for job training or organizing the labor market.

Created in 1919, the International Labor Organization (ILO) became a think tank for issues of unemployment. Between 1919 and 1931, the ILO adopted three conventions and seven recommendations regarding unemployment insurance, job placement, public works, and measures enacted to avoid foreign competition. In 1933, convention number 44 of the ILO institutionalized unemployment insurance. However, this convention was only ratified by Great Britain and Switzerland. In the case of France, the right to work and the right to rest were reaffirmed in March 1944 by the program of the National Council of Resistance which called for the implementation of a "complete social security plan aiming to provide all citizens with the means to survive in all cases in which they are unable to secure work."[13] Nevertheless, while the creation of social security through the decrees of October 4 and 19, 1945 enshrined within French law the idea that with work comes access to social rights, these rights initially only covered health care and retirement. And it was not until 1958 that the National Interprofessional Agreement signed between employers and unions created an unemployment insurance system for employees in industry and commerce.

Since unemployment insurance was perceived as compensation promoting the return to work and the mobility of the labor force, the Law of July 13, 1967 set up a body to provide job counseling and placement: the National Employment Agency. Depending on the economic situation and the ideological configurations of the time, unemployment insurance was sometimes seen as being a form of compensation meant to offset the loss of a job and the search for a new one and sometimes as a benefit that was conditional upon an active search. As the post-war boom came to a close and the so-called "economic crisis" set in, the significant decline experienced by the industrial sector meant that unemployment became a lasting, widespread phenomenon. The compensation system was now subject to increasingly venomous attacks highlighting its cost or budget deficit as well as its inefficiency. In the eyes of its critics, the system only produced more "welfare recipients" and was incapable of reducing unemployment rates. This recurrent criticism gradually led to unemployment compensation being made conditional upon the active return to work as stipulated by both the Law of February 13, 2008 which merged the National Employment Agency and the unemployment insurance system to create a unified Employment Hub and the convention of February 19, 2009 which made unemployment insurance a "benefit to help return to work."

Thus, superimposed upon the question of the right to work was the question of access to jobs, and alongside the insurance system appeared institutions meant to match unemployed individuals with existing job openings. In the interval, the massive rise in youth unemployment at the end of the 1970s would come to justify as well as to impose this approach to the problem.

Youth Unemployment as a Problem of Adapting to the Labor Market

Youth unemployment has been the subject of particular attention since the 1930s. The question was placed on the agenda of the nineteenth session of the International Labor Conference in 1935, and in recommendation number 45, the ILO suggested extending the length of training and raising the legal working age in order to resolve the problem of an over-saturated youth labor market. It also recommended that union organizations and employer organizations come together to create centers for professional training as well as the launch of public work relief programs specifically dedicated to youths.

But it was not until the late 1960s that youth unemployment became a real target of political action. In France, professional training programs specifically aimed at the youth population were tested under the aegis of the Association for the Professional Training of Adults, the Ministry of Labor, the Ministry of Education, the non-profit sector, and Young Worker Hostels. It was within the context of these programs that the distinction between integration into the workplace and broader social integration was first made, and the Schwartz Report, which served as the basis for the creation of Youth Employment Centers, would call for these two forms of integration to be handled together.

With the economic crisis of the 1970s and the massive growth in the number of out-of-work youths, this question was once again the target of government action. On an international level, the neoliberal wave of the early 1980s changed the way in which the access of youths to employment was perceived: from then on, it became a question of adapting them to the labor market.[14] In a recommendation published in June 1983 entitled *Youth Employment*, the European Economic and Social Committee highlighted the fact that unemployment among youths had seen unprecedented growth in the last five years (65 percent) in the countries of the European Economic Community (EEC). Determining that out of the 12 million young people living in the EEC at the time, 5 million were without jobs, the study cited various factors as possible explanations for this situation: "Inexperience, maladaptation, delays in training or lack of training, sociocultural attitudes and burdens, a situation and a structure of the labor market that is ill-suited to the nature of the problem or the expectations of the youths."[15] This list marks the first appearance of a rhetoric insisting on the incompatibility of the educational system with the job market, thus limiting policy intervention to demand rather than supply.

In France, the context was marked by a sharp rise in the youth unemployment rate (the number doubled between 1975 and 1977) as well as by a decrease in the value of vocational degrees. In an effort to combat the problem, the first interministerial internship training program for people aged 16–23, who were registered with the National Employment Agency and lacked any professional qualification, was launched in 1977. Based on the idea that internships were a prerequisite to employment, the program envisaged three different types of training: retraining when the initial training was ill-suited, qualification when the base training was sufficient, and pre-training when it was not. In conjunction with this, the Decree of June 4, 1975 created the possibility for on-the-job training for youths between the ages of 16 and 25 who were out of school and did not possess any professional qualifications. Lasting a minimum of six months, on-the-job training was coupled with support from the state including free classes, reimbursements for the training, and subsidies to pay the youths employed. For young people in particular, the launch of National Employment Pacts (NEP) in 1977 signaled the beginning of the war on unemployment with measures for training, specific job contracts, and direct help with hiring. At the same time, the definition of an unemployed youth was expanded to include anyone between the ages of 16 and 25, no matter what their status, qualifications, or educational level.

After its rise to power in 1981, the left went about implementing its Youth Future Plan. The program preserved the main provisions of the National Employment Pacts while systematizing and fixing the methods of categorization. Those youths who did not have problems with education or social integration were directed to professional qualification programs, while those who experienced both problems were steered into internships that were meant to lead to a job or professional training. Intended as a short-term solution following the elections of May 1981, the program was replaced in 1982 by the creation of Information and Guidance Centers and Youth Employment Centers, thereby making some of these previous provisions permanent while institutionalizing the role of municipalities in the war on unemployment.[16]

Integrating Youths into the Workplace and Society

In 1981, Bertrand Schwartz handed then Prime Minister Pierre Mauroy a report entitled *The Professional and Social Integration of Youths*. In the face of rising youth unemployment due to the restructuring of the industrial sector and the expansion of the service sector,[17] the report recommended that the state rely on the local structures which had grown out of its urban policy (*politique de la ville*) to implement a policy of integration. Youth Employment Centers and Information and Guidance Centers (IGCs) were initially created on a trial basis by the Decree of March 26, 1982. They were to cover the entire country and depended on funding from the state, which defined the general framework of their activities and urged the municipalities to set them up. On the national level, Youth Employment Centers and IGCs reported to the Interministerial Delegation for the Integration of Youths which was attached to the Ministry of Labor. The role and function of these institutions were further reinforced by the Law of December 19, 1989 which established the National Council of Youth Employment Centers, a joint consultative body that brought together representatives from the Youth Employment Centers as well as the various ministries. Youth Employment Centers were essentially financed by the state and the local governments. The five-year Law of December 20, 1993 decentralized the professional training of young people by delegating responsibility to the regional governments which then became the main actors in this policy.

Conceived of as structures meant to respond in a comprehensive manner to the needs of youths who are out of school and out of work, Youth Employment Centers were intended to contribute to the implementation of local integration policies by helping youths define their career plans, by finding them jobs, by enrolling them in training classes, or by referring those "farthest from employment" to other public services which would aid in the development of career plans.

Because of changes in the labor market, Youth Employment Centers located in urban areas are mainly used by those from low-income backgrounds. Since this social class is largely fed by labor migration from North Africa and sub-Saharan Africa, those who enroll at the centers are likewise often from immigrant families and racialized as "black" or "Arab."[18] As a result of discriminatory hiring practices,[19] the majority of the youths who visit by the centers are therefore prone to being victims of racial discrimination.[20] Youth Employment Centers therefore have the unstated goal of combating such practices. In addition to these activities, Youth Employment Centers also provide more extensive social support. The "health center" found in every facility[21] offers walk-in psychological support and helps to refer youths to other medical services. And financial aid disbursed under certain conditions can be used to help them pay for public transportation or qualifying training programs.

Youth Employment Centers were thus conceived of as being a "one-stop shop," and the principle of comprehensive support was reaffirmed, on the one hand, in the charter adopted by the National Council of Youth Employment Centers in 1990, and on the other, in the council's Protocol 2000 which was published in 2000. Although the youth services division of the Regional Inspectorate of Labor and Employment had already conceived of incorporating the social aspect into integration by the end of the 1940s, it was the emphasis placed on comprehensive support that gave Youth Employment Centers their specific feature by breaking with a policy focused solely on the workplace integration that had defined the 1976 Plan of Prime Minister Raymond Barre and the 1977 Youth Employment Plan.

While the autonomy granted to employment assistance has served to create the category of "employment intermediary," it has at the same time played an integral part in the establishment of a sharp distinction between Youth Employment Centers and the National Employment Agency—or Employment Hub, as the facility is known today. The fact that Youth Employment Center counselors see themselves as having a greater social responsibility in comparison to their Employment Hub colleagues reflects this division. The former lay claim to what they call the "social aspect of their job," which they consider as being more closely tied to the area or neighborhood, and which they view as the main value of their activity. It is also this dimension of their profession which in their eyes gives "more human" or "more in-depth" relationships with the youths, and a number of counselors liked to point out that this was the reason why they had chosen to work for a public employment service.

Yet Youth Employment Centers were increasingly seen as institutions whose main goal was merely to find jobs for youths rather than to take a societal approach. Efforts to strengthen the ties between training and employment and thereby optimize career development among youths resulted in the 1991 creation of institutions called "Crossroads for Employment and Training." Under a 1995 agreement with the state, Youth Employment Center counselors can now zero in on issues of employment by working more closely with the National Employment Agency, which placed one of its counselors at their disposal.

This transformation of the role of Youth Employment Centers is also reflected in the methods used by its principal funders to evaluate their activities and therefore in the methods chosen by the administration to assess the work accomplished by the various counselors. Whereas in the first two decades of its existence it was the number of youths assisted which determined the amount of funding received by the institution,[22] the subsidies allocated to Youth Employment Centers have since the early 2000s been based on the number of youths who have found jobs. And along with this shift from activity to outcome, the amount of pairing between youth demand and job supply has increased.

The Reconfiguration of Professional Ethics

A Reorganized Institution

The Youth Employment Center where I conducted my fieldwork was created in 1989. Its current director was previously a counselor, then a program manager at the same center. Located in a large town in the Paris region where 11 percent of the population is foreign born and where a significant proportion of those with French citizenship are descendants of immigrants,[23] the Youth Employment Center served out-of-work youths who had for the most part been subject to forms of discrimination. The unemployment rate in this department (9.2 percent in the first half of 2011) was higher than the average for the entire Paris region (8.1 percent).[24] Between 2008 and 2010, the number of unemployed in the town studied rose by 31.9 percent.[25] On average, 2,000 youths were enrolled at the Youth Employment Center and in 2010, counselors had provided assistance to 1,741 persons.

Signed with the state in 2007, the long-term agreement made job placement the main criterion for evaluating the activities and efficiency of the Youth Employment Center as a tool for integrating youths into the workplace. Similarly, human resources departments assess the work of the counselors by taking into consideration the number of youths assisted who have found jobs. A conflict of values consequently exists between, on the one hand, the counselors who stress the "social aspect" of their work and its qualitative nature and, on the other hand, the administrators who favor the idea of "professionalism" to designate the part of a counselor's work that can be subject to statistical assessment.

The fact that performance evaluations are based on the number of young people "placed in a job" creates a feeling of unease among the counselors. "Generalist" counselors have the job of welcoming the youths and assisting them as they use the services provided by the Youth Employment Center. They work with them to develop professional goals; they make sure that they receive social support by preparing applications for financial aid, or by putting them in contact with other services, and they refer them to either training classes or other specialized programs run by the Youth Employment Center (career guidance, work mentorship, local plan for integration and employment, etc.). "Generalists" thus focus less on job placement and feel slighted by the current evaluation method which gives them the impression that most of what they do "doesn't count." This feeling of worthlessness is reinforced by the reorganization of the Youth Employment Center into departments since 2002 with on one side the "welcome center" where the "generalists" are to be found, and on the other the various specialized services. But while the division of staff into departments does not at all reflect the type or level of academic degree held by the counselors, the working conditions in the various departments are hardly the same, from either a quantitative or qualitative point of view. A "generalist" on average assists around four hundred youths, whereas a "specialist" is responsible for just forty. And even though youths assisted by "specialists" can experience significant difficulties, they have been seen first by "generalists," who meet with and assess anyone who visits the Youth Employment Center before enrolling them in the center's programs, or directing them to other social services. This screening role implies that they are the ones who must explain to some candidates why their requests were denied, and that they must be prepared to deal with the sometimes violent reactions these explanations elicit. Thus, despite the organization of the center into specific departments, there has been no implementation of performance evaluations specific to each department or adapted to the work of the individual counselors, which is why generalists regard the system as being unfair to them and as evidence of a lack of consideration for their work.

The Managerialization of Practices

With a masters degree in psychology from the National Conservatory for Arts and Crafts, Charlotte was recruited as a generalist counselor in June 2010, first on a one-year contract, then as a full-time staff member in September 2011. When initially hired by the Youth Employment Center, she was in her thirties and already had ten years' experience in employment assistance, having previously worked for an organization helping those enrolled at the National Employment Agency, and then for a temporary employment agency.

Commenting on her experience in professional integration, she explained how gradual changes in the way the work performed by counselors was evaluated had come to place greater emphasis on job placement at the expense of social support: "At the time I was hired, you had specific funding depending on what your job was. For example, if you had career goals, then you worked specifically on career plans. You had the goal of getting the youths hired, but you didn't focus that much on it." Then she highlighted the effects that these evaluation methods had on the way the counselors did their jobs:

> The problem is that it's more and more a question of profitability and productivity, and even more so of immediate hire when it's impossible to achieve that without working beforehand on a career plan to identify goals, to see if the plan is realistic and reasonable based on an overall assessment of the person: the situation, the context, the needs of the person, which takes a lot of time. You have to work on a lot of things first.

She also added that it was not so much the resources that were lacking today but the time that was devoted to both social support (for example, seeing if the young person had proper housing, could benefit from parental support, etc.) and career guidance (at a moment when due to the economic and social situation, these youths were precisely the ones in need of this type of assistance).

The defining of statistical goals based solely on job placement thus conflicts with the conception that counselors have of their work. They view their activity as promoting professional integration, which implies focusing on the living conditions of the job seekers. Moreover, the counselors have to manage the distribution of financial aid depending on the budget allocated to them, which leads to beneficiaries being selected in a particular way.

Created after the riots in the fall of 2005, social integration contracts are a form of state funding, which aims "to promote the integration of youths into the workplace by removing the obstacles to hiring and by developing or restoring the autonomy of the youths to achieve their own integration. It can comprise of guidance, qualification, or the acquisition of professional experience."[26] The youths enrolled at the employment center are entitled to this funding for a year and may renew it once subject to the approval of their counselor. The overall amount per youth per year may not exceed 1,800 euros and the monthly amount is limited to 450 euros. Every year, the Youth Employment Center received a general grant for social integration contracts, which was the main resource used by counselors to finance in a relatively stable way a youth's training or job search.

In 2010, the Youth Employment Center in this study received 11,642 euros from the state. The counselors at the center must consequently adhere to two contradictory demands: not to spend the budget too quickly so that it lasts the entire year, but to spend all of it so that they receive the same amount next year. Thus, in addition to their "placed in job" number, the counselors must also keep track of their "social integration contract number."

Another "generalist," Cecilia, highlighted the strict controls implied by this constraint: "The goal is to have five social integration contracts per counselor. You can't have any less. Otherwise the state takes away our funding." And with the case of a young man who had decided to go into engineering after studying sociology in college still freshly on her mind, she added: "It's interesting giving someone like Fabien a social integration contract because he is ready to be placed in a job and this counts as a positive outcome without having to spend too much." Thus, instead of being used to provide financial assistance for training or living costs while seeking a job, the contracts serve to finalize the career path of a young man who would not have much trouble finding a job and who, in the words of Cecilia, would "get by just fine on his own." As a result, it is the qualitative objective, not the situation of the young person which determines whether or not he or she will receive the corresponding grant.

Charlotte likewise explained how these statistical demands had transformed the way in which counselors go about their job, but she also highlighted the fact that due to this, people like Fabien, who do not face serious issues and have relative ease finding a job, are more likely to be helped:

> The way you're evaluated is based on the instructions you're given. If you have to hand out 15 social integration contracts because otherwise the budget won't be renewed, your work will not really be evaluated based on its quality. The quality of the work you do is rarely evaluated and I think that there's less of a concern for people with major social problems because in the end that's not what counts."[27]

The fact that those with the most social resources are also those best served by the Youth Employment Center stems from the way in which requests for financial aid are evaluated by the heads of the institution. The example of the social integration contracts thus reveals a general tendency to handle cases in a manner that is increasingly blind to the social conditions of those who turn to the center for assistance. Decisions regarding the allocation of the contracts were made during monthly meetings chaired by Élisabeth. She was in charge of the "assistance, social integration contracts, career guidance, and health center" department and also played the role of human resources director for this department. Only those "generalists" submitting social integration contracts applications were in attendance. Camille presented the first case to her supervisor:

CAMILLE: She's a young woman who is already taking training classes but hasn't received any financial aid. So she would like to get some help, bearing in mind that she's already solved the problem of daycare for her daughter and that her husband only has a temporary job. [Lowering her voice a little] OK, it's true that he doesn't earn enough and that he's appeared before the excessive debt commission ....

SUPERVISOR: Do you think she'll work once she's done?

CAMILLE: Absolutely! She figured out daycare on her own.

SUPERVISOR: How much does she want?

CAMILLE: 880 euros. She said that she and the training center were going to come up with a repayment plan.

Élisabeth seemed reluctant to give the entire amount. She asked for the opinions of the others. They did not have much to say. Camille continued to praise the qualities of the young woman: "She's very hard-working and very ambitious. She'll do what she says she'll do. Plus, we just saw a help-wanted ad for a job in her field of training." Élisabeth decided to give her 450 euros.

The second case presented by Camille was of a young woman asking for 600 euros in order to "finish her vocational degree." Élisabeth took a look at her file and remarked: "She got her degree by correspondence, hats off to her!" Camille continued to say that she had made every appointment while another counselor highlighted the fact that she had a "coherent plan." Élisabeth decided to give her 450 euros as well. Then came the case of a young man assisted by Cecilia who was asking for 300 euros so he could finish taking driving lessons.[28] Élisabeth, who knew the youth, remarked that he had "significant cognitive difficulties," but that he had "already received financial assistance to get his permit." She insisted on knowing why he was asking for help again. She also wanted to know the reasons that had prompted Cecilia to apply for that amount. Cecilia explained that it was meant to cover his living expenses, to which Élisabeth responded: "300 euros is a lot just for that." The other counselors all argued in favor of the youth, and in the end the head agreed to give him "150 euros this month and 150 euros next month," claiming that "he'll learn more" than if he were given 300 euros all at once.

While the financial aid was ultimately given to the youth Cecilia had been assisting, it is striking that struggling young people arouse suspicion while graduates have an easier time receiving aid. Stuck in a results-based mentality which makes the granting of funding conditional on the number of youths who have found a job, the head of the Youth Employment Center tends to favor those who show the most promise and who have the most social resources. In this sense, the current situation is made worse since it becomes generalized, a tendency seen in the creation of programs like "mentorships," in which the personalized support of engineers, human resource managers, or retired business owners are reserved for "the cream of the crop" or—more accurately—for the least needy of the needy.

It would, however, be wrong to attribute this trend solely to a question of resources without relating it to the values of autonomy and responsibility underlying the decisions. Given the budgetary restrictions and the managerialization of practices, the promotion of these two values essentially means that young people are chosen according to the promise they show with respect to the "feasibility" of their career plans and their chances of successfully finding a job. Thus, during a meeting to determine the allocation of scholarships from the departmental government, the applications from the Youth Employment Center were examined according to the same criteria that the applications of students from much more privileged backgrounds were. At no point during the meeting was it mentioned that a young man whose one parent earned the minimum wage and whose other parent had a government-subsidized job might be in more urgent need of assistance to pay for a training program or to get a driver's license than a young woman whose parents were both physicians and who was applying for funding to open up an equestrian center. Moreover, applications were assessed and funding was granted mainly based on the feasibility of the project and on the money the youth could put forward to finance his or her project.

Selecting the Youths

Budgetary restrictions and performance evaluations tied to the number of job placements have transformed the work of the counselors. Without saying it and sometimes without even realizing it, Youth Employment Centers favor applicants who are "the closest to employment" or who are the least in need. This selection process casts doubt on the principle of unconditional welcome (that is to say, the act of enrolling any youth between the ages of 16 and 25 who is out of school and looking for a job or training) which along with the notion of comprehensive support still supposedly forms one of the two cardinal values of this service. Certain counselors like Charlotte, for instance, were aware of this: "They keep subtly telling you to focus only those who can manage and who can manage without you. They don't say it like that, but the work you're asked to do has you focus on those who are the most employable and who meet all the criteria." This tendency also explained for her the reason why the Youth Employment Center was increasingly looking to hire people with business backgrounds to work as counselors. So when a youth bears certain social characteristics—namely class, gender, race, and age—to which the criteria currently in use remain blind, the evaluation is based on criteria devised by each counselor individually, which also opens the door to discriminatory practices.

The transformations that the Youth Employment Center has experienced have therefore reconfigured the assistance provided in finding jobs. Counselors must not only advocate for comprehensive support while at the same time focusing on job placement, they must also claim to extend an unconditional welcome to any youth who satisfies the center's enrollment criteria while at the same time choosing some and turning away others. The problem for counselors lies in the contradiction between the affirmation of the principles which they consider the values of their profession and the demands imposed on them by the evaluation of their performance. This problem is even greater because the reconfiguration of the way in which the Youth Employment Center functions has gone unnoticed or rather has remained unspoken. On the one hand, the head was herself a former counselor attached to the principles of comprehensive support and unconditional welcome and she saw her work as resisting the transformations experienced by her profession. On the other hand, and more fundamentally, to admit such a shift would mean to acknowledge the Youth Employment Center is nothing more than an "Employment Hub for youths," in Charlotte's words.

As a result, the counselors must "make up," as they say, reasons to turn away those who are not accepted in the program. And the leeway of the counselors becomes in fact a vehicle for internalizing the institutionally imposed constraint. Hence discourses of disqualification insisting on the verbal and sometimes physical abuse experienced by counselors from youths "who have nothing to do with the Youth Employment Center." The counselors thus resort to evaluation methods in which the political meaning of their function is reinterpreted through a moral categorization of the young people: those who deserve help and those who should be disciplined.

The counselors tend to view their work as that of teaching responsibility. For instance, Cecilia did not immediately tell the youths that they might be entitled to financial aid. She preferred to see what their behavior during meetings revealed of their involvement and their desire to take responsibility for themselves. She wanted to find out if they were respectful, punctual, and hard-working. She also said that she liked to find out whether they had done any research on the financial aid that they might be entitled to, which was a way for her to gauge whether they were in a process of achieving self-sufficiency or if they would simply wait for their problems to be taken care of for them. Others sought to determine whether the youths were motivated by need or interest, dividing them into two categories: those who "only come for the money" and who, according to the receptionist, "prevent the counselors from doing their job," and those truly motivated by the guidance and general support offered by the Youth Employment Center. In all these cases, the moral nature of categories employed implies that the youths are not viewed as possessors of social rights that they are exercising but as applicants whose merits are to be evaluated.

Redefining Professional Subjectivities

By redefining the principles on which the moral position of the counselors is based and by modifying the methods used to evaluate the youths who come to the Youth Employment Center, these transformations have also led to differentiated forms of professional positioning since counselors justify their practices and their professional ethics in their own individual way.

After having conducted a group information session, Mounir met with the youths one on one. Samira was in her twenties. She stated multiple times that she was motivated. She had been referred to the center by the National Employment Agency for help in devising a career plan as well as getting her driver's license. She wanted the Youth Employment Center to assist her not only in finding a training program to become a nurse's aide, but also in getting the necessary financial support. Mounir told her that she would have to wait three months before the "Youth Employment Center's partners" would give her the funding, to which Samira instantly replied: "Three months! But I pay 650 euros a month in rent and my unemployment benefits run out in three months!" Without batting an eye, the counselor proceeded to explain that at the Youth Employment Center, she could take a career guidance class in order to get "acquainted with what a nurse's aide does." Samira listened, but the expression on her face betrayed her impatience and anxiety. Undoubtedly thinking of how she could speed up the process and obtain financial aid more quickly, she said that she was willing to work at the airport where she had already worked before. Mounir replied: "We'll discuss this at our next meeting." He scheduled an appointment and the interview was over. Once the woman had left, the counselor expressed his skepticism as to the supposed urgency of the situation. He had the impression that it was an attempt to put pressure on them. He then told one of his colleagues who had sat in on the interview: "She waves her rent about in front of us and wants to speed things up by taking the first job that comes along. It's 'any job's fine so long as it pays.' She's going about it the wrong way because she doesn't have a background in health care." And, as if to make more explicit to his young colleague the meaning of their action, he added: "She hasn't even developed a plan yet."

Although commonly understood as any activity performed in return for money, the definition of work is here replaced by something more akin to self-realization. The counselor's comments indicate a moral conception of work's intrinsic value, one in which work is less associated with a means to earn a living and more tied to a form of self-fulfillment or self-cultivation. While this view can be explained by the more general shift in the profession's focus from one centered on social work to one based on psychology, it can also be attributed to the background and political positioning of Mounir.

A "generalist" counselor in his mid-fifties, he began "working in the social field" in 1994 after he had been let go from a private company. He had studied first in Algeria and then in France and had a master's degree in the sociology of work as well as another in education. In his conversations with his colleagues, he liked to come across as an intellectual, citing academic texts or newspaper articles and opining on contemporary political and social issues. A very approachable person, he was also always responsive to the youths he assisted, agreeing to see one youth who showed up without an appointment just before lunch or finding the time to respond to the request of another. He was likewise very attentive during interviews, always making sure that he understood the situation of the person he was meeting with. Seeking to validate these youths, he explained to them that what they were experiencing was due to the accidents of life. He told one of them that he faced problems because he "never received any real guidance" and that he should not underestimate his skills by looking for unskilled jobs—the young man had stated that he wanted to apply for a job as a baggage handler at the airport—when he had a vocational certificate.

Mounir was thus deeply invested in the social aspect of his work. He considered his role as primarily one of helping the youths develop their career goals and not just one of referring them to employers: he appreciated, for example, when one youth explained his job search in the form of a cover letter. Similarly, putting the brakes on Samira's request was in his opinion an attempt to make the young woman think her plans through since a hasty decision on her part ran the risk of failing again or of limiting her to only temporary jobs.

He would also often cite the notion of comprehensive support as defined in the Schwartz Report and loved to point out frequently that the main responsibility of a counselor when assisting in the job search was to take into "consideration the social environment in which the youth has grown up." That was why he criticized the administration's decision in 2002 to reorganize the center into different departments which resulted in a distinction being made between the "generalists" attached to the "welcome center" and those working for specialized services like employer outreach or mentorships. Like many of his colleagues, he also criticized the fact that the performance evaluations introduced by the long-term agreement were only based on the number of youths each counselor managed to place in a job.[29] These new forms of evaluation called the principle of comprehensive support into question and therefore devalued the work performed by the "generalists." According to Mounir, counselors devoted 60 percent of their time to problems related to the difficult living conditions experienced by the youths and their families: "We're dealing with the *lumpenproletariat* here. For many families, the main source of income is welfare and the skill level remains very low." He had the impression that this part of his activity went unrecognized.

But this feeling of worthlessness diversely affects the way in which counselors view their jobs. Simply put, veteran counselors like Mounir and relatively new ones like Charlotte, whose comments revealed a reflection on the political meaning of her actions and sometimes union involvement, defend the principle of comprehensive support. Conversely, for counselors like Cecilia or Camille, who had been recently hired on fixed-term contracts and wished to see their jobs made permanent, things were quite different.

Cecilia was still in her twenties. With a master's degree in French as a foreign language, she had taught French to high school students learning the language, then a Spanish course, and then had worked for a year in Mexico for the Alliance Française. Comparing her various previous jobs, she stated that she had liked teaching and that being a counselor was not her "calling." Nevertheless, she still wanted to be hired on a permanent basis because the greater stability would make up for the step down that her current position represented in comparison to her job as a teacher. While most counselors who worked at the Youth Employment Center sought to make a distinction between themselves and job center counselors, Cecilia emphasized the distinction between her work and that of a social educator working with youths. Describing an EU exchange program with an employment center in Spain that she participated in, she commented at length on how she differed from such educators who accompanied her on the trip. She first highlighted what she thought of as a fault in their educational approach: "They asked the youths to do things that they themselves didn't do. For example, showing up on time." But she criticized them most of all for their excessive empathy and closeness with the young people, whereas she made every effort to "set boundaries" and to find the right distance: "I remember one of the educators being disappointed with one of the youths. My job's not to be disappointed!" Implying that the relationship she built with them was not emotional and that she had no illusions about those whom she helped, she then added: "The educators would say that they can't trust the youths anymore. Well, I don't trust them right from the start. I don't trust them at all."

Similarly, when she explained what her job as counselor consisted in, Cecilia insisted on the difference between her work and that of her colleagues, referring to one who had been working for twelve years and was on sick leave for several weeks after being attacked during an on-site job meeting. The youths assigned to this counselor had been distributed among the "generalists," and Cecilia had taken a few of them on. She again criticized the empathy—too much in her eyes—that her colleague had shown to some of the youths who "only came for the money," without seeming to understand that the financial assistance was conditional on actively searching for a training program or a job. She suggested that the lack of boundaries encouraged these young people to act as though they were helpless. She tried instead to set boundaries by making the aid conditional on what for her seemed like evidence of their commitment and involvement: their diligence and their punctuality. Thus, she claimed to have told one of the youths assisted by the other counselor who had asked for money to pay for transportation and other necessities as well as for an social integration contract: "We're not a bank!" before adding in order to justify her refusal: "You missed all your appointments!" She believed that financial aid should not be given out freely and that the counselors should be demanding. Otherwise, "it ruins our image," she said.

Cecilia therefore used the need to uphold the credibility of the institution and to avoid its abuse to justify her oversight. Her comments thus echo the classic discourse of institutions that distribute funds to the unemployed:[30] boundaries had to be set—an expression that cropped up in the comments made by several counselors as well as department heads at the Youth Employment Center—and there had to be various ways to measure the "actual effort to find a job"—in this instance the diligence of the youths. Thus, Cecilia considered her work similar to that of an Employment Hub counselor, even adding that "it would be better if the counselors didn't have to manage the money" because, according to her, the financial aid given by the center is both a source of problems and a burden: "That's what often makes them lose their temper: the institution takes its time making payments and the youths turn against us." Hence, Cecilia thought that it would be more efficient and more productive if the "money aspect" were kept separate from the "professional and social integration aspect."

So there are two conflicting approaches to the work performed by Youth Employment Centers. One is based on a public health model and operates out of public interest without posing any conditions. The other follows the correctional model of disciplining through incentives and restrictions. But while some counselors claim to ascribe to the first model, they are also in part socialized in the mentalities and practices of institutions of social control which operate according to the second approach. This tension is even more important because it reflects the intermediary position of the counselors who are forced to anticipate the expectations of employers and the norms of the labor market, even if it means condoning the discriminatory selection of youths.

A Practice in Tension

Serving as Intermediaries between Youths and Employers

Juliette, one of the counselors in the "business center" department, had Pierre and Luc do mock telephone interviews as part of a "fast track to employment" workshop. She explained to them that "it should last two or three minutes" and that "the goal is to snag a face-to-face interview." Pierre, who wanted to work at a call center, went first. He described his background, mentioned his skills, and ended by highlighting what he would bring to the company: "I would be an asset because I have good interpersonal skills. My strengths are diction and the ability to convince." After he was finished, Juliette first asked Luc what he thought of Pierre's performance, then she made her own comments: "You kept saying that your résumé would speak for you. You need to talk more about your experiences, and instead of saying 'I am able to,' say 'I know how to.' You have to go on the offensive with what you say!"

As intermediaries between the labor market and the youths they assist, counselors have the task of familiarizing them with what they perceive as being the dominant values in the world of business. A large part of the work done by counselors with the youths thus consists in educating them or rather teaching them about themselves. In order to "make a good impression," the youths learn not only how to prove that they are hard-working, motivated, and responsible, but also how to highlight their qualities and practical skills. Since they are often applying for jobs like salesperson, telemarketer, stock person, or home health aide, the youths, especially young women, must also learn how to point out their physical resources by learning to present themselves and appear attractive without seeming vulgar according to the middle-class criteria the counselors generally use.[31]

Lucie, another counselor with the "business center," led a session of the "fast track to employment" workshop in which about a dozen men and women were participating. During the group activity part of the workshop, she distributed a handout listing the classic questions asked during a job interview. She advised them to go on the Internet and research the company. Then she added: "Use concrete examples to back up your strengths." She next suggested that the youths do mock interviews among themselves while she met with each of them one-on-one. Bénédicte, the first to meet with her, was a black woman in her twenties. She had a child and wanted to be a "cashier." Lucie asked her to discuss her experience: "I'm supposed to talk about what I've done?" "Yes, what you liked and what you didn't like." "Customers!" Lucie said nothing. The young woman went on to say that she had worked for 15 months at a medium-sized store, then

she stopped: "I don't know what to say." Lucie asked her again if she had liked
the job. Bénédicte said yes but also mentioned a few tasks which had stressed her
out. She paused: "I don't know what to say about the job!" "There was a customer
relations part to it, right?" "Yes." "And what about your strengths?" "Um … I'm
a good listener." "And you're honest too." "Yes" "You already have a child. Do
you see yourself having another? What would be your schedule and when would
you be available to start?" The young woman stuttered. Lucie next asked her
how she envisaged her future, and Bénédicte replied that she wanted to take
classes to become a daycare assistant but that she was unable at the moment for
financial reasons. Bénédicte added that she had brought with her two types of
résumés: one to apply for jobs as a cashier, the other to apply for other jobs "just
because." The interview ended, and once the young woman had left, Lucie gave
her verdict: "She is not ready to work."

The workshops like the ones described show the forms of ethos seen as
corresponding to the expectations of potential employers. If Lucie discredits
Bénédicte on account of her hesitation, it is because the young woman gave the
impression of not knowing what she wanted or was looking for. In order to convince
a potential employer, a job applicant has to know how to show determination,
which according to the counselors means having a precise, well-defined career
plan. As one counselor explained: "It's important for the youths to consider why
they are interested in a particular job. They need to understand that they can't
do everything." By questioning them about their likes and dislikes, he tried to
determine what their motivation was.

The criterion of motivation seemed internalized by the youths: they attempted
to show it in their various interactions with their counselors. Some simply
insisted that they were motivated. Others were afraid that too many temporary
jobs "wouldn't seem hard-working"—thus highlighting the fact that the pressure
is unequally distributed among the various contracting parties in precarious
employment situations. Still others asserted their sense of responsibility and
autonomy, while a final group insisted on the methodical way that they went about
looking for a job by demonstrating their organizational skills (the different forms
needed to apply for a job were filed in separate folders with several copies at the
ready) as well as the reasoning behind their approach, especially when it came to
choosing a training program.

But at the same time, the way in which the counselors determined the motivation
of the youths also led to misunderstandings. In fact, while the former evaluated the
latter's desire to work a certain job, most youths were primarily looking to show
their general determination to find any job. Yet, as was the case with Lucie and
Bénédicte, the counselors would also ask the youths who were in the beginning
stages of developing a career plan if they had any backup plans. In this sense, the
youths are likewise made to believe that they must be open to accepting any job
offer. Hindered by their lack of skills as well as by the stigmatization that they
endure, they sought to counteract the image of being lazy people who were
reluctant to work and took advantage of handouts by stressing their readiness to do

anything. But that willingness gave the counselors the impression that they had a rather vague and undefined career plan.

Firmin was a young black man originally from the Caribbean. He showed up to a meeting with Julien dressed in track suit pants and a hoodie. He wore a baseball cap and had a series of piercings in one of his eyebrows. He held his cell phone in his hand. Firmin had a certificate in auto-mechanics and stated that he did not want to accept any more temporary jobs. The counselor read aloud some job offers and said to him: "Tell me when you hear one that interests you." Throughout the interview, he tried to get Firmin to figure out what interested him by asking him to explain each time why he liked or did not like a job. The meeting ended, and as soon as Firmin left, the counselor commented on the way in which he had conducted himself. He concluded by saying: "As for appearance, I'll need to talk to him about that next time."

Learning this new ethos likewise relies on a change in one's manner of being, which translates into particular attention being paid to body language, dress, and the image that one projects of oneself insofar as it carries with it social significance, not only because the projected image indicates the social class one belongs to, but also because it is associated with forms of racialization. The counselors might, for example, recommend that a young black man stop wearing the baseball cap, tracksuit, or baggy jeans that he regularly sports and adopt "proper" attire because the clothes he wears bear racial significance, thereby designating racializing markers as part of "appearance." Similarly, conforming to a certain image of femininity allows a young woman to avoid in part the racialization and class ascription she will be subject to. In this way, counselors favor certain class, race, and gender norms in an attempt to modify or reduce the disqualification that the youths experienced. Such practices are a sort of social slip that reveals the way in which class, race, and gender ascriptions are socially produced. While the counselors were not necessarily cognizant of the consequences of their actions, their practices nevertheless demonstrate how identity labels interact and are realized in accordance with social situations.[32]

In other words, since they cannot force employers to hire the youths they are responsible for, the counselors try to make the latter conform to the expectations of the former by erasing the markers which contribute to their exclusion from the labor market. Asked how the question of racial discrimination is handled, the head of the Youth Employment Center summed up this social reshaping by saying: "We tell our youths not to look like who they are."

Paradoxes

As a result of their intermediary position and the role that they play in normalizing the labor market, Youth Employment Center counselors often find themselves in a paradoxical situation. Eager to place as many youths in jobs as possible, they seek to make them conform to the expectations of potential employers who are assumed to be prejudiced. This practice is especially harsh because it unwittingly justifies the control exerted over them. Anxious to avoid situations in which the youths might find themselves confronted with discriminatory practices, the counselors can decide not to send them to certain employers. In doing so, they unwillingly contribute to the reproduction of social inequalities which, depending on the situation, take the form of racial,[33] age, or gender discrimination. The selection criteria of the employers are thus somewhat validated by institutions meant to help in finding jobs.

But this situation is all the more apparent in the case of Youth Employment Center counselors because they have a specific image of business and the private sector that is heavily dependent on managerial theories. This image derives in part from their training and their professional experience. Even though they made up a small percentage of the center staff, some of the counselors had worked in human resources departments before choosing to do social work. Others had always worked in the field but complemented their master's degrees in sociology or psychosociology with a few classes in management. But this image also derives from the center's privileged position within the field of employment as a public employment service responsible for a segment of the population which has difficulties entering the labor market. Lacking the respect of private employers (who almost never attend the various job fairs hosted by the Youth Employment Center), the counselors mainly worked with their colleagues at the Employment Hub, a few heads of training programs, social workers, and certain local elected officials. Because they felt illegitimate in relation to certain employers, they had a greater tendency to consider managerial theories as the main method of acculturating the youths (and themselves) to the world of business. That is why in a program like the career guidance classes offered by the center, the youths were asked starting in the second session to define their career goals based on a typology commonly used in managerial literature, the RIASEC model,[34] or to reflect upon the notion of "skills" by distinguishing between "skill set" and "personal skills." But it is also this use of managerial theories which puts counselors in the paradoxical situation of unwittingly or unwillingly (re)producing social inequalities since notions like that of skills, motivation, or suitability also allow for arbitrary exclusionary practices to be seen as acceptable and entirely justified, as was clearly the case for youths who identified as Muslim.

Following a meeting with the different department heads, the center's director explained how recent budgetary cuts had transformed the work methods of the counselors. She spoke in general terms and noted the forms of constraint they were subject to given the expectations of employers, using an emblematic figure to illustrate her point: "For example, it's impossible to tell a girl who wears a headscarf that she can find a job in retail."

A few months later, Juliette commented on the youths she had assisted as part of the "candidate pool" program during a break. The program sought to put youths in touch with employers recruited by "business center" counselors. It was an application of the so-called "supply and demand intervention" method. Conceived of as a means to combat racial discrimination, the method matched a single candidate chosen by the counselor with a job offer, thereby doing away with any form of competition during the recruitment stage. After the counselor had succeeded in "getting the job offer," he or she then tried to "sell the candidate," to "avoid any questions which might ruin the process," and to negotiate, for example, a trial period in the event that the employer proved hesitant.

Juliette illustrated the ambiguities of this method through an example:

> This young guy had a certificate in business relations. He was extremely hard-working and very dependable, but the problem was that he had a beard, a Muslim beard, and there was no way employers would want him if he had a beard. I told him to shave it or to trim it, but he wouldn't listen and told me that he would be ashamed to do that, that it would be a disgrace. Because of that, he decided to take a job as a sales assistant, a job he was overqualified for … I tried to get him to change his mind. I told him that he was taking the job away from someone who didn't have a certificate and therefore couldn't apply for other jobs. That seemed to make him think.

Then the counselor compared the case of this youth with that of a young woman who wore a headscarf and who, for her part, had "come to terms with the fact that in order to find a job she would have to remove her headscarf." She added: "This young girl had her own beliefs, but when she worked, she understood that she had to conform to what was expected of her."

Juliette gave the impression that she accepted this state of affairs: youths were required to conform to the expectations of employers and in this specific instance to the overriding values of society. Yet what she said next in the conversation revealed just how much the discomfort she felt and the moral dilemma she experienced could be explained by her own personal background. She had received a dual degree in psychosociology and urban sociology from the University of Paris-8, which was known for its strong political leanings to the left and support for the Third World, due to the teaching—ahead of its time in comparison to other French universities—of courses dedicated to gender theory and postcolonial studies, as well as for its high rate of recruitment of students from the northern banlieues who were themselves subjected to forms of racialization and identity labeling. Juliette's master's degree in urban sociology focused on juvenile delinquency. This had been what piqued her interest in the question of integration into the workplace—"as a solution to delinquency"—and what made her first think about the question of morality and the role of religion in the lives of youths. Firmly committed to progressive causes, she stated that after a background in human resources, she had decided to work at the Youth Employment Center because she was "interested in the social." Elected union representative in the fall of 2011, she was also very involved in defending workers' rights. Her own family background was also an important element. Very close to her maternal grandmother who had in part helped to raise her, she explained that she had been greatly influenced by the stories of her grandmother's childhood in Tunisia. The daughter of a colonial official who, Juliette liked to point out, spoke Arabic, her grandmother had instilled in her an interest in differences. She mentioned several times just how much her grandmother's narratives and her own subsequent trips to Tunisia had played a role in her personal life, stating that it was one of the things which had cemented her relationship with the father of her children, himself the descendant of an Italian family from the suburbs of Tunis.

After some back and forth in the conversation, Juliette distanced herself from the discourse that she thought she had to use in order to do her job. Conceding that "having a beard doesn't make someone any less competent," she admitted the illegitimate and therefore discriminatory nature of this selection criterion. She agreed with the idea that she should not even have had to talk to the youth about his beard and that doing so was somewhat invasive. As the conversation continued, her face began to exhibit her discomfort and her sense of powerlessness. These feelings were also reflected in the words she kept repeating: "We'll see, we'll see," as if to say that she wished she could come up with a solution which did not require the young man to shave his beard or to accept a job he was overqualified for, but that she did not know what to do. The next day, she brought up the issue again and commented on the expectations of the employers and their discriminatory practices: "Employers are always judging! Racial discrimination, gender discrimination, discrimination against people with disabilities or because of religion, it's a total joke!" Then she added, presenting this not as a behavioral norm the youths had to conform to, but as what goes unsaid or the fool's bargain on which her work is based: "Even if you understand on an analytic level the desire to identify with the youths, you have to make them understand that they have to adapt to what is expected of them." Through this example, Juliette underscored the ambiguity of a situation in which the counselors are made to highlight the racial meaning of physical or clothing markers and to justify the discriminatory actions of the employer by invoking a sort of realism with regard to the way that the labor market works.

Nevertheless, counselors themselves at times generate a racializing and stigmatizing discourse based for the most part on a form of culturalism in which the understanding of the other is limited to what one thinks about the other's culture. In the various conversations with Julien, he mentioned several times how his colleagues were able to racialize the youths they assisted and thereby condone the forms of identity ascription. He explained that he was attuned to this issue: "I have a background of my own," he said without going into further detail. He later revisited his personal story during lunch one day, stating that his father was from Gabon but that he had never known him and had only recently reconnected with his half-siblings. He remarked on the comments some of his colleagues would make about the youths. He found them to be particularly shocking and related them to the reactions he himself had experienced, for instance, when his colleagues assumed that he would know how to handle a "youth from the projects" because of his background or when all eyes turned to him the moment a cell phone ring began playing a rap song during a meeting. "One time, the counselors said about an Indian person: 'We have to take her; she won't make any trouble.' Or there was another time when they said about someone from the Caribbean: 'He'll take some time because they don't work at the same pace over there.'" He also explained how what he called "questions of representation" would crop up during meetings or in the discrepancy between the description of a youth provided by his colleagues and what he observed for himself when he met him.

That was the case for Yann, a 20-year-old who had recently arrived from Guadeloupe. He had been referred to the special program for difficult cases by Cecilia who had painted a "catastrophic" picture of the young man during a debriefing with Julien. According to her, Yann had problems with "boundaries": he was never on time for appointments and, more generally, "he has a problem keeping track of time." Yann was clueless and seemed completely irresponsible, which showed in the way he acted and looked, especially in his "cornrows" which Cecilia mentioned several times. But during his meeting with Julien, Yann spoke very clearly about his school background and the family difficulties he had experienced. He spoke fluent English because he had stayed in the United States for a while, and he wanted to use this language to find a job that would allow him to get himself set up before moving on to something he was more passionate about: opening up a fashion boutique. As soon as Yann had left, Julien exclaimed: "I thought he was an amazing kid! He didn't match the description that Cecilia gave me and unlike what another counselor told me, he wasn't complicated at all. Of course, there might be some problems that might pop up later, but I found him to be very well composed."

The remarks counselors would make about certain youths echoed those that would be termed "ordinary racism":[35] comments about the laziness of a person from Martinique who worked at the post office or various Asian jokes made directly in front of a Korean counselor were par for the course during meals or coffee breaks. But what was without a doubt even more striking was the fact that remarks intended to help youths value themselves in fact reinforced their identity ascriptions.

During the "fast track to employment" workshop run by Lucie, one of the women who participated was originally from Côte-d'Ivoire. She wished to work as a nurse's aide in a hospital, and it was apparent from her mock interview that she took a very methodical approach to finding a job. The counselor asked her first to introduce herself and then to explain what motivated her. The young woman hesitated a little before venturing: "I am used to taking care of elderly people back home in my country and I realized that I was really interested in it." The interview continued. Lucie seemed satisfied by the answers she was given. She encouraged the young woman, saying: "I really liked it when you talked about your home country." Then, once the woman had left, she added: "That was good. It's true that girls like her work well with elderly people. It's a question of culture. It's part of their culture."

In addition to the questions of ordinary racism or common culturalism present in these episodes, we see how as a result of the importance placed on valuing certain qualities may lead to their essentialization, especially in the case of youths from the Youth Employment Center who are seen as being barely employable.

Conclusion

By considering the practices of the counselors and emphasizing how these practices affected the youths, I have endeavored to show the way in which a logic based on qualitative assessment combines with a normative logic at a Youth Employment Center. My analysis of the way the question of material means intersects with that of the values and norms which define the mindset of the institution and determine the actions of its counselors also reveals the transformations that have taken place in employment policies.

The history of the ways in which the question of the right to work has been problematized has allowed us to re-situate employment assistance within a broader configuration in which the handling of unemployment is no longer viewed as a type of insurance granting unemployed individuals social rights, but instead as a form of help given to individuals who are made to conform to the expectations of potential employers. In other words, dealing with unemployed persons, initially formulated in terms of a right to work, has come to be thought of in terms of access to employment. So in addition to the insurance aspect, there is also an assistance aspect destined for persons who are designated as least employable and in which the granting of aid is made conditional on the disciplining of the beneficiaries. In a configuration like this, it is the youths with the most social resources and "the closest to employment" who are the best supported by the Youth Employment Center. The others are regarded not as being unemployed but as being "unemployable" and an attempt is made to transform them in order to find them a job "despite everything," as if they were being done a favor, thereby justifying the precarious nature of the jobs they are given.[36]

This reformulation of the question of the right to work explains the use of moral categories when evaluating the youths assisted by the Youth Employment Center. Since these youths are no longer considered legitimate beneficiaries of the social benefits to which they are entitled, counselors use moral qualities to determine whether or not they deserve to be granted aid. As a result, these youths are stigmatized as being welfare recipients, even though it is the state administration that places them in this position.

This moralization of the youths' support is all the more exaggerated because the counselors are themselves subject to evaluations. They are easily reproached for not making good use of the resources at the Youth Employment Centers' disposal. Moreover, some have increasingly precarious work situations which cause them to conform even more strictly to the demands of the institution. As a result, counselors have become even more demanding of the youths in an effort to set themselves apart and escape the uncertainty of their own status.

Notes

1 For example, in 1996, continuing education in the workplace affected 56 percent of all businesses in Germany, and vocational training represented 1.2 percent of payroll costs (Dubar 2004, 50).

2 On this point, see Sébastien Chauvin (2010). Based on a participant observation study conducted over the course of two years among day laborers, the research analyzes the disqualification experienced by these workers and the role of job intermediary played by day labor agencies. He demonstrates the way in which the precarity of these workers becomes apparent both in the permanent possibility that these agencies might hire them and in the uncertainty created by at-will employment.

3 This is what Nicolas Duvoux (2009a) shows in his work on welfare recipients.

4 For an analysis of the intersection of these two issues through the history of the "social question," see Robert Castel (1995).

5 See Agulhon (1973: 44).

6 See the speeches on the right to work delivered before the National Assembly (Agulhon 1984).

7 In pre-industrial societies, the "social question"—meaning the capacity of a society to maintain its cohesion—was conceived of through policies which aimed to repress or contain beggars and vagabonds (Castel 1995). It was only after the political and industrial revolutions of the eighteenth century that the figure of the marginal person changed and took the form of the proletarian (Castel speaks of "wage earner") whose only commodity is his labor.

8 The first texts to introduce an analysis of unemployment in macro-economic and social terms were by William Beveridge, particularly *Unemployment: A Problem of Industry* which was published in London in 1909.

9 By "governmentality," Michel Foucault designates "the ensemble formed by the institutions, procedures, analyses, and reflections, the calculations and tactics that allow the exercise of this very specific albeit complex form of power, which has as its target population, as its principal form of knowledge political economy, and as its essential technical means apparatuses of security" (Foucault 1997a: 219–20). The governmentalization of the state proceeds from a reconfiguration of the question of power. So in addition to the issue of sovereignty, there is a concern for the life of individuals and its continuous permanent supervision (Foucault 1997b). This transformation is based on a type of specific rationality, produces the same types of particular knowledge, and relies mainly on the administrative apparatus (Foucault 1997c; Lascoumes and Le Galès 2005).

10 See Topalov (1994).

11 Bronislaw Geremek has shown how the representations—which he analyzes as forms of response to social and economic mutations—of the poor have at various times been able to mix repression and charity by relying on the distinction between "good poor" and "bad poor" (Geremek 1987).

12 In the various countries of the European Union, oversight of the unemployed has increased since the 1990s. In a context of a deteriorating job market and political demands to reduce public spending, the distinction between the "real" and the "fake" unemployed has been endowed with new meaning and importance (Dubois 2007).

13 The National Council of Resistance program can be found in French online: http://fr.wikisource.org/wiki/Programme_du_Conseil_national_de_la_R%C3%A9sistance.

14 A wave also reinforced on an international level by the election of Margaret Thatcher in the UK in May 1979 and the election of Ronald Reagan in the US in November 1980.

15 Economic and Social Committee of the European Community (1983).

16 Dubar et al. (1987: 37–66).

17 For an analysis of the effects of the restructuration of the industrial sector on the children of workers, refer to works by Stéphane Beaud and Michel Pialoux (2012). In his work on crack dealers in East Harlem, Philippe Bourgois has shown that the expansion of the service sector and the fact that the qualities promoted by this sector conflict with those prevalent in what he calls "street culture" have led to the exclusion of a significant fringe of lower-income and often racialized youth from the legal labor market (Bourgois 2001: 149–209).

18 The concept of racialization serves to designate the social processes by which in a given political and social configuration certain characteristics—they could be phenotypical but are not limited solely to the question of skin color—justify the assignment of one group to a minority position by another (Murji and Solomos 2005; Fassin 2010: 147–72).

19 Silberman and Fournier (2006). See also the initial results of the study *Trajectoires et origines* (Equipe TeO 2010: 58–9).

20 *Trajectoires et origines* emphasizes that the "risk of unemployment is significantly higher for descendants of immigrants from Turkey (1.3), sub-Saharan Africa (1.7), Morocco or Tunisia (1.6), or Algeria (1.8) and for immigrants from sub-Saharan Africa (1.7) or Algeria (1.8) than it was for native French." This study also noted that "there are few differences between the risks of unemployment for the populations of this age group depending on whether one is an immigrant or a descendant of immigrants" (ibid.: 59).

21 In the Youth Employment Center where the fieldwork was conducted, the health center was set up in 1993.

22 This is what Xavier Zunigo points out (2007: 43).

23 Besides immigrants from North Africa and sub-Saharan Africa, this town had also received a significant influx of immigrants from Southeast Asia.

24 Source: INSEE.

25 Source: Employment Hub. This number refers to Category A unemployed, meaning unemployed individuals enrolled at the hub and looking for a job.

26 A description of the social integration contract can be found on the website for the Ministry of Labor and Employment: www.travail-emploi-sante.gouv.fr/.

27 The notion of "quality of work" designates among the counselors at the youth employment center the attention paid to the living conditions of the youths in an effort to determine if they have any bearing on the job search. This phrase, which is often confused with "social assistance," also refers to the time taken to devise a career plan with the youth and to find a job that fits the youth's profile (which conflicts with the idea that the youths must be matched with existing jobs). The indifference evident in the actions of the counselors, as described by Charlotte, can be seen as the product of a form of bureaucratic rationality which finds its justification in what the western nation state symbolizes and in the established daily forms of social, cultural, and racial exclusion (Herzfeld 1992).

28 The process of obtaining a driver's license in France requires significantly more investment in terms of both time and money than it does in the United States.

29 The introduction of project management based on statistical performance evaluations and an individualization of responsibilities characterized the managerial wave experienced by the business world in the 1980s (Boltanski and Chiapello 1999).

30 See Dubois (2007).

31 See Hochschild (1983).

32 Using an ethno-methodological approach as their theoretical basis, Sarah Fenstermaker and Candace West attempt to show the imbrication of gender, race, and class relations by highlighting the fact that these forms of ascription are not only to be viewed as individual properties, but as the product of interactions (West and Fenstermaker 1995).

33 The intermediary position of counselors at the youth employment center places them in a position of "co-producing" racial discrimination (Noël 2004).

34 Developed by John Holland, an engineer and professor of psychology at the University of Michigan in the 1950s, this typology divides individuals into six types of work profiles: realistic, investigative, artistic, social, enterprising, and conventional (hence the acronym RIASEC). Based on a cognitive and behavioral approach to psychology, the RIASEC model seeks to steer individuals toward jobs that are supposed to match their psychological profile.

35 The notion of ordinary racism designates the process which integrates categories of perception and racist preconceptions into daily practices. Ordinary racism is characterized by the banalization of these categories of perception and these preconceptions as well as by the forms of racial labeling which structure social relations. Vaguely present in all sorts of practices but most often formulated in an indirect manner or by playing on ambiguity—which allows it to shield itself from attack—ordinary racism flies under the radar and is not always detectable as such in societies in which the display of racism is more often associated with acts of verbal aggression or physical violence towards certain groups (Essed 1991).

36 In his work on day laborers in the United States, Sébastien Chauvin concludes by defining the "precariat" as "a new class of 'unemployablized' workers who despite everything are hired and hired, as if it were a favor" (Chauvin 2010: 339)

Conclusion
Raisons d'État

Didier Fassin

"The state is not a cold monster; it is the correlative of a particular way of governing," states Michel Foucault in one of his lectures at the Collège de France. "The problem is how this way of governing develops, what its history is, how it expands, how it contracts, how it is extended to a particular domain, how it invents, forms, and develops new practices."[1] In other words, one should not first posit the existence of the state and then examine how it manifests itself, but "start with these concrete practices" in order to discover at the end of the inquiry what part of it is the "*raison d'État*," understood as the rationality of the manner of governing. "Let us suppose that universals do not exist": it is this radical intellectual experience, this "theoretical and methodological decision" which the philosopher invites us to consider in our rethinking of the state—not as a universally identifiable entity, but instead as practices in permanent transformation.

Our approach has been inspired by that decision. In efforts to understand the state, we have focused our attention on institutions and professions, on those agents who in implementing the policies of the state simultaneously transform or reinvent them, and above all on the relationships developed with the populations construed as publics.[2] Thus, it is through the practices of those who represent it in their various capacities that the state gradually takes form. The entire state? Of course not. We have analyzed only a fraction of the many facets of its action: police patrolling poor neighborhoods, magistrates judging young offenders, determining the fate of undocumented foreigners, or ruling on requests for asylum, prison administrators and guards assigned to supervise inmates, probation officers meant to prevent possible repeat offenses, social workers assisting troubled adolescents and job counselors helping young adults find employment, psychologists and psychiatrists caring for teenagers thought to be in need.

Although this motley group in no way exhausts the diversity of the domains in which the state intervenes, it nevertheless offers a certain sociological coherence. The professions and institutions discussed here are those that deal first and foremost with social categories that are relatively difficult to qualify or even to name, but generally correspond with working-class people of immigrant origin or belonging to minorities. The resulting practices constitute the government of the "social question," to use a term inherited from the nineteenth century. However, this "new social question"[3] differs from the old one in that the relationship of domination which characterizes it adds to social class a racial component with a religious dimension often inscribed within a colonial genealogy, a fact that has long been ignored.

If the social question can be defined as the way in which the social is problematized at a given historical moment or, in other words, the way in which it is construed as a problem through themes such as poverty, marginality, insecurity, punishment, solidarity, nation, then it must be acknowledged that this social question is inherently a moral one as well: each of these themes implies a reference to values and an expression of sentiments concerning both the social categories concerned and the responses to the problems they experience or to the disorders they may create. Thus, the problematization of precarity and inequality necessarily implies the production of judgments on the merits of the poor or the legitimacy of the disparities and the manifestation of affects with regard to the suffering of the former or the reduction of the latter. The agents whose daily activities we have described and analyzed in this book mobilize values of good and bad, right and wrong, true and false, and feelings like compassion or indignation, empathy or suspicion, admiration or hostility. These values and feelings are all the more strongly expressed because they are inscribed within an asymmetrical relationship between the agents and their public, between those who confer power and resources and those who are dependent on them.

But these various forms of moral mobilization and the tensions, conflicts, or dilemmas to which they give rise should not be analyzed solely on the level of the personal experience of the agents, who in their daily work are confronted by situations which call for action on their part. Indeed, they always echo the values and sentiments prevalent within the public realm and political discourse and interact with the practices of these agents. The stigmatization of young people from the banlieues, the discrediting of the accounts of asylum seekers, the toughening of sentences handed down to delinquents, the distrust of welfare systems and their beneficiaries, the invocation of personal responsibility to the detriment of social causes constitute a sort of moral climate which influences the activities of the police, magistrates, prison guards, parole officers, social workers, or psychiatrists charged with responding to the problems that concern these populations. That is why we have insisted throughout our analyses on the importance of grasping how the agents think and act simultaneously with what is said and done in the public sphere and political world.

By discussing what we have called moral subjectivities and moral economies and by following the ideas and practices as well as the values and sentiments present in the institutions involved in law enforcement, the justice system, the penal world, social work, and mental health, we were able to grasp not one but several *raisons d'État*, that is to say, the various rationalities at work concomitantly and in part concurrently in the government of the social question. Of these rationalities, we have proposed genealogies, dating back to the eighteenth century and sometimes even further, as well as ethnographies, allowing for an understanding of how they are implemented today. More specifically, we have studied the major transformations which took place over the course of the last three or four decades in the way problems are posed and solutions put forth within French society. Thus, three figures emerge from a triple rationality: the welfare state, the penal state, and the liberal state.

If by welfare state it is meant the public effort in favor of distributive justice, the last few decades have been marked by its retreat in France as well as the rest of Europe.[4] This evolution is remarkable in two respects. On the one hand, it reverses a movement toward the extension of social rights which had characterized the post-war years and seemed to define a European vision of national solidarities long contrasted with the United States model. On the other hand, it occurred within a context of rising unemployment and increasing disparities, in other words, at a time when the need for social protection was especially crucial. With regard to this general trend, France occupies an average position when compared to the rest of the western nations with certain domains like health care, whose extension was pursued up until the last decade resisting more than others.[5] This entrenchment of inequalities and weakening of solidarities affect the most fragile populations: immigrants and their children are the first victims of underemployment and pauperization, both of which are exacerbated by spatial segregation and racial discrimination. The illegitimacy of the populations furthermore becomes an argument for delegitimizing the welfare state which supposedly unduly or unfairly benefits certain categories, with concentric circles of disqualification affecting at first undocumented foreigners, then legal immigrants, and finally, all welfare beneficiaries.

Alongside this decline, the penal state, if one designates as such public action devoted to retributive justice, has experienced unprecedented expansion.[6] The repressive shift accompanied by a phenomenon of mass incarceration at first concerned the United States, but it has spread, although to a much lesser degree, to the majority of western countries. France again falls in the middle internationally, but the rapid rise in prison population seems all the less justified, given the fact that serious crime has regularly decreased over the past half-century.[7] The punitive turn essentially affects working-class populations and in particular immigrants and minorities, beginning with the youth: the first victims of job insecurity, residential segregation, and unfair treatment are also the first targets of this disciplinary trend. The implementation of the penal state in France can be witnessed in three institutions: police, courts, and prisons. Law enforcement agents, and in particular, special units such as the anti-crime squads, are concentrated in poor neighborhoods, where their prerogatives have notably increased, while their deontological authority has been suppressed. The judicial system, under pressure from the injunctions and criticisms of the government, applies increasingly strict laws which permanently extend the realm of crime to new minor infractions and impose mandatory sentencing for repeat offenders. Finally, the penal system must cope with a considerable increase in the prison population, a consequence of more frequent convictions and longer sentences, the effects of which are only partially mitigated by various probation measures. To complete the picture, one should also consider the measures that pertain specifically to foreigners, namely airport waiting zones and administrative detention centers which are just as much places of imprisonment and whose capacities have grown in accordance with the government's deportation quotas. Finally, asylum proceedings themselves have undergone a dramatic evolution, with the proportion of those granted refugee status plummeting to one-fifth of what it was thirty years ago, thereby meaning that once their appeals have been exhausted, the remaining four-fifths slide into illegality.

However, merely capturing the shift from a social to a penal state leaves us with a partial understanding of the transformations of the *raisons d'État*. Other rationales are at work, rationales in which a twofold project of reform can be discerned. First, institutions undergo democratic reform, including the power given to the liberty and detention judge over custody procedures, the systematization of legal counsel for asylum seekers in preparation for their hearings, the presence of a lawyer during prison disciplinary or probation proceedings, the recognition of certain prerogatives of inmates—all provisions stemming from a European policy guaranteeing individual rights and therefore the necessity for each country to integrate these new obligations into its legislation at the risk of being found guilty of non-compliance by European courts. Second, individuals are supposed to reform themselves as part of their transformation within these various institutions, with social worker reports scrutinizing the offender's past before trials, with the insistence on damages being paid and treatment being followed in the assessment of inmates for probation or parole, with training for job seekers at youth employment centers that emphasizes their appearance, with educational programs in Youth Protective Services, with psychiatric evaluations for troubled adolescents—all measures whose primary goal is to develop a sense of responsibility with regard both to acts already committed as well as life in the future. Democratization and individualization thus constitute the two components of this political project which aims to form moral subjects under the rule of law.[8] The decline of the welfare state and the rise of the penal state are coupled with a liberal state which, on the one hand, substitutes these retreating social protections with an expectation that individuals take responsibility for themselves and, on the other hand, regulates the repressive apparatus through the establishment of legal guarantees. "Liberal" therefore must be understood here in a political and even moral rather than economic sense,[9] one inherited from classical philosophers for whom the defense of formal liberties implies that free individuals be held accountable for their acts.

Hence, three *raisons d'État*. It would of course be tempting to look for ideological unity in this triptych and to propose a "functionalism of the worst" showing how each rationale is inevitably in the service of the others.[10] The decline of the social would feed the excesses of the penal, which the liberal argument would in turn legitimize. Analyzing from a distance could lend itself to such a project—and there is no shortage of examples in sociological literature. Our ethnographic inquiry nevertheless resists this totalization. That is not to say that relationships cannot be established among the three rationalities. For example, when in the name of maintaining public order, the police operating in housing projects actually recall and reproduce an unequal social order through discriminatory and brutal practices, the state substitutes the penal state for the welfare state. Numerous illustrations of other such relations could be cited. But they would not establish a homogenous architecture, let alone a single architect, even if within this context of growing inequalities, increased erosion of protections, stiffening of punishments, and erasure of social causalities, the dominant classes have done more than resist: they have enriched and consolidated themselves, benefiting from evolutions that have been detrimental to the disadvantaged.

However, the observation of the agents' practices as well as the analysis of public discourse and public action reveal often complex rationales that are sometimes surprisingly contradictory, sometimes simply dissonant or different. More severe prison sentencing guidelines are accompanied by a reinforcement of the rights of inmates. The introduction of the possibility to try minors as adults in certain situations coexists with the development of educational measures for delinquent adolescents. The suspicion toward asylum seekers, which translates into a remarkable drop in the rates of granting refugee status, does not prevent the implementation of legal aid permitting claimants to be better defended on appeal, which has notable effects on the proportion of people whose applications are in the end accepted. But the discordances and variations in the practices of the state are not only evident in the definition of policies, they are also revealed in the work of the agents. Liberty and detention judges can oppose the illegal practices of the police in arresting undocumented immigrants. Social workers from Youth Protective Services tend to tone down the deviances which could penalize those in their care even more when brought before the magistrates. Psychiatrists at a Home for Adolescents use their skills to alleviate the social pressures, notably those of school, which weigh heavily on teenagers torn by their multiple obligations. The *raisons d'État* are therefore not just intelligible through legislative texts and political statements. They are equally as intelligible in the mistakes, waverings, resistances, and confrontations of agents who implement public action.

To take into account the tensions at the heart of the state between the coherences and contradictions, between the over-determination of the action and the indetermination of the agents, between the macro-power of the law and policy makers and the micro-powers of the agents in the institutions is to implement what Michel Foucault called a "critical morality."[11] The critique of the *raisons d'État*, such as we have endeavored to present through this lengthy inquiry into the government of the social question, supposes that we grasp both the broad historical movements—the retreat of the welfare state, the expansion of the penal state, the development of the liberal state—and the modest local actions—the day-to-day work of agents of who sometimes reinforce the general evolutions, sometimes contest, reorient, or relax them. But if the critique itself stems from an analysis in terms of morality, then it is not enough to be interested in the values and sentiments, in the deontology of the professions, and in the ethics of the actors.

We must also be consequentialist or in other words we must also consider the consequences of what the state and its agents do, notably in the two domains which have been remarkably ignored by Foucault himself: injustice and inequality. At the end of our journey into the heart of the state, we contend that it is according to these two criteria, which are both moral and political, that contemporary societies should ultimately be judged.

Notes

1 In the January 10, 1979 lecture on the birth of biopolitics (2004 [2008]: 1–25), Michel Foucault responds to potential criticism that he does "without a theory of the state" by stating that in fact for him it is not a question of "starting off with an analysis of the nature, structure, and functions of the state," but of operating an "identification of the gradual, piecemeal, but continuous takeover by the state of a number of practices, ways of doing things, and, if you like, governmentalities" (ibid.: 76–7).

2 In this respect, our approach shows strong similarities with the recent project on the ethnography of the state dubbed "stategraphy" by Tatjana Thelen, Larissa Vetters, and Keebet von Benda-Beckmann (2014).

3 The phrase has been coined by Pierre Rosanvallon (1995) and Robert Castel (1995). It is worth noting that the importance of immigrants and their children in the constitution of the new social question and consequently both the colonial legacy and the racial implications are not taken into account in their analysis (Fassin and Fassin 2006).

4 The phrase "welfare state" is preferred here to the literal translation of the French "*État social*," which is central to the analyses of Robert Castel (2003). Analyzing its retreat at the European level and drawing from a significant wealth of literature, Walter Korpi (2003) relates the phenomenon with the fact that strong political divisions tied to the existence of parties based on class, which had permitted the development of the welfare state, have almost all disappeared to the extent that it is sometimes easier for governments on the left side of the political spectrum than those on the right to carry out reforms that aim to reduce social protection and rights.

5 According to Daniel Schraad-Tischler (2011), who uses a complex indicator combining rates of poverty, employment, education, health, and social cohesion, France ranks tenth out of the 31 nations belonging to the Organization for Economic Cooperation and Development in terms of "social justice," behind countries from northern Europe, but ahead of countries from Eastern and Southern Europe as well as the United States.

6 The phrase "penal state" was notably proposed by Loïc Wacquant (2004) for the United States where the prison population has quintupled in the last 25 years. Contesting the interpretation that this evolution is the product of a policy of economic neoliberalism which handles poverty by incarcerating the poor, Willem de Koster, Jeroen Van der Waal, Peter Achterberg, and Dick Houtman (2008) consider the phenomenon to be linked to a "new political culture," which values authoritarianism and a response to a demand for social order.

7 According to Roy Walmsley (2011), with 96 prisoners for every 100,000 inhabitants, France falls exactly in the middle for western European countries, noticeably higher than the Scandinavian countries and Germany, but clearly lower than Italy, Spain, and Britain, and far behind Israel, Russia, and the United States, whose respective rates of incarceration are 325, 568, and 743 per 100,000. An in-depth study of French prisons was recently published (Fassin 2015).

8 The survey directed in Italy by Andrea Muehlebach (2012) on the reforms of the welfare

state and the implementation of a neoliberal morality invites works of international comparison.

9 The distinction between the political and moral sphere and the economic sphere is actually ambiguous in classical liberalism since individual freedom is closely associated with private property. Bernard Harcourt (2011) has established an intellectual genealogy of the relationships among freedom, the police, and the market.

10 By this expression, José Luis Moreno Pestaña (2011) means the tendency to consider everything tied together with each part serving to validate the others in the service of a hidden design.

11 In his March 7, 1979 Lecture, Michel Foucault (2004 [2008]: 185–213) attacks the "inflationary critique" of the state which at the time seemed a generalized "denunciation" of any state form viewed as oppressive, if not totalitarian. Though times have changed, the necessity of a critique which avoids the "elision of actuality" remains.

Glossary

Anti-crime squad (*brigade anti-criminalité, BAC*)
Anti-crime squads are special police units created in 1994 to operate in so-called "sensitive neighborhoods." There are more than three hundred units in France, mostly targeting misdemeanors. Their existence has been controversial since the mid-2000s due to their discriminatory practices.

Banlieues
The term "banlieues," for which the plural carries a negative connotation, refers to disadvantaged suburban areas mostly inhabited by low-income individuals with high rates of unemployment and a high percentage of whom are immigrants. It cannot be translated as "suburbs," since it corresponds demographically and sociologically to what would be called the "inner city" in other countries with the same stigmatizing undertone. To render this complex reality, the French word has been kept in the text without italics.

Brief social report (*enquête sociale rapide*)
A brief social report is an investigation conducted by psychologists or social workers accredited by the judicial system to gather the information about the family, social context, and criminal history of a person accused of an offense. It is based on a short interview and read by the judge during the hearing in immediate appearance trials.

Child Welfare (*Aide sociale à l'enfance, ASE*)
Child Welfare is a public administration, the mission of which is to protect children and ensure their safety. Social workers intervene to prevent abuse against them as well as to assist their parents in situations of economic or legal precarity. They work closely with other institutions such as juvenile court judges and Youth Protective Services.

Civic responsibility classes (*stage de citoyenneté*)
The civic responsibility classes were introduced by the Law of April 9, 2004. They are part of a community rehabilitation program providing young persons convicted of misdemeanor offenses like resisting arrest or insulting an officer with an alternative to prison.

Constitutional Council (*Conseil constitutionnel*)
The Constitutional Council was established in 1958 as the highest public authority in charge of upholding the French Constitution. It is composed of nine judges

appointed every three years to serve a term of nine years. Three are nominated by the president of France, three by the president of the Senate, and three by the president of the National Assembly. It also includes former presidents of France. Its role is mainly to determine the constitutionality of laws prior to their final adoption, and to supervise national elections.

Council of State (*Conseil d'État*)
Established in 1799, the Council of State has two functions: an administrative advisory role to assist the government in drafting new legislation and an adjudicative role since it is the French state's highest court of appeals.

Court of Audit (*Cour des comptes*)
The Court of Audit is a public institution in charge of auditing organizations and administrations, including the French government, to assess the use of public financial resources and the good governance of public institutions. It has the dual function of a comptroller's office and of an auditor general's office.

Court of Cassation (*Cour de cassation*)
The Court of Cassation was established in 1790 as the highest court of appeal for civil and criminal matters. Its role is limited to ensuring that proper legal procedure is followed during the appeals process. It does not rule on the substance of a case.

Department (*département*)
Departments are administrative divisions initially created during the Revolution of 1789. There are 96 departments in metropolitan France and 5 overseas. They are mostly in charge of social welfare, middle schools, and local public infrastructure. The governing body of the department is dual, with the prefecture, representing the state, and the *Conseil général*, a departmental assembly composed of elected representatives.

Deportation decision (*obligation de quitter le territoire français, OQTF*)
The deportation decision is defined by the Law of July 24, 2006. It is the main legal measure to deport undocumented immigrants. Depending on the case, it may require the person to leave the country immediately or within thirty days.

Detective (*police judiciaire*)
Placed under the supervision and control of a magistrate, detectives work closely with the justice system. These police or gendarmerie agents are empowered to record illegal acts and to gather the evidence necessary to arrest culprits.

Employment Hub (*Pôle emploi*)
The Employment Hub succeeded the National Employment Agency in 2008 as the French administration in charge of counseling and helping unemployed persons in their search for a job or training.

Examining magistrate (*juge d'instruction*)

Examining magistrates are judges in charge of investigating criminal allegations. They work in collaboration with the police to collect evidence regarding the case. Once compiled, the file is transmitted to a court.

Felony (*crime*)

French penal law classifies penalties according to the sentence incurred. An offence is considered a felony (*crime*) if the incurred sentence exceeds ten years of imprisonment or a fine of over 75,000 euros.

Gendarmerie (*gendarmerie*)

The gendarmerie is a military force in charge of law enforcement mostly in rural areas and small towns, whereas the national police operate in urban areas. It is under the supervision of the Ministry of Defense.

Home for Adolescents (*Maison des adolescents*)

These facilities were created in the early 2000s as multidisciplinary services involving psychiatrists, psychologists, social workers, and special educators to respond to the specific problems posed by teenagers confronted with a series of difficulties at school and more generally in their relations with institutions. Most of the young people served are from disadvantaged neighborhoods and have an immigrant background.

Immediate appearance trial (*comparution immédiate*)

Immediate appearance trials are legal proceedings that allow for a person to be tried soon after being taken into police custody. They correspond to cases for which the offender was caught *in flagrante delicto* and the elements of evidence are sufficient for rapid adjudication. Most cases involve drug use, traffic violations, domestic violence, and other misdemeanors.

Immediate execution of sentence (*mandat de dépôt*)

The immediate execution of sentence is a decision made by the judge who orders the detention of the person held in pre-trial custody or who has been given a prison sentence. The alternative would be, respectively, release pending trial or sentence adjustment.

Immigrant detention center (*centre de rétention administrative, CRA*)

The immigrant detention center is a specific site of imprisonment for foreigners who are due to be deported.

In flagrante delicto (*flagrant délit*)

This legal term is used when someone is caught in the act of committing an offense. In France, this sort of case typically leads to an immediate appearance trial.

Insulting an officer and resisting arrest (*outrage et rébellion*)
These offenses have steadily risen in the last two decades as a result of both a deterioration in the relationship between law enforcement agents and the population and incentives from the Ministry of the Interior to increase the number of indictments for such offenses.

Liberty and detention judge (*juge des libertés et de la detention, JLD*)
The liberty and detention judges were instituted under the Law of June 15, 2000. Their role is mostly to assess the necessity and legality of the incarceration of an individual prior to being charged, while awaiting trial, or being held in an immigrant detention center.

Magistrates adjudicating asylum (*formation de jugement*)
A *formation de jugement* is the phrase used to designate the three magistrates who adjudicate cases of asylum seekers at the National Court of Asylum.

Mandatory minimum sentence (*peine plancher*)
The Law of August 10, 2007 introduced minimum sentences for offenses in cases of recidivism. The Law of August 14, 2011 extended its use.

Misdemeanor (*délinquance*)
The French judicial system considers misdemeanors (*délinquance*) as offenses that correspond to a maximum sentence of less than ten years in prison and a fine amounting to less than 75,000 euros.

Municipality (*municipalité*)
Municipalities are the smallest level of the French administrative division. There are 36,000 municipalities of various sizes, from small villages to large cities.

National Court of Asylum (*Cour nationale du droit d'asile*)
The National Court of Asylum (formerly called the *Commission des recours des réfugiés*) was instituted by the Law of November 20, 2007. It hears appeals of decisions made by the French Office for the Protection of Refugees and Stateless Persons (OFPRA).

Precarity (*précarité*)
Précarité is a notion that was introduced into French public debates in the 1990s to characterize the objective as well as subjective situations where individuals face economic and social insecurity in a context of massive unemployment. Distinct from poverty, precarity implies uncertainties regarding the future, instability of work contracts, loss of social links, and even sometimes legal issues regarding residence permits. Recently adopted in the English sociological vocabulary, it is distinct from precariousness, which refers to the existential fragility of life.

Prefecture (*préfecture*)
A prefecture is the capital of a department. The term is also used metaphorically to designate the administrative representative of the French state at the departmental level. It stands in contrast to the *Conseil général*, which is the department's locally elected representative body.

Probation and Reentry Services (*Service pénitentiaire d'insertion et de probation*)
Probation and Reentry Services are units of the Prison Administration established in 1999 with the ultimate objective of reducing criminal recidivism. They are composed of social workers and probation officers, some of whom work in the prison system, where they assist inmates in devising reentry plans, while the majority are in charge of persons on parole or probation.

Prosecution in real time (*traitement en temps réel*)
Prosecution in real time arose from local initiatives at the end of the 1990s. It was designed as a tool to streamline the management of penal justice by reducing the time required to process the cases. It includes two steps: the decision of the public prosecutor to have the case immediately brought to trial and the immediate appearance trial leading to a sentence being handed down on the same day. It is proven to produce much more severe punishment than the normal legal procedure with a police or judicial investigation.

Rapporteur
At the National Court of Asylum, the rapporteurs are young staff members often with legal backgrounds who prepare reports regarding appeals made by asylum seekers after having been denied refugee status by OFPRA. The report, which concludes with a recommendation regarding the decision to be made, is read at the beginning of the hearing.

Region (*Région*)
Regions are administrative units consisting of several departments. They were officially created in 1972. There are 22 regions in metropolitan France and 5 overseas regions. A reform was proposed in 2014 that would reduce their number and increase their jurisdiction at the expense of departments. Regions are mostly in charge of economic development, spatial planning, local transportation, and high schools. The governing body is dual, with the regional prefecture, representing the state, and the *Conseil régional*, an assembly composed of elected representatives.

Residence permit (*carte/titre de séjour*)
A residence permit is a document which allows a foreigner to stay in a country legally. In France, there are different types of residence permits. The *carte de séjour temporaire* is granted for one year, while the *carte de résident* lasts ten years. The conditions for receiving a residence permit are presented in the articles L-311-1 ff.

of the Code of Entry and Residence of Aliens and the Right to Asylum (CESEDA). Residence permits are issued by the *Préfectures*.

Security housing unit, SHU (*quartier disciplinaire*)
In France, every jail has a security housing unit, where inmates are locked up as a result of either an immediate decision (preventive confinement), usually after an act of violence or resistance, or a sentence of the disciplinary board (punitive confinement). Prisoners can be sentenced to a maximum of 30 days of confinement.

Sensitive urban zone (*Zone urbaine sensible, ZUS*)
The so-called "sensitive urban zones" were defined in 1996 as public housing with particularly high levels of unemployment and poverty, where special social policies were to be implemented. More than 4 million inhabitants live in Sensitive urban zones, mostly located in the neglected banlieues of large cities.

Sentence adjustment (*aménagement de peine*)
Sentence adjustments are issued by specialized judges (*juge de l'application des peines*) under specific circumstances. These adjustments seek to develop alternatives to imprisonment either by avoiding it completely or by reducing its duration.

Sentencing judge (*juge de l'application des peines, JAP*)
Sentencing judges were created in 1958 to guarantee the principle of individualized sentences. They decide the way in which prison sentences can be adjusted to individual situations and possibly converted into other sanctions.

Special educators (*éducateurs spécialisés*)
Belonging to the broad sector of social work, special educators monitor and supervise children, youths, and sometimes adults who experience various sorts of problems: social, legal, psychological, or educational. They work in public institutions such as Youth Protective Services or Homes for Adolescents, and until recently in prisons.

Supervised release (*placement extérieur*)
Supervised release corresponds to one possible sentence adjustment intended to avoid or to reduce time in prison. It is a form of parole or probation allowing for a more gradual reentry into society through work, training courses, or medical treatment. The person is monitored by a private organization under the supervision of a judge.

Waiting zone (*zone d'attente pour personnes en instance, ZAPI*)
Foreigners who are not admitted into the French territory upon their arrival are held in waiting zones, most often in airports or ports. Non-admitted immigrants can be detained up to 96 hours by administrative decision only, but the liberty and

detention judge can extend this duration. In most cases, the person is deported back to their point of origin, except if their application for asylum has been accepted under an emergency procedure. The largest waiting zone is located at Roissy-Charles de Gaulle Airport.

Youth Employment Center (*Mission locale*)
Youth Employment Centers were initially created in 1982 to provide counseling to out-of-school and unemployed youths between the ages of 16 and 25. Although a major objective is to help them find a job or training, counselors must also pay constant attention to the living and health conditions of those whom they assist.

Youth Protective Services (*Protection judiciaire de la jeunesse, PJJ*)
Youth Protective Services are units of the Ministry of Justice dedicated to the supervision, support, protection, and rehabilitation of both juvenile delinquents and minors in need. The department employs educators, psychologists, and social workers who collaborate with juvenile judges to define the best sentence (prior to the judgment) or to assist minors (once they have been judged). Youth Protective Services agents are civil servants present in both custodial and non-custodial institutions.

Bibliography

Abrams, Kathryn (2002) "Fighting fire with fire: rethinking the role of disgust in hate crimes," *California Law Review*, Vol. 90, No. 5, pp. 1423–64.

Agulhon, Maurice (1973) *L'Apprentissage de la République (1848–1852)* (Paris: Seuil).

—— (1984) *1848. La révolution démocratique et sociale*, Vol. 3 (Paris: EDHIS).

Akoka, Karen (2011) "L'archétype rêvé du réfugié," *Plein droit*, Vol. 90, pp. 13–16.

Alain, Marc and Pruvost, Geneviève (2011) "Police: une socialisation professionnelle par étapes," *Déviance et société*, Vol. 35, No. 3, pp. 267–80.

Ancel, Marc (1954) *La Défense sociale nouvelle* (Paris: Cujas).

Ariès, Philippe (1960) *L'Enfant et la Vie familiale sous l'Ancien Régime* (Paris: Plon).

Astier, Isabelle (2007) *Les Nouvelles Règles du social* (Paris: PUF).

Aubouin, Michel, Teyssier, Arnaud, and Tulard, Jean (2005) *Histoire et dictionnaire de la police du Moyen Âge à nos jours* (Paris: Robert Laffont).

Aubusson de Cavarlay, Bruno (1985) "Hommes, peines et infractions. La Légalité de l'inégalité," *L'Année sociologique*, Vol. 35, pp. 275–309.

Bailleau, Francis, Cartuyvels, Yves, and de Fraene, Dominique (2009) "La criminalisation des mineurs et le jeu des sanctions," *Déviance et société*, Vol. 33, pp. 255–69.

Barbot, Janine and Dodier, Nicolas (2012) "De la douleur au droit. Ethnographie des plaidoiries lors de l'audience pénale du procès de l'hormone de croissance contaminée," in Cefaï, D., Berger, M., and Gayet-Viaud, C. (eds.) *Du civil au politique. Ethnographies du vivre ensemble*, pp. 289–322 (Brussels: Peter Lang).

Barnes, John A. (1994) *A Pack of Lies: Towards a Sociology of Lying* (Cambridge: Cambridge University Press).

Barré, Marie-Danièle and Aubusson de Cavarlay, Bruno (2008) *Dynamique du contentieux administratif. Analyse statistique de la demande enregistrée par les tribunaux administratifs (1999–2006)* (Guyancourt: CESDIP).

Barrett, Robert (1998) *La Traite des fous. La construction sociale de la schizophrénie* (Le Plessis-Robinson: Les Empêcheurs de penser en rond).

Bastard, Benoît, Mouhanna, Christian, and Ackermann, Werner (2007) *Une justice dans l'urgence: le traitement en temps réel des affaires pénales* (Paris: PUF).

Baudelot, Christian and Establet, Roger (2006) *Suicide. L'envers de notre monde* (Paris: Seuil).

Baudelot, Christian and Gollac, Michel (2003) *Travailler pour être heureux? Le bonheur et le travail en France* (Paris: Fayard).

Beaud, Stéphane (2002) *80% au bac, et après? Les enfants de la democratization scolaire* (Paris: La Découverte).

—— and Pialoux, Michel (2012 [1999]) *Retour sur la condition ouvrière. Enquête aux usines Peugeot de Sochaux-Montbéliard* (Paris: La Découverte).

Beccaria, Cesare (2009 [1764]) *On Crimes and Punishments*, Newman, Graeme R. and Marongiu, Pietro (trans.) (New Brunswick, NJ: Transaction Publishers).

Becker, Howard Saul (1997 [1963]) *Outsiders: Studies in the Sociology of Deviance* (New York: The Free Press).

Berlière, Jean-Marc and Lévy, René (2011) *Histoire des polices en France de l'Ancien Régime à nos jours* (Paris: Nouveau Monde Éditions).

Bernardot, Marc (2008) *Camps d'étrangers* (Bellecombe-en-Bauges: Croquant).

Bigo, Didier (1996) *Polices en réseaux. L'expérience européenne* (Paris: Presses de la Fondation nationale des sciences politiques).

Bittner, Egon (1980) *The Functions of the Police in Modern Society* (Cambridge, MA: Oelgeschlager, Gunn & Hain Publishers).

Blanc-Chaléard, Marie-Claude, Douki, Caroline, and Dyonnet, Nicole (2001) *Police et migrants France, 1667–1939* (Rennes: Presses universitaires de Rennes).

Blanchard, Emmanuel (2004) "La dissolution des Brigades nord-africaines de la Préfecture de police. La Fin d'une police d'exception pour les Algériens de Paris (1944–1953)?," *Bulletin de l'Institut d'histoire du temps présent*, Vol. 83, pp. 70–82.

—— (2011) *La Police parisienne et les Algériens 1945–1962* (Paris: Nouveau Monde Éditions).

Bohmer, Carol and Shuman, Amy (2008) *Rejecting Refugees: Political Asylum in the 21st Century* (London: Routledge).

Boltanski, Luc and Chiapello, Ève (1999) *Le Nouvel Esprit du capitalisme* (Paris: Gallimard).

Bonelli, Laurent (2008) *La France a peur. Une histoire sociale de "l'insécurité"* (Paris: La Découverte).

Bonneau, Jean (2007) Projet associatif. Association de politique criminelle appliquée et de réinsertion sociale: www.apcars.org/wp.../projet-associatif- apcars.pdf.

Bosworth, Mary (2007) "Creating the Responsible Prisoner: Federal Admission and Orientation Packs," *Punishment and Society*, Vol. 9, pp. 67–85.

Bouagga, Yasmine (2012) "Le métier de conseiller d'insertion et de probation: dans les coulisses de l'État pénal?," *Sociologie du travail*, Vol. 54, No. 3, pp. 317–37.

Boucher d'Argis, Antoine-Gaspard (1751–80) "Police," in Diderot, Denis and Le Rond d'Alembert, Jean (eds.) *Encyclopédie, ou Dictionnaire raisonné des arts et des métiers*, Vol. 12, p. 911 (Paris).

Bourdieu, Pierre (1998 [1989]) *The State Nobility: Elite Schools in the Field of Power*, Clough, Lauretta C. (trans.) (Cambridge: Polity).

—— (ed.) (1999 [1993]) *The Weight of the World: Social Suffering in Contemporary Society*, Ferguson, Priscilla Parkhurst (trans.) (Cambridge: Polity).

—— (2012) *Sur l'État. Cours au Collège de France 1989–1992* (Paris: Raisons d'agir/Seuil).

Bourgois, Philippe (2001) *En quête de respect. Le crack à New York* (Paris: Seuil).

Brodkin, Evelyn (2011) "Policy Work: Street-level Organizations under New Managerialism," *Journal of Public Administration Research and Theory*, Vol. 21, Sup. 2, pp. i233–i251.

Butler, Judith (1997) *The Psychic Life of Power: Theories in Subjection* (Stanford, CA: Stanford University Press).

Carrier, Nicolas (2010) "Sociologies anglo-saxonnes du virage punitif," *Champ pénal/Penal field*, Vol. 7: http://champpenal.revues.org/7818.

Castel, Robert (1983) "De la dangerosité au risque," *Actes de la recherche en sciences sociales*, Vol. 47, No. 1, pp. 119–27.

—— (1995) *Les Métamorphoses de la question sociale. Une chronique du salariat* (Paris: Fayard).

—— (2003) *L'Insécurité sociale. Qu'est-ce qu'être protégé?* (Paris: Seuil/La République des idées.)

Céré, Jean-Paul (1999) *Le Contentieux disciplinaire dans les prisons françaises et le droit européen* (Paris: L'Harmattan).

Certeau, Michel de (2011 [1980]) *The Practice of Everyday Life*, Rendall, Steven (trans.) (Berkeley, CA: University of California Press).

Chamboredon, Jean-Claude (1971) "La délinquance juvénile, essai de construction d'objet," *Revue française de sociologie*, Vol. 12, No. 3, pp. 335–77.

Chantraine, Gilles and Cauchie, Jean-François (2005) "De l'usage du risque dans le gouvernement du crime," *Champ pénal/Penal field*, Vol. 7: http://champpenal.revues. org/80.

Chauvaud, François (2006) "Repris de justice et incorrigibles: les figures du récidiviste au France de l'imaginaire judiciaire (France, XIXe)," in Briegel, F. and Porret, M. (eds.) *Le Criminel endurci. Récidive et récidivistes du Moyen Âge au XXe siècle*, pp. 251–62 (Geneva: Droz).

Chauvenet, Antoinette, Benguigui, Georges, and Orlic, Françoise (1993) "Les surveillants de prison: le prix de la sécurité," *Revue française de sociologie*, Vol. 34, No. 3, pp. 345–66.

Chauvenet, Antoinette, Gorgeon, Catherine, Mouhanna, Christian, and Orlic, Françoise (2001) "Entre social et judiciaire. Quelle place pour le travail social de milieu ouvert?" *Archives de politique criminelle*, Vol. 1, pp. 71–91.

Chauvenet, Antoinette, Monceau, Madeleine, Orlic, Françoise, and Rostaing, Corinne (2005) *La Violence carcérale en question. Rapport de recherche GIP, mission de recherche Droit et Justice* (Paris: CNRS-EHESS).

Chauvin, Sébastien (2010) *Les Agences de la précarité. Journaliers à Chicago* (Paris: Seuil).

Chevalier, Louis (1958) *Classes laborieuses et classes dangereuses* (Paris: Plon).

Chevandier, Christian (2012) *Policiers dans la ville. Une histoire des gardiens de la paix* (Paris: Gallimard).

Christin, Angèle (2008) *Comparution immédiate. Enquête sur une pratique judiciaire* (Paris: La Découverte).

Cicourel, Aaron (1968) *The Social Organization of Juvenile Justice* (New York: Wiley).

—— (1981) "Notes on the integration of micro and macro-levels of analysis," in Knorr-Cetina, K. and Cicourel, A. (eds.) *Advances in Social Theory and Methodology: Toward an Integration of Micro- and Macro-sociologies*, pp. 51–80 (Boston, MA: Routledge & Kegan Paul).

Clark, Michael (1971) "The Moral Gradation of Punishment," *Philosophical Quarterly*, Vol. 21, No. 83, pp. 132–40.

Clemens, Elisabeth and Cook, James (1999) "Politics and Institutionalism: Explaining Durability and Change," *Annual Review of Sociology*, Vol. 25, pp. 441–66.

Cohen, Mathilde (2009) "L'épreuve orale. Les magistrats administratifs face aux audiences de reconduite à la frontière," *Droit & société*, Vol. 72, pp. 387–410.

Colera, Christophe (2001) "Tribunaux administratifs et cours administratives d'appel: Évolution sociologique et effets sur la jurisprudence," *Droit & société*, Vol. 49, pp. 873–94.

Comité économique et social des Communautés européennes (1983) *L'Emploi des jeunes* (Brussels: Avis).

Conley, John M. and O'Barr, William M. (1998) *Just Words: Law, Language, and Power* (Chicago, IL: University of Chicago Press).

Conseil Lyonnais pour le respect des droits (2008) "Rapport sur les comparutions immédiates à Lyon," unpublished document, 30 pp.

Corrigan, Philip and Sayer, Derek (1985) *The Great Arch: English State Formation as Cultural Revolution* (Oxford: Blackwell).

Coutant, Isabelle (2005) *Délit de jeunesse. La justice face aux quartiers* (Paris: La Découverte).

—— (2012) *Troubles en psychiatrie. Enquête dans une unité pour adolescents* (Paris: La Dispute).

Coutin, Susan (1995) "Smugglers or Samaritans in Tucson, Arizona: Producing and Contesting Legal Truth," *American Ethnologist*, Vol. 22, No. 3, pp. 549–71.

Daniel, Valentine and Knudsen, John (1995) *Mistrusting Refugees* (Berkeley, CA: University of California Press).

Darmon, Muriel (2009) *Devenir anorexique. Une approche sociologique* (Paris: La Découverte).

Das, Veena and Poole, Deborah (2004) "State and Its Margins: Comparative Ethnographies," in Das, V. and Poole, D. (eds.) *Anthropology in the Margins of the State*, pp. 3–33 (Santa Fe, NM: School of American Research Press).

Daston, Lorraine (1995) "The Moral Economy of Science," *Osiris*, Vol. 10, pp. 2–24.

De Koster, Willem, van der Waal, Jeroen, Achtenberg, Peter, and Houtman, Dick (2008) "The Rise of the Penal State: Neo-liberalization or New Political Culture," *British Journal of Criminology*, Vol. 48, pp. 720–34.

Delarue, Jean-Marie (1991) *Quartiers en difficulté. La relégation* (Paris: Syros).

Delmas-Marty, Mireille (1986) *Le Flou du droit. Du code pénal aux droits de l'homme* (Paris: PUF).

Delwit, Pascal, De Waele, Jean-Michel, and Rea, André (1998) *L'Extrême droite en France et en Belgique* (Brussels: Complexe).

Devresse, Marie-Sophie (2006) "Réflexivité, responsabilité et position du justiciable dans le processus pénal consenti," in Digneffe, F. and Moreau, T. (eds.) *La Responsabilité et la responsabilisation dans la justice pénale*, pp. 369–74 (Brussels: De Boeck et Larcier).

d'Halluin-Mabillot, Estelle (2012) *Les Épreuves de l'asile. Associations et réfugiés face aux politiques du soupçon* (Paris: Éditions de l'EHESS).

Donzelot, Jacques (1997 [1977]) *The Policing of Families* (New York: Pantheon Books).

—— (2006) *Quand la ville se défait. Quelle politique face à la crise des banlieues* (Paris: Seuil).

Douglas, Mary (1986) *How Institutions Think* (Syracuse, NY: Syracuse University Press).

Dubar, Claude (2004) *La Formation professionnelle continue* (Paris: La Découverte).

Claude, Dubar, Elyzabeth, Feutrie, Michel, Gadrey, Nicole, Hedoux, Jean, and Verschave, Édouard (1987) *L'Autre Jeunesse. Des jeunes sans diplôme dans un dispositif de socialisation* (Lille: Presse universitaire de Lille).

Dubois, Vincent (2012 [1999]) *The Bureaucrat and the Poor: Encounters in French Welfare Offices* (Farnham: Ashgate Publishing).

—— (2007) "État social actif et contrôle des chômeurs: un tournant rigoriste entre tendances européennes et logiques nationales," *Politique européenne*, Vol. 21, pp. 73–95.

—— (2009) "Le paradoxe du contrôleur. Incertitudes et contraintes dans le contrôle des assistés sociaux," *Actes de la recherche en sciences sociales*, Vol. 178, pp. 28–49.

Durkheim, Émile (1986 [1900]) "The Concept of the State," in Giddens, Anthony (ed.) *Durkheim on Politics and the State*, pp. 32–72 (Stanford, CA: Stanford University Press).

Duthé, Géraldine, Hazard, Angélique, Kensey, Annie, and Pan Ké Shon, Jean-Louis (2009)

"Suicide en prison: La France comparée à ses voisins européens," *Population et sociétés*, Vol. 462, pp. 1–4.

Duvoux, Nicolas (2009a) *L'Autonomie des assistés. Sociologie des politiques d'insertion* (Paris: PUF).

—— (2009b) "L'injonction biographique dans les politiques sociales. Spécificité et exemplarité de l'insertion," *Informations sociales*, Vol. 156, pp. 114–22.

Economic and Social Committee of the European Community (1983) *Youth Unemployment*: http://aei.pitt.edu/cgi/export/42815/HTML/aei-archive-42815.html.

Ehrenberg, Alain (1998) *La Fatigue d'être soi. Dépression et société* (Paris: Odile Jacob).

Elisha, Omri (2008) "Moral Ambitions of Grace: The Paradox of Compassion and Accountability in Evangelical Faith-based Activism," *Cultural Anthropology*, Vol. 23, No. 1, pp. 154–89.

El Qadim, Nora (2008) *Le Tribunal administratif de Paris à l'épreuve des évolutions du contentieux des étrangers depuis 2007: Changement juridique et impact organisationnel* (Paris: Institut d'études politiques de Paris).

Enguéléguélé, Stéphane (2010) *Justice, politique pénale et tolérance zéro* (Paris: L'Harmattan).

Équipe TeO (2010) *Trajectoires et origines. Enquête sur la diversité des populations en France, premiers résultats* (Paris: INED): https://www.ined.fr/fichier/s_rubrique/19558/dt168_teo.fr.pdf.

Essed, Philomena (1991) *Understanding Everyday Racism: An Interdisciplinary Theory* (Newbury Park, CA: Sage).

Faget, Jacques (2008) "La fabrique de la décision pénale. Une dialectique des asservissements et des émancipations," *Champ pénal/Penal field*, Vol. 5: http://champpenal.revues.org/3983.

—— (1992) *Justice et travail social: Le Rhizome pénal* (Toulouse: Érès).

Farcy, Jean-Claude (2006) "Qui sont les récidivistes parisiens au XIXe siècle?," in Briegel, F. and Porret, M. (eds.) *Le Criminel endurci. Récidive et récidivistes du Moyen Âge au XXe siècle*, pp. 187–234 (Geneva: Droz).

Fassin, Didier (2001) "Charité bien ordonnée. Principes de justice et pratiques de jugement dans l'attribution des aides d'urgence," *Revue française de sociologie*, Vol. 42, No. 3, pp. 437–75.

—— (2002) "L'invention française de la discrimination," *Revue française de science politique*, Vol. 52, No. 4, pp. 403–23.

—— (2005) "Compassion and Repression: The Moral Economy of Immigration Policies in France," *Cultural Anthropology*, Vol. 20, No. 3, pp. 62–387.

—— (2009) "Les économies morales revisitées," *Annales. Histoire, sciences sociales*, Vol. 6, pp. 1237–66.

—— (2010) "Ni race, ni racisme. Ce que racialiser veut dire," in Fassin, D. (ed.) *Les Nouvelles Frontières de la société française*, pp. 147–72 (Paris: La Découverte).

—— (2012a) "Vers une théorie des économies morales," in Fassin, D. and Eideliman, J.-S. (eds.) *Économies morales contemporaines*, pp. 19–47 (Paris: La Découverte).

—— (2012b) "Toward a Critical Moral Anthropology," in Fassin, D. (ed.) *A Companion to Moral Anthropology*, pp. 1–17 (Malden, MA: Wiley-Blackwell).

—— (2013a [2011]) *Enforcing Order: An Ethnography of Urban Policing* (Cambridge: Polity).

—— (2013b) "The Precarious Truth of Asylum," *Public Culture*, Vol. 25, No. 1., pp. 39–63.

—— (2015) *L'Ombre du monde. Une anthropologie de la condition carcérale* (Paris: Seuil).

—— and Eideliman, Jean-Sébastien (eds.) (2012) *Économies morales contemporaines* (Paris: La Découverte).

—— and Fassin, Éric (2006) *De la question sociale à la question raciale? Représenter la société française* (Paris: La Découverte).

—— and Kobelinsky, Carolina (2012) "Comment on juge l'asile. L'institution comme agent moral," *Revue française de sociologie*, Vol. 53, No. 4, pp. 657–88.

Faubion, James (2011) *An Anthropology of Ethics* (Cambridge: Cambridge University Press).

Faugeron, Claude and Le Boulaire, Jean-Michel (1988) "La création du service social des prisons et l'évolution de la réforme pénitentiaire en France de 1945 à 1958," *Déviance et société*, Vol. 12, No. 4, pp. 317–59.

Feeley, Malcom and Simon, Jonathan (1992) "The New Penology: Notes on the Emerging Strategy of Corrections and Its Implications," *Criminology*, Vol. 30, No. 4, pp. 449–74.

—— (2003) "The Form and Limits of the New Penology," in Blomberg, Thomas G. and Cohen, Stanley (eds.) *Punishment and Social Control*, pp. 75–116 (Hawthorne, NY: De Gruyter).

Ferlay, Nadine (2011) *Les Travailleurs de l'ombre: Enquête sur les travailleurs sociaux de l'administration pénitentiaire*, 2 vols. (Paris: UGFP-CGT).

Fernandez, Fabrice (2010) *Emprises. Drogues, errance, prison: figures d'une expérience totale* (Brussels: Larcier).

—— (2011) "Le théâtre des fumeurs de crack. Mise en scène émotionnelle et voilement/ dévoilement de soi," *Ethnologie française*, Vol. 44, No. 4, pp. 707–15.

—— and Lézé, Samuel (2011) "Finding the Moral Heart of Carceral Treatment: Mental Health Care in a French Prison," *Social Science and Medicine*, Vol. 72, No. 9, pp. 1563–9.

——, Lézé, Samuel, and Marche, Hélène (2008) *Le Langage social des émotions. Études sur les rapports au corps et à la santé* (Paris: Anthropos-Economica).

——, Lézé, Samuel, and Strauss, Hélène (2010) "Comment évaluer une personne? L'expertise judiciaire et ses usages moraux," *Cahiers internationaux de sociologie*, Vol. 128–29, pp. 179–206.

Fossé-Polliak, Claude and Mauger, Gérard (1983) "Les loubards," *Actes de la recherche en sciences sociales*, Vol. 50, pp. 49–68.

Foucault, Michel (1979 [1975]) *Discipline and Punish: The Birth of the Prison*, Sheridan, Alan (trans.) (New York: Vintage Books).

—— (1985 [1984]) *The History of Sexuality*, Vol. 2: *The Use of Pleasure* (New York: Pantheon Books).

—— (1988) "Morale et pratiques de soi," in *Dits et écrits, 4, 1980–1988*, pp. 555–661 (Paris: Gallimard).

—— (2003 [1999]) *Abnormal: Lectures at the Collège de France, 1974–1975*, Davidson, Arnold I. (ed.), Burchell, Graham (trans.) (New York: Picador).

—— (1997a) "Governmentality," in *Essential Works of Foucault, 1954–1984*, Vol. 3: *Power*, pp. 201–22 (New York: The New Press).

—— (1997b) "*Omnes et Singulatim*: Toward a Critique of Political Reason," in *Essential Works of Foucault, 1954–1984*, Vol. 3: *Power*, pp. 298–325 (New York: The New Press).

—— (1997c) "The Political Technology of Individuals," in *Essential Works of Foucault, 1954–1984*, Vol. 3: *Power*, pp. 403–17 (New York: The New Press).

—— (2003) *Sécurité, territoire, population. Cours au Collège de France 1977–1978*, Paris: Seuil/Gallimard.

—— (2004 [2008]) *Naissance de la biopolitique. Cours au Collège de France 1978–1979*, Paris: Seuil/Gallimard.

Frader, Laura (2006) "Depuis les muscles jusqu'aux nerfs: Le Genre, la race et le corps au travail en France, 1919–1939," *Travailler*, Vol. 16, pp. 111–44.

Froment, Jean-Charles and Kaluszynski, Martine (eds.) (2011) *L'Administration pénitentiaire face aux principes de la nouvelle gestion publique: Une réforme en question(s)* (Grenoble: Presses universitaires de Grenoble).

Gander, David (2006) "La répression pénale des récidivistes à Genève au XVIIIe siècle," in Briegel, F. and Porret, M. (eds.) *Le Criminel endurci. Récidive et récidivistes du Moyen Âge au XXe siècle*, pp. 137–52 (Geneva: Droz).

Garapon, Antoine (1997) *Bien juger. Essai sur le rituel judiciaire* (Paris: Odile Jacob).

Garcia-Parpet, Marie-France (1996) "Représentations savantes et pratiques marchandes," *Genèses*, Vol. 25, pp. 50–71.

Garland, David (2001) *The Culture of Control: Crime and Social Order in Contemporary Society* (Chicago, IL: University of Chicago Press).

Geremek, Bronislaw (1987) *La Potence ou la pitié. L'Europe et les pauvres du Moyen Âge à nos jours*, Paris: Gallimard.

Goffman Erving (1986 [1974]) *Frame Analysis: An Essay on the Organization of Experience* (Boston, MA: Northeastern University Press).

Good, Anthony (2007) *Anthropology and Expertise in the Asylum Courts* (Abingdon: Routledge-Cavendish).

Graham, Mark (2002) "Emotional Bureaucracies: Emotions, Civil Servants, and Immigrants in the Swedish Welfare State," *Ethos*, Vol. 30, pp. 199–226.

Gras, Laurent (2008) *La Socialisation professionnelle des conseillers d'insertion et de probation* (Agen: ENAP): www.enapp.justice.fr/eleves/ representations.php.

Hacking, Ian (2008) *Entre science et réalité: la construction sociale de quoi?* (Paris: La Découverte).

Hall, Peter and Taylor, Rosemary (1996) "Political Science and the Three New Institutionalisms," *Political Studies*, Vol. 44, pp. 936–57.

Harcourt, Bernard (2001) *Illusion of Order: The False Promise of Broken Windows Policing* (Cambridge, MA: Harvard University Press).

—— (2011) *The Illusion of Free Markets: Punishment and the Myth of Natural Order* (Cambridge, MA: Harvard University Press).

Herbert, Steve (1996) "Morality in Law Enforcement: Chasing 'Bad Guys' with the Los Angeles Police Department," *Law & Society Review*, Vol. 30, No. 4, pp. 799–818.

Herlihy, Jane, Gleeson, Kate, and Turner, Stuart (2010) "What Assumptions about Human Behavior Underlie Asylum Judgments?," *International Journal of Refugee Law*, Vol. 22, No. 3, pp. 351–66.

Herzfeld, Michael (1992) *The Social Production of Indifference: Exploring the Symbolic Roots of Western Bureaucracy* (New York: Berg).

Heyman, Josiah McConnell (2000) "Respect for Outsiders? Respect for the Law? The Moral Evaluation of High-scale Issues by US Immigration Officers," *Journal of the Royal Anthropological Institute*, Vol. 6, pp. 635–52.

Hirschman, Albert (1970) *Exit, Voice, and Loyalty: Responses to Decline in Firms, Organizations, and States* (Cambridge, MA: Harvard University Press).

Hochschild, Arlie (1983) *Managed Heart: Commercialization of Human Feelings* (Berkeley, CA: University of California Press).

Hughes, Everett (1971) *The Sociological Eye: Selected Papers* (Chicago, IL: Aldine-Atherton).

Hunt, Allan (2003) "Risk and Moralization in Everyday Life," in Ericson, R.V. and Doyle, A. (eds.) *Risk and Morality*, pp. 165–92 (Toronto: University of Toronto Press).

Inspection générale des services judiciaires (2009) *Évaluation du nombre de peines d'emprisonnement ferme en attente d'exécution* (Paris: La Documentation française).

Ion, Jacques and Ravon, Bertrand (2005) *Les Travailleurs sociaux* (Paris: La Découverte).

Jobard, Fabien (2002) *Bavures policières? La Force publique et ses usages* (Paris: La Découverte).

—— (2010) "Le gibier de police, immuable ou changeant?," *Archives de politique criminelle*, Vol. 32, pp. 93–105.

—— and Névanen, Sophie (2007) "La couleur du jugement," *Revue française de sociologie*, Vol. 48, No. 2, pp. 243–72.

Kellens, Georges (2000) *Punir, pénologie et droit des sanctions pénales* (Liège: Éditions juridiques de l'Université de Liège).

Kelling, George L. and Coles, Catherine M. (1998) *Fixing Broken Windows: Restoring Order and Reducing Crime in our Communities* (New York: Free Press).

Kensey, Annie and Benaouda, Abdelmalik (2011) "Les risques de récidive des sortants de prison. Une nouvelle évaluation," *Cahiers d'études pénitentiaires et criminologiques*, Vol. 36.

Klockars, Carl (1980) "The Dirty Harry Problem," *Annals of the American Academy of Political and Social Science*, Vol. 452, pp. 33–47.

Kobelinsky, Carolina (2012) "L'asile gay: Jurisprudence de l'intime à la Cour nationale du droit d'asile," *Droit et société*, Vol. 82, pp. 583–601.

Korpi, Walter (2003) "Welfare State Regress in Western Europe," *Annual Review of Sociology*, Vol. 29, pp. 589–609.

Lagroye, Jacques and Offerlé, Michel (2011) *Sociologie de l'institution* (Paris: Belin).

Laidlaw, James (2002) "For an Anthropology of Ethics and Freedom," *Journal of the Royal Anthropological Institute*, Vol. 8, No. 2, pp. 311–32.

Larminat, Xavier de (2012) "La probation en quête d'approbation. L'exécution des peines en milieu ouvert entre gestion des risques et gestion des flux," Ph.D. diss., Université Versailles-Saint Quentin, CESDIP-Université de Versailles-Saint-Quentin.

Lascoumes, Pierre (1977) *Prévention et contrôle social: Les Contradictions du travail social* (Paris: Masson).

—— and Le Galès, Patrick (2005) *Gouverner par les instruments* (Paris: Presses de Sciences Po).

——, Poncela, Pierette, and Lenoël, Pierre (1989) *Au nom de l'ordre. Une histoire politique du code pénal* (Paris: Hachette).

Latour, Bruno (2002) *La Fabrique du droit. Une ethnographie du Conseil d'État* (Paris: La Découverte).

Lazega, Emmanuel (1999) "Le phénomène collégial: Une théorie structurale de l'action collective entre pairs," *Revue française de sociologie*, Vol. 40, No. 4, pp. 639–70.

Le Caisne, Léonore (2008) *Avoir 16 ans à Fleury. Ethnographie d'un centre de jeunes détenus* (Paris: Seuil).

Lechien, Marie-Hélène (2001) "L'impensé d'une réforme pénitentiaire," *Actes de la recherche en sciences sociales*, Vol. 136, pp. 15–26.

Lee, John Alan (1981) "Some Structural Aspects of Police Deviance in Relations with Minority Groups," in Shearing, C. (ed.) *Organisational Police Deviance*, pp. 49–82 (Scaborough, ON: Butterworth).

Lévy, René (1985) *Du flagrant délit à la comparution immédiate: La Procédure d'urgence d'après les statistiques judiciaires (1977–1984)* (Paris: CESDIPP).

L'Heuillet, Hélène (2002) "La généalogie de la police," *Cultures & conflits*, Vol. 48, pp. 109–32.

Lhuilier, Dominique (2007) *Changement et construction des identités professionnelles: Les travailleurs sociaux pénitentiaires* (Paris: Direction de l'administration pénitentiaire).

Liebling, Alison (2000) "Prison Officers, Policing and the Use of Discretion," *Theoretical Criminology*, Vol. 4, No. 3, pp. 333–57.

Lipsky, Michael (2010 [1980]) *Street-Level Bureaucracy: Dilemmas of the Individual in Public Services* (New York: Russell Sage Foundation).

Loescher, Gil (1993) *Beyond Charity: International Cooperation and the Global Refugee Crisis* (Oxford: Oxford University Press).

Luhmann, Niklas (2001) *La Légitimation par la procédure* (Laval, QC: Presses de l'Université Laval).

Lutz, Catherine (1986) "Emotion, Thought, and Estrangement: Emotion as a Cultural Category," *Cultural Anthropology*, Vol. 1, No. 3, pp. 287–309.

Lynch, Mona (1998) "Waste Managers? The New Penology, Crime Fighting, and Parole Agent Identity," *Law & Society Review*, Vol. 32, No. 4, pp. 839–70.

Mahmood, Saba (2009) *Politique de la piété. Le Féminisme à l'épreuve du renouveau islamique* (Paris: La Découverte).

Millet, Mathias and Thin, Daniel (2005) *Ruptures scolaires. L'École à l'épreuve de la question sociale* (Paris: PUF).

Ministère de la Justice (2008) *Annuaire statistique de la justice 2007–2008.*

—— (2009) *Annuaire statistique de la justice 2008–2009.*

—— (2010) *Annuaire statistique de la justice 2009–2010.*

Mohammed, Marwan and Mucchielli, Laurent (eds.) (2007) *Les Bandes de jeunes. Des "blousons noirs" à nos jours* (Paris: La Découverte).

Monjardet, Dominique (1994) "La culture professionnelle des policiers," *Revue française de sociologie*, Vol. 35, pp. 393–411.

—— (1996) *Ce que fait la police. Sociologie de la force publique* (Paris: La Découverte).

Moreno Pestaña, José Luis (2011) *Foucault, la gauche et la politique* (Paris: Textuel).

Mouhanna, Christian (2011) *La Police contre les citoyens* (Nîmes: Champ social).

Mouton, Eugène (1887) *Le Devoir de punir. Introduction à l'histoire et à la théorie du droit de punir* (Paris: Cerf).

Mucchielli, Laurent (2002) "Misère du débat sur 'l'insécurité,'" *Hommes et libertés*, Vol. 118, pp. 46–9.

—— (2003) "Délinquance et immigration en France: un regard sociologique," *Criminologie*, Vol. 36, No. 2, pp. 27–55.

—— (ed.) (2008) *La Frénésie sécuritaire. Retour à l'ordre et nouveau contrôle social* (Paris: La Découverte).

Muehlebach, Andrea (2012) *The Moral Neoliberal: Welfare and Citizenship in Italy* (Chicago, IL: University of Chicago Press).

Muel, Francine (1975) "L'école obligatoire et l'invention de l'enfance anormale," *Actes de la recherche en sciences sociales*, Vol. 1, pp. 60–74.

Muel-Dreyfus, Francine (1983) *Le Métier d'éducateur* (Paris: Minuit).

Muir, William Kerr (1977) *Police: Street Corner Politicians* (Chicago, IL: University of Chicago Press).

Murji, Karim and Solomos, John (eds.) (2005) *Racialization: Studies in Theory and Practice* (Oxford: Oxford University Press).

Napoli, Paolo (2003) *Naissance de la police moderne. Pouvoirs, normes, société* (Paris: La Découverte.

Noël, Olivier (2004) *Jeunesse en voie de désaffiliation. Une sociologie politique de et dans l'action publique* (Paris: L'Harmattan).

Noiriel, Gérard (1988) *Le Creuset français. Histoire de l'immigration, XIXe–XXe siècles* (Paris: Seuil).

—— (1991) *La Tyrannie du national. Le droit d'asile en Europe (1793–1993)* (Paris: Calmann-Lévy).

—— (2005) "De l'enfance maltraitée à la maltraitance. Un nouvel enjeu pour la recherche historique," *Genèses*, Vol. 60, No. 3, pp. 154–67.

—— (2007) *Immigration, antisémitisme et racisme en France, XIXe–XXe siècles: Discours publics, humiliations privées* (Paris: Fayard).

O'Brien, Patricia (1982) *The Promise of Punishment: Prisons in Nineteenth-Century France* (Princeton, NJ: Princeton University Press).

Ottenhof, Reynald (2001) *L'Individualisation de la peine. De Saleilles à aujourd'hui* (Toulouse: Érès).

Pédron, Pierre (1995) *La Prison et les Droits de l'Homme* (Paris: LGDJ).

Perrot, Michelle (1975) "Délinquance et système pénitentiaire en France au XIXe siècle," *Annales ESC*, Vol. 30, pp. 67–93.

Petit, Jacques-Guy, Castan, Nicole, Faugeron, Claude, Pierre, Michel, and Zysberg, André (1991) *Histoire des galères, bagnes et prisons, XIIIe–XXe siècle. Introduction à l'histoire pénale de la France* (Toulouse: Privat).

Peyrefitte, Alain, Schmelck, Robert, and Dumoulin, Roger (1977) *Réponses à la violence: Rapport à M. le Président de la République* (Paris: Comité d'études sur la violence, la criminalité et la délinquance).

Philippe, Robert (2009) *Peine, récidive et crise sécuritaire. La peine dans tous ses états, colloque en l'honneur de Michel van de Kerchove*, Facultés universitaires Saint-Louis, October 16–17.

Pinell, Patrice and Zafiropoulos, Markos (1978) "La médicalisation de l'échec scolaire, de la pédopsychiatrie à la psychanalyse infantile," *Actes de la Recherche en Sciences sociales*, Vol. 24, pp. 23–49.

Pruvost, Geneviève, Coulangeon, Philippe, and Roharik, Ionela (2004) *1982–2003: Enquête sociodémographique sur les conditions de vie et d'emploi de 5 221 policiers. Rapport final.* Paris: Ministère de l'Intérieur.

Reiner, Robert (2000) *The Politics of the Police* (Oxford: Oxford University Press).

Reiss, Albert (1971) *The Police and the Public* (New Haven, CT: Yale University Press).

Renneville, Marc and Carlier, Christian (2008) "Chronologie relative au milieu ouvert et à ses personnels," *Criminocorpus*: www.criminocorpus. cnrs.fr/article389.html.

Rhodes, Lorna A. (2004) *Total Confinement: Madness and Reason in the Maximum Security Prison* (Berkeley, CA: University of California Press).

Rigouste, Mathieu (2009) *L'Ennemi intérieur. La Généalogie coloniale et militaire de l'ordre sécuritaire dans la France contemporaine* (Paris: La Découverte).

Robert, Philippe and Lascoumes, Pierre (1974) *La Crise de la justice pénale et sa réforme* (Paris: SEPC).

Robert, Philippe and Pottier, Marie-Lys (1997) "'On ne se sent plus en sécurité.' Délinquance et insécurité: Une enquête sur deux décennies," *Revue française de science politique*, Vol. 47, No. 6, pp. 707–40.

——— (2004) "Les préoccupations sécuritaires: une mutation?," *Revue française de sociologie*, Vol. 45, No. 2, pp. 211–41.

Rosanvallon, Pierre (1990) *L'État en France de 1789 à nos jours* (Paris: Seuil).

——— (1995) *La Nouvelle Question sociale. Repenser l'État-providence* (Paris: Seuil).

Rostaing, Corinne (2007) "Processus de judiciarisation carcérale: Le Droit en prison, une ressource pour les acteurs?," *Droit & société*, Vol. 67, pp. 577–95.

Rousseau, Cécile and Foxen, Patricia (2006) "Le mythe du réfugié menteur: Un mensonge indispensable?," *L'Évolution psychiatrique*, Vol. 71, No. 3, pp. 505–20.

Roussel, Louis (1989) *La Famille incertaine* (Paris: Odile Jacob).

Roux, Guillaume, Roché, Sebastian, and Astor, Sandrine (2011) *Minorities and Trust in the Criminal Justice: French Case Study* (Grenoble: Pacte/CNRS).

Roux, Sébastien (2012) "La discipline des sentiments. Responsabilisation et culpabilisation dans la justice des mineurs," *Revue française de sociologie*, Vol. 53, No. 4, pp. 719–52.

Salas, Denis (2007) *La Volonté de punir: essai sur le populisme pénal* (Paris: Hachette Littératures).

Saleilles, Raymond (1898) *L'Individualisation de la peine. Étude de criminalité sociale* (Paris: Alcan).

Salle, Grégory (2009) *La Part d'ombre de l'État de droit: La Question carcérale en France et en République fédérale d'Allemagne depuis 1968* (Paris: Éditions de l'EHESS).

Sallée, Nicolas (2010) "Les éducateurs de la Protection judiciaire de la jeunesse à l'épreuve de l'évolution du traitement pénal des jeunes délinquants," *Champ pénal/Penal field*, Vol. 7.

Sbriccoli, Mario (2006) "Periculum previtatis. Juristes et juges face à l'image du criminel méchant et endurci (XIVe–XVIe)," in Briegel, F. and Porret, M. (eds.) *Le Criminel endurci. Récidive et récidivistes du Moyen-Âge au XXe siècle*, pp. 25–42 (Geneva: Droz).

Schnapper, Bernard (1983) "La récidive, une obsession créatrice au XIXe siècle," in *Le Récidivisme, 21ème congrès de l'Association française de criminologie*, pp. 25–64 (Paris: PUF).

——— (1991) *Voies nouvelles en histoire du droit: La Justice, la famille, la répression pénale, XVIe–XXe siècle*, Vol. 18 (Paris: PUF).

Schraad-Tischler, Daniel (2011) *Social Justice in the OECD: How Do the Member States Compare?* (Gütersloh: Bertelsmann Stiftung).

Schwartz, Olivier (1990) *Le Monde privé des ouvriers. Hommes et femmes du nord* (Paris: PUF).

——— (2010) "Faut avoir une force mentale?," in De Singly, F., Giraud, C., and Martin, O. (eds.) *Nouveau Manuel de sociologie*, pp. 204–13 (Paris: Armand Colin).

Scott, James C. (1990) *Domination and the Arts of Resistance: Hidden Transcripts* (New Haven, CT: Yale University Press).

Sekhon, Nirej (2012) "Redistributive Policing," *Journal of Criminal Law and Criminology*, Vol. 101, No. 4, pp. 1171–226.

Serre, Delphine (2001) "La 'judiciarisation' en actes. Le Signalement d'enfant en danger,'" *Actes de la recherche en sciences sociales*, Vol. 136–37, pp. 70–82.

——— (2009) *Les Coulisses de l'État social. Enquête sur les signalements d'enfant en danger* (Paris: Raisons d'agir).

——— (2011) "Gouverner le travail des assistantes sociales par le chiffre?," *Informations sociales*, Vol. 167, No. 5, pp. 132–9.

Silberman, Roxanne, and Fournier, Irène (2006) "Les secondes générations sur le marché du travail en France: une pénalité ethnique ancrée dans le temps. Contribution à la théorie de l'assimilation segmentée," *Revue française de sociologie*, Vol. 49, pp. 45–94.

Simmel, Georg (1950 [1908]) "The Secret and the Secret Society," in Wolff, Kurt H. (ed.) *The Sociology of Georg Simmel*, pp. 305–76 (New York: The Free Press).

Singly, François de (1996) *Le Soi, le couple et la famille* (Paris: Nathan).

Skolnick, Jerome (1994 [1966]) *Justice without Trial: Law Enforcement in Democratic Society* (New York: Macmillan College).

—— and Fyfe, James (1993) *Above the Law: Police and the Excessive Use of Force* (New York: The Free Press).

Sparks, Richard and Bottoms, Anthony (1995) "Legitimacy and Order in Prisons," *British Journal of Sociology*, Vol. 46, No. 1, pp. 45–62.

Spire, Alexis (2004) "Les réfugiés, une main-d'œuvre à part? Conditions de séjour et d'emploi, France 1945–1975," *REMI*, Vol. 20, No. 1, pp. 23–38.

—— (2008) *Accueillir ou reconduire. Enquête sur les guichets de l'immigration* (Paris: Liber).

Stinchcombe, Arthur (1997) "On the Virtues of the Old Institutionalism," *Annual Review of Sociology*, Vol. 23, pp. 1–18.

Terrio, Susan (2009) *Judging Mohammed: Juvenile Deliquency, Immigration, and Exclusion at the Paris Palace of Justice* (Stanford, CA: Stanford University Press).

Thelen, Tatjana, Vetters, Larissa, and Benda-Beckman, Keebet von (2014) "Stategraphy: Towards a Relational Approach," *Social Analysis*, Vol. 58, No 3.

Thin, Daniel (1998) *Quartiers populaires. L'École et les familles* (Lyon: Presses universitaires de Lyon).

Thoits, Peggy A. (1985) "Self-labeling Processes in Mental Illness: The Role of Emotional Deviance," *American Journal of Sociology*, Vol. 91, pp. 221–49.

Thompson, Edward Palmer (1971) "The Moral Economy of the English Crowd in the Eighteenth Century," *Past & Present*, Vol. 50, pp. 76–136.

Topalov, Christian (1994) *Naissance du chômeur. 1880–1910* (Paris: Albin Michel).

Tournier, Pierre-Victor and Robert, Philippe (1991) *Étrangers et délinquance: Les Chiffres du débat* (Paris: L'Harmattan).

Traïni, Christophe (2010) "Des sentiments aux émotions (et vice-versa). Comment devient-on militant de la cause animale?," *Revue française de science politique*, Vol. 60, No. 2, pp. 335–58.

Valluy, Jérôme (2009) *Rejet des exilés. Le Grand retournement du droit d'asile* (Bellecombe-en-Bauges: Éditions du Croquant).

Van Maanen, John (1978) "Observations of the Making of Policemen," in Manning, P. and Van Maanen, J. (eds.) *Policing: A View From the Street*, pp. 292–308 (Santa Monica, CA: Goodyear).

Vera Institute of Justice (1972) *Programs in Criminal Justice Reform. Vera Institute of Justice Ten-year Report, 1961–1971* (New York: Vera Institute of Justice).

Verdès-Leroux, Jeannine (1978) *Le Travail social* (Paris: Minuit).

Vial, Monique (1990) *Les Enfants anormaux à l'école. Aux origines de l'éducation spécialisée (1882–1909)* (Paris: Armand Colin).

Viennot, Camille (2012) *Le Procès pénal accéléré. Étude des transformations du jugement pénal* (Paris: Dalloz).

Vigarello, Georges (2005) "L'intolérable de la maltraitance infantile. Genèse de la loi sur la protection des enfants maltraités et moralement abandonnés en France," in Fassin, D.

and Bourdelais, P. (eds.) *Les Constructions de l'intolérable: Études d'anthropologie et d'histoire sur les frontières de l'espace moral*, pp. 111–27 (Paris: La Découverte).

Vimont, Jean-Claude (2004) *La Prison. À l'ombre des hauts murs* (Paris: Gallimard).

Wacquant, Loïc (2004) *Punir les pauvres. Le Nouveau gouvernement de l'insécurité sociale* (Marseille: Agone).

—— (2008) "Ordering Insecurity: Social Polarization and the Punitive Upsurge," *Radical Philosophy Review*, Vol. 11, No. 1, pp. 9–27.

Waddington, P.A.J. (1999) "Police (Canteen) Sub-culture: An Appreciation," *British Journal of Criminology*, Vol. 39, No. 2, pp. 287–309.

Walmsley, Roy (2011) *World Prison Population* (London: International Centre for Prison Studies).

Weber, Florence (2008) "Une enquête dans l'histoire. Le travail à-côté, apogée d'une culture ouvrière européenne," in Arborio, A.-M. et al. (eds.) *Observer le travail. Histoire, ethnographie, approches combinées*, pp. 201–14 (Paris: La Découverte).

Weber, Max (1994 [1919]) "The Profession and Vocation of Politics," in Lassmann, Peter and Speirs, Ronald (eds.) *Weber: Political Writings*, pp. 309–69 (Cambridge: Cambridge University Press).

West, Candace and Fenstermaker, Sarah (1995) "Doing Difference," *Gender and Society*, Vol. 9, No. 1, pp. 8–37.

Westley, William (1970) *Violence and the Police: A Sociological Study of Law, Custom, and Morality* (Cambridge, MA: MIT Press).

Wilson, James Q. (1968) *Varieties of Police Behavior: The Management of Law and Order in Eight Communities* (Cambridge, MA: Harvard University Press).

Yvorel, Jean-Jacques (2012) "Le discernement: Construction et usage d'une catégorie juridique en droit pénal des mineurs. Étude historique," *Recherches familiales*, Vol. 9, pp. 153–62.

Zarca, Bernard (2009) "L'éthos professionnel des mathématiciens," *Revue française de sociologie*, Vol. 50, No. 2, pp. 351–84.

Zocchetto, François (2005) "Juger vite, juger mieux? Les procédures rapides de traitement des affaires pénales: état des lieux," Rapport de la mission d'information de la commission des lois du Sénat.

Zunigo, Xavier (2007) "La gestion publique du chômage des jeunes de milieu populaire. Éducation morale, conversion et renforcement des aspirations socioprofessionnelles," Ph.D. diss., Sociology, EHESS, Paris.

—— (2008) "L'apprentissage des possibles professionnels. Logiques et effets sociaux des missions locales pour l'emploi des jeunes," *Sociétés contemporaines*, Vol. 70, pp. 115–31.

List of Contributors

Didier Fassin is the James D. Wolfensohn Professor at the School of Social Science at the Institute for Advanced Study in Princeton. The founding director of IRIS (Institut de recherche interdisciplinaire sur les enjeux sociaux), he is also a director of studies at the École des hautes études en sciences sociales in Paris. Laureate of an advanced grant of the European Research Council, he directed the program "Toward a Critical Moral Anthropology" upon which the current volume is based. He is interested in political and moral anthropology, the study of the state, the epistemology of ethnography, and the implication of a public social science.

Yasmine Bouagga is a Teaching Assistant and Postdoctoral Researcher in sociology at the Université Paris Dauphine and a member of IRIS (Institut de recherche interdisciplinaire sur les enjeux sociaux). Her research focuses on criminal law, justice, state institutions and their public. Her Ph.D. dissertation explored the implementation of reforms aiming at the so-called "humanization" of prisons and aligning them on the principles of the rule of law. She is currently developing a comparative sociology of punishment, social control and moral controversies related to security policies.

Isabelle Coutant is a Researcher in sociology at the CNRS (Centre national de la recherche scientifique), and a member of IRIS (Institut de recherche interdisciplinaire sur les enjeux sociaux). Over the past twenty years, she has studied the transformations of the working class in contemporary France and more specifically the consequences of its precarization with regards to the experience of young people. Her research has focused in particular on the relations of the latter with justice and psychiatry.

Jean-Sébastien Eideliman is an Assistant Professor in sociology at the Université de Lille 3, and a member of CERIES (Centre de recherche individu-épreuves-société). His research focuses on disability, mental health, family and teenagers. After completing his Ph.D. on the ethnography of parents facing mental disabilities, he analyzed the moral and emotional issues involved in institutional support for teenagers with social and psychological problems. He currently studies the life course of children with hyperactivity disorders.

Fabrice Fernandez is a Research Fellow in sociology at the ANR (Agence nationale de la recherche), and a member of the Centre Max Weber at the Université de Lyon. His primary research interests involve drug addiction, mental illness and the penal system. He completed his Ph.D. on the use of drugs, in particular among inmates. His current research focuses on the moral and emotional issues involved in relationships of domination.

Nicolas Fischer is a Researcher in political science at the CNRS (Centre national de la recherche scientifique), and a member of CESDIP (Centre d'étude du droit et des institutions pénales). His research focuses on immigration policies and detention institutions. He completed his Ph.D. on detention centers for migrants in France, and subsequently worked on immigration courts. He is now undertaking research on the political and legal issues involved with the death penalty.

Carolina Kobelinsky is a Research Fellow in anthropology at the Casa de Velásquez in Madrid. After having completed her Ph.D. on the experience of waiting among asylum seekers in France, she analyzed the adjudication process at the French National Court of Asylum. She now studies migrant mortality at Europe's southern borders, examining the management of dead bodies and the imaginaries of death at the border.

Chowra Makaremi is a Researcher in anthropology at the CNRS (Centre national de la recherche scientifique), and a member of IRIS (Institut de recherche interdisciplinaire sur les enjeux sociaux). Her research focuses on the anthropology of law and the state, and processes of subjectivation at the margins. After completing a Ph.D. on border confinement for undocumented migrants, she studied criminal courts in France, especially immediate appearance trials. She is currently researching the genealogy of state violence in post-revolutionary Iran.

Sarah Mazouz is a Marie Curie Fellow at the Humboldt Universität in Berlin and a member of the Institut für Europäische Ethnologie, where she is conducting a project on dual citizenship in Germany. After having completed a Ph.D. on anti-discrimination policies and the naturalization process in France, she studied youth employment centers. Her current research focuses on citizenship policies, bureaucratic practices, and the sociology of law, as well as racialization, gender, and corresponding modes of subjectivation.

Sébastien Roux is a Researcher at the CNRS (Centre national de la recherche scientifique), and a member of LISST (Laboratoire interdisciplinaire solidarités, sociétés, territoires). His research focuses on policies pertaining to young people, parenting, gender and sexuality. After having completed his Ph.D. on the anthropology of sex tourism in Thailand, he analyzed the moral issues involved in juvenile delinquency policies in France. He currently studies transnational adoption, focusing on the interrelationships between bodies, nations, intimacies, and ethics.

Index